CONSTITUTIONS AND CONSTITUTIONAL TRENDS SINCE WORLD WAR II

CONTRIBUTING AUTHORS

JOSEPH DUNNER
Professor of Political Science
Grinnell College, Grinnell, Iowa

CARL J. FRIEDRICH
Professor of Government
Harvard University and Radcliffe College, Cambridge, Massachusetts

FERDINAND A. HERMENS
Professor of Political Science
University of Notre Dame, Notre Dame, Indiana

EDWARD G. LEWIS
Associate Professor of Political Science
University of Illinois, Urbana, Illinois

KARL LOEWENSTEIN
Professor of Political Science
Amherst College, Amherst, Massachusetts

JOHN BROWN MASON
formerly Professor of Political Science, Oberlin College, Oberlin, Ohio; at present, Chief, Civic Activities Branch, Office of Political Affairs, Internal Political and Governmental Affairs Division, Office of the High Commissioner for Germany

ROBERT G. NEUMANN
Assistant Professor of Political Science
University of California, Los Angeles, California

ADAM B. ULAM
Assistant Professor of Government
Harvard University, Cambridge, Massachusetts

ARNOLD J. ZURCHER
Professor of Political Science
New York University, New York, New York

Constitutions and Constitutional Trends since World War II

An Examination of Significant Aspects of Postwar Public Law with Particular Reference to the New Constitutions of Western Europe

EDITED BY
ARNOLD J. ZURCHER
NEW YORK UNIVERSITY

NEW YORK UNIVERSITY PRESS
WASHINGTON SQUARE · NEW YORK
LONDON: GEOFFREY CUMBERLEGE · OXFORD UNIVERSITY PRESS

COPYRIGHT 1951 BY NEW YORK UNIVERSITY

Printed in the United States of America

PREFACE

THIS Book consists of a series of essays on the postwar constitutions written by eight of America's outstanding specialists in comparative public law. The essays are an outgrowth of papers that were prepared for a two-day round-table discussion group on the postwar constitutions at the Annual Meeting of the American Political Science Association recently held in New York City. Subsequently the papers were entirely rewritten and greatly elaborated. Much new material was incorporated, and the various authors developed their respective topics more systematically and also more comprehensively than was possible in the forum which originally inspired their efforts. In order to enhance the reference value of the book, the texts of the more representative new constitutions and public documents have been incorporated in the Appendix. The result, although hardly a systematic legal or philosophic commentary on the new postwar documents, will nevertheless furnish the student with a satisfactory comparative introduction to such a commentary and provide him with significant interpretations and analyses of at least the more novel institutional aspects of the governmental and administrative patterns that have emerged since World War II.

All involved in this project owe a debt of gratitude to New York University Press for its entrepreneurship in undertaking production of this volume. Much of that debt is owed to the Secretary of the Press Committee on Management and Supervisor of Printing at New York University, Miss Jean B. Barr, for her careful editing of the manuscript and for planning and designing this book. Grateful acknowledgment is also made of the work of her colleague, Miss Anne Koreny. The French Embassy in the United States kindly permitted use of the official English translation of the French Constitution and provided the editor with copies. The English translation of the Italian Constitution is that provided by Messrs. Howard McGaw Smyth and Kent Roberts Greenfield and is reprinted from

Preface

pages 46 ff. of *Documents and State Papers,* I, No. 1 (April 1948), published by the United States Department of State. The text of the Bonn Charter comes from the official translation of the Military Government. Finally, the editor wishes to thank his secretary, Mrs. Muriel P. Gaines, for assistance given without stint in the physical preparation of the manuscript for the printers.

It is perhaps unnecessary to add that neither New York University nor the American Political Science Association bears any responsibility for the views expressed in the subsequent pages. Neither is there any corporate responsibility on the part of editor and authors for views expressed therein. Each author is solely responsible for what he has contributed; and for the views expressed in that personal contribution he, and none other, receives whatever censure or praise those views may elicit from the public.

ARNOLD J. ZURCHER

New York, 1951

TABLE OF CONTENTS

Preface . . . . *page* v

1

Introduction 1
ARNOLD J. ZURCHER

2

The Political Theory of the New Democratic Constitutions . 13
CARL J. FRIEDRICH

3

Electoral Changes after World War II 36
EDWARD G. LEWIS

4

The Position of the Representative Legislature in the Postwar Constitutions 67
EDWARD G. LEWIS

5

Stabilization of the Cabinet System in Western Europe . . . 81
JOSEPH DUNNER

6

Local Autonomy in France and Italy 95
FERDINAND A. HERMENS

7

Functional Autonomy after World War II 116
FERDINAND A. HERMENS

8

Federalism—The Bonn Model 134
JOHN BROWN MASON

vii

Contents

9

The British Commonwealth as an Example of a Multinational State System 154
ADAM B. ULAM

10

Constitutional Documents of East-Central Europe . . *page* 175
ROBERT G. NEUMANN

11

Reflections on the Value of Constitutions in Our Revolutionary Age 191
KARL LOEWENSTEIN

Appendixes 225

   A. Constitution of the French Republic 226

   B. Constitution of the Italian Republic 248

   C. Basic Law of the Federal Republic of Germany . . . 283

   D. Statute of Westminster, 1931 325

   E. Communique and Declaration of the Commonwealth Prime Ministers' Conference 329

   F. Statute of the Council of Europe 331

Index 343

1

Introduction

By Arnold J. Zurcher
NEW YORK UNIVERSITY

IN the period between the two World Wars, written constitutions had apparently declined in popular esteem and lost much of their erstwhile significance as symbols of political unity or as instruments of political discipline. Faith in the efficacy of such instruments, which attained a high point in the nineteenth century, had by no means been entirely dissipated; nevertheless there were few who shared the belief of a Paine, a Condorcet, or some other late eighteenth-century intellectual that written constitutions might be used to codify a rational and progressive political order or to discourage the abuse of political power. Such a belief, if exhibited in contemporary juristic or philosophic writing, would probably have been diagnosed as a form of nostalgia for outmoded ideas or as rather pronounced naïveté. And if the interbellum generation was not quite ready to take up the extreme views of Edmund Burke and dismiss written constitutions as digests of anarchy or the outpourings of impractical and disgruntled revolutionaries, it included many jurists and politicians who were even more contemptuous than Burke and who displayed that contempt by dismissing the latest imitation of the art of the Abbé Sieyès as a document possessing little more significance than a political platform or a "public-relations handout" of the party or coalition in power.

Reasons for this decline of faith in constitutions are not far to seek. Much of the explanation resides in the impact of the various international and domestic crises that afflicted the past generation, especially the two world conflagrations and the social and economic convulsions attributable in whole or part to the great depression

Arnold J. Zurcher

of the 1930's. In nation after nation the accepted constitutional pattern proved to be inadequate—or at least appeared to be inadequate—to meet the political needs of so parlous a period. People became acquainted with various kinds of "crisis" or "emergency" regimes; they became conditioned to the exercise of governmental powers not warranted by traditional conceptions of constitutional authority. Often the provisions of a nation's fundamental statute, when not ignored altogether, underwent tortured interpretations and, by a violation of every canon of construction, were made to sanction unprecedented exertions of political power. Not only did this aggravate the semantic confusion so characteristic of current political thought and action on both the Western and Eastern sides of the Iron Curtain; it also brought into contempt the idea that the written constitution established standards for political action and placed limitations upon political discretion. Where the written constitution enjoyed the status of a judicially enforceable limitation upon the political departments of the government, as in the United States, the document sometimes was alleged to be an instrument for frustrating the aspirations for social reform which popular majorities regarded as legitimate. As Professor Neumann makes clear on a subsequent page, contemporary authoritarian states, by prostituting both the symbolism and the text of written constitutions, contributed significantly toward the declining reputation of such documents and their loss of public respect. Cumulatively, the effect of this interbellum experience, when added to the somewhat questionable record of stability enjoyed by some written constitutions in the nineteenth century, notably in France, goes far to explain the low estate to which such instruments had fallen in recent years.

Against this backdrop, events since World War II present something of a paradox. For at precisely the time when faith in written constitutions appeared to have reached its nadir, the world witnessed an outpouring of such documents that is without parallel. Not even the periods of most violent revolutionary upheaval, like those of 1789, 1850, or 1919, witnessed a greater number of efforts to reduce the basic concepts of national polity to written form. Revival of

Introduction

constitution-writing has, moreover, not been limited to Europe. On the contrary, many of the documents have come from the peoples of Asia and Indonesia. Having struck off the shackles of Western political control and become masters in their own house, these peoples have followed Western precedent, even as Japan and China did earlier, and reduced the principles of their newly established statehood to the confines of a single organic statute. Eastern pursuit of Western precedent in this respect has, indeed, been almost too faithful; for the Eastern constitution-writers appear to have absorbed also the Western penchant for prolixity and constitutional "gobbledegook." As a result of this too faithful imitation, India has acquired the unenviable reputation of having formulated what is probably the longest written constitution in history. Its printed English version covers some two hundred pages exclusive of supplementary schedules which account for some fifty additional pages.

At first glance, this extraordinary contemporary outpouring of the product of constituent assemblies might imply a renascence of faith in constitutions. Many supporters of free government, particularly those who interpret free government as limited government, fervently hope that such is the case. That hope, however, ought not to be taken too seriously. The fact is that both the circumstances attending the drafting of the new public documents and much of their content suggest they are in great measure the product of habit—a kind of tacit response to historical conditioning. With the exception of Britain, which is already surfeited with the symbols of statehood, most contemporary states appear to regard possession of a written constitution as a kind of necessary part of the formal impedimenta of statehood. Especially is this true of states that have just acquired their sovereignty. For them it is almost an indispensable symbol: it is the sign of their independence and political maturity; a necessary part of the lares and penates of their newly found statehood.

That habit bears considerable responsibility for this most recent deluge of constitutions, and not a renewal of faith in such documents, seems confirmed by the relative lack of enthusiasm with which various peoples have greeted the labors of their constituent assemblies. On a subsequent page, Professor Loewenstein testifies to this absence of enthusiasm. He emphasizes the allegedly "fading importance" of written constitutions among Western European societies which he characterizes as "tired, neurotic, cynical, and disenchanted." Among Western peoples, he suggests, constitution-writing after World War II was a business that was attended to as a matter of duty and without enthusiasm. Professor Friedrich, who also comments, is somewhat more optimistic, or perhaps less pessimistic, in his appraisal of the significance of the new documents. For him the solons of the postwar constituent assemblies are restrained revolutionaries. They represent a so-called "third force" who do have aspirations; but those aspirations are such eminently conservative ones as peace and security. For these conservative revolutionaries of Professor Friedrich, fashioning the refurbished constitutional structures of the postwar world is undoubtedly a process more significant than a mere ritual, but it is apparently not much more significant.

The relative indifference of the postwar constitution-makers is reflected in their work. These new constitutions may be "new" in a chronological sense, but their substance rarely justifies that adjective. Some "advances" have been made. Suffrage has been extended to women in certain Romance states of Europe. Judicial enforcement of the constitution against legislatures has gained ground in Italy and Germany; and even France has tried to set up nonjudicial machinery to enforce her organic law against a legislature that, under previous republican dispensations, has always been regarded as omnipotent. Here and there an alleged "strengthening" of the executive has occurred, use of the popular referendum has been extended, and some further experimentation with second chambers and advisory "economic" councils has taken place. Also, as we shall note later, some new efforts have been made, on paper at least, to exploit federal and regional principles in the interests of a greater degree of local political responsibility and to assimilate erstwhile colonial territory to a municipal constitutional system. In general, however, the post-1945 documents remind the reader of those that made their début in 1919 or thereabouts. These later

Introduction

documents abound in the clichés of nineteenth-century constitutionalism; they recapitulate with boring fidelity the orthodox formulas descriptive of the representative parliamentary system of government; they are full of vacuous injunctions to public authority to practice benevolence toward the individual. These latter sentiments sound as noble as when they were first expressed a century ago or when they were systematically catalogued in the Weimar Constitution a generation ago. Everyone applauds them as everyone applauds the ideal of a sinless world, but of their precise meaning there is more than a little doubt.

What is especially noteworthy is the almost complete absence of any solutions or prescriptions for the solution of the difficult issues posed by some of the currently favored policies of government. Virtually nothing, for example, appears concerning the administrative and economic problems of contemporary "welfare" politics. Bills of rights may be replete with promises of public beneficence, but they remain curiously silent about how such promises are to be fulfilled. They say little if anything about the standards to be observed in rendering public assistance, nothing about the economic problem of ways and means, and next to nothing about the problem of administration. Related problems resulting from the collectivistic revolution and public economic intervention are likewise passed over in silence. The managerial responsibilities of state enterprise; problems of administrative and budgetary autonomy of such enterprise; the extension of democratic control over vast new areas of public responsibility; the limitations inherent in public planning; the direction and management of economic life which flow from direct public controls over finance, production, and distribution—these are the substance of some of the great constitutional problems of the day. Yet reference to them in the new documents is only sporadic. By and large they are passed over in silence.

Equally ineffective has been the constitution-maker's effort to cope with the problem of concentration of power in the state, again because the problem has been largely ignored. Those efforts that have been made seem largely artificial. At any rate the treatment of this major problem in the postwar documents, reviewed in

Arnold J. Zurcher

Professor Hermens' papers on functional and local autonomy and Professor Mason's discussion of German federalism, is not reassuring. It is possible that Italian efforts to promote a new level of local government called the "Region" betokens a direct attack upon the contemporary evil of bureaucratic centralism that is slowly sapping the integrity of political amateurism at the local level. But, again, it remains to be seen whether this Italian reform is more than a paper gesture. As for German federalism, no honest observer can assert that this represents a bona fide German formula of governmental deconcentration; at least he can make no such assertion until Allied control is removed and Germans are masters in their own house. At the moment the West German Federal Republic looks suspiciously like a form of government dictated by the Allied, and especially the French, foreign offices and hardly a genuine expression of the kind of state that the Germans themselves would erect.

Inadequate solutions, or the lack of solutions, for problems like the foregoing, are undoubtedly also due to the popular apathy toward constitutions and the general lack of faith in their significance to which reference was made earlier. But there is another, and an even more alarming, explanation. Stated most succinctly, it is a lack of social consensus. It is the absence of any underlying agreement among social groups about the scope and purpose of government and the relation of government to society.

It is true, of course, that in the existing free societies of Western Europe and other parts of the world the very formation of these new constitutions, and their ratification after discussion and debate, suggest that social compromises have been secured and unity of a sort established. Nevertheless that unity is basically a false one; it is an illusion. In many instances the constitutions are masterpieces of semantic tact; they are compendiums of formulas, principles, and generalities that obscure the absence of agreement on significant detail or that, at best, provide only tentative solutions for bitterly contested issues. Too often the constitutions consist of words and phrases that divide men least; of brittle formulas that sound well but offer little in the way of concrete guides to action. To many

Introduction

of these formulas parties of the extreme right and left may have given their formal assent. But like the Communist support of the special position of the Roman Catholic Church in Italy's Constitution, the assent represents a purely tactical step. It is an expression of political opportunism, not of constitutional conviction.

Nor is the situation much better among the parties of the so-called "center." In the political lists they may tolerate one another with some decorum and they may agree on what might be termed the processes of free government, but on the goals of the contemporary state they are often as far apart as the more extreme groups. Political clericals, secular, procapitalist liberals, conservative agrarians, Marxian socialists whose color ranges from claretlike red to pastel pink, and miscellaneous groups whose primary aim seems to be their own aggrandizement at the expense of society—these constitute an alleged "center." But they constitute a center chiefly because they occupy a position between extremes. They are largely incapable of any long-term constructive action, and it is misleading to refer to them as a "third force" or a "vital center" or to apply to them any other label that suggests a conception of corporate unity or a sense of common purpose.

In short, the great liability of the new constitutions is the lack of moral unity in the societies that have promulgated them. It is the absence of anything approximating Rousseau's concept of a "general will." It is the failure to achieve agreement among parties and interest groups on any fundamental common aims and the failure to acknowledge that there are values upon which parties must agree, at least tacitly, not to disagree for fear of bringing the state itself into jeopardy. To reiterate, it is the failure to secure consensus.

It is in this lack of consensus, quite as much as in popular apathy and toleration of the habitual, that we find the explanation for much that is tentative and superficial in the postwar constitutions. Here is the primary reason for the repetition of hackneyed phrases and orthodox formulas. Here is the most persuasive explanation of the failure to assess the impact of collectivism upon personal and group freedom and economic efficiency. In short, here is the reason why the provisions of the new constitutions are so often the "warmed-over" product of the constitutional assemblies of another generation. Glittering generalities can secure the support of politicians of almost any camp, particularly when such generalities are hallowed by long use. So can tried and tested constitutional formulas, however hackneyed. But any attempt to press forward toward the unknown, or perchance toward the unpopular, constitutes a political liability. It is best avoided and left for future resolution. Otherwise cracks are likely to develop in the thin veneer of habit and traditional loyalties that, temporarily at least, hold groups together.

Failure to come to grips with some of the real problems of the contemporary state is not the only liability attributable to the lack of social and moral unity in the community. Probably a more serious danger, because it is more imminent, is the likelihood that the absence of consensus will paralyze the political process in free societies and prevent even the elementary discharge of public business. Western parliamentarism may have developed an excellent procedure for facilitating and encouraging the art of compromise. But none of the parliamentary arts and mechanics can compensate for the absence of social consensus. Indeed, to be effective, parliamentary arts and mechanics must assume consensus. Because of the schisms which afflict free society, parliamentary regimes face the possibility that the arts of parliamentary compromise will prove inadequate and that government by parliamentary majorities will break down. If such a breakdown occurs parliamentary states, new and old, will again find it necessary, as in the 1930's, to depart from constitutional normality and legality and resort to extralegal, makeshift arrangements in order merely to maintain authority. In other words, the penalty for the failure to secure at least a minimum of social unity may well be the breakdown of the elementary processes of government by consent and the administration of further doses of "emergency" or "crisis" government.

That the constitution-makers fear such a breakdown is only too apparent. Their fears are implicit in the various constitutional clauses that seek to give mechanical stability to parliamentary government. Typical are those clauses that require a special procedure to place upon the agenda motions critical of the cabinet or

Introduction

likely to bring about the cabinet's downfall; that arbitrarily delay voting upon such motions and demand extraordinary affirmative majorities for their adoption; and that seek to make dissolution of parliament available to the cabinet in order to curb the more reckless ambitions of opposition party groups. The essays by Professors Dunner and Lewis consider at greater length these efforts to give a somewhat artificial stability to the postwar parliamentary regime. Suffice it to say here that all these efforts are poor substitutes for united and disciplined majorities. That these substitutes can keep the ship of state afloat, when the shoals of real controversy are reached, is doubtful. As previously indicated, one of the discernible trends in the new Western constitutions is the rejection of the historic French doctrine of parliamentary supremacy. Inchoate concepts of a constitutional separation of powers, an allegedly more vigorous executive authority, and, above all, the embryo, if not the fetus, of judicial review of legislative action in Italy and Germany mirror this conservative trend. In one sense this is but another reflection of the distracted and divided political community of our time: it reflects the desire of minorities to erect safeguards against potentially hostile majority coalitions. The decline of the legislature's historic constitutional position is also expressive of the fear that a government which focuses its powers in legislative majorities may not function at all and that, hence, for the safety of the commonwealth, other areas of authority, as august or nearly as august as the legislature, must be groomed. Some of the more conservative groups of the West, like the De Gaullists in France, constantly champion such a view, urging an independent executive to compensate for anticipated parliamentary anarchy. Other groups may not be so explicit about the matter, but their fears of governmental instability are as abiding, even if they formally reject the De Gaullist solution.

Whatever the weaknesses of the new constitutions, as respects the internal affairs of state, they may still achieve stability of sorts if the communities that have adopted them can be given reasonable security against external aggression. Even the nonexpert can understand that the threat of such aggression is another shadow cast

Arnold J. Zurcher

upon the postwar settlements within each individual state and that this shadow is even more enveloping and more menacing than the shadow cast by the lack of domestic unity.

Solution of this problem of world order is obviously beyond the competence of any particular state. Nevertheless, the national constitutional arrangements, which these essays describe, impinge formally upon the broader problem of maintaining world order on more than one point. Where they do, moreover, we discover at least the rudiments of a sense of national responsibility for global peace and stability and explicit admissions that the sovereign discretion of the national state must be appropriately limited. Such is the purport, for example, of the constitutional provisions explicitly accepting the principles of international law and the formal offer, in certain of the new documents, to limit municipal sovereignty, on a reciprocal basis, to the extent required for the establishment of effective collective-security arrangements. The new French Constitution, which is perhaps most explicit on this latter point, declares that France will go as far as any other state in accepting such limitations on national sovereignty as may be necessary to the defense of peace (see the Preamble). Clauses such as these denote a new sense of national responsibility for international organization and suggest that the constitution-makers, however uninspired they may have been, were at least aware of the urgency of the international problem.

Equally worthy of comment are the efforts that have been made to integrate into some formal or semiformal constitutional association a metropolitan national state and its erstwhile dependent territories. Oldest contemporary example of this phenomenon is the British Commonwealth of Nations, now officially known simply as the Commonwealth, which was formally originated after World War I. Professor Ulam devotes his essay to the rapidly changing character of this multinational structure, particularly to the changes since 1945, and the effect these have had upon the formal legal description of the Commonwealth provided in the Statute of Westminster. Since the last global conflict, the world has witnessed the efforts of both the Dutch and the French to create similar

Introduction

organizations. The French effort, officially known as the French Union, occupies much space in the new French Constitution and is obviously regarded as a most important part of the new national dispensation.

These multinational structures may be but the last gasps of dying empire; on the other hand, if they should succeed, their contribution to world political integration and world order can be considerable. They can bring into effective, if limited, association many diverse peoples and cultures; establish forums for the discussion and decision of common problems, particularly those of extranational significance; and provide logical steppingstones to broader, and ultimately universal, organization.

Similar in significance are the steps taken by the Western European nations to promote European constitutional integration. Agitation for such integration, small in volume but persistent since World War I, grew after World War II and resulted in the creation of the Council of Europe at Strasbourg. The Consultative Assembly of this Council may be nothing but a debating society at this writing, but the conception of a permanent multinational organization of the states of Europe and plans for extranational projects, economic, cultural, and political, are writ large upon the records of the Council's debates and that of its committees. That conception is also well articulated in the recent parliamentary debates of member states of the Strasbourg Assembly and even in the actual constitutions of some Western European nations. Since World War II, European union has ceased to be merely a vague ideal and has become a concept of public law.

These extranational developments in public law and the effort to integrate political nationalism in a broader juridical order constitute, probably, the most progressive aspect of the product of constituent assemblies after World War II and compensate somewhat for the prevailing lack of originality. They indicate awareness of the fact that the stability of domestic constitutional arrangements, whether innately good or bad, is peculiarly dependent upon the international climate. They are evidence of broad popular acceptance of the proposition that peace and sta-

Arnold J. Zurcher

bility within particular states depend upon the maintenance of global peace. Indeed, acceptance of that proposition represents probably the most important advance in political understanding which has been made in the past fifty years, a half century otherwise singularly reactionary in its political practice and singularly unimaginative in its political theory.

This awareness of the dependence of an orderly state upon an orderly world can well mean the salvation of the new constitutional settlements, inherently dubious though their outlook may be. The content of the new documents may be hackneyed, and the documents may scarcely lay claim to the faith of people or challenge their patriotism. Their governmental and administrative arrangements may be threatened by the paralysis of social and moral disunity. But if, contrary to present indications, global conflict is not imminent and if, over the long pull, Fortune be reasonably benign and this new national will to sacrifice sovereignty for international order has a chance to assert itself, these postwar national constitutional settlements may survive indefinitely. Like the constitution of the Third French Republic, which certainly began operations under the most adverse auspices, these new documents may yet enjoy a degree of longevity and acquire a vogue among their respective peoples that will confound their critics, including this one, and surprise even the most optimistic observers.

2

The Political Theory of the New Democratic Constitutions

By Carl J. Friedrich
HARVARD UNIVERSITY

ANY attempt to assess the political theory of the new constitutions is confronted with the problem whether to treat the constitutional documents as prima-facie evidence or to search for underlying trends that these documents may or may not express. When Charles A. Beard threw out his challenge concerning "the economic interpretation" of the American Constitution—a challenge which in later years he sought to soften considerably—he implied, if he did not state explicitly, that the words the constitution-makers at Philadelphia used were modeled upon their economic interests and the views which stemmed from them. In an interesting detailed application of this general thought, Walton Hamilton and Douglass Adair in their *The Power to Govern* argued that the word "commerce" must be interpreted in accordance with what "commerce" meant to the fathers: that a broad, mercantilist notion was what the constitution-makers "intended" to have understood in the commerce clause. An examination of the political thought of the new constitutions in such exacting and refined terms would be a Herculean task, little short of an intellectual and social history of Continental Europe during the last two generations. All that is being attempted here is to indicate the broad framework of general ideas on politics into which these constitutions are set.[1]

[1] The constitutions to be considered here include the French Constitution of 1946, the Italian Constitution of 1947, and the German Basic Law of 1949—with occasional references to the German *Land* constitutions of 1946 to the present; attention is also given to the emergent Constitution of Europe. Regarding leading

Carl J. Friedrich

The very phrase "political theory" is intended to provide a limiting concept. The new constitutions deal with a great many matters, not strictly "political" in the sense in which that term has come to be specialized for purposes of modern political science. Everything today is "political," of course. But "political" in the stricter sense is confined to the organizational pattern of government, the control relationships, if you please, its functioning processes, and the like. In this sense, the new constitutions represent restorations, rather than revolutions, although they are stases or overturns in the Aristotelian sense. And, yet, closer inspection reveals a revolutionary change of unintended proportions, which I am proposing to designate by the term "negative revolutions."[2]

The revolutions of 1640 and 1789 were carried forward with a positive enthusiasm for freedom. The drama and the failure of both revolutions were dominated by this fact; both revolutions provided the stage for long-drawn-out struggles to write a constitution. Each

---

commentaries for the French Constitution, mention might be made of Maurice Duverger, *Manuel de droit constitutionnel et de science politique* (5th ed.; Paris, 1948), Julien LaFerriere, *Manuel de droit constitutionnel* (2d ed.; Paris, 1947), Georges Burdeau, *Manuel de droit public—les libertés publiques, les droits sociaux* (Paris, 1948), Marcel Prélot, *Précis de droit constitutionnel* (Paris, 1948); for Italy, Oreste Raneletti, *Istituzioni di diritto pubblico* (13th ed.; Naples, 1948), P. B. di Ruffia, *Diritto costituzionale (lo stato democratico moderno)* (Vol. I; Milan, 1949); on the Italian Constitutional Assembly, V. E. Orlando's *La costituzione della repubblica italiana*, which gives textual extracts and an interesting introduction by the editor, is valuable; the Italian text is contained in the volume published by the general secretariat of the Chamber of Deputies in 1949, entitled *L'assemblea costituente*, which also contains other legislation in summary; for Germany, no good commentaries have yet made their appearance. Three divergent American accounts may be mentioned, however: A. Brecht, "The New German Constitution," *Social Research*, XVI (December 1949), 425–73; Hans Simons, "The Bonn Constitution and Its Government," *Proceedings* of the Twenty-sixth Institute of the Norman Wait Harris Memorial Foundation, pp. 204–14; and Carl J. Friedrich, "Rebuilding the German Constitution," *American Political Science Review*, XLIII (1949), 461–82 and 704–20. The text of the important constitutional documents is contained in *Germany Under Occupation, Illustrative Materials and Documents*, eds. Pollock, Meisel, and Bretton (Ann Arbor, 1949). See also, for a general discussion of the constitutions within the longer perspective of constitutional development, Carl J. Friedrich, *Constitutional Government and Democracy* (Boston, 1950), and the literature cited there at length.

[2] See for this the author's "The Negative Revolutions and the Union of Europe," in *Perspectives on a Troubled Decade*, eds. Bryson, Finkelstein, and McIver (New York, 1950), pp. 329 ff.

Political Theory of New Democratic Constitutions

produced a crop of such constitutions, and eventually a dictator emerged to carry on by force and authority what could not be arranged by co-operation. But the lesson of the struggle for constitutional freedom was not lost; the idea of the rights of man was not dead. In the United States, a group of small, seemingly inconsequential, colonies got together and merged the ideas of both revolutions, forged them into a lasting charter: the Constitution of the United States. In England and in France the same impulse produced constitutional systems in the course of the next generation, and these systems remained.

The same cannot be said for the revolution of 1917. In impulse and in effect it was anticonstitutional. The dictatorship of the proletariat was, in the revolutionary vision, not linked to a constitutional democracy but to a direct democracy of the Rousseauistic model; yet no corresponding realistic appreciation of the limits, as far as size and spirit are concerned, characterized the vision. Both the revolutionaries themselves and the Fascist reaction they brought on stressed total authority and accepted coercion and violence thinly disguised by alleged necessities and dangers.

But now a strange turn has occurred. Out of the battle of revolutionaries, counterrevolutionaries, reactionaries, and innocent bystanders, a third force has emerged. And this third force is spreading. It is recapturing the impetus of the revolutions of 1640 and 1789. In France, in Italy, even in Germany, constitutions have been written by men who are certainly far from the "mad inspiration of history" which Trotsky called a revolution. These constitutions are not the result of any positive enthusiasm for the wonderful future; they flow rather from the negative distaste for a dismal past. What these odd revolutionists are saying primarily is: "No." They do not want Fascism and dictatorship. They do not want Communism and dictatorship. They do not want liberalism and the anarchy of the "free market" and its enterprises growing into gigantic monopolies. What, then, *do* they want? The answer seems to be: "We want peace. We want a chance to live and *if* possible to live well. We want something better than either free enterprise or the planning economy. We insist that there must be an order beyond Communism and Fascism, and we want to try to work it out." That is why I propose to call these revolutions "negative."

France affirms the rights of man of 1789, Italy affirms the rights and duties of Mazzini's good citizen, Germany affirms the dignity of man and abolishes the death sentence and compulsory military service. Are these not positive beliefs? Certainly they once were. In 1789, the Declaration of the Rights of Man was expected, however, to usher in the millennium. Did the makers of the French Constitution of 1946, reaffirming these rights, share such expectations? Hardly. They only knew that such a program would be less bad than what they rejected: the weakness and confusion of the Third Republic, the glum serfdom of the Vichy dictatorship, the terror of the Communist comrades. Similar observations apply to the other two democratic constitutions. When read with the cynicism of the twenties, or the ideological spectacles of Marxist orthodoxy, these constitutions have, in fact, a hollow ring. There does not pulse in them that passion, based upon the weird mixture of romanticism and scientism, which animated constitution-makers from 1789 to Weimar.

Are the negative revolutions a species of restoration? Do they seek to rebuild what was once there? Admittedly, neither Charles II nor Louis XVIII ever restored the past either; they just tried. But their policies and programs did express the exhaustion of a generation that was tired of enthusiasm, tired of ideas, tired of change. It might seem as if the same exhaustion were sweeping Europe today. Yet, there is a sign that this analogy does not hold, and this sign provides a possible key to the situation. Genuine enthusiasm is felt in many quarters of Europe for the possibility of effective unification. Underlying the strictly practical and pragmatic grounds there exists an undercurrent: a vivid sense of cultural unity and community. It found striking expression in the French Assembly debate that settled Germany's admission to the European Union. This sense of unity, this idea of European culture, unlike the shadowy and somewhat disturbing concept of world culture (behind which lurks the Soviet Russian slogan of world revolution), corresponds to vividly felt realities in spite of the bitter conflicts, and to some extent even because of them.

Political Theory of New Democratic Constitutions

When T. S. Eliot, during World War II, appealed to the Germans, pleading with those among them who would yet acknowledge the common culture of Europe, he said: "The dominant force in creating a common culture between peoples each of whom has its distinct culture, is religion . . . I am simply stating a fact." This fact has found striking expression in the new constitutions through the stress laid upon the dignity of man. The way in which this broad concept is interpreted is decisively related to the unity of Europe and distinguishes present European trends from both the Soviet Union and the United States. For this dignity of man is interpreted in all European constitutions to mean freedom of expression *and* socialization or, perhaps more broadly, social responsibilities. The first sets off Europe from the Soviet Union, the second from the United States. Maybe it will prove unrealizable. But when taken together with the common recognition of European unity, and the willingness to surrender national sovereignty to such higher unity, it may yet revolutionize Europe and the world.

The political theory of the new constitutions that are democratic [3] in the traditional Western sense (the "people's democracies" are here excluded, because their constitutions are façades to a much greater extent than constitutions necessarily are) revolves, then, around four major focal points which distinguish them from their

---

[3] Throughout this chapter the word "democratic" is used in the prevailing Western sense, which was adumbrated by the American Government through its occupation authorities in an effort to differentiate itself clearly from the Soviet position, on July 9, 1946. It stressed, *inter alia*, (1) frequent popular elections in which "not less than 2" parties effectively compete, these parties to be "voluntary associations," (2) guarantee of basic rights, (3) "rule of law"; see for this Carl J. Friedrich and others, *American Experiences in Military Government in World War II* (New York, 1948), App. C. Consideration is focused upon the constitutions of France, Italy, and Germany, the latter term referring to Germany under Western occupation whose constitution (Basic Law) claims to represent all Germany, from a democratic standpoint, just as the republic that has been erected in the Soviet zone claims to do from a Communist ("people's democracy") standpoint. It might have been well to include also the constitutions of the several German states *(Länder)*; there are twelve of them, and all but three have constitutions that resemble the Basic Law sufficiently to reinforce the analysis given here.

Austria was permitted to reactivate the constitution of 1929, to annul at the same time all laws made after March 5, 1933, and especially the Fascist Constitution of 1934—an inadequately noted and belated recognition that Fascism came to Austria at the same time it came to Germany, though in attenuated form. The constitutional situation in Austria deserves and requires separate analysis.

predecessors: (1) reaffirmation of human rights; *but* (2) efforts to restrict these rights in such a way as to make them unavailable to the enemies of constitutional democracy; (3) stress upon social goals and their implementation through socialization; *but* (4) efforts to circumscribe these goals and their implementation in such a way as to prevent the re-emergence of totalitarian methods and dictatorship. With reference to all four aspects, a comparison reveals that, generally speaking, they are most explicit in the German Basic Law, and least so in the French Constitution of 1946, the Italian Constitution occupying a middle ground. This fact is in keeping with the relative depth of the totalitarian impact, comparatively, in the three countries, as well as with the time sequence of the three constitutions: 1946, 1947, 1948. This sequence deserves attention, because it suggests that we are here face to face with an emergent trend still in the process of crystallization.

At this point the question may well be asked: What right have we to consider the French, the Italian, and the German Constitutions together? Is not the political theory of a constitution bound to be affected by preceding political experience? So put, a certain divergence is explainable: the more intense the experience with Fascism, the more poignant is the political theory of the new constitution. This reflection reinforces the point made earlier about the time sequence. Furthermore, Fascism represents a pattern of ideological reaction to Communism, and we face in any case the related problem of Communist danger. In this respect, France and Italy are today more vulnerable than Germany, considering the breadth of electoral support in these countries for Communism (approximately 30 per cent as against 8 per cent in Germany); but Germany is confronted with the impact of Communist control in the Soviet-occupied zone and the threat of a war in which the country would forthwith be overrun by victorious Soviet armies. These armies would no doubt establish "people's democracies" in their wake, and hence every German, so the saying goes, has his Communist friend, as a re-insurance policy.

Another common ground of these three constitutions is the Rousseauistic tradition regarding democracy that the three countries share to a large degree. What I mean by this tradition is not necessarily something to be found in Rousseau himself, but something associated with his work and thought since the French Revolution: radical majoritarianism. It is the view that the majority, as such, provides an implicit and indubitable "legitimacy" in the determination of public policy and general laws. Reinforced by Jacobinism in France, by Mazzini in Italy, and by Kant and the Kantians in Germany, this view inclines to reify the concept of the general will in terms of actual votes taken in elections, referendums, and the like. That is to say, with a general skepticism about the capacity of man to free himself of such prejudice-creating frameworks as his class and economic interest goes the conviction that the general decisions in the body politic result from an act of will, rather than rational deliberation. Also involved is a tendency to disregard (*a*) the degree of reversibility of decisions, and (*b*) natural limits to any decision, resulting from the inherent conditions with which the decision is concerned.[4] But politically decisive is the disregard for the minority, including the individual. There is little understanding in this tradition of the delicate balance between the majority's and minority's "rights" in a free society and the persistent difficulties inherent in any scheme which sets out to achieve this balance in such a way that neither of two undesirable results arises: (*a*) that the minority is tyrannized over by the majority, (*b*) that the majority is prevented from acting by the recalcitrant minority. Much of the best thought of constitutional theorizing in English-speaking countries has, as everyone knows, gone into the exploration of these issues; Harrington and Locke, the *Federalist* and John Stuart Mill, and a host of others have tried to resolve the numerous problems posited by what I once called "one majority against another: *populus semper virens*." This problem is, of course, at the heart of constitutional liberty, as Kant well knew and made explicit in spelling out the implications of Rousseau's

[4] For a more detailed discussion of these problems, see my *The New Image of the Common Man* (Boston, 1942; new ed., 1950), chap. iv; for a contrary view, see Edwin Mims, Jr., *The Majority of the People* (Toronto, 1941), and Willmore Kendall, "The Majority Principle and the Scientific Elite," *The Southern Review*, IV, No. 3 (1939). Neither author deals with (a) above.

concept of the general will.[5] But Continental European democrats, in the tradition of the Jacobins, have tended to neglect these problems, with the result that constitutionalism has been a weak ingredient in their democratic ideology.

It is not possible to consider constitutional provisions in detail, let alone the debates in terms of which their meaning becomes clear. It must suffice to indicate some broad lines of analysis to be implemented by the other essays that follow. Relatively small is the influence of British and American constitutional experience upon these new constitutions, in spite of the manifest "success" of these models in mastering the political tasks with which men, working with and through them, have had to deal. Vague excuses, such as "America is different" and "Britain's parliamentary system is inimitable," served to insulate native thought habits from undue disturbance by these Anglo-American traditions. In Germany, this propensity to stick to local habits was, of course, reinforced by the brutal fact of occupation, which made it unattractive for a politician seeking popular approval to appear to copy the occupants' ideas on democracy in detail; it was bad enough to have to "democratize" under instructions. For the Social Democrats, the unscrupulous propaganda of the Communist party exploiting this weakness was a prime factor in making them move with the greatest circumspection in all matters of this kind. Whatever the reasons, the influence of British and American constitutional thought was certainly quite limited.

There is, however, one important feature of American constitutionalism that has taken hold of Continental European theorists to an unprecedented extent, and that is the idea of making the courts, or at least a judicial body, the guardian of the constitution, rather than the legislative and/or executive authorities. Here again, the French provisions are less pronounced than the German and Italian ones. Austria has had a limited constitutional judiciary under its constitution of 1929, now revived.[6] It has always been recognized

[5] See for this my *Inevitable Peace* (Cambridge, 1948), as well as Professor Lewis W. Beck's Introduction to his selections of Kant.

[6] See Ludwig Adamovich, *Grundriss des oesterrischischen Verfassungsrechts* (4th ed.; Vienna, 1947), esp. pp. 303 ff., where the narrow limits of judicial review in Austria are indicated.

Political Theory of New Democratic Constitutions

in the United States that the existence of a federal system greatly contributes to the need for, and the vitality of, a judicial guardianship over the constitution. The absence of such a federal system in France, its emasculated form in Italy with its regions, and its presence in both Austria and Germany undoubtedly explains to some extent the difference, in stress and emphasis, upon judicial review. The French organized merely a "constitutional committee" consisting of the president who presides, the presiding officers of the two houses of the legislature, and ten members of the houses—seven from the lower, three from the upper—who are chosen annually by proportional representation. It is obvious that such a body, modeled upon a proposal once advanced by Sieyès, is still very close to the legislature (as are similar ones in a number of the German states). Actually, by the end of 1949, it had met only once. By contrast, the Italian Constitution, definitely implemented by a constitutional law, set up a constitutional court (Arts. 134–137) consisting of lawyers (jurists) who serve for twelve years and are nominated one third by the president, one third by parliament, and one third by the judiciary. They may not be parliamentarians. The German Basic Law likewise provides for a constitutional court (Arts. 92–94), but half its members are elected by the *Bundesrat* and half by the *Bundestag,* and its jurisdiction is more fully described. Since the law envisaged by the Basic Law has not yet been adopted, it remains to be seen whether an attempt will be made, as has been the case in some of the *Länder,* to emasculate the court by excluding individual litigants and similar procedural devices. The German Basic Law shoulders the constitutional court with the task of determining who has abused various basic rights "in order to attack the free, democratic basic order" and provides for the court's pronouncing the extent to which any such attackers have forfeited these basic rights. While the intention of this provision (Art. 18) is laudable, insofar as it seeks to prevent to some extent the re-emergence of Fascist-Communist attempts to twist constitutional freedoms into anticonstitutional tools, the article is a dangerous weapon. In the light of experience in older constitutional democracies, it is certainly well that this weapon be placed in judicial, rather than executive, hands.

Carl J. Friedrich

This recognition of judicial protection for constitutional charters is of fundamental significance for the political theory of the new constitutions: not only does it relate clearly to the broader and deeper appreciation of the importance of civil rights, but it also clearly signalizes a recognition of the constitution as a fundamental law in a manner not customary in Continental Europe before. It represents a departure from the older, radically majoritarian, position noted earlier in this paper.

Returning now to the general issue of the reaffirmation of human rights, this trend in European constitutional thought is marked, specifically, by a tendency to put such rights into more forthright language than has been customary since the French Revolution. The reason is apparent enough: Fascist and Communist perversion of general paper declarations has shown how useless such declaratory rights can be. The "constitutions" of the *Länder* in the Soviet zone of Germany, for example, contain high-sounding lists of such rights, but their interpretation is left to a committee of the Communist-dominated parliament. While it would be futile to assume that, under Russian bayonets, judicial safeguards would be any better, the complete concentration of power in the hands of a majority party, so called, reveals the central issue of these rights: How can they be enforced? There are, of course, still such qualifying phrases as suggest interpretation of these constitutional rights by legislation (e.g., Italian, Arts. 14, 21, freedom of the press: "contrary to good custom," etc.; German, Arts. 2, 4, 8, 10). The rather numerous references to such laws in the German case would be more objectionable if the Basic Law did not also provide (Art. 19) that "in no case may a basic right be altered in its essential core *(Wesensgehalt).*"[7]

Both constitutions conceive of these rights as not limited to the

---

[7] We are concentrating in this discussion upon the Italian and German provisions, because the French relegated the statement of basic rights to the preamble. However, the earlier French draft that was rejected by the voters on May 5, 1946, *did* contain such a bill of rights, which to a considerable extent fits into the analysis above (not, however, into the anti-Communist part of it). Cf. Georges Burdeau, *Manuel de droit public.* The authoritative *Précis de droit constitutionnel* by Marcel Prélot, a member of the constitutional committee, entirely discards the preamble and speaks of the rights having been "eliminated," and in the author's view rightly so.

individual but as social and economic in their ramifications. In fact, the Italian Constitution, like the discarded French draft, elaborates these social and economic aspects into a broad pattern; the German Basic Law is briefer, but the fundamental outlook is the same. Thus the state appears as the collective assisting in the realization of all these rights, rather than as the antagonist of the individual's self-expression. Education and family life (Italian, Arts. 29–34; German, Arts. 6–7) and the care of the indigent and the underprivileged are thus seen as social rights, while the right to work, and to social security (Italian, Arts. 35–38; German, Art. 12) when unable to work, take their place alongside the right to organize and to conduct strikes (Italian, Arts. 39–40); they are followed, rather than preceded, by the right of private initiative and of property. But these former individual or natural rights are now carefully circumscribed by such expressions as that they must not be contrary to social utility or do damage to security, freedom, or human dignity (Italian, Arts. 41–42; German, Arts. 14–15). These matters deserve the greatest attention; it is easy to laugh off such broadly sketched social philosophy as in no sense a guarantee of individual rights. Those individual rights, the freedoms of expression, and of personal security and privacy, also find their place in these constitutions and at times are carried to much greater length than in older constitutions (e.g., contrast the German Basic Law guarantee, Arts. 3–4, that no one may be compelled to serve militarily against his conscience, with Italian, Art. 52). But there is a definite effort made in these constitutions, as had been done earlier in the Weimar Constitution and in the Austrian Constitution of 1929, to anchor the human rights of the "welfare state" in the constitution. In conclusion, it might be noted that parties are recognized as instrumentalities of democracy and that these parties themselves need to be democratic (Italian, Art. 49; German, Art. 21).

The need for preventing the enemies of the constitutional order from utilizing such broadly conceived rights for the purpose of destroying the constitution itself is more marked in the German, than in the Italian, Constitution. In the latter, it is merely proclaimed that all citizens have a duty to be faithful to the Republic and to observe the constitution and the laws. The German Basic Law, on the other hand, proposes, as already noted, to put the enemies of the constitution beyond its protective frame. It goes so far as to attempt to provide (Art. 143) a criminal sanction against attacks on the constitution, written apparently with direct reference to Hitler's seizure of power "from within." Similar provisions are found in the several *Land* constitutions.

Socialization and planning are given constitutional sanction in all three constitutions, and there can be no doubt that the political theory of these constitutions encompasses these modern approaches. While rather controversial, they constitute, according to prevailing opinions, extensions rather than perversions of constitutionalism. This is not the place to elaborate such an idea,[8] but there can be no doubt that the makers of these constitutions entertained the hope that such a solution could be found. Thus, Article 25 of the French Constitution provides for an economic council which, apart from advisory legislative duties, "must be consulted in the adoption of a national economic plan for full employment and the rational utilization of resources." Likewise, the Italian Constitution envisages such an economic council (Art. 99). The German Basic Law, in its long list of legislative competencies of the *Bund* (Arts. 74-75), includes socialization and planning among these federal activities. Before the Basic Law came into being, a socialization law, representing a compromise between Christian and Social Democrats, had already been formulated and passed by the legislature of *Land* North-Rhine-Westphalia (in September 1948) but was suspended by the British in order not to anticipate federal legislation in this field; a similar situation prevails in Western Berlin. Likewise, Hesse passed a Shop Council Law, involving the principle of workers' participation in management, similarly suspended by the Americans. This law, too, represented a Christian and Socialist compromise. Finally, the Bizonal Economic Council prepared a "deconcentration law," which is being brought forward under the Basic Law's enabling clause in this field. All these activities, no less than the socialization measures in France and Italy, show that these consti-

---

[8] *Constitutional Government and Democracy*, chap. xxiii.

tutional provisions represent a broad sweep of political thought, as do efforts to develop national planning, like the Monnet Plan. They have been greatly strengthened by the pressure for implementing the Marshall Plan. But political theory is no longer unaware of the totalitarian potentialities of a socialized and planned economy. It would be very misleading, however, to pretend that these constitutions or their makers had as yet made any very striking contribution to the solution of the problems of the rival claims of freedom and authority under such conditions. A slogan, the "social-market economy," is making itself heard in connection with the German Basic Law, but whether it will turn out to be more than a "conjunction of opposites" remains to be seen.

The slogan of a "social-market economy" *(soziale Marktwirtschaft)* has certainly become the target of numerous angry attacks by German Social Democrats. In these "broadsides" the underlying conflict between the two major elements supporting European democratic constitutionalism is finding vigorous expression. It is important to bear in mind that all three constitutions (as well as the German *Land* constitutions) are the result of compromises between these Christian and Socialist Democrats, united primarily by their common hostility toward the totalitarianism of right and left (with some significant differences of emphasis in this respect also). But beyond this common adversary, the approaches of the Christians and the Socialists are rather widely divergent. It is not only that the Christians assign a maximal role to religion in the ordering of social relations—from which an emphasis on education and the like stems—whereas the Socialists, while no longer doctrinaire atheists, prefer to leave religion a private matter and build the constitution upon a civic spirit; but, in keeping with this theoretically significant divergence in their general outlook, the Christians tend to minimize the role of the state in social betterment, while the Socialists consider it decisive. Such compromise legislation as the socialization law, passed in September 1948 in North-Rhine-Westphalia (but suspended by the British occupation authorities), was very difficult to achieve because of this radical divergence in viewpoint; a mixture of the two outlooks is reflected in the law's essential provisions. It is, in this connection, worth while to note the difference in terminology: Continental Europeans often speak of socialization as different from nationalization, in the sense that the latter involves the "state" as owner and manager, whereas the former does not necessarily do so.

This basic divergence in attitude toward the degree of creative potentiality of state action is reflected, in turn, in the two parties' different attitude toward federalism. The Christian Democrats favor whatever degree of regional and local autonomy can be secured under prevailing conditions. Communal autonomy in France, regional autonomy of the provinces in Italy, and states' rights federalism in Germany are merely three cognate expressions of the same underlying partiality for "grass-roots democracy," as Americans like to call it. There are, of course, considerable differences of opinion within the Christian Democratic movements, but the general trend cannot be doubted. The Socialist Democrats, on the other hand, even if not outright centralists, incline toward the solving of social problems by means of state action in all fields. Yet their ideology contains a distinct paradox in this general outlook, for, while favoring the state, they do not favor "bureaucracy"; they are forever insisting that the civil service must be "democratized" and thus brought within the general framework of their "civic responsibility" pattern of political theorizing.

But whether the Christian Democrats and the Socialists work together in a coalition, as in France, Italy, and a number of German states, or whether they confront each other as government and opposition, as in the Federal German Republic and other German states, it is in any case clear that the continuing process of molding constitutional developments is largely the result of their recurrent compromises. For a constitution consists not merely of the compromise arrived at, when its formal provisions were drafted, but of the ever-changing interpretation for its provisions provided by those in power as the political situation unfolds. Perhaps these compromises would not be possible if there were not increasing pressure from the partisans of totalitarian solutions inside and outside these countries; no one knows. The essential fact remains that the divergent theorizing of the Christian and Socialist Democrats coalesces into a compromise practice under these constitutions, and that in the course of this development there is unfolding a "common ground" of constitutional democratic theory which is more moderate than the viewpoints of either of the theoretical contestants.

To round out the analysis, one might mention some governmental institutions that represent, at least negatively, a taking of stock of European constitutional thought and an attempt to transcend the challenge of totalitarianism. For one, the establishment of a Council of the Judiciary in both France and Italy, to weaken the bureaucratic hold of the justice ministry upon courts, is noteworthy. French desire to emulate the British Commonwealth policy has found expression in the very interesting French Union, through which effective participation in government of all those living under French law is eventually going to be brought about. Italy has also made an attempt, albeit a feeble one, to get away from overcentralization by the recognition and organization of regions with a measure of autonomy; while Germany, partly under Allied pressure but also responding to ancient traditions, has re-established a thoroughgoing federalism which, freed from the Prussian incubus, may prove a workable scheme and more truly federal than the Weimar Republic or even the *Kaiserreich*. Germany's Basic Law has also made an interesting attempt to avoid the instability of governments resting upon coalitions in a parliament by making votes of lack of confidence depend upon the opposition uniting in putting forward a new chancellor, and giving the chancellor the right to dissolve. But this provision (Art. 67) may lead to a dangerous stalemate, since another article provides that a majority consists of the majority of all members of parliament (Art. 121), which suggests that obstructionist minorities, even though they cannot agree on a chancellor, may thwart all legislation by staying away.[9] The diffi-

---

[9] These provisions are given especial attention by Brecht, *op. cit.* Actually, similar provisions have worked reasonably well in Württemberg-Baden; they have now also been incorporated into the new constitution of North-Rhine-Westphalia. See, for an interesting comparative analysis, Friedrich Glum, *Das parlamentarische Regierungssystem in Deutschland, Grossbritannien und Frankreich* (Munich, 1950), esp. chap. xiii. Dr. Glum takes a critical view of this new system, which he believes will end

culty is enhanced by the weakness of emergency powers under the Basic Law. This is a countertrend in Germany; in France and Italy the emergency powers have been strengthened, and these provisions have already proved their value. Up to the end of 1950 this problem was not serious, because behind any such powers of the German Government there stood the authority of the occupying powers who, under the Occupation Statute, had reserved to themselves the right to resurrect their "full authority," not only in the interest of their own security and obligations, but also "to preserve democratic government in Germany" (Occupation Statute, Art. 3). But if the Occupation Statute should be abrogated, without any radical amendment in the Basic Law to correct this weakness, a very serious situation might develop. The abuse of Article 48 of the Weimar Constitution by the antidemocratic elements around Hindenburg in 1932–1933 has obscured the fact that, as had been intended, this article served the constitutional system when it was under very serious attack in 1923. Both the Communist rebellion in Saxony that year and the so-called beer-hall *Putsch* could probably not have been handled successfully by a government that had had at its disposal only the powers which the Basic Law provides in the case of an emergency. Nor could the *Länder* be expected to step into the breach; their constitutions also contain rather inadequate emergency-power provisions. This is notably true of the two largest states, Bavaria and North-Rhine-Westphalia.[10] Under the circumstances, it is to be hoped that the United States, Great Britain, and France will, under any kind of negotiated security treaty, maintain some sort of prerogative in the handling of emergencies.

Perhaps the most startlingly novel aspect of these constitutions is their abandonment of the idea of national sovereignty as a central presupposition of their political theory. Here, again, the constitutional provisions are increasingly radical, as we compare the French,

---

by leading to minority cabinets that will have to yield to a determined anticonstitutional opposition (cf. pp. 333 ff.).

[10] Art. 60 in the latter constitution only provides for the special case in which the *Landtag* (legislature) is prevented from sitting. The Bavarian provisions resemble those of the Basic Law.

Political Theory of New Democratic Constitutions

the Italian, and the German documents. The French Constitution states that "on condition of reciprocal terms, France shall accept the limitations of sovereignty necessary to the organization and defense of peace" (preamble). The Italian Constitution, in Article 11, provides that Italy "consents, on conditions of parity with other states, to limitations of sovereignty necessary to an order for ensuring peace and justice among the nations; it promotes and favors international organizations directed toward that end." The Basic Law's Article 24 elaborates this thought by the following: "(1) The Federation may, by legislation, transfer sovereign powers to international institutions. (2) For the maintenance of peace, the Federation may join a system of mutual collective security; in doing so it will consent to those limitations of its sovereign powers which will bring about and secure a peaceful and lasting order in Europe and among the nations of the world. (3) For the settlement of disputes between nations, the Federation will accede to conventions concerning a general, comprehensive obligatory system of international arbitration." It will be noted that paragraph (2) specifically makes reference to *Europe* as an area to which the national sovereignty might yield its various rights. While this provision does not preclude participation in the looser kind of league that the United Nations constitutes, it unquestionably is intended to be a more inclusive commitment.[11] This tendency was reasserted by a resolution in the Bonn Parliament, passed in July 1950, instructing its delegation to the Consultative Assembly of the Council of Europe to "work for the establishment of a government and parliament of Europe" and authorizing it "to transfer to such government and parliament all such authority as other European governments and parliaments were prepared to transfer to it." The resolution passed 362 to 40. The French Parliament, likewise, has gone on

[11] Whether membership in the United Nations entails an infringement of national sovereignty has been a subject of dispute. The Charter explicitly states that the member states are "sovereign"—as did the United States Articles of Confederation (in Art. II). On the other hand, member states can be committed to actions involving war without their consent, except for those states that exercise a veto power in the Security Council. Yet what this commitment actually amounts to, the Korean crisis has revealed. It seems fair to conclude that, at present, the United Nations Charter leaves member states sovereign; moves to alter this situation have so far not succeeded.

record in supporting its government in its efforts to establish a government of Europe, and the foreign-policy debates of the French Council and Assembly are full of references to this idea, as are the resolutions of political-party congresses. The M.R.P.F. *(Gaulliste)*, for example, has adopted a radical plank supporting a government and parliament for Europe.

All these developments point toward what seems to be a central development of political thought in Continental Europe; namely, the establishment of a federal government for Europe as a whole supported by a European "nation." This European sentiment has grown very rapidly in the course of 1949 and 1950 and in many ways constitutes a revolutionary development. It is the positive projection of the negative revolutions that occurred in France, Italy, and Germany. By the end of 1950, this novel constituent power had become very active. Transitional institutional forms had been set up in the form of the Council of Europe, consisting of Ministers and a Consultative Assembly, with headquarters at Strasbourg. At the same time, the Schuman Plan, so called, had led to the draft of an international "government" of the coal and steel industries of France, the Benelux, Italy, and Germany (Federal Republic). Plans were afoot for the establishment of a European army and for a "government" of agriculture. These developments represent what is called the "functional" approach as contrasted with the "federal" approach of the Council of Europe and the more far-reaching plans to convert the latter into a government of Europe. The issue of functionalism versus federalism has been hotly debated and is not settled, by any means. What concerns the student of political thought is the radical turning away from nationalism involved in all these developments and the substitution of a regional internationalism. This regional internationalism could, and in quite a few minds does, involve a new "nationalism" on a broader plane. As it is customary to speak of Chinese or Indian "nationalism," meaning thereby the sentiment of allegiance and political support for the broad cultural entities of China and India, so European culture is very much the focal point of attention of the European movement. Perhaps one should speak of "culturism" rather than nationalism.

On the other hand, the peoples of Europe are being referred to, from time to time, as a "nation" already, and a number of the characteristic elements of nationalism are present in much of the thinking and arguing over the "Pan-Europe" of the future. But this Europe-in-the-making must, in view of the diversity of its "national" subcultures, try to organize itself federally. This means that constitutionalism has suddenly acquired new life and significance, for a federal state cannot be organized, except on a constitutional basis. Its characteristic division of powers (or competencies) along regional lines, *i.e.,* between the federal authorities and the local constituent units (states, *Länder,* cantons, etc.), presupposes a written document. This document must be protected by adequate sanctions and calls for continuous interpretation by some kind of judicial body.[12] Such a federal union will not come into existence without a vigorous constituent power, sufficient to overcome local vested interests, sentiments, and ideology. Within the Consultative Assembly at Strasbourg, in the meeting in August 1950, all this was proposed, but the demand for the election of a constituent assembly was thwarted by opposition in the Council of Ministers, especially opposition by Britain. Britain, which is governed under an ancient and deep-rooted constitution, has not experienced the rise of such a constituent will to create a new constitutional order as is found on the Continent. Her constitutional tradition is "organic," in the sense that the *grown,* as contrasted with the *made,* constitution appears to her people the sound and natural process. No federating of discordant elements under outside pressure was involved in the process either—the union with Scotland having been brought about by quasi-dynastic methods. This view is sensible, if there is adequate *time* for the growth. For actually "growth" is a slow accumulation of rules and institutions over a long period of time. But there are situations when a new organization has to be created *at one time.* This sort of event is characteristically involved in the founding of federal states as they emerge from a preceding congeries of independent units. The Europeans who insist upon the federal, as

[12] See the theory of federalism given in my *Constitutional Government and Democracy,* previously cited, chap. xi.

against the functional, approach are convinced that such a time has arrived for them. They have come to this view mainly for three reasons: first, the need for achieving some measure of military security in the face of the Soviet Union, without so much dependence upon the United States as is at present required; second, the need for much larger market areas unimpeded by tariffs, foreign exchanges, and the like; and, third, the desire to eliminate the destructive intra-European warfare (and, at present, reconstruction to overcome its effects). In other words, European union has a military, an economic, and a broad political objective in view. To each of these major objectives there corresponds a series of activities, roughly N.A.T.O., O.E.E.C., and the Council of Europe. But behind these immediate objectives, and giving them meaning and significance, is the sense of European culture as a precious heritage to be preserved, a vital challenge to be met.

A great deal of theorizing is going on in Europe at the present time concerning these developments. This theorizing is essentially constitutional in nature. It has significantly intensified the grasp of the inherent meaning of constitutionalism as a system of effective regularized restraints upon a legally organized government. Past Fascist experience, as well as the specter of Soviet dictatorship, have combined to focus attention upon a number of interrelated propositions: that the German problem cannot be solved without a united Europe within which Germany may develop economically and otherwise; that the Communist problem cannot be solved without a united Europe, one that will have a large and prosperous economy; that the Fascist problem cannot be solved without a united Europe in which the appeal of emotional mass nationalism will be attenuated by supranational allegiance. This supranational allegiance found expression in the adoption of a charter of basic rights at Strasbourg in August 1950. The charter represents the thought of the three constitutions we have already studied. It is not novel, any more than they are. Ancient truth, *das alte Wahre* in Goethe's sense, has been embodied in this document. And yet there is something profoundly significant, from the standpoint of political thought, in this common action. *Si duo faciunt idem, non est idem.* It is fulfillment

Political Theory of New Democratic Constitutions

of the universalism of the English and French revolutions. Both are here being transcended; their specifically local and national orientations have been left behind, and a more truly human embodiment has been given to these ideas. For if all Europeans are now equal before the law, it means that they all acknowledge themselves to be equal to each other. National conceits and pretensions are being laid aside, or at any rate recede into the background.

Before concluding this general sketch of the political theory of the new European constitutions of a Western democratic type, it seems important to note one rather striking divergence from the American, if not from the British, climate of opinion. Nowhere on the Continent is there to be found any genuine "belief in the common man," as that belief is taken for granted in the United States. In fact, the very term is nonexistent and hence untranslatable. This extraordinary personification of American democratic traditions is, throughout Continental Europe, confused with the mass man. Attacks upon the mass man, such as Ortega y Gasset's, have achieved very wide currency among Europeans of presumably democratic convictions. Not only Europe's deep attachment to culture, but the Marxist insistence upon the class-conscious elite (in the socialist sector), and the corresponding elite notions in the catholic tradition, have combined to prevent the rise of any such confidence in the common man's ability to deal with common concerns of the community as is generally accepted in America, even by people with sophisticated ideas about the workings of democracy. Somehow, this lacuna in European democratic thought seems related to the exaggeration of the majority's views on one side and to the role of the state on the other. In both cases, we must recognize in European democratic theory a stronger emphasis upon the collective aspects of society and government and a corresponding weakness, when it comes to the individual. Characteristically, European parliaments make quite inadequate provisions for the contact between the citizen and his representative. European party leaders tend to become rather authoritarian, as soon as they have achieved a measure of status and leadership. The resulting reaction of the people at large is one of indifference, cynicism, and even

Carl J. Friedrich

antidemocratic (though not necessarily prototalitarian) sentiments. Whether a belief in the common man could be generated to remedy these defects seems doubtful. As the gentleman was the embodiment of England's ideal of man in an aristocratic age, so the common man seems America's personal "mirror of man." Some of the more thoughtful European theorists appreciate the weakness resulting from the absence of such a personal projection of democratic ideals, especially in the face of an aggressive totalitarian challenge. But is that enough?

In sum, the negative revolutions that have occurred in Western Europe as a result of the victory of British and American arms over Fascism are animated by a spirit of reconstruction. The political theory associated with these revolutions and with the resulting constitutions is one of moderation and compromise. It seeks to transcend the totalitarian challenge, not by a blind appeal to the past, but by a patient effort to recapture the essentials of human freedom and dignity. The political thought of the negative revolutions is motivated by the social and economic ills of an aging industrial society, rent by violent revolutionary claims for radical improvement. Yet, on the whole, it is still true that Continental Europeans stress abstract principles, rather than specific procedures and concrete solutions. Quite a few years ago, John Stuart Mill wrote:

The common-places of politics, in France, are large and sweeping practical maxims, from which as ultimate premises men reason downwards to particular applications, and this they call being logical and consistent. For instance, they are perpetually arguing that such and such a measure ought to be adopted, because it is the consequence of the principle on which the form of government is founded; of the principle of legitimacy or the principle of the sovereignty of the people.[13]

It is a curious but undeniable fact that these observations still hold true to a remarkable degree, not only of France, but of Italy and Germany as well. If Mill thought that "it would be often a much stronger recommendation of some practical arrangement, that it does not follow from what is called the general principle of the

---

[13] John Stuart Mill, *Logic* (1st ed.; London, 1843), II, 618.

Political Theory of New Democratic Constitutions

government, than that it does," I believe that this thought is as "weird" and "incomprehensible" to Europeans today as it was nearly a hundred years ago. From which it follows that the political *theory* of these constitutions is probably a good deal more important than an Englishman or American is likely to assume. This reflection may serve as a humble excuse for seeking to elucidate the theorizing of those who have developed these new constitutions: rejecting the totalitarian dictatorship, they are groping for workable principles of social order with genuine theoretical concern.

Electoral Changes after World War II

By Edward G. Lewis
UNIVERSITY OF ILLINOIS

HOW people vote and how their representatives speak for them are vital aspects of democracy, because while democracy is an idea, it is also machinery. And a democracy built out of faulty machinery is itself faulty. So a study of the electoral process and of the representative legislature of a state is, actually, a study of how democratic that state is.

The constitution-builders in postwar democracies knew that this was true, so they built their electoral and representative systems most carefully. In only a few countries have the electoral and legislative systems been twisted away from democracy—from majority rule. South Africa is one of these. But the over-all trend is toward improved representation.

Different countries have become a part of this trend by different routes. This is to be expected, because governments are a part of the tradition of the country—of its way of life, its customs, and its aspirations. But, fortunately, there are not as many routes to improved legislative representation as there are democratic countries. Instead, there are mainly two: those used in the so-called two-party parliamentary countries and those used in the multiparty parliamentary countries.

In the two-party countries, mainly Great Britain and the Commonwealth countries, the route to improved representation has been, with few exceptions, through slight changes and improvements in the existing system.

In Great Britain itself, in the postwar period, there was no major change in the underlying idea of the representational system. It is

Electoral Changes after World War II

now, more than ever, founded on the single-member district. Each electoral area now sends one representative to Parliament. This means, though, that the number of members a party has in the House of Commons may not be at all proportional to the number of people who voted for that party in the country. In fact, if parliamentary representation even closely equals the party's voting strength in the country, it is an accident. This can be demonstrated by the February 1950 general election statistics. The spectacular example is the Liberal party. Nearly nine per cent of those who cast ballots voted for Liberal candidates—about two and one-half million votes—but the Liberal party won only seven tenths of a per cent of the seats in the House of Commons. Of course, the Labour and Conservative parties fared better. For Labour, forty-five per cent of the votes won fifty-one per cent of the seats, and for the Conservatives, forty-two per cent of the votes won forty-eight per cent of the seats.[1] But 186 members were elected by a minority of the voters of their district.[2] These were in multiparty districts where, with at least three parties putting up candidates, the victor received more votes than his rivals, but not a majority of the votes.

The British have recently made a number of changes in this imperfectly representative single-member district system, but their effect is to make it more symmetrical than it used to be rather than to change its basic aspects. Up until World War II some odd historical remnants had upset the symmetry of the system—a few plural votes were allowed.[3] For example, some people voted twice because they had business property in one voting area and lived in another. Others voted twice because, in addition to voting for a representative from their home district, they had a university degree that allowed them to vote for one of the twelve university members of the House of Commons. But although the actual

---

[1] These calculations are based on the summaries of the *Manchester Guardian Weekly*, March 2, 1950, p. 3.
[2] *Parliamentary Debates (Commons)*, 5th series, vol. 472, col. 143.
[3] Slightly less than 200,000 people probably voted twice in the 1945 general election. See R. B. McCallum and A. Readman, *The British General Election of 1945* (London, 1947), pp. 220, 275–76.

number of people who voted twice was small, the idea of plural voting was anomalous in a democracy.

This anomaly was removed, at least for the moment,[4] by the Representation of the People Act of 1948.[5] By it, the principle of "one man one vote" was finally put into effect in Great Britain. Both the university constituencies and the business plural votes were wiped out.

A number of other minor changes in the election system were effected through this same act. These were mainly recommended by a Speaker's Committee on electoral reform and the redistribution of seats. The House of Commons set up this committee by a resolution of February 2, 1944, introduced by the coalition government.[6] Thirty-two peers and members of Parliament made up the committee. They were selected roughly in proportion to party strength, but also to represent various shades of opinion, different types of constituencies, and all parts of the country. The committee met twenty times. Its terms of reference show how sweeping its recommendations could be. These terms were:

> To examine, and, if possible, submit agreed resolutions, on the following matters:—
> (a) Redistribution of seats.
> (b) Reform of franchise (both Parliamentary and local government).
> (c) Conduct and costs of Parliamentary elections, and expenses falling on candidates and Members of Parliament.
> (d) Methods of election.[7]

The committee's major recommendation was that a general redistribution of seats should take place as soon as possible. And to do this it recommended that boundary commissions be set up to redraw the boundaries of electoral areas. Furthermore, it recommended that these commissions should be instructed to reconsider

---

[4] The 1950 Conservative party election manifesto, "This Is the Road," calls for a restoration of the university constituency. See British Information Services Publication I.D. 970, p. 17. This is a reprint of the Conservative manifesto.

[5] 11 & 12 Geo. VI, c. 65.

[6] The parliamentary history and recommendations of the Speaker's Committee are found in Cmd. 6534, *British Parliamentary Papers* (cited hereafter as *B.P.P.*), 1943–1944, vol. III, p. 213. Cmd. 6543, *B.P.P.*, 1943–1944, vol. III, p. 221.

[7] Cmd. 6534, previously cited, p. 2.

Electoral Changes after World War II

the boundaries of electoral districts not less than every three nor more than every seven years. The commissions were to be nonpartisan.

These Speaker's Committee recommendations were put into effect by the House of Commons (Redistribution of Seats) Act of 1944.[8] At the time this Act was discussed in the House of Commons, Herbert Morrison, for the Labour party, called it the culmination of the electoral reforms that began with the great reform act of 1832.[9] It was indeed as important as this because it set up permanent machinery for redistribution of seats, in the form of the boundary commissions. The earlier reforms along this same line had been piecemeal, and no machinery previously existed for a periodical review of electoral boundaries. The 1944 Act removed this major defect of the British representational machinery.

The Speaker's Committee, however, did not recommend the "one man one vote" principle. In fact, by a vote of twenty-five to six it explicitly rejected it.[10] It also voted unanimously to continue the university constituencies, and voted twenty-one to eight to allow one business and one residential vote. Even so, as we have seen, the Labour government abolished the plural vote by the Representation of the People Act of 1948.[11]

Thus the British electoral system has been improved, but always within the framework of the single-member district. The British Government has given very little thought to the introduction of proportional representation as a cure for the distorted majorities produced by the single-member district system. The 1944 Speaker's Committee was asked to recommend the adoption of proportional representation, but by a vote of twenty-four to five it decisively

---

[8] 7 & 8 Geo. VI, c. 41.
[9] *Parliamentary Debates (Commons)*, 5th series, vol. 406, col. 1646.
[10] Cmd. 6534, previously cited, pp. 6 and 8.
[11] Many other minor changes were made by this Act, in such fields as corrupt and illegal practices and registration of voters. It also assimilated the local and the parliamentary franchise. This Act was based partly on the Speaker's Committee report already cited (note 6 above), but also on the interim and final reports of the Departmental Committee on Electoral Reform (Cmd. 6606, *B.P.P.*, 1944–1945, vol. V, p. 59. Cmd. 7286, *B.P.P.*, 1947–1948, vol. XI, p. 727. Cmd. 7004, *B.P.P.*, 1946–1947, vol. XI, p. 377).

rejected the idea.[12] For years, of course, the Liberal party has asked for proportional representation. The obvious reason for this is that, by it, the party would gain many seats in the House of Commons. For example, the use of proportional representation in the 1950 elections would have given the Liberals about fifty-four seats in the House of Commons instead of the nine the party actually received under the single-member district system, assuming that the popular votes had been the same.

More recently, however, proportional representation has been at least suggested in the House of Commons by no less a dignitary than Mr. Winston Churchill, as leader of the opposition. He proposed that a "Select Committee" should be set up to inquire into the whole question of electoral reform but that "it should be based not on the numbers of Members here, but upon the numbers of votes recorded by the electorate for the three parties which are represented in the House."[13] For the Labour government, Mr. Morrison called this suggestion both unparliamentary and unconstitutional. Nothing came of it.

But the British Government's dislike for proportional representation has not always been reproduced in the Commonwealth. Thus, in 1948 the Australian Parliament, departing from British precedent, enacted a proportional-representation statute for selecting Senators, members of the Australian upper house.[14] This change grew out of the Representation Act of 1948.[15] This Act increased the size of the House of Representatives (the lower house) from seventy-four members to one hundred and twenty-one. And, according to the Australian Constitution, the Senate must be one half the size of the House. Hence, the Senate was increased in size from thirty-six members to sixty. By this change, each state elected ten members, whereas formerly it had elected six.

But this Act increasing the size of the Senate could not be put into operation at once. This was because the terms of the Senators were staggered—one half went out of office at intervals of three

[12] Cmd. 6534, previously cited, pp. 7–8.
[13] *Parliamentary Debates (Commons)*, 5th series, vol. 472, cols. 143–44.
[14] Commonwealth Electoral Act 1948 (Act no. 17 of 1948).
[15] Act no. 16 of 1948.

Electoral Changes after World War II

years. Hence each state, for the 1949 elections, had three Senators whose terms had not yet expired. That left seven new senatorial posts to be filled in the elections by the proportional-representation system.

This change to proportional representation was attacked by the Australian Liberal party—then in opposition—as a piece of rank partisanship. The Act, it said, was in fact a racket.[16] Undoubtedly the effect of the Act was to keep the Labour party in control of the Senate while it lost control in the House. The explanation for this is that, at the time of the passage of the Act, the Labour party had fifteen of the eighteen seats of Senators whose terms had three more years to run. Through the use of the proportional-representation system it was likely that the seven new Senators from each state would be nearly evenly split—say four for the Liberals and three for Labour—because the popular support of the parties was nearly the same. Thus the Liberal party coalition, even though it was successful in the House elections, could not win control of the Senate. In fact, the election turned out very nearly as the opposition Liberals had predicted, except that in one state the Labourites won four instead of three seats.[17]

Even though the Liberal party opposed the method of introduction of proportional representation in 1948, it proposed two years later to extend and modify the system. And as the Labour government's act had momentarily benefited the Labour party in the Senate, so this new proposal would momentarily have helped the Liberal party. The new proposal[18] was that, on double dissolutions (that is of the House and Senate at the same time), the ten Senators to be elected from each state should be divided into two groups of five each, one group to be elected for three years and the other for six. This proposal was made, the Liberal government said, to get a workable majority in the Senate. Mr. Menzies, the Liberal Prime Minister, said that if ten Senators were elected in one group

---

[16] Commonwealth of Australia, *Parliamentary Debates*, 1946–1948, vol. 196, p. 1001.

[17] *Round Table*, no. 158 (March 1950), p. 181.

[18] Introduced May 4, 1950; passed by the House of Representatives on June 7, 1950; rejected by the Senate. See *Keesing's Contemporary Archives* (London), VIII (August 12–19, 1950), 10900.

as the existing law required, instead of being split into two, a close election could well result in a stalemate—five Senators from each party. By the new proposal, in a close election, each group of five Senators might split three to two. Thus, the party with a bare majority of the votes would win six seats in each state. This would create a workable majority in the Senate.

Obviously this proposal of Mr. Menzies makes proportional representation no longer proportional; that is to say, it exaggerates the majority of the winning party. But it also helps to solve one of the major weaknesses of proportional representation—the unworkably slender majority that results when two major parties, in a two-party country, are almost evenly balanced. So, although the Australian scheme departs from the ideal of proportional representation, it might at least produce a dependable majority.

Some proportional representation was also introduced in one other British Commonwealth country—the newly independent member of the family, Ceylon. There, while the lower house is elected by the single-member district system, the upper house or Senate is partly chosen by proportional representation. The Senate has fifteen of its thirty members appointed by the Governor, but the remaining fifteen are selected by proportional representation, using the single transferable vote system.[19]

The inspiration for using proportional representation in the Ceylon Senate came from Great Britain, however, and not from the Ceylonese themselves. In Ceylon, in fact, a second house was not wanted by local leaders, although these leaders did say that, after independence, the Ceylon legislature might create a second house. The Soulbury Commission, a group sent from England to make recommendations about the government of Ceylon, introduced the idea of the existing second house.[20]

But these are only minor postwar experiments with proportional representation. Apart from these, many British Commonwealth countries remain firmly attached to the single-member district sys-

---

[19] See the Constitution of Ceylon, Art. 9 (2), in Amos J. Peaslee, *Constitutions of the Nations* (Concord, N. H., 1950), I, 381–82.

[20] For an extended discussion of this point, as well as of the drafting of the Ceylon Constitution, see Cmd. 6677, *B.P.P.*, 1945–1946, vol. X, p. 319.

Electoral Changes after World War II

tem, at least in their lower houses. For example, the Ceylon system, for the lower house—the House of Representatives—is a single-member district system. It is somewhat like the British. The idea for it came from the Ceylon ministers who drew up a draft constitution; and this part of their constitution was accepted by the Soulbury Commission. By this constitution, a Delimitation Commission draws the boundary lines of the electoral districts. This commission is appointed by the Governor-General. Its members must not be actively engaged in politics. The commission must follow certain rules in drawing districts. It must make the districts approximately equal in population (about 1 to 75,000); but it must also consider transportation, physical features, and the community or diversity of interests of the area. If a substantial minority group lives in an area, the commission must provide it with some representation. After the commission has drawn its lines, the Governor-General puts the recommendations into effect by proclamation. If, after the commission has drawn its lines and after the elections have been held, any important racial, religious, or other interest group is not represented in the legislature, the Governor-General may appoint members to the House of Representatives, not to exceed six (Art. 11). Needless to say, these powers of the Governor-General are used on the advice of responsible ministers.

The Indian Constitution also contains what amounts to a single-member district system for electing members of the House of the People, the lower house.[21] But, curiously enough, the Indian Constituent Assembly, which drew up the constitution, was chosen in part by proportional representation, by the Hindu, Moslem, and Sikh groups of the provincial legislatures. This scheme was proposed by the so-called British Cabinet mission to India in 1946.[22] Its recommendation was to allot to each province the number of seats to which it was entitled on the basis of one representative for each one million people; then the province's seats were to be divided among the General (Hindu), Moslem, and Sikh groups on the

[21] Art. 67. The constitution is printed in O. P. Aggarawala and S. K. Aiyar, *The Constitution of India* (Delhi, 1950). The draft constitution is printed in Peaslee, *op. cit.*
[22] See Cmd. 6821, *B.P.P.*, 1945–1946, vol. XIX, p. 127.

basis of population. Thereafter, the members of the provincial legislatures, divided by communal groups, were to select the Constituent Assembly members by proportional representation. But the members of the provincial legislatures had themselves been elected under the arrangements made by the Government of India Act of 1935.[23] This Act provided for a district system of election, although some of the districts had two or three members. This system had been worked out by the Marquess of Lothian's committee in 1932.[24] The Lothian committee also recommended that only a limited number of people should be allowed to vote. This recommendation was put into effect. Those who could vote had to meet property and educational requirements, and, in 1937, thirty million Indians met these requirements.[25]

The result of this complicated electoral pattern was that the Indian Constituent Assembly, which became the Indian legislature for the first years of the new constitution, was indirectly elected. And it in turn was chosen by voters who met extensive property and educational requirements. Because millions of Indians were illiterate, and not used to the idea of democratic elections, the immediate use of full adult suffrage would have been impractical. The new constitution, however, does provide for adult suffrage; and the legislature is empowered by it to write a new law that will make this full adult-suffrage provision effective.

Pakistan's electoral situation is much like that of India. Pakistan, too, has used its Constituent Assembly as a legislature.[26] That body had also been elected following announcement of the British Cabinet mission's plan of 1946. The Pakistan Constituent Assembly, however, has been much slower about writing its constitution. In the meantime, before the constitution goes into operation, Pakistan is governed under the amended Government of India Act of 1935.

---

[23] Particularly Schedule I (25 & 26 Geo. V, c. 42).
[24] House of Commons Paper 112 (1), *B.P.P.*, 1932–1933, vol. V, p. 661.
[25] For a full account of the provincial electoral procedure in 1946 (and earlier) under the Government of India Act of 1935, see F. O. Bell, "Parliamentary Elections in Indian Provinces," *Parliamentary Affairs* (London), I (Spring 1948), 20–28.
[26] This was provided for in the India Independence Act of 1947, Art. 8 (1), 10 & 11 Geo. VI, c. 30.

Electoral Changes after World War II

The amendments make the dominion independent of the British Parliament and set up the Governor-General as a typical British Commonwealth ceremonial executive. But the real governing power, of course, rests with the Prime Minister and his Cabinet, who are in turn responsible to the Parliament, that is, the Constituent Assembly, until a constitution is written.

Others of the Commonwealth countries still using the single-member district system have made minor mechanical improvements in it. For example, Canada made her system more accurately representative by a Representation of the People Act, 1947.[27] This Canadian change, however, required an amendment to the British North America Act. The old arrangement under that Act tied representation in the rest of Canada to Quebec's representation. The Liberal government wanted to cut the representation system loose from this tie. It argued that such a scheme was artificial. The important thing, it said, was that the provinces should be evenly represented, on the basis of population. It therefore pushed through the Canadian Parliament an amendment to the British North America Act; and afterwards this amendment was approved, almost without comment, by the Parliament in Great Britain.[28]

This amendment provided for a readjustment of the Canadian representation after each census. The readjustment formula was complicated. First, the House of Commons was fixed at 255 members. The government decided on this figure, it said, because in the redistribution about to be made only one province—Saskatchewan—would lose a representative.[29] The other provinces either retained the existing number of representatives or gained some. Then the total census population was to be divided by 254. The resulting electoral quotient was divided into the population of each province, and the result of this division, disregarding remainders for the moment, represented the number of seats given to that province. The remaining seats—those not already apportioned—were allotted, beginning with the province having the highest remainder, until

[27] Chap. 71 of 1947.
[28] In the British Statutes, 9 & 10 Geo. VI, c. 63. Presumably British parliamentary action was taken under provisions of the Statute of Westminster, 1931.
[29] Dominion of Canada, *Debates, House of Commons*, vol. II, 1946, p. 1937.

45

the total of 254 was reached. There were a few deviations from this formula. The Yukon has one representative, although its population is far short of the electoral quotient. Also, no province was to receive less representation than it had in numbers of Senators. By this exception Prince Edward Island, with four Senators, received four members of the House of Commons, although its 1941 census population was so small that it normally would have received two members.

Once the number of representatives for each province had been calculated, then the really difficult political problem came up. How should the electoral boundaries within the provinces be drawn? Here the Canadians did not follow the British system. Instead, they set up a special committee of the House of Commons to do the work. The committee, established in 1947, was built on partisan lines. The government and the opposition whips nominated its members in proportion to party strength.[30] Furthermore, the government party gave the commission few instructions to guide it. The two principal instructions were that county and municipal organization lines should be followed as far as possible, and that in general rural constituencies could have smaller populations than urban constituencies.[31] The reason given for this last was that urban constituencies were normally more vocal and had the leading newspapers in them, so that their views could be expressed adequately even though they had fewer representatives.

The decisions of this special committee were written into the Representation Act of 1947, an Act that was not passed without a good deal of partisan argument. Some of those whose constituencies had been changed feelingly charged the government with gerrymandering.[32] It is undoubtedly true that this Canadian distribution system can be manipulated to favor the party in power.

Several irate Canadian members of the House of Commons asked why the British nonpartisan system was not used. They also praised New Zealand's relatively nonpartisan boundary-commission system for redistribution of seats. But, in New Zealand, even with an

[30] Dominion of Canada, *Debates, House of Commons*, vol. I, 1947, p. 739.
[31] *Ibid.*, pp. 692–93.
[32] Dominion of Canada, *Debates, House of Commons*, vol. VI, 1947, pp. 5568 ff.

Electoral Changes after World War II

almost nonpartisan boundary-commission system, there had been, in 1945, a minor revolution in the single-member district system. This revolution was the abandoning of the "country quota." Since 1881 the New Zealand electoral system contained a purposeful over-representation of the rural voters. In 1881, for example, they were given a bonus of 33.5 per cent; in 1887, 18 per cent; and, since 1889, 28 per cent.[33] Under this old system, the country population was fictitiously increased by 28 per cent before the electoral district boundaries were drawn.

But in the Electoral Amendment Act of 1945,[34] the New Zealand Labour government abolished this "country quota." After this Act, the electoral districts had to have an approximately equal number of adults, excluding Maoris and some others, such as convicts. The actual drawing of the electoral district lines is done by the seven-man representation commission. Three of its members are nonpolitical; the other four are appointed by the House of Representatives. The commission must follow the instructions in the Act: (1) The North and South Island representation must be in proportion to the respective populations; (2) the districts must be as nearly equal as possible; but (3) due consideration must be given to existing electoral district boundaries (excepting those before the Act went into effect), community of interest, communication facilities, and topography. Once the lines are drawn, the commission's report is published in the government *Gazette;* objections are heard by the commission; and then the final commission report is proclaimed by the Governor-General. The report goes into effect immediately, ready for the next election. Parliament must be given a copy of the report, but the report is not debated unless Parliament demands debate. A commission device very like this had previously operated in New Zealand, although there had been a North Island and a South Island commission—each one having three nonpartisan, ex officio members, and two appointed by the House of Representatives.[35]

The Union of South Africa also uses a nonpartisan boundary

---

[33] *New Zealand Official Yearbook, 1947–1949* (Wellington, 1950), p. 16.
[34] No. 10 of 1945.
[35] See Electoral Act of 1927, no. 44.

47

commission to draw constituency lines,[36] but it is not this part of the South African electoral system that has attracted world-wide attention in the postwar period. The burning problem in South Africa, rather, is that of the franchise itself. This franchise problem is only one aspect of the *apartheid* (or "separateness") policy of the ultranationalist government of Dr. Malan. Dr. Malan is trying to solve the racial color problem in South Africa by a most rigid segregation system. And because most of the unskilled labor in South Africa is done cheaply by native and colored workers, his plan creates enormous economic as well as other difficulties. Many of the native and colored people, although already segregated, live in and around the larger towns; the *apartheid* plan calls for a division of South Africa into separate native and white areas. Thus, the franchise changes are only a small part of this much larger program of the Nationalists.

The background of the native and colored franchise problem in South Africa, however, goes back to the South Africa Act itself. That Act was written by a National Convention, which met in 1908. One of the compromises of that convention was about the colored and native vote in the Cape Colony (natives and colored people were not allowed to vote in other colonies). The colonies that did not allow natives to vote were adamant in demanding that native suffrage be prohibited everywhere. The Cape Colony was equally firm in defending its wider suffrage. The upshot was that the Cape gave up its wish to have colored people seated in the new Parliament; it also did not have the colored people counted for distribution of seats in Parliament. But, in exchange, both natives and colored people were permitted to remain on the voter's lists in the Cape. Furthermore, this compromise was "entrenched" in the South Africa Act by the requirement that a two-thirds vote of both houses, meeting together, should be required for changing this part of the Act.[37]

In 1936 this particular "entrenched" clause was amended by the

---

[36] See Union of South Africa Act, 1909, Art. 38, and later amendments, particularly Act no. 30 of 1942.
[37] See *Cambridge History of the British Empire* (New York, 1936), VIII, 633 ff.

Electoral Changes after World War II

Representation of Natives Act by the needed two-thirds vote.[38] By this amendment the native (but not the colored) voters in the Cape lost the privilege of voting for the ordinary members of the House of Assembly, the lower house. In return, though, the natives could vote for three Europeans to be their representatives in the House of Assembly. For these elections, the Union of South Africa was divided into three "circles" or electoral districts. Also, the natives could choose four European Senators to represent them, and for this choice an electoral college system was set up. A further feature of the Act of 1936 was the creation of the Natives Representative Council. Six of its members were official, representing the government, four native members were nominated by the Governor-General, and twelve were elected indirectly by the natives themselves. This Council, meeting irregularly, could only consider and report on matters of interest to natives. Its reports, however, did have to be presented to Parliament.[39]

Somewhat similar in principle to the native representation act of 1936 was the Asiatic Land Tenure and Indian Representation Act of 1946. One section of this Act provided that the Indians of Natal (where one quarter of a million of them lived) and of the Transvaal (having about 25,000) could elect three European members to the House of Assembly to speak for them. They could elect one Senator, and the Governor-General would nominate another Senator also to represent them. These Senators must be European. Although the Indians in South Africa are in many cases descendants of Indians brought in from 1860 onwards, most of them had not formerly voted. Only in the Cape had the Indians been placed on the common voter's roll. The new Act was, however, not actually put into effect; and in 1948 it was repealed by the Nationalist government on the ground that the Indians ought not to have any representation. This was but one more part of their *apartheid* policy.

This same policy of *apartheid* had been the emotional electoral battle cry of the Nationalists. They used it to edge to victory in

---

[38] Act no. 12, of 1936.
[39] For a brief description of the native problem, see *Official Yearbook of the Union of South Africa, no. 23 of 1946* (Pretoria, 1947), chap. xi.

1948, but their victory was a qualified one. Their opponents, the United party, actually received a majority of all the votes, but the Nationalists won the plurality of the seats in the House of Assembly. Partly this was the result of three-way splits in single-member districts, and partly it was the result of an overrepresentation of the rural constituencies, in which the Nationalist strength was greatest.[40]

With a slender plurality in the House of Assembly, the Nationalists were dependent upon the votes of the Afrikaner party for accomplishing their program of *apartheid*—including the franchise reform; but on this the Afrikaner leader, Mr. Havenga, refused to agree until the voters should clearly show their desire for a change.

Dr. Malan, therefore, said that he would consider the 1949 provincial elections an indication of the voters' views on *apartheid* and particularly on the franchise question. In these elections the voters cast their ballots in the same way they had in 1948. Again the United party received a majority of the votes, but the Nationalists won a majority of the provincial council seats.[41] This, said Dr. Malan, was a clear mandate from the voters for electoral reforms. He therefore set out on his program. In this, one of the major objectives was to strike the Cape colored voters from the common electoral register. But here Dr. Malan had a constitutional problem to overcome because the Cape colored franchise was one of the "entrenched" clauses of the South Africa Act. To change it, apparently, Dr. Malan needed a two-thirds vote of both houses, and this he could not get.

[40] The votes and seats for the May 26, 1948, elections were as follows:

	Seats	Votes
United party (Smuts)	65	524,230
National (Malan)	70	401,834
Afrikaner (Havenga)	9	41,885
Labour	6	27,360
Others	0	71,940

These figures are from the *Annual Register* (1948), p. 114.

[41] The results of the March 10, 1949, elections were as follows:

	Seats	Votes
United party	78	592,000
National	86	453,000
Independent	3	63,000
Labour	3	22,000

See *The Times* (London), March 12, 1949, p. 4.

Electoral Changes after World War II

But Dr. Malan did not think that a two-thirds vote was actually necessary. He said that the Statute of Westminster of 1931 had freed the Union of South Africa from bondage to the British Parliament. The British Parliament had passed the South Africa Act and had therefore imposed the two-thirds rule in the "entrenched" clauses. Thus, now that South Africa was free, it could change any part of its constitution by a simple majority. The opposition United party pointed out that this argument was at least dubious because it was a South African National Convention that had actually written the South Africa Act. Furthermore, that convention had agreed upon "entrenching" the Cape colored vote as one of the conditions for forming the Union.[42]

Without the consent of the Afrikaner party, Dr. Malan could not change the constitution even by a majority vote, much less two thirds, because he lacked the majority. But he could still take some steps toward *apartheid*. One of these dealt with the Natives Representative Council. The Minister of Native Affairs, who was legally responsible for calling its meetings, announced on January 4, 1949, that no further meetings would be called.[43] But this action was not as drastic as it appeared because the Council had almost ceased to function some years earlier. Dr. Malan's action, therefore, was more a declaration of principle than a change of behavior. At the time the Council was abandoned, however, the Minister of Native Affairs said that a more effective ethnic link with the natives would someday be established.

We have already noted another of Dr. Malan's steps to *apartheid*: his repeal of the Indian representation system. But here again the action only formally accomplished what had already been done informally. The Indian Act had not been put into effect by the Smuts government.

The Nationalists had to take several steps more before they could accomplish one of their major objectives; that is, getting the colored voters off of the common roll in the Cape. They still had to

[42] *Journal of the Parliaments of the Empire*, XXX (1949), 141–46.
[43] See *Round Table*, no. 158 (March 1950), pp. 182–84. There was a meeting of the Council in December 1950, but it adjourned sine die. See *The Times* (London), December 6, 1950, p. 6, and December 8, 1950, p. 5.

get a majority of the seats in the House of Assembly even if they assumed they could make this constitutional change by a majority vote rather than by the constitutional two thirds. So Dr. Malan continued to build his majority. A part of this process was the annexation of Southwest Africa. By a careful manipulation of the electoral districts, six more Nationalists were elected from Southwest Africa to the House of Assembly. Each of these members represented half as many voters as the usual representative did in the rest of the Union. And with these additional six, the Malan government had close to a majority of the seats and might shortly, with the support of a few of the Afrikaner party, place the *apartheid* changes into effect. The issue remains unsolved, however, at this writing.

Except for the Union of South Africa, it can be said that the two-party countries, which means substantially Great Britain and the Commonwealth countries, have improved their representational system in the postwar years. But almost always this has been done within the framework of the single-member district system—a system that is often representationally defective.

But other democratic countries do not fit into the two-party category. In most of them many parties are usual, and the way in which their legislature is elected greatly influences the position and strength of each party. One acerb observer has said that the very existence of parliamentary government in one of these countries, namely, France, is dependent upon the electoral system.[44] Indeed, it may well be true that the existence of democracy in France depends on the details of the electoral system. This is because political opinions in that country in the early postwar years have been split into three large groups—those on the extreme left, the Communists, with about one third of the votes; those on the extreme right, the De Gaullists, with another third of the votes; and those in the middle, divided into several parties. The left and the right—two thirds of the voters—firmly oppose the present form of the French government, if their party's programs can be believed. Hence, if

[44] Raymond Aron, "Will the Mode of Election Determine the Future of the Fourth Republic?" *France illustration*, no. 166 (December 18, 1948).

Electoral Changes after World War II

the electoral system actually reproduced the political complexion of the country, the present parliamentary democracy in France might well be changed.

The present electoral system can be changed easily enough, too, if a majority of the legislators can agree on the same change. This is because the constitution of 1946 provides that the machinery of elections is to be fixed by law. The only constitutional requirements are that both chambers must be elected on a territorial basis, that the National Assembly (the lower house) be chosen by universal, direct suffrage, and that the Council of the Republic (the upper house) be elected by universal, indirect suffrage.[45]

Within this very simple framework, then, the legislators can build almost any electoral system they desire. In the first flush of liberating enthusiasm, before the party strife had become too great, the legislators passed the electoral law of October 5, 1946.[46] This provided for the selection of National Assembly members. It set up a list system of proportional representation. By it, each electoral area (usually the department) elected several candidates, in proportion to its voting strength. In each area the voter was required to vote only for one party list; he could not split his vote among several candidates on different party lists. He could, however, show his preference for different candidates on his own party's list. To take care of this possibility, the law provided that if one half the voters for a particular list should depart from the order of preference set up by the party, then the voters' preference should be counted; otherwise, the voter could show that he supported his party and his party's order of preference by marking his ballot in a party column. In practice, in the 1946 elections, the voters generally accepted the party's order of listing of candidates.

The French use a typical system for counting the proportional-representation ballots. This is a responsibility of an electoral commission of which the president of the Departmental Civil Court is chairman and two other judges and two prefectural representatives

---

[45] Art. 6. The constitution is reprinted in L. H. Laing and others, *Source Book in European Governments* (New York, 1950). See also Appendix A, p. 226.

[46] Law 46-2151. Excerpts are in Laing, *op. cit.*, pp. 114 ff.

are members. The commission uses the system of the highest average for counting. Under this system, the commissioners count the ballots for each party list and then distribute the total number of seats among the different successful parties. To do this they give the first seat to the party with the largest vote. Then they divide that party's number of votes by one seat plus one. If the quotient is still larger than the total vote of any other party, the second seat goes to the same party. If not, the second seat goes to the party having the highest remaining vote. After this, as the law states, seats are granted successively to that party "list for which the division of the number of votes for the list by the number of seats already granted to that list, plus one, gives the highest result" (Art. 13). The candidates on each list are declared elected in the order that the party has put them on the ballot, unless half the voters have altered that order; if this happens, the commission declares the candidates elected in the order set up by the voters.

This electoral system has greatly strengthened the control of the larger parties over their Deputies, because the party, in making out the lists of candidates, controls the order of preference and hence the order of election. It also encourages the formation of larger parties, because each party list must have as many candidates as seats. The single independent candidate cannot get his name on the ballot.

Another feature of this electoral system is that it breaks the personal contact between the Deputy and his district. This contact may be quite strong under the single-member district system, because the legislator knows his own district and many of his people know him. But, under the 1946 French system, the districts were each likely to have four or five representatives and some had as many as eleven.[47] This relationship also helps to strengthen the party's hold over the Deputy, because the party is likely to keep a much more careful watch over the Deputy than his constituents can.

Of course, the major advantage of this system is that it mirrors the political opinions of the voters far more accurately than the single-member district system does. This is the most powerful

[47] Table 2 of the Law of October 5, 1946.

argument for proportional representation, but it is a costly advantage. The cost is almost always a coalition government; and often one result of coalition government is a weakened and less responsible Cabinet.

Because of the political results of the 1946 electoral system for the French National Assembly, there have been frequent suggestions for changes. Each suggestion for change usually sets up a scheme advantageous to the proposer, yet each of the changes is in line with some phase of earlier French electoral experience. The most frequently suggested change is the so-called uninominal vote with a second ballot. This system was greatly favored during the Third Republic. Under it France would again be divided into single-member districts. On the first ballot all parties could present candidates. If no candidate received a majority of the votes, there would be a second balloting. On this second ballot, a plurality would be sufficient for election.

The center parties, with one exception (this is the Popular Republican Movement, the M.R.P.), favor this system. They like it because their local connections are good and because they can often combine with each other on the second ballot to elect a moderate candidate. The M.R.P., however, among the moderate parties, resolutely opposes this system. Its members are fearful that, because their party is mainly a postwar party, it will lose out under this system. Their local connections are poor. They are also afraid that their clericalism—they are the modern Catholic Action party—will make them the target of many electoral bargains on the second ballots. This is because they know that for years clericalism has been the whipping boy for the radical parties.[48]

The other major political groups—representing nearly two thirds of the voters, if the balloting in October 1947 is to be considered as representative—disagree completely with the second-ballot system. One of these groups, the Communists, prefers the pure proportional representation system. For them, as for the M.R.P., this system is a source of electoral strength. They feel that all electoral bargains will be made against them. Proportional repre-

[48] *The New York Times,* October 6, 1950, p 1.

sentation is their ticket to success. The other extremist group—the De Gaullist Rally of the French People—wants a departmental list system with a second ballot. Thus, if it won the majority of the departmental votes, it would get all the seats from that department; and, on second ballots, it could compromise with other anti-Communist parties. The De Gaullists, of course, favor this system because they think it might give them a working majority in the National Assembly.

Meanwhile, there has been no real agreement among major groups of French parties on reform of the electoral system. On February 28, 1951, the Cabinet of Mr. René Pleven resigned because of the failure of the majority parties to agree on a new electoral law. Shortly thereafter, at the end of March 1951, a compromise electoral law was worked out. Its principal feature was the use of a departmental list system of election, with one ballot. There was to be no run-off election. If one list—made up either by one party or a group of parties working together—obtained a majority of the departmental votes, this list was to have all the seats of the department. (These seats were to be distributed among the grouped parties of the list on the basis of proportional representation.) If no list or grouped list received 50 per cent of the votes, the seats were to be distributed by the proportional-representation system of highest averages. The most populous departments—Seine, and Seine and Oise—were excepted from this system.[49] Applied in the elections of June 17, 1951, this law greatly favored the middle parties which, with 52 per cent of the vote, won 401 seats, the extreme right and left, with 48 per cent of the vote, winning only 224 seats.

The French upper house, the weak Council of the Republic, is selected by a different system. It is complicated and indirect. Here again the parties in power when the electoral law was written safeguarded their own special positions. The effect of the system is to strengthen the center parties at the expense of the extreme right and left.

The electoral system for the Council of the Republic was set up

[49] See *Le Monde,* March 23, 1951, p. 1, and March 24, 1951, p. 4.

Electoral Changes after World War II

by the law of September 23, 1948.[50] It provides for an electoral college very much like that used for electing Senators in the Third Republic. Each department's membership in the Council of the Republic varies according to the size of its population. The members are chosen by the electoral colleges, half of them every three years. The colleges are made up of (1) the departmental deputies to the National Assembly, (2) the general councilors of the department (somewhat like local government representatives), and (3) delegates from municipal councils. These last electors are by far the most numerous in the electoral colleges. For this reason they really control the selection of most of the members of the Council of the Republic. Thus, rural sections of the country have great influence in the elections. In elections to the Council of the Republic in November 1948, two thirds of the electoral-college members came from rural municipalities of 3,500 or less population; and these two thirds represented half the people of France. The other half of the people, therefore, were represented by only one third of the electoral-college members.[51] Understandably, the parties of the center and the right were the greatest gainers from this arrangement.

Thus in France, although there is now complete adult suffrage, the electoral system has been consistently fixed for partisan purposes. This partisanship can hardly be avoided. Moreover, perfectly good and logical arguments can be used to support either proportional representation, or the list system, or the single-member district system of representation. None of these is completely satisfactory. None of them can be said to be the most democratic, in the sense of expressing the majority's will most effectively.

Elsewhere on the Continent of Europe the same electoral problems arise. The Italians have solved their particular problem rather differently from the French. The Italian Constitution, like the French, is brief in describing the electoral system; details are filled in by law. But the constitution does stipulate certain simple suffrage re-

[50] Law 48-1471. The first Council of the Republic, however, was elected following a slightly different system—that established by the law of October 27, 1946 (Law 46-2383). This law was passed by the second Constituent Assembly.

[51] *Manchester Guardian Weekly,* October 21, 1948, p. 14.

quirements. It says that "all citizens, men and women, who have reached the age of majority, are electors." It explains that "the vote is personal and equal, free and secret. Its exercise is a civic duty." [52] Having established these general voting requirements, the constitution goes on to set up the general conditions for electing the Deputies and Senators. For the Deputies, it states: "The Chamber of Deputies is elected by universal and direct suffrage, in the proportion of one deputy for 80,000 inhabitants or for fractions greater than 40,000" (Art. 56). For the Senate the electoral basis is regional. "To each Region is attributed one senator for 200,000 inhabitants or for a fraction greater than 100,000." The Senators are also elected "by means of universal and direct suffrage" but by voters who have reached the age of twenty-five.[53] The electoral laws, based on these constitutional provisions, deal separately with the Chamber of Deputies and the Senate.

For the Deputies, the electoral law is that of February 5, 1948.[54] By this law the country is divided into thirty-one electoral districts. The voters in each one of these districts elect as many Deputies as their numbers permit them to elect. The actual voting is by a proportional-representation list system. By it each voter has one vote. But, unlike the original French arrangement, each party does not have to nominate as many candidates as there are seats to be filled in the region. On the other hand, no party may offer a list in which the total number of candidates falls short of the number of seats to be filled by more than three. Within each list the voter may, if he does not like the official order of candidates on his list, show his preference for three or four candidates of the list.[55]

Counting of the ballots takes place under the control of a court of appeals or a lesser court in the chief town of each electoral region, and distribution follows the pattern usual to list systems of propor-

[52] The constitution is printed in translation in *Documents and State Papers* (United States Department of State, 1948), I, 46–63. It is also printed in Appendix B, p. 248.

[53] Arts. 57 and 58. An exception to the regular rule of distribution of Senators is made for the Val d'Aosta. This area is the subject of special sections of the laws on the selection of Senators and Deputies.

[54] No. 26 of 1948. The most important provisions of this law are translated in Laing, *op. cit.*

[55] Three for lists of fifteen or less; four for sixteen and over.

tional representation on the Continent. Remnant votes, that is, votes of parties insufficient to elect a candidate, are exploited in an unusual way. They are collected for the individual parties from all over Italy, and additional seats are then allotted on a national basis. These remainders are even collected from the parties that did not have enough votes to elect a candidate in most of the regions, provided that the party had secured the election of at least one candidate in one electoral region. Under the remainder system the small party generally stands a better chance of gaining satisfactory representation, provided it is strong enough to win a seat in at least one locality.[56]

In the first election under this new law, that of April 19, 1948, the Christian Democratic party won a majority of the seats, although its popular vote was less than a majority—48 per cent in fact. The other large group, the Popular Front parties, also gained. Its popular vote was 30.7 per cent and it won 32 per cent of the seats. But the smaller parties received fewer seats than their popular votes would indicate they should have. For example, the popular vote for the Republican party was 2.5 per cent, but it won only nine seats, or 1.5 per cent of the total. The Republicans' vote should have given them fourteen seats under a strictly proportional system. This sort of proportional representation, obviously, is not exactly proportional, since it produced a majority government where a majority did not quite exist.

The Italian Senate is selected by a combination of several electoral systems. One of these is used to fill five seats. For these, the President of the Republic names citizens who have distinguished themselves in the scientific, artistic, social, and literary fields. These are appointed as Senators for life. Former Presidents of the Republic will constitute another category of lifetime Senators.[57] Still other appointed members of the first republican Senate are certain former members of the Constituent Assembly.[58]

The greatest number of the Senators, however (237 out of 345),

[56] In the 1948 elections under this law, there were twenty-two seats distributed on the national level, from among a total of 574 seats (*Manchester Guardian Weekly*, April 29, 1948, p. 5).
[57] Art. 59 of the constitution.
[58] Constitution, Transitional Provision III.

were elected following the procedure set up by the electoral law of February 6, 1948.[59] Like the Deputies, the Senators are elected by regions and, as we have seen, the constitution establishes the number of people to be represented by each Senator; that is, one Senator for each 200,000 people, or one for a fraction over 100,000. Each of these regions is divided into electoral districts, one for a Senator. This means that the senatorial system makes some use of the single-member district system. But it is only a limited use, for a candidate is elected only if he receives 65 per cent of the votes cast in his electoral district. Very few achieve this majority; hence most of the elective seats are filled by a modified system of proportional representation, which supplements the majority formula. All seats not filled under the 65 per cent majority rule in the single-member districts are pooled for an electoral region. Electoral officials add up the total vote for each party group of candidates and award available seats to each group according to the standard procedure of the list system of proportional representation. Each party's list vote is divided by one, then by two, then by three, and so on. The resulting quotients are arranged in descending order, and the seats allotted in this order. The next job is to distribute the party's assigned seats to its candidates. This is done by multiplying each candidate's actual votes by 100 and dividing the product by the number of votes in the candidate's district. Actually, this formula gives the percentage of the total vote of each district that the candidate received. The candidates on each party list are arranged by these percentages, and the seats are allotted within each list in the descending order of percentages.

Because of this use of a combination of a single-member district system for some seats and proportional representation for the rest, the senatorial elections do not produce strictly proportional results. For example, in the 1948 elections, the Christian Democrats received 47.9 per cent of the popular votes for the Senate, but received 55 per cent of the number of elected Senators. On the other hand, the other major parties received their seats on a strictly proportional basis. For example, the Popular Front parties received 31.2 per cent

[59] Law no. 29. Partially translated in Laing, *op. cit.*

Electoral Changes after World War II

of the popular vote and exactly the same percentage of the elected seats in the Senate. The Socialist Unity party received 5.1 per cent of the popular vote and 5.06 per cent of the seats, and so forth.

Thus, the Italians have skillfully altered the traditional proportional-representation formulas, and the result has been to favor the largest parties. In the 1948 election, as we have seen, the Christian Democrats—the largest party—received a majority of the elected seats in both the Chamber and the Senate. Yet the party's popular vote was slightly less than a majority for each chamber. Nevertheless, even with this misrepresentation of party strength, the Italian system gives a truer picture of the voters' party opinions than a single-member district system usually does.

The West German electoral system is even more a hybrid of proportional representation and the single-member district system than the Italian, and it is even more favorable to the large parties. The Bonn Basic Law—the temporary German equivalent of a constitution—contains only a few statements on elections. Hence, the major features of the electoral system are set up by the legislature, and they are thus easily changed. The Basic Law does require that Deputies for the *Bundestag,* or lower house, be elected by the people by universal, free, equal, direct, and secret suffrage.[60]

The details of the electoral system were fixed by a directive of the Bonn Parliamentary Council—the group that wrote the Bonn Charter—on May 10, 1949. The various *Länder* (geographical units comparable to the states of the United States) promulgated the law on June 15, 1949. They made some slight changes in the Parliamentary Council's directive at the request of the Western military governors.[61] This electoral law for the *Bundestag* combines the single-member district system and proportional representation. By it, 60 per cent of each *Land's* Deputies are elected from single-

---

[60] Art. 38 (1). The Basic Law is printed in *Germany, 1947–1949* (United States Department of State Publication no. 3556, March 1950), pp. 283 ff. It is also printed in Laing, *op. cit.*

[61] *Germany, 1947–1949,* pp. 310 ff. This document contains a translation of the electoral law as promulgated on June 15, 1949, together with annotations showing changes made in the May 10 directive after correspondence with the military governors. The June 15 version is printed, in large part, in Laing, *op. cit.,* pp. 422 ff.

member districts, and the remaining 40 per cent are elected by proportional representation (Art. 8). In the single-member districts, the candidate who gets the most votes is elected; that is, the person with a plurality or better. For the proportional-representation seats, all the votes received by a party in the *Land* are added together, and this figure is used for assigning seats to the party lists by a system very like that used for the French National Assembly.[62] Once the number of seats to which each party is entitled has been determined, the seats already won by that party in the single-member districts are deducted from the party's total. The remainder constitutes the number each party may distribute to its candidates. If a party wins less than 5 per cent of the *Land* vote, its votes are not considered unless that party has gained one of the district seats of that *Land* by a plurality. Obviously this provision discriminates against the small party.

This law of June 15, 1948, governed the *Bundestag* elections of August 14, 1949. In these elections, the largest parties gained at the expense of the smaller ones. Yet it has been calculated that the political picture would not be greatly changed if full proportional representation had been used instead of the hybrid system actually used.[63]

The members of the German second chamber, the *Bundesrat,* are chosen by a quite different system. This system is not unlike the one used for the second chambers of the Second Empire (1871–1918) or of Weimer (1918–1933). The Bonn *Bundesrat* consists of members of the governments of the *Länder,* and they are appointed and recalled by their governments.[64] These members only roughly represent the same number of people. Each *Land* has three votes; if it has more than two million people, it has four votes; if over six million people, five votes. Thus, the smaller *Länder* are overrepresented; but this is a persistent tendency in many legislative systems.

A summary of electoral changes all over Western Europe and in

[62] See pp. 53–54.
[63] For a detailed analysis of the outcome and statistical calculations, see Otto Kirchheimer and A. H. Price, "Analysis and Effects of the Elections in Western Germany," *Department of State Bulletin,* XXI (1949), 563–73.
[64] Basic Law, Art. 51.

Electoral Changes after World War II

the British Commonwealth countries shows that proportional representation has made headway. But in almost every proportional-representation system changes have been made so that an increased majority can be obtained. Meanwhile, the single-member district remains entrenched. Especially is this true in countries whose constitutions survived World War II. It was in the countries with new constitutions that the modified proportional-representation systems made headway.

In several postwar constitutions, a direct connection between the voters and the public has been re-established by the referendum. By it, the voters themselves make certain major policy decisions. The countries using this system usually apply it to constitutional amendments, but there are examples in which it has been used for other major policy decisions. Even the British Commonwealth countries have come to make some use of this device. This is noteworthy because the time-honored principle of their parliamentary democracy is that it is representative and not direct; that is, the voters speak through their elected representatives but do not legislate directly.

After World War II the possibility of using the referendum was discussed rather extensively in Great Britain. One suggestion that it be used came from Mr. Winston Churchill while he was coalition Prime Minister in 1945. His idea was that the British voters should be polled about the question of the length of life of the coalition Parliament. They were to be asked whether a new Parliament should be elected after VE day, or whether the elections should be postponed until VJ day.[65] Mr. Attlee, for the Labour party, strongly opposed the suggestion. He thought the plebiscite system was closer to the Nazi system than to the British.[66]

Although the idea did not advance beyond the suggestion stage in Britain itself, it was applied to the Newfoundland constitutional question in 1948. This concerned the governmental fate of Newfoundland: whether it should continue under a colonial commis-

---

[65] This was proposed in a letter from Mr. Churchill to Mr. Attlee. The letter is printed in *The Times* (London), May 22, 1945, p. 4.
[66] *Ibid.*

sion government, go back to dominion status, or join Canada. These weighty questions were discussed by a Newfoundland constitutional convention, but no agreement could be reached. The British Government thereupon suggested that the local voters be polled by a referendum. The suggestion was subsequently applied, and Newfoundland's voters were queried on whether they wished to continue colonial government, regain dominion status, or join Canada.[67]

The British Government also suggested the use of a referendum in some of the Indian provinces to decide whether those provinces should join Pakistan or India.[68] More than once, then, the British Government has used the referendum, though not in Britain proper.

Commonwealth countries have also expanded use of the referendum in the postwar period. New Zealand, for example, has held a referendum on race-track betting. This was under the Gaming Poll Act.[69] The machinery for holding the referendum was written into the Act itself. A similar arrangement was made for the referendum held in 1949 on the compulsory military service question.[70] In Australia, likewise, the referendum continues to be used, several constitutional amendments having been submitted to the voters by this means since 1945.[71]

Certain Continental democracies use the referendum in much the same way as Australia; that is, for constitutional amendments. But most of them, unlike Australia, have other methods for amending the constitution. The French, for example, can amend their constitution if two thirds of the members of the National Assembly vote to adopt the amendment or if three fifths of each house—the National Assembly and the Council of the Republic—adopt the amendment. But if only an ordinary majority of the Parliament agrees to the amendment, then a popular referendum is used as the final step.[72] Also, a referendum is needed for amendments dealing

[67] *Parliamentary Debates (Commons)*, 5th series, vol. 448, cols. 208–10.
[68] See Mr. Attlee's statement to the House of Commons on June 3, 1947. Cmd. 7136, B.P.P., 1946–1947, vol. XIX, p. 11, esp. pars. 11 and 13.
[69] *New Zealand Official Yearbook, 1947–1949* (Wellington, 1950), p. 789.
[70] *Keesing's Contemporary Archives*, VII (June 4–11, 1949), 10036.
[71] See *Journal of the Parliaments of the Empire*, XXVII (1946), 379, 387; also *Annual Register* (1948), p. 103.
[72] Constitution of 1946, Art. 90.

Electoral Changes after World War II

with the existence of the Council of the Republic unless that body agrees to the amendment. In a larger sense, however, the referendum has played an enormous part in recent French history. This is in connection with the entire constitution-making process. It was the French voters themselves who rejected the first constitution in 1946 and the French voters, again, who approved the present constitution. Thus, in France the voters have been directly consulted on the awesome job of constitution-making; it is therefore hardly surprising that they should be consulted on the less formidable job of constitution-changing.

The German Basic Law, unlike the French Constitution of 1946, was not approved directly by the voters. Instead, the component parts of the state, that is, the *Länder,* approved the Bonn document; and it was the members of the *Land* assemblies rather than the *Land* voters who made the decision.[73] But the ultimate decision on the Bonn government was not actually made either by the *Land* assemblies or by the West German voters; rather, it was made by the Western Allied occupation authorities. This fact cannot be forgotten. Its importance was underscored by the Military Governors themselves. At the very time they approved the West German Basic Law, they also issued their Occupation Statute. By it they reserved "the right ... to resume, in whole or in part, the exercise of full authority."[74] Thus, the Bonn Charter operates on the sufferance of the occupying powers.

This Bonn Charter, however, makes use of the referendum as well as of the initiative, the latter another of the mechanisms of direct democracy. One article of the Bonn document states that "all state authority emanates from the people"; but this authority is to be exercised "in elections and plebiscites" as well as in separate legislative, judicial, and executive organs. Here the plebiscite, or referendum, is put on equal terms with elections for exercising state authority. The Bonn Charter, however, contains very few other statements about the referendum. One of these few deals with changing the boundaries of certain *Länder* (Art. 29). But

[73] See *Germany, 1947–1949,* p. 281.
[74] *The New York Times,* April 11, 1949, p. 9.

this section was explicitly reserved for final consideration by occupation authorities. Nor does the amending process involve a referendum, as it may do in France. The Bonn Basic Law simply requires two thirds of the members of the *Bundestag* and two thirds of the votes of the *Bundesrat* in support of an amendment (Art. 79). This section of the Charter is also explicitly controlled by the occupation authorities. No amendment may go into effect without their approval.[75] In fact, the Bonn Charter uses the referendum much less than did the Weimar Constitution of 1918, even though the Weimar Constitution served as the model for Bonn.

Finally, Italy's Constitution calls for the referendum and other direct democratic devices rather frequently. Fifty thousand electors may present a proposal to the legislature (Art. 71); and a popular referendum is authorized for the partial or total abrogation of a law if a half-million electors or five Regional Councils request it (Art. 75). Voters are enjoined against the use of this device for the possibly popular purpose of protesting against tax laws, the budget, pardons, amnesties, or treaties; but it can be used if new Regions are to be created or old ones to be fused (Art. 132). It is also a part of the amending procedure when less than two thirds of each of the chambers have voted for a constitutional change or if one fifth of the members of either chamber or 500,000 voters or five Regional Councils request the referendum be applied (Art. 138).

A survey of both the Continental European postwar constitutions and the British Commonwealth laws and constitutions clearly indicates that the referendum is making headway. The same observation applies to the other device of direct democracy, the initiative, although less emphatically. By and large, however, these gains are, up to now, merely the implications of constitutional provisions. Actual application of the devices has been rare except, surprisingly enough, in certain of the Commonwealth countries.

[75] Occupation Statute, Art. 5.

4

The Position of the Representative Legislature in the Postwar Constitutions

By Edward G. Lewis
UNIVERSITY OF ILLINOIS

IF democracy means governmental control by a majority of the voters, then an all-powerful legislature representing the current majority is vital to democracy. But if that legislature is limited in its powers by a constitution, so democracy is limited. This is because a majority of the voters, speaking through their legislature, are themselves thereby limited in their activities. Many statesmen and scholars insist that democracy must be more than majority rule. At its base, they say, is respect for individual rights. In their view, an unlimited majority would be as tyrannous as one-man rule, and the lack of limitations would violate an essential part of democracy —the freedom of the individual.

In all the new postwar democratic constitutions limitations are put on pure majority rule. In all of them these limits take the form of bills of rights, though in Great Britain and some of the Commonwealth countries the formal constitutional structure still emphasizes the omnipotence of the majority, as represented by the legislature. This does not mean that individuals are less free or more likely to lose their freedom, but it does mean that the protections of the individual take a different form. They take the form of ordinary laws that the legislature may change at any time. The British Bill of Rights, however, even though it can be changed by Parliament, is an important part of the British system of government. Any fundamental change in it is extremely unlikely. In fact, it has lasted much longer (since 1689) than bills of rights written into

Edward G. Lewis

Continental constitutions. In measuring the democratic character of a country, the living force of tradition must be remembered.

There are, therefore, two central questions to be asked to discover the type and amount of democracy existing in a country. One of them is about the formal structure of the legislature: To what extent does it let the expressed opinions of the majority of the voters operate? To answer this question, the formal structure and operation of the legislature must be looked at. For example, what are the powers of the upper and lower house? Which house is the more powerful and which one represents the existing desires of the majority of the voters the more effectively? The second fundamental question is about the formal constitutional limitations on the legislature: What subjects are taken away from ordinary majority control? What organizations limit the legislature?

On both these questions the answer is that the postwar trend is in line with prewar democratic developments. Nevertheless, increasingly, the Continental countries use some form of "constitutional court" removed from direct majority control as a legal check on the legislature.

In Great Britain, trends discernible before World War II continue. Apart from one important structural change, namely, a further weakening of the House of Lords, there have been only minor changes. The British Government thus remains true to its traditional concept of the omnipotence of Parliament, always remembering that Parliament is the House of Commons, the House of Lords, and the King. But the Parliament Act of 1949 [1] did strengthen the power of the already enormously powerful House of Commons.

The most remarkable fact about this new Parliament Act is not the substitution of the one-year suspensive veto of the Lords for the two-year veto. This change is in accord with the trend established by the Parliament Act of 1911, which originally "clipped the wings" of the House of Lords by cutting its veto to two years. What is more remarkable is the fact that the major parties nearly came to an agreement on an extensive change in the structure of the House of Lords. Tentatively, at least, the party leaders agreed,

---
[1] 12, 13, 14 Geo. VI, c. 103.

for example, that the structure be modified so that no party should have a majority. They also agreed that the members of the House of Lords should not necessarily be hereditary peers but that most of them should be "Lords of Parliament" appointed on a non-hereditary basis.[2]

These tentative agreements went by the board because the area of disagreement was crucial to the Labour party. That party insisted that the period of the Lords' suspensive veto be limited to nine months after the third reading in the Commons, the reading by which the House of Commons finally approves a bill. The Conservatives insisted that twelve months elapse after the third reading in Commons. Labourites favored the lesser period because they feared three additional months would bring on another parliamentary session and extend the period beyond twelve months. Because of this, the Labour party discarded the tentative agreement and directed its members to vote for the one-year veto between the second reading in one session and the final reading in the subsequent session.[3] Thus, the predominance of the House of Commons is reinforced and the British come close to a one-house legislature in fact if not in law.

This does not mean that they have lost or will lose their individual liberties. These liberties are as safe as the voters want them to be. So long as the British legislators and the British voters keep their great respect for the centuries-old tradition of their government, the liberties are as safe as they always have been. This is not to say that the individual liberties have always remained the same. Their content changes with changing times, but the core of individual liberty remains.

Among the minor changes in the House of Commons procedure are various amendments in the rules or standing orders by which the House governs itself.[4] By one of these the House set up a

---

[2] For details of the agreement, see Cmd. 7380, *British Parliamentary Papers* (cited hereafter as *B.P.P.*), 1947–1948, vol. XXII, p. 1001.

[3] *Parliamentary Debates (Commons)*, 5th series, vol. 456, col. 820.

[4] The most extensive revisions were made in 1947 and 1948. See the Report of the Select Committee on Standing Orders, House of Commons Paper 192, *B.P.P.*, 1947–1948, vol. IX, p. 603.

business committee to allot a specific amount of time for discussion to various parts of bills. This committee has power only over bills on which a time limit for discussion has already been fixed by the House; that is, for those bills the government wants to speed up. A similar arrangement is made in the standing committees on bills for the discussion of which a specific time has been allotted. In these there is now a business subcommittee, which allots a prearranged amount of time for each part of the bill.

Another relatively new development in the House of Commons is the Select Committee on Statutory Instruments. It was set up first in 1944 and originally known as the Select Committee on Statutory Rules and Orders. It has the power to draw the attention of the House to any Statutory Instrument "which imposes charges, is not open to challenge in the courts, makes unusual or unexpected use of the powers conferred, has been unjustifiably delayed in publication, or for any special reason requires elucidation."[5] The purpose of this committee is to handle the difficult problem of delegated legislation that grows out of the great increase in governmental activities. As the government controls more and more parts of economic life, so the need for detailed rules and regulations increases. The House of Commons cannot itself meet this need. For example, it is not expert enough to fix in detail how the laborers and their foremen get on with each other in the coal mines. This sort of regulation comes from the Ministry of Fuel and Power or the National Coal Board. The House, therefore, has actually delegated some legislative powers to the ministry. There are many other reasons why the House delegates legislative power. But this very delegation raises a problem for the House: How can it check on the use made of this discretion? This is where the Select Committee on Statutory Instruments goes into action.

As we have seen, this Select Committee may only draw the attention of the House to the existence of a Statutory Instrument that it thinks breaks the rules. To do more than this, for example, to recommend definite action to the House, would be unparlia-

[5] Third Report of the Select Committee on Procedure, House of Commons Paper 189, *B.P.P.,* 1945–1946, vol. IX, p. 241.

mentary, since the making of policy is the function of the ministry. If a select committee were to make suggestions attacking the policy of the government, a question of confidence in the government would surely arise. Thus, the role of the Committee on Statutory Instruments is limited.

The British Parliament, therefore, does not differ greatly from the prewar model. The same observation may be made about the Commonwealth Parliaments. In the older Dominions, for example, while there have been discussions about the relationship between the upper and the lower houses, few definitive changes have been made.[6]

Even the new Commonwealth legislatures have not departed far from the standard Commonwealth parliamentary pattern. This pattern, however, limits them more than the mother Parliament is limited. In most instances the source of these limitations is a written constitution. This is the case in India. By the constitution which was approved in November 1949, a two-house legislature was set up. But the lower house or House of the People, which is directly elected, is decidedly more powerful than the upper house, the Council of States (largely elected by the state legislative assemblies). The House of the People is paramount because money bills and financial measures are passed by it alone. Likewise, disagreements between it and the Council of States are settled by a joint meeting in which, of course, the House of the People is the more powerful because it has twice as many members as the Council of States. Further, the constitution specifically makes the Prime Minister responsible only to the House of the People.[7]

Nevertheless, limits are placed on the House of the People. Most importantly, the Supreme Court of India, whose members serve during good behavior, can review the constitutionality of legislative acts. In addition, the Indian Constitution contains an elaborate

[6] In New Zealand, however, the second chamber was abolished, January 1, 1951. See *Round Table*, no. 161 (December 1950), pp. 99 ff. For relevant discussion in South Africa, see *Journal of the Parliaments of the Empire*, XXVII (1946), 938–44.

[7] For the text of the constitution, see O. P. Aggarawala and S. K. Aiyar, *The Constitution of India* (Delhi, 1950).

bill of Fundamental Rights, and this also limits the action of the legislature. Furthermore, because the governmental structure is federal, the controls of the central legislature are limited. Decidedly, then, the Indian legislature lacks the legal omnipotence of the British Parliament.

The legislature of Ceylon, another of the new Dominions, is also limited by a constitution. Amendments to the basic law require a two-thirds majority of all the members of the House of Representatives, rather than an ordinary majority. Also, the legislature is forbidden to pass laws regulating religious beliefs. In respect to general legislation, the House of Representatives is the more powerful of the two houses. The constitution states that the Prime Minister is responsible to Parliament; but the Senate (upper house) can be overruled by the House of Representatives because the Senate can only delay ordinary bills for two sessions and money bills for only one month.[8]

Pakistan, the third new Dominion in the British system, had not produced a constitution by the end of 1950. It has operated since the partition of the subcontinent under a modification of the Government of India Act of 1935. Textual changes were made in this Act following establishment of an independent government within the Commonwealth framework. Otherwise the structure is the same as it was. This means that the Pakistan Constituent Assembly, which temporarily is also the Pakistan legislature, is bound by the many and detailed limitations of the Government of India Act. Pakistan's Prime Minister has issued a general statement about the contemplated provisions of the proposed new constitution.[9] He says it will protect the rights of religious minorities and that other fundamental rights, such as equality of status, and opportunity of social, economic, and political justice, will be safeguarded. Always, however, these rights will be subject to law and the "public majority." The government will also be federal in form. Hence, it would appear that the Pakistan Government will be one of limited

[8] For the constitution, see Amos J. Peaslee, *Constitutions of the Nations* (Concord, N.H., 1950), I, 367–408.
[9] Quoted in *India and Pakistan Yearbook* (Bombay, 1949), p. 604.

powers and that its legislature will be confined within the bounds of a federal constitution.

On the Continent of Europe, as in the British Commonwealth, the constitution-builders have, in the main, followed traditional patterns. Even so, none of the new constitutions is a slavish copy of its democratic predecessor. Partly this is because constituent assemblies tried to improve on the old models; partly, also, it is because existing political pressures required changes.

The French constituent assemblies are a good example. The first French Constitution of 1946 was written by a somewhat leftist assembly, which planned a one-house legislature. Socialists and Communists strongly favored this feature, whereas the Popular Republican Movement, most of the other parties holding over from the Third Republic, and the rightists opposed it. The Communists liked one house because it offered an easy way to take over the government. They hoped to form a momentary coalition with the Socialists and transform the government into a Communist people's democracy.[10]

However, on May 5, 1946, the French voters rejected this constitutional draft by 10,583,724 votes to 9,453,675. The campaign leading to this rejection had been focused mainly on two features of the proposed document. One of these was the weak executive, which General de Gaulle, the first postwar president, especially opposed. The other was the one-house legislature.[11]

Only the second of these institutions was changed by the Second Constituent Assembly, which met on June 11, 1946. The voters approved the second constitutional draft on October 12, 1946, by 9,257,432 to 8,125,295 votes. The revised legislature, like that in the Third Republic, has two houses. The more powerful is the National Assembly. As we have seen, the voters elect its members directly, and, except for the constituent amending power, it exercises the sovereignty of the French people (Art. 3). Indeed, the constitution

[10] For a most comprehensive account of French constitution-making in 1946, see Gordon Wright, *The Reshaping of French Democracy* (New York, 1948).

[11] For a valuable brief discussion of these points, see R. K. Gooch, "Recent Constitution-making in France," *American Political Science Review*, XLI (1947), 429–46.

puts relatively few limitations on the Assembly's power. It is not expressly limited by a long bill of rights, the famous Declaration of 1789 being given no more than passing mention in the preamble of the constitution. The constitution also provides that "the National Assembly alone shall adopt the laws" and that "it may not delegate this right" (Art. 13).

Under the new dispensation, moreover, Ministers are responsible only to the National Assembly and not to the other house, a departure from the practice under the Third Republic. Less fundamental parts of the new French Constitution add to the ascendancy of the National Assembly. The premier (officially called the President of the Council) can only be formally appointed by the President of the Republic (the ceremonial executive) after the premier has submitted his program of action to the National Assembly. In practice this requirement of advance approval of the new premier's program has been a major stumbling block in the setting up of new ministries. The National Assembly also keeps a continuing control over the premier and his Ministers. For this reason it has often been said that the French Government is really run by the Parliament, whereas the British Government is run by the Cabinet. Indeed, legislative pre-eminence in the French Government shows up in the National Assembly's own rules. The timetable of debates, for example, is arranged by a committee of the National Assembly. In Great Britain, on the other hand, the chief whip—a Minister—arranges the timetable in consultation with the opposition whip. Likewise, the French legislative commissions can make important changes in the laws proposed by the Ministers, whereas the British standing committees generally confine their work to minor improvements. In these and many other ways, the National Assembly remains master of the ministry.

But, for all its great powers, the National Assembly must occasionally reckon with the upper house or Council of the Republic, which is not completely powerless. The constitution requires that it concur in a declaration of war. The Council may also send proposed laws to the National Assembly, although these may not contemplate reduction in revenues or increased expenditures. On proposed laws, already passed by the National Assembly, the Council of the Republic has at the most a two-month suspensive veto. The least time it can delay a proposal, under urgency rules, is for as long as the National Assembly has itself taken to consider and vote on a measure. Clearly, then, the Council of the Republic has some few functions; but it is considerably weaker than the old Senate of the Third Republic.

Another limitation on the National Assembly is the constitutional committee. It is headed by the President of the Republic and consists of the presiding officers of both the National Assembly and the Council of the Republic, in addition to the ten members selected by the two houses. The important function of this committee is to determine if laws passed by the National Assembly actually imply amendments to the constitution. It examines laws at the request of the Presidents of the Republic and the Council of the Republic, supported by a majority of the Council. If it thinks that a law does amend the constitution, the National Assembly is asked to reconsider the measure; if Parliament holds to its earlier action, the regular amending procedure must be followed before the law becomes effective (Arts. 91, 92, and 93).

There are still other constitutional limitations on the National Assembly. It is not free, for example, to upset governments on the spur of the moment, because the Constituent Assembly wrote delaying clauses into the constitution in connection with questions of confidence. By these clauses, a question of confidence can only be put after the Council of Ministers has discussed it; furthermore, only the President of the Council can put it, and one full day must elapse after its presentation to the Assembly before it is voted upon (Art. 49). The motion of censure—prepared by those who oppose the government—must likewise be given to the National Assembly one full day before it is voted upon (Art. 50). These are provisions that were supposed to quiet sudden storms, although in spite of their existence cabinets have fallen about as frequently as they did under the Third Republic.

One other device in the new French Constitution is intended to increase the stability of the Cabinet. This is the dissolution article (Art. 51). By its terms the Council of Ministers, with the consent of the President of the National Assembly, may decide to dissolve the National Assembly if two Cabinet crises have occurred on questions of confidence or motions of censure within an eighteen-month period. After the President of the Republic has proclaimed the dissolution, new elections take place within a month. This article was designed to restrain the National Assembly from lightly passing motions to bring down cabinets. Such a restraining article had not been included in the constitution of 1875. Under the provisions that did exist the President of the Republic could dissolve the Chamber of Deputies if the Senate approved. This had been done after the events of May 16, 1877. The incumbent President of the Republic, who was a reactionary, and an almost equally reactionary Senate dissolved the Chamber of Deputies in the hope that a new chamber would bring back the monarchy. The result was quite the opposite, but the memory of this episode was so strong that throughout the rest of the life of the Third Republic dissolution was never used again. Without the dissolution power, however, the only solution to a Cabinet crisis was a new Cabinet. This gave the individual Deputies a good deal of irresponsible freedom in voting against the government, because the fall of a Cabinet did not threaten legislative tenure or raise the specter of election expenses. Undoubtedly, the fact contributed to Cabinet instability under the Third Republic; and it was awareness of this fact that led to an attempt to rehabilitate the practice of dissolution in the new constitution.

The National Assembly is assisted by two other constitutional agencies, the Economic Council and the Assembly of the French Union. The first of these is a functional body whose members come from labor, industry, agriculture, co-operatives, overseas territories, intellectual societies, and other groups. Its powers are purely advisory. On the crucial economic issue of the budget, it cannot make recommendations. However, its advice must be asked on the French "economic plan," and it may look into proposals on its own initiative if they fall within its province; that is, proposals of an economic or social character.[12] The National Assembly must hear

[12] Law 46–2384 of October 27, 1946. Partially reprinted in L. H. Laing and others, *Source Book in European Governments* (New York, 1950), p. 123.

the viewpoint of the Council, but it need not follow it. The Assembly of the French Union is also, in a sense, a functional body whose members are selected because of their expert knowledge about colonial affairs. It may only deal with matters affecting overseas territories, and its role is advisory.

The Italian Constitution of 1947 provides quite a different solution of the problem of legislative structure. In Italy, both houses of the legislature—the Chamber of Deputies and the Senate—have almost equal powers. Both must directly approve bills concerning constitutional and electoral matters, the delegation of legislative power, the ratification of treaties, and the approval of expenditures.[13] The constitution also provides that the government is responsible to both chambers, not merely to the Chamber of Deputies. But this responsibility is tied to motions of confidence, not to ordinary legislative proposals. Thus, if a Cabinet proposal is voted down by either or both chambers, the Cabinet need not resign. Furthermore, a three-day period must elapse before a vote on a motion of lack of confidence. A motion of lack of confidence passed against a Cabinet may lead to dissolution and new elections for either or both chambers (provided that the President of the Republic is not within less than six months of the end of his term). New elections are ordered by the President of the Republic with the support of the Prime Minister and of the president of the chamber that is being dissolved. Thus, the device of dissolution and the delay on voting motions of no confidence are both available to the Italian Ministers to restrain legislators from lightly voting against the Cabinet.

There are other more direct restraints on the power of the Italian Parliament. It is prohibited from taking away from the citizens a great number of civil and other fundamental rights. The list of these rights and corresponding duties is impressive, but many of the rights need legislation before they begin to operate.

The Italian legislature is also limited by a Constitutional Court. Significantly enough, this tribunal is described in the constitution in

[13] For a trenchant analysis of the new Italian Constitution see Mario Einaudi, "The Constitution of the Italian Republic," *American Political Science Review*, XLII (1948), 661-76.

the section headed "Constitutional Guaranties," not in the section headed "The Judiciary." Its important work, as the section heading makes clear, is not strictly judicial, but instead is political: that of safeguarding the constitution against violation by the different governmental agencies. This includes Parliament. According to the constitution, this court decides disputes about "the constitutionality of laws, and of acts having the force of law, emanating from the state and the Regions; on conflicts arising over constitutional assignment of powers within the state, between the state and Regions, and between Regions; on impeachments of the President of the Republic and of the Ministers, according to the norms of the Constitution" (Art. 134).

The fifteen judges who perform these potentially important functions are appointed by each of the three major branches of the Italian central government: one third by the President of the Republic (of course with ministerial approval), one third by the legislature in joint session, and one third by the ordinary and administrative judges. All the judges appointed to this court must have had extensive judicial training, as ordinary or administrative judges, as university professors of law, or as lawyers of twenty years' practice. They serve for twelve years and are not immediately re-eligible.

Italy's legislature does not differ radically from still another new Continental Parliament, that of Western Germany. This body, which consists of the popularly elected *Bundestag,* or lower house, and the much less powerful second chamber, or *Bundesrat,* is limited by the rules of the occupation authorities as well as by the limitations of the Bonn Basic Law. Among the most important of the latter limitations are a long list of Basic Rights. This list deals with freedom of opinion, of the press, of teaching, of assembly, secrecy of the mails, of property, and the right of asylum. Each of these particular freedoms is forfeited by a person if he uses them to attack the "free, democratic basic order." Here the Bonn authors tried to protect the very existence of democracy against attacks from the political left and right. The vital job of applying this safeguard of democracy was given to the Federal Constitutional

Court, which thus serves to restrict the discretion of the legislature. The Constitutional Court decides on the interpretation of the Basic Law "in the event of disputes concerning the extent of the rights and duties of the highest federal organs" and also on "the formal and material compatibility of federal law or *Land* law with this Basic Law" (Art. 93).

Of course, the federal system itself acts as a limitation on the Bonn legislature. The Charter contains many explicit grants of power to the central government, in such matters as foreign affairs, citizenship, coinage, customs, and commercial unity. But the list of concurrent powers on which both the central and *Land* governments may act is long, and deals with such important matters as civil and criminal law, public welfare, economy, and labor. Apart from the powers expressly given to the central government, the *Länder* have legislative power. They must, however, always "conform to the principles of the republican, democratic and social state based on the rule of law" (Art. 28).

Within this limiting framework, then, the legislature carries on its work. Of the two houses of the legislature, the *Bundestag* is much the more powerful, although the *Bundesrat* can exercise certain restraints. For example, the *Bundesrat* must sometimes consent to changes in the territory of the *Länder* and it may begin impeachment proceedings. However, on most ordinary legislation the *Bundesrat* has only a kind of suspensive veto. Although Cabinet bills must first be submitted to it, an opinion must be given within three weeks. After a bill has been passed by the *Bundestag,* the *Bundesrat* considers it. Within a period of two weeks the *Bundesrat* may demand a joint conference, and the conference may ask the *Bundestag* to reconsider. If a majority of the *Bundesrat* should veto a bill, a majority of the *Bundestag* must repass it. This majority needed to repass is raised to two thirds if the *Bundesrat's* veto was supported by two thirds. The *Bundesrat* also participates in the amending process. An amendment of the Basic Law can only be passed by two thirds of the members of the *Bundestag* and two thirds of the votes of the *Bundesrat.*

The *Bundesrat,* however, does not directly control the fate of the German Chancellor and the ministry. This is the special responsibility of the *Bundestag;* and the working out of this responsibility is carefully described in the Bonn Charter. Certainly this problem is the central one in a parliamentary government. Under the Bonn arrangement, the *Bundestag* may express its lack of confidence in a Chancellor by electing his successor by a majority vote. Thereupon the *Bundestag* requests the federal President to appoint this successor, and he may not refuse this request (Art. 67). As in France, there is a "cooling-off" period. In Germany it is forty-eight hours. This period of time must elapse between a no-confidence motion and the election of a new Chancellor. Thus, the *Bundestag* cannot be completely capricious in upsetting a government; it must be ready to substitute one that will have majority support. If a stable majority cannot be constructed in the *Bundestag,* then the Chancellor may request the federal President to dissolve the *Bundestag.* The Charter provides, however, that this right of dissolution lapses if a majority of the *Bundestag* elects a new Chancellor (Art. 68).

From the foregoing it may be seen that the representative legislatures of the postwar democratic countries do not differ greatly from their prewar prototypes. Except in Italy, the trend toward unicameralism has continued. Here and there evidence may be offered to indicate a trend toward restricting legislative power and curbing the legal supremacy of parliamentary majorities. In several states minor structural changes have been made based on the prewar and wartime experience of those who wrote the constitutions. In sum, these changes are not challenging and certainly not revolutionary. Now that the heroic period of postwar constitution-making has come to a close, the legislators are faced with a much more difficult problem than drafting basic documents. Their problem is to use the existing legislative machinery to settle the enormous postwar social, political, and economic issues. The continued existence of the democratic form of government depends upon their success.

Stabilization of the Cabinet System in Western Europe

By Joseph Dunner
GRINNELL COLLEGE

THE cabinet system of government is usually defined as that form of government in which the cabinet, as the "real" executive, is legally responsible to the legislature for policies and administration. The tenure of the members of the cabinet depends upon the legislature. If major policies or administrative acts of the cabinet are disapproved by the legislature, the ministers must resign or dissolve the legislature and stake their continuance in office on the outcome of a new general election. The members of the cabinet are customarily members of the legislature. In fact, they represent the leading core of either the majority party or a coalition of parties forming a majority in the legislature. As parliamentarians, they serve as a sort of steering committee in the legislature. As members of the executive branch, they serve as heads of the various administrative departments. In contrast to the presidential type of government, in which the president as the "real" executive is independent of the legislature in regard to his tenure and, to a considerable degree, his policies and acts, cabinet government, in the persons of the cabinet ministers, emphasizes the interdependence of legislative and executive functions.

The cabinet system of government originated in England as an outgrowth of the Privy Council of the King. While the members of the British Cabinet are at once the working executive, the guiding agency in legislation, and the leaders of the majority party inside and outside of Parliament, this concentration of responsibility and power in the governing party is matched by a unique responsiveness to the voice of the parliamentary minority, a free press, and the general public.

Owing to British traditionalism, the remnants of aristocratic organization that continue to influence British political life,[1] and the regular alternation of two major political parties, able and willing to shoulder the responsibilities of government, the cabinet system in England proved so successful that it was adopted, with some modifications, by most of the states of the European Continent.

Very few of the Continental European nations have, however, ever succeeded in developing fully the subtle and yet fairly simple interrelationship of British constitutionalism with a cohesive, efficient executive leadership, tempered and controlled by a vigilant representative body. While on the European Continent, as in Britain, the contest of political parties created that individual and collective responsibility of cabinet ministers which lies at the root of parliamentary government, the absence of the gentlemanly character of British politics and a traditional multiplicity of large and small parties nearly always militated against a smooth and satisfactory operation of the cabinet system.

As a rule, ministries in France, Italy, and Germany, as well as in a number of other European countries, have to be formed as coalitions by representatives of a number of parties, which compete with one another for popular support. A government so constituted often is unable organically to harmonize, in its political and administrative policies, even the more essential interests of the groups upon which it is compelled to rely. It is from this condition of things that there arose the remarkable frequency of ministerial crises and cabinet changes in the pre-Fascist era of France, Italy, and Germany. This resulted in a popular demand for stable and clearly recognizable government leadership, and, in turn, such a demand, perverted by demagogues, resulted in the emergence of totalitarian structures.

After World War II, public opinion in France, Italy, and Germany

[1] Cf. Carl J. Friedrich, *Constitutional Government and Democracy* (Boston, 1950).

Stabilization of the Cabinet System

considered new constitutions necessary to underscore a fresh approach to political life. But it must be kept in mind that governmental systems are not created *de novo*. The crucial problem upon which the constitutional debates of the postwar years in Western Europe have been centered is the precise character of the relationship between the executive and legislative branches of government. In attempting to find a more satisfactory solution to this problem, the framers of the new constitutional documents evolved a number of interesting new devices. Yet the connection of the new documents with the past is quite apparent. The more carefully one examines the position accorded in the new basic laws to the head of state, the head of government and the ministers, and to the legislative bodies, and the more one analyzes the various procedural and substantive checks on the parliamentary control of the executive, the more one is reminded of the French proverb, *Plus ça change, plus c'est la même chose.*

Under the constitution of 1875, the President of the French Republic theoretically enjoyed supreme executive powers. In actual fact, however, his powers were of no real significance. His official decrees had to be countersigned by a responsible minister. His suspensive veto over parliamentary acts was allowed to fall into disuse. While he sat as chairman of the Council of Ministers, he had no vote. Poincaré once remarked, *"Je suis un manchot constitutionnel."* While the Kings of France reigned and governed, the French presidents traditionally neither reigned nor governed. After the collapse of the Vichy regime, fear of De Gaulle's alleged dictatorial ambitions resulted in the "tripartisme" of M.R.P. (Christian Democrats), Socialists and Communists formally transferring many of the more important executive powers, once attributed to the President of France, to the President of the Council of Ministers, as the French prime minister or premier is known (Art. 47 of the constitution).

Under the constitution of 1875, the most important governmental function of the President of the Republic was his selection of a new premier whenever a ministry fell. The constitution of 1946 reduces this appointive power of the President of France by providing that formal presidential appointment of a premier and ministers must be preceded by submission of the executive program to the National Assembly and a vote of confidence for the ministerial candidates (Art. 45, 3, and Art. 46). While the constitution of 1875 gave the President of the Republic the initiative of the laws, concurrently with the members of the Chamber of Deputies and the Senate, the new constitution stipulates that only the President of the Council of Ministers and the members of Parliament shall have the initiative in legislation (Art. 14).

The constitution of the Third Republic did not limit the chances for re-election of the President of France. The new constitution, like the old one, stipulates a term of seven years, but adds, "He can be re-elected only once" (Art. 29, 2). In one minor respect only has the office of the President of France been somewhat strengthened. Under the new constitution, as under the constitution of 1875, the President of the Republic sits without a vote as chairman of the Council of Ministers. But this presidential prerogative is extended by the stipulation that "he shall order the minutes of their meetings to be recorded and shall keep them in his possession" (Art. 32). As a national leader who must keep out of the storms of partisan politics, the President of France affords badly needed continuity in government. If he is a forceful individual, he can become the interpreter of past policies and the arbiter in Cabinet deliberations. Beyond that he must not venture.

By comparison, the new Italian Constitution of 1947 gives the President of the Republic rather extensive executive powers. They are symbolized by the provision that the President of the Council of Ministers and the ministers, before assuming their office, shall swear an oath in the hands of the President of the Republic (Art. 93 of the Constitution). Of more material significance is the right of the President of Italy to dissolve one or both of the chambers at any time and as often as he deems necessary, except during the last six months of his term, when he should be prevented from a possible manipulation of the forthcoming presidential elections (Art. 88).

Italy's head of state, like the President of France, is elected for

Stabilization of the Cabinet System

seven years at a joint session of both houses of Parliament. While the French Constitution says nothing about the mode of election,[2] the Italian Constitution prescribes the secret ballot and a two-thirds majority. After the third ballot, however, an absolute majority suffices (Art. 83, 3). Like the President of France (Art. 37), the Italian President can send messages to the chambers (Art. 87, 2); he also promulgates the laws (Art. 87, 5). Under the new French Constitution, the President's appointive powers, applying to Councilors of State, members of the National Defense Council, chiefs of the central administrative services, general officers of the armed forces, and ambassadors and government representatives in France's overseas territories, are to be exercised at Cabinet meetings (Art. 30). This can only mean that the appointments must have the approval of the Cabinet. In the fields traditionally within the jurisdiction of the parliamentary head of state, the Italian President is allowed to act alone although countersignature is necessary.

Under the Weimar Constitution of 1919, which undoubtedly was ever present in the minds of the framers of the Bonn Basic Law of 1949, the office of the popularly elected *Reichspräsident* was of overriding significance. In fact, it was this office that provided the legal mechanisms for the change of Germany from a parliamentary democracy to the Hitlerian dictatorship. While the *Reichspräsident* could not initiate ordinary legislation, he had the power of governing by emergency decree (the well-known Article 48 of the constitution of Weimar), and he had the power to dissolve the *Reichstag* (Art. 25).

Under the Bonn Basic Law, the federal President is deprived of an independent popular base. He "shall be elected, without discussion, by the Federal Convention" (Art. 54), which consists of the popularly elected deputies of the *Bundestag* (Federal Diet) and an equal number of specially elected delegates of the *Länder* (state) parliaments. His term in office is five years. Immediate re-election is admissible only once. Under the Basic Law, the federal President

---

[2] An agreement, accepted by all major parties and confirmed by Parliament on January 16, 1947, required the secret ballot and an absolute majority for the election of the first President of the Fourth Republic.

has the privileges customarily accorded to the head of state in a parliamentary democracy. The ill-fated experiment of the constitution-makers of 1919, in attempting to fuse elements of the American presidency with the British monarchic tradition, has obviously been discarded by the constitution-makers of 1949 in favor of a presidential office closer to French and Italian models.

If the new Italian Constitution weakens the position of the President of Italy by comparison with the position enjoyed by the King under the *Statuto* of 1848,[3] and if the French and West German documents likewise reduce somewhat the power of the head of state, the French and Italian Constitutions, as well as the Bonn Basic Law, have tried to compensate by strengthening the position of the Cabinet in its relationship with the legislative bodies.

As was the case under the constitution of 1875, the "real" executive in the new Fourth Republic of France is the Council of Ministers. In contrast to the constitution of 1875, however, the constitution of 1946 establishes a certain hierarchy in the membership of the Council of Ministers by making the President of the Council somewhat more than a *primus inter pares*. It is significant that he, and no longer the President of the Republic, directs the armed forces and co-ordinates all measures of national defense (Art. 47). It is he who shall secure the execution of the laws. He alone can put the question of confidence before the National Assembly (Art. 49). The requirement that the program of the premier be accepted by an absolute majority of the National Assembly before the premier's appointment serves to enhance the power of the legislature in relation to the President of the Republic; at the same time this requirement also increases the stability of a Cabinet whose program has been approved. Altogether, such departures from the constitution of 1875 as were made in the new French system result from the dual objective of increasing the power of the National Assembly and the efficiency of the ministerial team as an executive committee of the Assembly.

---

[3] "To the King alone belongs the executive power" (Art. 5). The legislative power shall be exercised collectively by the King and two Houses, the Senate and the Chamber of Deputies (Art. 3).

Stabilization of the Cabinet System

Three times—under Napoleon I, under Napoleon III, and during the Vichy period—France had succumbed to a dictatorial perversion of its constitutionalism. If the constitution-makers of 1946 were to bring about greater ministerial stability than characterized the French Cabinets of the Third Republic, they had no intention of diminishing the controlling role of the Assembly in its relations with the executive.

Under the constitution of 1875, the Council of Ministers depended for support not only on the Chamber of Deputies but on the Senate as well (Art. 6). Since the composition of the membership as well as the policies of the two chambers were often at variance, the very formation of a Cabinet was, at times, next to impossible. French experience with a strong upper house during the Third Republic caused the "tripartisme" to create a scheme of parliamentary organization reminiscent of the days of the French Revolution and the Second Republic. While the new French Constitution reserves a limited amount of legislative initiative to the Council of the Republic, the National Assembly has the sole legislative authority (Art. 13). Under the constitution of 1946, the Ministers are not responsible to the Council of the Republic (Art. 48, 2).

Another attempt to harmonize added control of the executive by the Assembly with increased ministerial stability can be seen in the constitutional treatment of the dissolution powers of the executive. Under the British system, general elections for Parliament can occur whenever the King, acting upon the advice of the Cabinet, dissolves the House of Commons. Through the device of dissolving Parliament, the Cabinet can fix the time of the election to gain the best advantage for bringing critical issues before the voters. On the other hand, the House of Commons can effectively dismiss a Cabinet by passing a resolution of "want of confidence." This in turn will almost always lead to general elections. As stated before, the fact that elections may be held at any time tends to make both the executive and the legislative branches of British Government highly sensitive to public opinion.

On the surface, the new French Constitution sanctions the power of the Cabinet to resolve parliamentary deadlocks by appealing the issues at stake to the nation in a general election. However, some unpopularity attaches to this device inasmuch as it was attacked by Socialists and Communists in both constituent assemblies as "antidemocratic." Moreover, the dissolution of the National Assembly is based on conditions that in actual practice destroy the effectiveness of the principle. First of all, no dissolution is permissible during the first eighteen months of the legislature (Art. 51, 2). Afterwards, it may take place only if, during another eighteen-month period, two ministerial crises have followed each other as the result of either a refusal of a vote of confidence (Art. 48) or of the passage of a motion of censure by an absolute majority of the Deputies (Art. 50). Even in this case the Cabinet needs the concurrence of the President of the Assembly. Moreover, the Assembly has a right of immediate political retaliation; for, in the case of dissolution, the President of the Council of Ministers must surrender his office to the President of the National Assembly, who appoints a new Minister of the Interior (head of the police forces in Continental Europe) with the approval of the Secretariat of the National Assembly (Art. 52).

While this limitation of official pressure during elections could, as such, be considered an improvement in constitutional technique, it is bound to increase the subservience of the Cabinet to the Assembly and its party blocs under the *"régime conventionnel"* of the Fourth Republic. It should also be kept in mind that an appeal of the Cabinet to the electorate can always be frustrated by the simple method of delaying a vote of nonconfidence or censure. Should the Cabinet, in such a situation, prefer to resign, it would, of course, lose its right to dissolve the Assembly.

This arrangement can be understood only if we remember that to many Frenchmen the dissolution of the legislature appears to signify a *coup d'état* rather than a means of determining the wishes of the electorate. It must also be remembered that the ever-shifting coalition governments secure most of their personnel from the same pool of ministerial candidates; or, in other words, that many ministerial candidates return to office time and again. Finally, it should be kept in mind that the senior members of the civil

Stabilization of the Cabinet System

service, legally protected from the operation of the spoils system, give France more administrative stability than the frequent Cabinet crises might indicate.

Under the new Italian Constitution, the Cabinet has ten days to consolidate itself and to organize its parliamentary support before it must present itself to the two chambers, the Senate and the Chamber of Deputies, for a vote of confidence (Art. 94). Three days—two more than in the French practice—must elapse before a motion of nonconfidence can be put to a vote. Moreover, the motion of lack of confidence must be signed by at least one tenth of the members of either of the chambers in which it is presented. A vote in opposition to the Cabinet by one or by both the chambers on a motion of the government does not carry with it the obligation of resigning (Art. 94); but it stands to reason that, if the Cabinet is defeated on major issues of policy, a vote of nonconfidence is likely to follow. In that event, the Cabinet must resign.

Although the Christian Democrats in the Constituent Assembly of Italy had hoped to make the dissolution power a presidential prerogative completely detached from the policies of the Cabinet, the act of dissolution, like every other presidential act, must be countersigned by the President of the Council of Ministers. While the present government, thanks to the elections of April 1948 which gave the Christian Democrats a majority of the seats in the Chamber of Deputies, enjoys rare stability, there is no such guarantee for the future. In Italy, as in France, the extremist parties to the left and right have been assisted greatly by the prevailing electoral laws.[4]

The two Italian chambers possess concurrent powers of legislation. As in France under the Third Republic, this raises the question of the influence that the co-existence of two legislative chambers

[4] On the basis of the list system of proportional representation, adopted by the Second Constituent Assembly on October 5, 1946, for the election of the Deputies of metropolitan France to the National Assembly, the Communists emerged as the strongest party in the Assembly. By contrast, in the elections to the Provincial Councils of March 1949, in which the traditional French plurality system was applied, the Communist party elected only 37 out of some 1,500 Provincial Councilors. In Italy, proportional representation is written into the constitution itself (Arts. 56–57).

may have on the continuity and stability of the executive branch. In view of the different composition of the Senate and Chamber of Deputies, reflecting different periods and slightly different modes of election, the possibility exists that, just as in the days of the Third Republic, one house may approve of the policies of the government while another may express a lack of confidence. In such a case the new constitution leaves the final decision in the hands of the President of the Republic. He can either accept the negative verdict of the one chamber and, following the resignation of the Cabinet, proceed to form a new one or dissolve the house that cast a vote of nonconfidence. In all likelihood, he will be guided by the political mood of the country as a whole and attempt to follow the house that reflects it more accurately. Italy under Fascism, like France under the Vichy system, experienced the weakening of parliamentary government through the practice of delegating important legislative powers of Parliament to the executive. While the French Constitution prohibits such delegation outright (Art. 13), the new Italian Constitution allows exceptions "for a limited time and for defined objectives" (Art. 76). Under the Fascist dictatorship, executive decrees had the validity of law. Under the new constitution, the government may issue decree laws only if it has received specific authorization from the chambers (Art. 77); moreover, on the day the decrees are issued, it must present them to the chambers for conversion into regular law. To prevent the executive from ruling the country by emergency decrees during a period of parliamentary crisis, the constitution demands that, even in the event of a dissolution, a special session of the chambers must be convoked within five days after the issuance of the decrees to permit the chambers either to sanction or to reject the decrees (Art. 77).

On the other hand, just as the dissolution provisions of the Italian Constitution allow the government to overcome an executive-legislative stalemate by presenting important issues to the electorate, the electorate itself retains a greater measure of legislative initiative than is granted the French voter. While the French Constitution limits the use of the referendum to constitutional amend-

Stabilization of the Cabinet System

ments (Art. 90), the Italian Constitution authorizes the President of the Republic to announce a referendum if 500,000 voters or five Regional Councils demand a total or partial abrogation of a law or any act having the force of law (Art. 75). No referendum is allowed, however, on tax laws, on the budget, on laws concerning amnesty and pardon, and on international treaties.

Generally speaking, the Italian Constitution has avoided the pitfalls of an almost omnipotent unicameral legislature such as exists in the French system. While Parliament is the supreme authority in the Italian nation, the executive holds a position of central influence in it.

Under the Bonn Basic Law the federal Chancellor occupies a position similar to that of the British Prime Minister and somewhat stronger than that of the heads of the governments of France and Italy. The Chancellor is elected by the *Bundestag* (Diet) on the proposal of the federal President (Art. 63). If, within a two-week period, a candidate cannot obtain a majority, he must be elected by a simple plurality. While the federal President is legally bound to appoint the person who has received a majority vote, he is free to refuse appointment to a candidate elected by a relative plurality. In that event, the President must dissolve the Diet and call for new elections.

As in the days of Weimar, the Chancellor selects his ministerial colleagues and determines the broad outlines of governmental policy. Like his French and Italian counterparts, he alone puts the vote of confidence before the Diet. Departing quite radically from the French and Italian Constitutions, the Bonn Basic Law stipulates that the Diet may remove the Chancellor only if it elects a successor by majority vote (Art. 67). If the Diet cannot produce a successor, the Chancellor, himself unable to marshal sufficient parliamentary support, may ask the federal President to dissolve the Diet. The presidential right of dissolution lapses, however, if the Diet elects a new Chancellor within a twenty-one-day time limit and thereby forestalls new federal elections. As Article 68 of the Basic Law, dealing with the dissolution of the Diet, leaves the decision on this matter in the hands of the Chancellor, it is theoretically possible that a Chancellor, as in the days of Von Papen and

Von Schleicher, could remain in office without ever having a majority. Moreover, since the federal President has the power to declare "a state of legislative emergency" (Art. 81, 1), the Chancellor, with the support of the President, can pass emergency laws that have been rejected by the Diet. It should be noted, however, that this power of the government to rule by emergency decrees is contingent upon the approval of the majority of the *Bundesrat* and that no constitutional amendment is allowed under the state of legislative emergency (Art. 81, 4). It is further understood that, after the expiration of a six-month period, a renewal of such a "state of legislative emergency" with the same Chancellor at the helm of the government is inadmissible (Art. 81, 3).

Obviously, all these provisions are intended to avoid the recurrence of situations that were so frequent in the days of the Weimar Republic, when the absence of a responsible parliamentary majority, willing to sustain the government, caused a general disappointment in the efficiency of the whole democratic process. The danger of these provisions, however, lies in the temptation they offer to a federal Chancellor to govern without a parliamentary majority, even where such a majority could be organized.

Like its two predecessors, the Imperial *Bundesrat* and the *Reichsrat* (National Council) of the Weimar Republic, the new *Bundesrat* (Federal Council) is composed of delegates appointed by the *Land* governments. Unlike the Italian Senate, it is not a true upper house, inasmuch as its share in legislation consists chiefly in assenting to Cabinet bills or postponing the promulgation of laws. But consent of the Federal Council is required in matters that concern the *Länder* (Art. 80, 2); and constitutional amendments need the support of two thirds of the members of both the Federal Council and the Diet. In regard to normal legislation, an absolute majority of the Federal Diet can override a suspensive veto of the Federal Council (Art. 77, 4). The Cabinet is dutybound to keep the *Bundesrat* "currently informed" on the conduct of federal affairs, although the Cabinet's primary responsibility is to the Federal Diet.

Like the Japanese Constitution of 1947, the Bonn Basic Law was

Stabilization of the Cabinet System

promulgated in the presence of foreign military authorities. As nations of proved energy and industry and, especially, in view of the East-West conflict, neither Japan nor Western Germany is a completely helpless pawn on the international chessboard. If the hopes and plans of the Western powers are fulfilled, the potentials of the two defeated nations will be released along democratic lines. Nevertheless, it stands to reason that the constitutional documents drawn up under the influence of Allied military administrations will be discarded or at least modified after a final peace settlement. In this respect it is significant that the framers of the Bonn Basic Law deliberately called their document a "Basic Law" and not a "Constitution."

If we were to find a common denominator in the new constitutional documents of Western Europe, it would be the emphasis that all of them place on the prerogatives of the popular assembly. While the Italian and German documents attempt to strike a certain equilibrium between the executive and an ultimately superior legislative authority, the French Constitution suggests a deliberate effort to deprive the executive of all independence from parliamentary rule.

This trend can be well understood as a reaction to the Fascist past of these countries and the "Gleichschaltung" of supreme legislative, executive, and judicial powers in the hands of the hierarchy of a totalitarian party clique. The re-emphasis on parliamentary supremacy must be viewed as the return to a utilitarian-liberal concept of the state. Although the protagonists of this concept usually mention the traditional trinity of power as the best safeguard against the abuse of power, they are probably quite aware of the fact that the lawmaking and administrative processes are closely interwoven and that a rigid separation of power is but *jeu et mystère*.

Every highly industrialized democracy has had to delegate the function to frame bills to the experts of the government bureaucracy, while Parliament retains the power to approve or disapprove these bills as regards their broad intent. It is certainly true that in the United States "the separation doctrine has served to maintain the principal attributes of the legislative significance of Congress."[5]

But it is also true that, in the more unified system of the executive-legislative relationships in Britain, Parliament has retained "the principal attributes" of legislative authority. The fact that private member bills rarely reach today the crucial second reading, while government bills virtually monopolize the timetable of the House of Commons, has been called "cabinet dictatorship." This is a matter of terminology, not to say a play on words; for it must not be forgotten that it is through the majority party in the Commons that the British Cabinet receives its power to assume legislative leadership, and that it is Parliament as a whole before which the members of the Cabinet have to justify their policies.

The main problem which confronted the framers of the postwar constitutional documents of France, Italy, and Western Germany was to work out a system that permits the legislative authority to supervise the legislative functions delegated to the executive branch without disturbing their efficacy. To assume that the few improvements in constitutional technique which have been pointed out could automatically produce the great measure of stability enjoyed by the British system would be an act of wishful thinking. In view of the traditional multiplicity of rather doctrinaire political parties in the Continental European nations, abetted largely by the electoral system of proportionate representation, there remains always the danger that the legislative assembly will become divided into so many factions that no stable majority can be found to support the executive.

The return of France, Italy, and Western Germany to the utilitarian-liberal concept of the state comes at a moment when we experience the resurrection of the totalitarian menace in the form of Soviet imperialism and its world-wide Communist agencies. In the final analysis, a successful revival of constitutionalism in France, Italy, and Western Germany will depend less on the constitutional machinery than on the dominant movements of thought and feeling in these countries.

[5] Arnold J. Zurcher, "The Presidency, Congress and Separation of Powers: A Reappraisal," *The Western Political Quarterly,* III (March 1950), 88.

6

Local Autonomy in France and Italy*

By Ferdinand A. Hermens
UNIVERSITY OF NOTRE DAME

THE political development of the Western world is characterized by the paradox that where central government is strong, as in Britain and the United States, local autonomy is well developed, and that where central government is weak, as in France and Italy, local autonomy is severely curtailed. Strength and self-confidence at the political center apparently engender a willingness to let local bodies lead a life of their own; weakness at the center breeds fear that local authorities might rival their national counterparts, or at least become too strong to be checked when checks are needed in the general interest.

Events in postwar France and, to a significantly lesser extent, in postwar Italy conform to this pattern. Both countries have a tradition of centralized government, born out of the original uncertainty of national unity. In both, the opinion that democracy, like charity, begins at home had gained ground at the end of World War II. Thus, the two new constitutions contain generous provisions for enlarged home rule. In France, where the national government is even weaker than it was during the Third Republic, nothing has come of these reforms; in Italy, where the national government is, for the time being, more forceful and coherent than in France, a measure of progress has been made.

In France, the Revolution deemed it necessary to break up the

---

* The preparation of this and the following chapter was made possible through the assistance of the Committee on International Relations of the University of Notre Dame. For material on France the author is indebted to Dr. Jacques Cadart, and for material on Italy to Professor Giuseppe D. Ferri and Mr. William H. Knight. The author alone is responsible for the conclusions reached.

old provinces and to replace them by eighty-three (at present ninety) small *départements,* which would permit the national government to "divide and rule." Still, the law of December 22, 1789, which effected this change, intended to institute self-government for the *départements* as well as for the municipalities. It proved impossible, however, to establish a new tradition of local home rule during a time of revolutionary disorders. In the words of Professor Sharp: "Administrative and financial chaos developed in many parts of the nation."[1] Therefore the Revolution resorted to centralizing measures, and Napoleon completed the process with the law of the 28 Pluvôise of the year VIII (1800). He introduced, in particular, the *préfet* who, as the representative of the central government, became the all but absolute ruler of departmental affairs and exercised strict control over the municipalities. The name "prefect" was new, but the office was a revival, for a smaller geographical unit, of the *intendant* who under the *ancien régime* had ruled over a *généralité.* Napoleon's centralizing legislation was partly reversed by the July Monarchy, which once again made the councils elective; but serious progress had to wait for the Third Republic. The law governing the basic aspects of departmental life was issued by the National Assembly in 1871 and the law governing municipal life in 1884, although both have been amended since that time, the latter more than the former. The medium of centralization is in both cases the prefect, appointed by the Minister of the Interior, whose function is twofold: He controls in some detail the self-government of the *département* and of the municipalities within its borders, and he is, to a limited extent, the head of the instrumentalities of the central government located within his *département.*

In the two French Constituent Assemblies of 1945 and 1946 the tendency toward decentralization was not universal. Edouard Herriot and most of the members of his Radical party, who had come to defend everything connected with the Third Republic as much as others opposed it, were afraid that radical measures of local autonomy might bring different parties into control in various parts of the country. The Communists favored autonomy, apparently

[1] Walter Rice Sharp, in William Anderson, ed., *Local Government in Europe* (New York, 1939), p. 112.

feeling that, while in the national government they could at best conquer a share, they might be able to dominate local and departmental government in certain areas. The Christian-Democratic M.R.P., unlike its counterparts in Italy and Western Germany, insisted on strict limitation of local autonomy.

The result was a compromise, contained in provisions which Gordon Wright has called "one of the most obscure chapters of the constitution"[2] (Arts. 85–89). The conflicts raging in the minds of the constitution-makers are readily apparent from the first sentence of Title X: "The French Republic, one and indivisible, shall recognize the existence of local administrative units." Still, the compromise would seem workable. Article 87 stipulates that the local and departmental councils (in this connection we can ignore the overseas areas) are to govern the respective units "freely." The execution of their decisions is to lie in the hands of the mayor of the commune (as all municipalities are termed, regardless of size, just as all are subjected to the same legal regulations) and in the hands of the president of the departmental parliament (the "general council") for the *département*. Subsequent plans to implement these constitutional provisions contemplate three sets of measures: First, there is to be decentralization in the sense of self-government of the *départements*. Second, there is to be administrative "deconcentration," meaning that all the agencies of the central government within the *départements* are to be grouped under the control of the prefect, with decisions made locally, so far as possible. Third, there is to be true municipal autonomy.

Before discussing concrete reform proposals, it may be well to note the shortcomings of the present setup. Thus, the *"exposition des motifs"* for the bill introduced by the M.R.P. in order to bring about departmental decentralization [3] states:

The general councils are, at the moment, hemmed in by a group of provisions which subject them to a narrow administrative tutelage.

[2] *The Reshaping of French Democracy* (New York, 1948), p. 241.
[3] Assemblée Nationale, première législature, session de 1947 (No. 2341), *Proposition de loi tendant à réorganiser l'administration départementale dans le cadre de la réforme administrative* . . . , présentée par M. De Tinguy et les membres du Mouvement Républicain Populaire, p. 2.

Ferdinand A. Hermens

Their deliberations are prepared by the prefects, discussed by the active participation of the administration, very frequently submitted to the approval of, and always executed by, the prefects alone.

The budgetary rules, and the rules governing financial control, double the effects of this administrative tutelage by adding a narrow financial tutelage.

When, on November 9, 1949, the National Assembly discussed the "Statute of the Personnel of the Communes," and it was charged that this law constituted an interference with local freedom, the Deputy, Waldeck-L'Huiller, the reporter of the Commission of the Interior, said:

The true interference with municipal autonomy, Mr. Minister, consists in the constant and abusive intervention, in the meddling so often denounced here of the superimposed powers of tutelage, which constitute an intolerable hampering, and which all of the mayors, who sit here (as members of the National Assembly) know well.[4]

Inasmuch as the legal relation between cities and provinces is basically the same in Italy as in France, the interference with municipal government by the prefects may be illustrated by what the mayor of an Italian town told this writer: The prefect's principal concern was uniformity. The town in question was a seaside resort. The mayor wanted to develop the city's water front and planned expenses along those lines. The prefect found it hard to understand why the city in question should engage in expenditures that the other cities in his province, which were not seaside resorts, did not contemplate. In this case the mayor proved to be sufficiently able personally, and influential politically, to get, in the main, what he wanted, but he resented the expense of time and energy required to meet objections of a purely bureaucratic nature. In France, where the prefect is supported by a much more powerful central bureaucracy (Rome cannot, of course, compare with Paris as a centralizing force), his weight is greater. The result is a corresponding lessening of local initiative. French cities and *départements* would, if granted the freedom promised them in the constitution, probably make

[4] *Journal officiel de la république française*, November 9, 1949, p. 6004.

mistakes from which they are now preserved by the tutelage of the prefect, but they might also develop a strengthened local and regional life; as a result, the energies of the people of France might not be drained off to their capital to the extent that they are at present.

In order not to make the prefects the villains of the piece of stymied local energies, we must emphasize that they constitute a body of men with excellent training and, as a rule, high qualifications. Their profession—the dignity of which is properly enhanced by a splendid uniform—is, next to the diplomatic service, the one that is most attractive to young Frenchmen who aspire to public service. The ambiguity of their position arises from the fact that they have both administrative and political functions, which causes Michel Debré to write that the career of prefect at present is "neither in the field of administration, nor in that of politics."[5] One might call them administrators who must permanently resort to political maneuvering if they are to achieve their task. They may want to keep within the framework of the law, but they will do well to be on good terms with the powers that be, not only in Paris, but also the Deputies and perhaps the Senators of their *département,* returning favor for favor, even though they may compromise their impartiality.

There is no lack of concrete plans for the implementation of Section X of the French Constitution. Thus, a bill providing for departmental decentralization was introduced in the name of the then Prime Minister, Paul Ramadier, and the then Minister of the Interior, Edouard Depreux, in 1947.[6] Its *"exposition des motifs"* constitutes a rather forceful restatement of the goals that the respective constitutional provisions were meant to reach. It is said that: "The reforms which are to be realized must be daring. Our democracy has reached maturity and it is necessary that our local bodies cease to be regarded as minors *(comme des personnes morales mineurs)*." To characterize the spirit of the reform, the authors of

[5] *La Mort de l'état républicain* (Paris, 1947), p. 84.
[6] Assemblée Nationale, première législature, session de 1947 (No. 1391), *Projet de loi relatif à l'organisation départementale.*

the bill quote the President of the Republic, Vincent Auriol, who in his book, *Hier-Demain,* wrote: "We must repudiate equally the centralizing Jacobinism which stifles initiative, the caesarian authoritarianism, which suppresses freedom, and the separatist autonomy which disperses the nation and mutilates the fatherland."

The authors proceed to assure the prefects that they will not become useless, that they will remain the representatives of the central government, and that deconcentration will give them new powers. On the other hand,

> the president of the general council receives generally the attributes with which so far the prefect was charged as agent of the *département*.
> It will be his task to arrange for the topics to be submitted to the general council, to carry out the decisions of this assembly, to nominate departmental officials, to administer the property of the *département,* and to represent it before the courts and in contracts.

Furthermore, while the law of August 10, 1871, does not attribute to the departmental assembly a general competence comparable to that given to municipal councils, and limits its powers to those enumerated:

> The present bill provides, on the contrary, that the general council through its deliberations regulate the whole of the affairs of the *département* as a territorial collectivity.
> The extension of the departmental liberties further implies a profound transformation of the regime of tutelage for which the constituent assembly has decided to substitute administrative control.
> This change of denomination means more than a mere change of terminology. It testifies to the desire to break with former conceptions, the maintenance of which has proven unacceptable.
> While tutelage has too often revealed a paralyzing character, control must limit itself to as few interventions as possible. . . .

Passage of this bill would, obviously, for the first time give real self-government to the French *départements,* but it is not expected in the immediate future.

"Deconcentration," the second part of the reform program, is to give to the prefects control over the activities of the agencies of the central government within the *département.* This measure is, as mentioned above, intended to compensate the prefects for the powers they would lose as a result of departmental self-government. The complaint has been made frequently that the various government agencies in the *départements* refer measures of only local interest to the ministries in Paris, a procedure which means the loss of much time and finally results in decisions being made by inexperienced young men in Paris. The prefects are said to contribute to this tendency by "opening an umbrella"; *i.e.,* by referring all kinds of minor decisions to the ministries in order to shield themselves against possible blame. A bill to remedy the situation was submitted to the National Assembly in the name of the then Prime Minister, Robert Schuman, and seven other ministers, on March 6, 1948.[7] It is rather short and delegates to the prefects the power of supervision over all offices of the central government located in the *département,* not only those of the Interior Department, with the exception, of course, of the administration of justice. Practically the same bill was submitted by Mr. Dreyfus-Schmidt, the reporter of the Commission for Administrative Reform, on January 20, 1949. How much such a bill, if adopted, would mean in reality is difficult to tell. It is interesting to note that the one important reform measure of recent years is the institution of the so-called "super-prefects";[8] *i.e.,* eight prefects charged with the task of co-ordinating government activities in the various regions of France. These officials continue, in a different manner, the supervisory functions exercised by the six regional prefects instituted by the Vichy government. Under present conditions, the "super-prefects" may be needed in order to bring order out of what would otherwise (as a result of the continuing multiplication of government functions) be administrative chaos; still,

[7] Assemblée Nationale, première législature, session de 1947 (No. 3705), *Projet de loi relatif aux pouvoirs des préfets et à la deconcentration administrative,* présentée au nom de M. Robert Schuman, président du Conseil des Ministres, par M. André Marie, Garde des Sceaux, etc. See also, Assemblée Nationale, première législature, session de 1949 (No. 6122), *Rapport fait au nom de la Commission de la Réforme Administrative sur le projet de loi relatif aux pouvoirs des préfets et à la deconcentration administrative,* par M. Pierre Dreyfus-Schmidt.

[8] For details, see Roger S. Abbott and Roger Sicard, "A Post-War Development in French Regional Government: The 'Super-Préfet,'" *The American Political Science Review,* XLIV (June 1950), 426 ff.

they could as properly be called agents of concentration as of deconcentration.

The third topic to be dealt with is the powers of the municipalities. A bill intended to enlarge them was introduced in the National Assembly on June 18, 1948, in the name of the Communist deputies.[9] It is rather lengthy but, on the whole, constitutes what appears to be a faithful interpretation of the intentions expressed in Article 88 of the constitution. The municipal councils are to be given complete powers; there is to be no more administrative tutelage by the prefect, although the acts of the municipalities must stay within the laws. Certain actions of the municipal councils are, however, to be submitted to the presidents of the departmental councils for their opinion or for their approval. The mayors are to obtain control over the municipal and rural police; the city of Paris is, in the main, to receive the same city government as the other French cities. It may be noted that the office of the "police prefect" for Paris would be abolished; none of those who have held this office has ever been popular with the Communists. The mayor would inherit his powers, although one wonders whether the Communists would be any better satisfied with a police under the control of Pierre de Gaulle (who became "Mayor of Paris," *i.e.,* President of the General Council of the Seine, after the municipal election of 1947) than they were with the department when it was headed by Jean Chiappe, a prewar official specializing in effective measures to repress Communist activities.

Municipal reform is to include further a change in the recruitment of municipal officials. Such a bill was introduced by Jacques Bardoux in the National Assembly of February 7, 1947.[10] It proposes certain reforms in the election of mayors and assessors; mayors, for example, could no longer hold office in the National Assembly and in the Council of the Republic. The rules of budgetary procedure would be more strict. Finally, provision is made to secure for the

[9] Assemblée Nationale, première législature, session de 1947 (No. 1731), *Proposition de loi relatif à l'organisation municipale,* présentée par Mm. Auguet, Waldeck L'Huiller . . . et les membres du groupe communiste et apparentés.

[10] Assemblée Nationale, première législature, session de 1947 (No. 492), *Proposition de loi relatif à l'administration municipale,* présentée par M. Jacques Bardoux.

technical employees of the cities a higher professional level; they would be recruited by a *concours,* with the intention of having as many of them as possible taken from among the graduates of the *facultés de droit.* It might be mentioned in passing that the prefect of the *département* is to recruit the local police, with approval by local authority wherever their functions are purely local. Mr. Bardoux, who introduced the bill, complains that the *gardes champêtres,* to whom in many rural municipalities the entire law enforcement is entrusted, are "impotent old men," entirely unable to exercise their functions. It will be seen that a bill of this kind, although intended to strengthen local government, would add to the body of national regulations with which municipalities have to comply.

This, then, is the general framework of the laws that would fill the structure established by Title X of the French Constitution. The bills themselves seem to be rather well drawn, and the enactment might, for the first time, give France real local self-government. However, the chances of these laws being passed (with the possible exception of the last one, dealing with municipal employees) is small. The Communists seem, at present, to be the only active supporters; the Socialists, who in the past took the same attitude, have deserted them. Communist sponsorship appears, to the majority of the National Assembly, to reflect on the content even of those measures which not a few of them advocated several years ago themselves, and which are even now, at least nominally, supported by the Assembly Commissions of the Interior and of Administrative Reform. Now it is true that wherever the Communists and their allies would secure control of local and provincial governments they could create more difficulties with the enlarged powers of these bodies than before. Two considerations are, however, disregarded by those who advance such arguments. In the first place, when Communists did secure the control of a municipality, before as well as after World War II, this generally had the result of making them unpopular; the devices of administrative chicanery to which they invariably resorted usually led to a loss of votes in the ensuing elections and, not infrequently, to a loss of control. In the second place, Communist power is, even on the local level, largely a function of proportional representation (hereafter referred to with the familiar abbreviation P.R.). This was demonstrated in the municipal elections of October 1947. In the cities with a population upwards of 9,000, P.R. was applied and, for the nation as a whole, the Communists preserved their position. In the smaller towns, the battle went differently. When subsequently the National Assembly discussed the system of voting to be used for the election of the Council of the Republic, the Communist spokesman, Demusois, said:

> It happened (as a result of the majority system) that in a very large number of municipalities . . . the Communist party saw itself excluded from the municipal council, although its candidates had secured forty-five per cent, forty-seven per cent, and even forty-nine per cent of the votes.[11]

It might be added that wherever the Communist candidates seemed likely to secure a majority this led to a degree of unity among the non-Communist voters (if not their parties) which could not have been created in any other way. Also, the majority system has the tendency of separating a good part at least of the "soft shell" from the "hard core" of the Communist vote: people who vote Communist for reasons of protest, but are not really Communists themselves, vote for more moderate candidates. This was clearly discernible in the elections to the General Councils held in March 1949. At a time when, in all elections held under P.R., the Communists still maintained (or even increased) their share of the popular vote, there was, for the first time, a perceptible decline in the Communist vote, from the 28.6 per cent obtained in the elections to the National Assembly to 23.5. The Communists won only 35 of the 1,508 seats at stake on this occasion, about two and a half per cent of the total; *i.e.,* one tenth of what, in the words of their central committee, a "just system of voting" would have accorded them. It should seem clear, then, that as long as municipal and departmental councils are elected under a majority system, no one need fear that the Communists would be placed in a position to use, for their own pur-

[11] *Journal officiel de la république française,* August 13, 1948, p. 5711.

poses, the added powers which *départements* and municipalities would obtain in case Section X of the French Constitution were implemented by legislative action.

The true reason for the inability of the French Government and Assembly to carry out the explicit directives of the constitution lies in their own weakness, which makes them afraid and incapable of effective reform measures in any field. This was pointed out, even if for reasons of his own, by the Deputy, Pierre Dreyfus-Schmidt, a member of a pro-Communist group, who, in the course of a brief debate in the National Assembly on February 17, 1949, reported the laws providing for administrative deconcentration and departmental decentralization on behalf of the Assembly's Committee on Administrative Reform, and found himself hampered by procedural objections of the then Minister of the Interior, Jules Moch. The latter said that some of the features of the law, as proposed by the commission and previously recommended by the Socialist Premier, Ramadier, were "particularly dangerous for the authority and the permanence of the state." When the Assembly, by a comparatively small majority, had recommitted the bill under consideration (the one providing for deconcentration), the reporter said:

> The ministers defend obstinately the bureaucracy *(les bureaux)* before this Assembly, without being aware of it. We have constantly to deal with demands by them which are in reality demands of the bureaucracy.
> Actually, we are being governed by the bureaucracy. As long as the ministers do not comprehend that it is their duty to impose the will of the Assembly on the functionaries who are under their orders, we shall be in the same position.[12]

In this particular case, the prefects are the bureaucracy whom Mr. Dreyfus-Schmidt had in mind; and the prefects object to the implementation of the constitution because, whatever else may be said about it, it could not be real without curtailing their power. In the France of today, even more than in the France of the Third Republic, no Minister of the Interior is strong enough to risk opposition by *"le corps préfectoral"* (the term indicates that the prefects,

[12] *Journal officiel de la république française,* Débats Parlementaires, Assemblée Nationale 2ᵉ séance du 17 février 1949, p. 652.

who, incidentally, are usually competent and well-trained officials, are similar in prestige to the diplomatic corps) as a whole. Mr. Moch could, of course, have given other reasons in defense of his position: The change of any system that has formed such strong roots in the political soil as has the French system of local government inevitably upsets routine to the extent of making for uncertainty during a period of transition; it would necessitate a revision of financial legislation in order to make municipalities and *départements* primarily dependent upon taxes for which they themselves are responsible. These difficulties are real, but they were anticipated and presumably discounted when the new constitution was adopted.

French failure to carry out the constitutional provisions for local autonomy strengthens the arguments of those who, like Michel Debré,[13] hold that the French political problem is one and that, as long as there is no strong government at the top, there will be no real self-government at the bottom. It might be added that Debré had, during the days of the Resistance when he headed the Comité Général d'Etudes, worked out in good time proposals that promised to secure the necessary result in the national as well as in the local field.[14] He failed in the latter because he failed in the former.

The Italian Constitution is bolder than the French in the extension of local autonomy, and a serious start, at least, has been made in the implementation of its provisions. These have little direct bearing on communes and provinces: Article 5 of the constitution

[13] *La Mort de l'état républicain;* see, in particular, the very interesting discussion of the problems of local reform on pp. 80 ff. Debré would like to make the *départements* more viable by reducing their number to between forty-five and fifty, and then give to them, as well as to the municipalities, real self-government. He is, apparently, inspired by the British example in the field of local and national government. The honest, if somewhat bitter, discussion of the French political system in this excellent book should commend itself to the political scientist for its author's knowledge of administrative detail and likewise for his sure grasp of general problems.

[14] For details, see Gordon Wright, *op. cit.,* pp. 36 ff., and Ferdinand A. Hermens, *Europe between Democracy and Anarchy* (Notre Dame, 1951), pp. 125 ff. Debré insists strongly on the need for a plurality system in French elections, which he would want to be applied in elections held in multiple-member constituencies, and also on the need for a workable right of dissolution. That the former cannot be applied successfully without the latter has been emphasized by Jacques Cadart (see his contribution to Maurice Duverger, *L'Influence des systèmes électoraux sur la vie politique* [Paris, 1950], pp. 137 ff.).

Local Autonomy in France and Italy

(contained in that depository of good intentions, the "Fundamental Principles") states: "The Republic, one and indivisible, recognizes and promotes local autonomy," and there follows a reference to decentralization and deconcentration; Article 128 refers to provinces and communes as "autonomous bodies," and Article 129 promises to make both of them organs of state and regional decentralization.

The meat of the clauses in the new Italian Constitution providing for extended local autonomy is to be found in Title V, Articles 114-133, which deal in some detail with the establishment of regions as new organs of government. When Italian national unity was established, the Piedmontese law of October 23, 1859, providing, on the French model, for small provinces with centrally appointed prefects at their head, was extended to the annexed territories. There remained, however, advocates of administrative decentralization, although they usually insisted that their demands be carefully distinguished from federalism, the latter being deemed dangerous to the country's newly won unity.[15] At the end of World War II, the general desire of promoting radical reforms, as well as the wish to do justice to the particular problems of peripheral areas, led to what could be turned into a constructive compromise between those in favor of the old centralism and those demanding bold steps in the direction of decentralization. The basically unitary structure of the state was reaffirmed, but the nineteen regions, into which the country was to be divided, were endowed with a set of limited powers which, it was hoped, would enable them to vitalize local energies, in particular in cultural, social, and economic matters.

Action was rapid in regard to the five peripheral regions. They occupy a status of their own, defined by separate laws, and motivated by special requirements. In Sicily a separatist movement was to be

[15] For a brief history of the demand for regional autonomy, see Giovanni Miele, "La regione," in Piero Calamendrei and Alessandro Levi, eds., *Commentario sistematico alla costituzione italiana* (Rome, 1950), II, 223 379. While Miele's approach is juridical, his comprehensive discussion of all aspects of regional government contains factual material that will be welcome to the reader interested in details. See also Nicola Sutherland, "The Problem of Administration in Italy," *The Journal of International 'Liberal' Exchange*, I (1950), No. 2, 31 ff.; Mario Einaudi, section on France and Italy, in Morstein Marx, ed., *Foreign Governments: The Dynamics of Politics Abroad* (New York, 1949), pp. 248-50.

headed off; in Sardinia strong demands for autonomy were recognized; in the Val d'Aosta a special status was to obviate the French territorial claims; in the Trentino-Alto Adige the formerly Austrian population was to be given satisfaction; and in Friuli-Venezia Giulia Yugoslav territorial claims were to be headed off. With the exception of the last named, the peripheral regions have been established; the inauguration of the fourteen regions for the rest of the country has, at the time of this writing, not yet taken place.

The provisions concerning the regions are complex. Article 117 of the constitution contains a long (if not too impressive) list of enumerated powers; the main items are control of urban and rural local police, public charities, roads, aqueducts, and public works. A commissioner of the central government resides in the capital of the region. Every law passed by the Regional Council must be submitted to him. He must approve it within thirty days, unless the central government opposes it. The latter may do so because of the presumed illegality of an act or because it conflicts with "the interests of the nation or those of other regions." In case of disapproval, the bill goes back to the Regional Council. If it is approved again with an absolute majority of its members, the central government may refer the issue either to the constitutional court to determine its legality or to the Chambers to determine the question of either the merits of the bill or of conflicts with the interests of other regions.

The organs of the region (Article 121) are the Parliament or Regional Council, and the Executive Committee or *Giunta*. The Council is elected under the terms of an election law established by the organs of the central government; this feature eliminates the possibility that some regions might experiment with different systems of voting, with considerable benefits resulting for the country. The Regional Council elects the members of the executive *Giunta,* as well as that body's president, from among its own members, which means that at least some of the principles of the parliamentary system are adopted. The degree of the possible central control of these agencies is indicated by the first two sections of Article 126, which read as follows:

Local Autonomy in France and Italy

The Regional Council may be dissolved when it performs acts contrary to the Constitution or commits grave violations of the laws, or if it fails to respond to the request of the Government to replace its Executive Committee *(Giunta)* or President when they have committed analogous acts or violations.

It may be dissolved when, by reason of resignations or through the impossibility of forming a majority, it is not in a position to function.

It may also be dissolved for reasons of national security.

It is obvious, then, that the powers which the central government has reserved for itself are substantial. They are strengthened by the degree of state intervention made necessary, in the opinion of many, by postwar events, in particular, the unrest fostered by Communist and, to a lesser extent, neo-Fascist agitation. There is one striking, if unusual, example in the fact that, in the region of Val d'Aosta, the state-owned Cogne works claim to employ eighty per cent of the industrial workers of the region, which gives the central government a strong lever of power against these particular regional authorities who have been endeavoring, rather successfully, to demonstrate that regional government can be carried on without conflict with the national government.

Difficulties for regional reorganization further arise out of the poverty of some of the regions. The regional governments of Sicily and Sardinia, and those to be formed in Southern Italy, may succeed in drawing attention to the needs of their respective areas, but if adequate remedial action is to be forthcoming the money will have to be provided by the central government. Article 119 of the constitution provides that the state will, by law, assign special contributions to individual regions; explicit reference is made to the needs of the South and of the islands. Meanwhile, opponents of regionalism point to the fact that the only immediate result of establishing the new institutions is new government machinery, consisting of nineteen new parliaments and governments, as well as the necessary employees for the new services. A saving might be effected if the provinces and the prefects were abolished. The only statute mentioning the abolition of the provinces is, however, that of Sicily, where this provision has not yet been carried out; in the other cases both provinces and prefects will, apparently, continue, although in Trentino-Alto Adige the two provinces actually have the characteristics of regions. It would, of course, be possible to abolish provinces and prefects insofar as they are organs of the state and to permit the continued existence of associations *(consorzi)* of communes for the area of the provinces. This was done in the former Prussian province of Westphalia where, after its merger into the state of North-Rhine-Westphalia, the **Landeshauptmann** continues to function as the co-ordinator of the welfare and educational activities carried on by the municipalities. If regional government in Italy develops true vitality, the provinces may, of course, atrophy even where retained by law, although developments to date do not point in this direction.

Prime Minister De Gasperi is, as a native of the Trentino, strongly in favor of regional decentralization, and he is determined to carry out the respective constitutional provisions. The obligation to hold elections for the regional parliaments within a year after the constitution went into effect has not, however, been met (except in the above-mentioned four peripheral regions). Much of the delay can be explained by the fact that an Italian government (even the De Gasperi government after the Christian-Democratic victory in the elections of April 1948) does not lead the Chamber in legislative work as the British Cabinet leads the House of Commons. Italian parliamentary commissions make substantial changes in the bills submitted by the government, and so do the two Chambers themselves. Thus, the First Permanent Committee of the Chamber made a detailed report on the government's bill for the establishment of the region, concluding that the official project was "from many points of view insufficient and full of gaps," [16] and submitting an alternative draft. The ironing out of such differences requires time at best, and the Italian Chamber and Senate were occupied with more urgent matters, with business being slowed down by Communist and left-wing Socialist obstruction.

[16] Camera dei Deputati, No. 211-A, *Relazione della I Commissione Permanente . . . sul disegno di legge presentato del Consiglio dei Ministri . . . Costituzione e funzionamento degli organi regionali,* presentata alla presidenza l' 11 novembre 1949, p. 1.

Local Autonomy in France and Italy

In the final resort the basic difficulty in implementing the constitutional provisions for decentralization is the same in Italy as in France. In both cases the government at the center lacks the strength required for making far-reaching changes in the administrative structure. In Italy, De Gasperi's victory in the elections of April 1948 placed him in a much more favorable position than was occupied by the Third Force cabinets in France; but in both cases the government was not strong enough to move against its own bureaucracy, and it was feared that the Communists might derive unwelcome advantage from decentralization. As French Communist influence is largely a result of P.R., it is interesting to note that Ivor Thomas wrote, in his comments on Italy's 1948 elections: "The Front (formed by the Communists and the left-wing Socialists) has suffered a major reverse which only proportional representation saved from being a major rout." [17] After such a "rout" on the national level, the representatives of the extreme left could hardly expect to do better in regional and local parliaments. Certainly, this would seem to be the lesson of the French municipal elections of October 1947 and the departmental elections of March 1949. There is, then, in both countries a key that could open the gates leading to political clarification on both the local and the national levels, but it is doubtful whether it will be used.

The obstacles to be overcome, before a way out of the difficulties created by P.R. is found, are illustrated by the events of Italy's *crisetta*, the "little crisis," which began when, on October 31, 1949, the right-wing Socialists left De Gasperi's Cabinet and was ended by the appointment, on January 27, 1950, of Prime Minister De Gasperi's sixth Cabinet. The "little crisis" became rather large; all the subjects on which the coalition partners differed were brought to the fore; the electoral system to be used for municipal, provincial, and regional elections was discussed with particular heat. The Christian Democrats had begun to challenge P.R. on the local level; it had been applied in municipalities with more than 30,000 inhabitants, whereas in those with a smaller population elections were held under the limited vote, each voter being allowed to vote for

[17] "The Italian Election," *The Contemporary Review*, CLXXIII (May 1948), 257.

four fifths of the councilmen. The Christian Democrats tried to extend the use of this system, although with modifications designed to meet the objections of the smaller parties. De Gasperi referred to "the difficulties experienced in communes where at present P.R. applies," comparing them with communes using the limited vote, "where no such inconvenience had to be lamented."[18] He could have mentioned the example of the city of Rome, where after the P.R. elections of 1946 no mayor could be elected, and the Council had to be dissolved, with a government commissioner appointed to run the city temporarily. Or he could have pointed to the city of Viareggio, where two parties obtained nineteen Council seats each, with two independents turning the scales. The Deputy Carignani commented: "No one can fail to see the precariousness of such an administration where the two independents . . . make rain or sunshine, laughing at the one side as well as the other."[19] It is needless to say that the cause of local autonomy suffers from such developments, as does the cause of regional autonomy by the splitting up of parties characteristic of the present Sicilian and Sardinian parliaments.

The representatives of the smaller parties in the coalition (Liberals, Republicans, right-wing Socialists) were impressed only by the fact that, in their opinion, P.R. alone would enable them to survive. The Liberals were particularly insistent, even though one of their leaders, the then National Councilor (subsequently President of the Republic), Luigi Einaudi, had in 1946 opposed P.R. in a speech in which, with supreme mastery of the subject, he had made a kind of grand tour of all the arguments in favor of that system of voting, leaving none of them standing by the time he finished.[20] Parties that have become small under P.R. rarely succeed in assessing cor-

---

[18] "Il programma definitivo esposto da De Gasperi," *Il giornale d'Italia,* January 20, 1950.

[19] Camera dei Deputati, No. 984-A, *Relazione delle I Commissione Permanente . . . sul disegno di legge . . . per la elezione dei Consigli Comunali,* presentata alla presidenza il 10 giugno 1950, p. 2.

[20] *Contro la proporzionale,* Discorso pronunciato alla Consulta Nazionale nella seduta dell' 11 febbraio 1946. Published as a pamphlet, Rome, 1946.

rectly their chances under a majority system, where more than numbers count and where the local prestige enjoyed by the members of Italy's smaller parties would weigh heavily in their favor. Nor was a proper evaluation of the facts promoted by the Christian-Democratic predilection for the limited vote. In a country with a two-party system as firmly established as in the United States, this can yield excellent results, as it has done for more than a generation in the city of Indianapolis, where it applies to the election of the city council. Where there exists a multiple-party system of the kind that the Italian system of voting, as used for the Chamber and the Senate elections, either creates or preserves, a party can secure the advantages conferred upon the strongest and the next strongest group without having to pay the price of moderation and decentralization, which the majority system in single-member constituencies necessitates. In Italy, the limited vote (unless modified by provisions in favor of a proportional division of the minority seats) means, for the time being, that the country's two strongest formations, the Christian Democrats and the "People's Bloc" of Communists and left-wing Socialists, have a monopoly of the seats. They can alter this result by forming coalitions with minor parties, but are unlikely to do so if they consider it unnecessary for success. The minor parties feel that such a monopoly for the major groupings is artificial, but they weaken their case by failing to realize the needs of political integration. In France, the return to the majority system in single-member constituencies for the departmental elections of March 1949 demonstrated that the majority principle favors large parties only to the extent that they are moderate, and that smaller parties, as the Radicals now are, can derive great advantages from the popularity of their candidates as well as from their strategic position, which enables them to attract support both from their right and from their left. The General Councils of the French *départements* are free from the difficulties besetting the P.R. parliaments of the regions of Sicily and Sardinia. While the latter, with their partisan bickering, weaken the case of local autonomy, the former, if given more responsibility, would be able to discharge it without difficulty.

Ferdinand A. Hermens

The Italian controversy concerning the electoral law for the municipalities was finally settled as follows:[21] In cities of up to 10,000 inhabitants the limited vote applies in its simplest form. Four fifths of the seats go to the strongest party, and one fifth to the runner-up. In the larger cities, two thirds of the seats go to the strongest party, or to the strongest combination of parties; the remainder are divided among all others according to P.R. Where a combination of parties secures two thirds of the seats, these are divided among them in proportion to the number of votes obtained by each party. The purpose was to make it possible for the smaller parties, in particular the Liberals, the Republicans, and the right-wing Socialists, to present lists of their own, link them to those of the Christian Democrats, and thereby to avoid "the great fear of these stormy times: the fear of the wasted vote."[22] This is the law under which the municipal elections of 1951 were held, and which enabled the moderate parties to take control of most of the cities won by the Communist-Socialist left in 1946 in spite of an increase of the leftist vote over the level attained in the national elections of 1948. This system maintains some of the essential aspects of the psychology guiding the voter under P.R.; besides, it fails to encourage the development of a "loyal opposition" that could operate as the safety valve, which Luigi Einaudi, in his above-mentioned speech, characterized as one of the principal requirements of democracy.

The electoral law[23] for the provinces provides that two thirds of the seats are attributed, in single-member constituencies, to the candidates with the highest vote, the remainder being used to reestablish as close a proportionality between votes and seats for each party as possible.

In Italy, then, as in France we can only conclude that the basic problems of national and local government are closely interrelated.

[21] For the text of the law, see "Norme per la elezione dei Consigli Municipali," *Gazzetta ufficiale della repubblica italiana,* March 2, 1951.

[22] Oronzo Reale, "La democrazia e i sistemi elettorali," *La voce repubblicana,* December 10, 1950.

[23] For the text, see "Norme per la elezione dei Consigli Provinziali," *Gazzetta ufficiale della repubblica italiana,* March 13, 1951.

Local Autonomy in France and Italy

Only if national governments are strong and stable will they have the incentive and strength to carry out reforms providing for a large measure of local autonomy; only if the agencies of local government are constituted in a manner tending to assure coherence and moderation can they inspire the confidence needed for an extension of their powers.

7

Functional Autonomy after World War II

By Ferdinand A. Hermens
UNIVERSITY OF NOTRE DAME

IN the preceding discussion of local autonomy in France and Italy we were moving on proved ground. What is being attempted in those two countries has been Anglo-Saxon praxis for a good many generations. Functional autonomy, on the other hand, takes us into a field almost entirely eschewed by the two oldest and largest democratic countries. Experiments in this direction have been attempted in the newer democracies, such as Weimar Germany and Czechoslovakia, and in France, where democracy never attained the strength and stability characteristic of it in the Anglo-Saxon countries. That a variety of dictatorships have claimed the successful establishment of functional autonomy only adds to the bewildering aspects of the issue.

A discussion of functional autonomy necessitates, more than that of any other topic in political science, clarity on fundamentals. In this case as in others it is, of course, essential that conclusions be based on the analysis of the concrete material pertaining to the issue;[1] but in a discussion of social and economic councils a mere listing of isolated facts risks, on account of the terminology involved, suggesting conclusions based more on ideological background than actual accomplishment. Let us bear in mind, then, that the customary formulation of the demands for functional autonomy in-

[1] The pertinent data are summarized and problems analyzed by Arnold J. Zurcher, *The Experiment with Democracy in Central Europe* (New York, 1933), pp. 252 ff.; Herman Finer, *The Theory and Practice of Modern Government* (rev. ed.; New York, 1949), pp. 543 ff.; Carl J. Friedrich, *Constitutional Government and Democracy* (rev. ed.; Boston, 1950), pp. 460 ff. The latter book contains, on pp. 649–52, a critical bibliography.

volves criticism of "political" democracy. It is said that existing parliaments, and the political parties which organize them, are not representative, or not sufficiently representative, of the economic interests of the country.[2] Where economic interests are made effective in political decisions, this is done through lobbying, which means that a public function is left in the hands of private groups. Furthermore, party leaders are amateurs, whom no training has prepared for the technical issues of modern society. Lastly, parliaments are overburdened, with the result that the executive has usurped too many parliamentary functions; an economic parliament could lighten the legislative load and give parliaments time to fulfill their essential tasks.

A discussion of these charges must begin by admitting that, if representation is taken to indicate a reflection of every interest in a country, political parties are not representative. If they were, the result would be anarchy rather than democracy. Proponents of functional representation, like those of proportional representation, are inclined to overlook the difference between society and the state. Society consists of individuals associated in a multiplicity of groups: families, neighborhoods, social classes, religious bodies, and the like. To represent all these groups on a minor scale in a parliament would leave us with nothing but their multiplicity and their mutual antagonism. We must go beyond this and find a principle by which the unity of action essential to the state can be established, and, in a democracy, this must be done on the basis of spontaneity rather than of coercion.

Political parties are the answer to this need. Their essence does not lie in the reflection, but in the reconciliation, of differences:[3]

[2] This and other charges are formulated brilliantly by Herman Finer in his book, *Representative Government and a Parliament of Industry: A Study of the German Federal Economic Council* (London, 1923). It is interesting to compare his change of approach to the subject as expressed in the new edition of his volume, *The Theory and Practice of Modern Government,* cited above, with that of his earlier work; while, in 1923, he gave expression to the notions current among British Guild Socialists, he expresses himself, in 1949, in the familiar terms of the political scientist who is aware of the need for integration.

[3] It is interesting to note that while Charles A. Beard, in his book, *An Economic Interpretation of the Constitution of the United States* (New York, 1913), took it

they find common denominators in the face of what John Locke called "the variety of opinions and contrariety of interests which unavoidably happen in all collections of men." To this integrating task our parties are suited, because the majority system forces them to attract, in a process of persuasion, voters from a large variety of different social groups. In addition to integration, elections organized by political parties under the majority system can fulfill the tasks of decision and the selection of a democratic elite. A decision results from the mere formation of a majority; the voters of the Anglo-Saxon countries know, on the evening of election day, to which party the conduct of their public affairs is entrusted. The need for a political elite has been sadly neglected by democratic theory, although Jefferson formulated the whole problem in classical terms when, in a letter to John Adams, he exposed the merits of a "natural aristocracy." [4]

A representation of interests is deficient on all these points. It limits itself to a juxtaposition of what exists in society of different and divergent forces, and offers no way of transcending them. It suffices to contemplate the formation of "economic parliaments" in order to make the basic difficulty apparent. Such bodies, supposedly organic and natural, do not arise spontaneously; they would never arise if there did not exist a government, formed on a different basis, that could bring them into existence. Even then, there is no general principle that such a government can follow. It is usually demanded, as is done explicitly in Article 99 of the new Italian Constitution, that "qualitative" as well as quantitative considerations are to be taken into account. "Quality" will, however, have to be determined without reference to any objective criterion. Guild history in the late Middle Ages shows that, where functional

---

for granted that political parties merely represent economic interests, he revised this view in his later volume, *The Republic* (New York, 1943), pp. 268–69, making allowance for the integrating function of a party and explicitly exonerating the leaders of the Federalist party from the charges of having served group rather than national interests.

[4] Letter written on October 28, 1813; see Saul K. Padover, *The Complete Jefferson* (New York, 1943), pp. 282–83. For a more detailed discussion of the views expressed above, see Ferdinand A. Hermens, "The 1938 Elections and the American Party System," *The Review of Politics,* I (April 1939).

Functional Autonomy after World War II

groups are not checked by a higher political authority, physical force is their final arbiter.[5]

Assuming that a functional parliament has been brought into existence and a division of its seats agreed upon, how are its decisions to be made? Unanimity will be the exception and hardly occur in important matters; use of the majority principle is inevitable but also incongruous. In the German *Reichswirtschaftsrat,* on one occasion, the scales between the iron-manufacturing and the iron-consuming industry were turned by the professional musicians. The situation will rarely be so grotesque, but the strange character of the principle involved will always be noted, and the authority of the vocational parliament will suffer. One wonders, in fact, why the term "parliament" is used at all for a gathering of people representing different economic interests. There can be little genuine debate among them; the life-giving principle of a political parliament is lacking.

Functional parliaments are in no stronger a position so far as the problem of a political elite is concerned. Political scientists, from Aristotle[6] to Harold Laski, have advised us of "the limitations of the expert." The latter is likely to be a specialist of such a narrow nature that his knowledge will have little relevance to a political decision. A businessman, or a trade-unionist, may be a master in the technique of his trade, and yet be entirely unaware of what it means to direct the interrelation of *all* trades (and of noneconomic political issues), which is the specific political task. When, in 1937, I discussed in Vienna the functioning of the economic section of the parliament of Dr. Schuschnigg with one of this body's government-appointed members, he said: "One of the members represents the Tyrolese dairy industry. When *we* talk about problems outside his special field, he sleeps. When *he* talks *we* sleep, because all he deals with is the technical details of his trade." This incident was adduced as an example of "the inferiority of democracy"; in reality, it proves only the incongruity of associating basically nonpolitical specialists with

---

[5] Take only the telling illustrations related in Henri Pirenne, *Belgian Democracy: Its Early Origins* (Manchester, 1915), pp. 174–80.
[6] *Politics* iii. 11.

Ferdinand A. Hermens

a political task. In the solution of those tasks the "amateur" is much more likely to be trustworthy than the specialist; if he fulfills the requirements of political leadership, he will be able to absorb the essentials of any technical problem in the same way in which the successful lawyer is able to absorb them.

Finally, is there much of a chance to avoid, through a vocational parliament, the danger of lobbying? In this connection it must first be borne in mind—as Harold Laski [7] has emphasized—that lobbying is one thing under a political system in which the individual member of a parliament is largely on his own, as he is in consequence of the separation of powers in our Congress and even more in our state legislatures. Lobbying is something else again where, as in England and in Canada, decisive power is in the hands of the party leaders (meaning, in the last resort, the Cabinet); mere sectional interests are, in that case, at a disadvantage, and logrolling is all but impossible. What there remains in the way of lobbying is so intimately connected with the essence of freedom that democracy will have to live with it. Certainly, the lobbyists will pay slight attention to a vocational parliament which commands so little prestige that its actions, usually limited to recommendations, may be safely ignored.

There remain the questions whether functional parliaments can provide political parliaments with technical advice not otherwise available, and whether they can help to overcome social conflicts, in particular to bring capital and labor together. It will be best to postpone the answer until after the examination of the functional parliaments created, or proposed, by the constitutions under consideration.

The French Economic Council was preceded by the National Economic Council, which was first established by decree in 1925 and subsequently placed on a broader basis by the law of March 19, 1936.[8] It appeared to be a basic defect of this institution that it had

---

[7] *Parliamentary Government in England* (New York, 1938), pp. 136–38.

[8] For a keen analysis of the constitutional functioning of this body and a presentation of its lessons (soon to be disregarded), see Georges Cahen-Salvador, "Le Conseil National Economique," *Droit social* (September–October 1946). Dr. Cahen-

no constitutional basis; as a result, it lacked prestige and could not be placed into organic contact with the legislative process. Article 25 of the new constitution fills this gap. The final phrasing of this article was preceded by considerable, though somewhat obscure, controversy over the nature of the Council.[9] The leftists generally wanted a technical council of advisers, representing central organizations. The M.R.P. wanted a "parliament of industry," and was—as were many others—fond of such terms as "economic and social democracy" and "industrial autonomy." These goals were to be reached by a Council that would have regional as well as national representatives. The views of the left prevailed in the main, and the 164 members of the present Council [10] are mostly appointed by central trade-unions, employers' associations, and the like. It should be noted that the membership of the Council is weighted toward employees; with forty-five members they form the largest single group, whereas, for example, there are only fourteen representatives of private industry and six representatives of nationalized enterprises, plus ten representatives of commercial establishments. It might be mentioned that there are ten representatives of *La Pensée française,* including scientists, economists, and so forth.

The functions of the Council are as follows:

First, the National Assembly may consult it on matters of economic and social policy, excluding the budget and international conventions.

Second, the government may ask its advice on the same topics; it *must* ask its advice on decrees intended to carry out laws on which the Council was consulted, as well as on the national plan.

Salvador, the Secretary-General of both the former and the present Council, placed a complete file of material at my disposal and discussed with me the pertinent problems. He is, of course, not responsible for my conclusions.

[9] Gordon Wright, *The Reshaping of French Democracy* (New York, 1948), pp. 240–41.

[10] The relevant legal texts were published by the office of the Conseil Economique in a pamphlet entitled *Textes constitutifs du Conseil Economique et règlement intérieur* (Paris, 1948). For the background and details concerning the present Council, see *France documents,* issue of September 1947, entitled *Le Conseil Economique;* also *La Documentation française, notes documentaires et études,* No. 908 (Le Conseil Economique, May 1948).

Ferdinand A. Hermens

Third, the Council may itself take the initiative to examine problems within its general competence and investigate them.

Fourth, it may, at the request of the parties and in accord with the interested ministers, act as an arbiter in economic or social conflicts.

It will be seen that emphasis was placed on the subordinate and advisory tasks of the Council. Still, its advice was to be made effective. The *Avis et rapports* of the Council are published as part of the *Journal officiel* and distributed to all members of the National Assembly and of the Council of the Republic. In the sessions of the respective committees of the National Assembly, the reporter of the Economic Council is to be heard; he may be heard in the debates of the National Assembly. A full record of the debates of the Council is published in the same format as the debates of the other three parliaments of the Fourth Republic.

How effective have these devices been in the few years that have elapsed since the establishment of the Council? At present, if one looks for unqualified praise, one must look to the writings of its president, Léon Jouhaux,[11] who speaks, of course, the language of diplomacy. On the other hand, it is typical that when, in its issue for July–August 1948, the magazine *Politique*[12] published two articles on the subject, which constitute the best critical evaluation available to date,[13] the editorial introduction contained this sentence: "Well received at the outset, it (the Council) has rapidly disappointed, and some foretell its disappearance, or its fusion with another council." Let us briefly relate the major points of criticism.

First, instead of trying to give competent technical advice, the Council tries hard to become the fourth parliament of the Republic, imitating, in organs and procedure, the National Assembly, the Council of the Republic, and the Council of the French Union. Inevitably, the Council engages in partisanship and is used by its

---

[11] "Le Rôle du Conseil Economique," *Revue française du travail* (August 1947).

[12] "Faut-il maintenir le Conseil Economique?"; Yves Archambeaud, "Conseil Economique et régime democratique"; Maurice Byé, "Le Présent et l'avenir du Conseil Economique."

[13] See also, however, Jacques Revol (pseudonym for a high official of the Council), "Le Fonctionnement du Conseil Economique," *Droit social* (April 1948).

constituent groups to secure publicity for their views. This is a development against which Georges Cahen-Salvador, the Secretary-General of the former *Conseil National Economique,* had given warning before the Council was established. It had been expected that the work of the new body, like that of its predecessor, would in the main be done in committee, without the disturbing influence of publicity. The present Council, however, disregarded all warnings. It meets in plenary session, lasting from two to three days each, every second week during the period when Parliament is in session. Thus, considerable opportunity is offered to partisan oratory. On March 10, 1948, for example, a representative of the co-operatives, Mr. Gaussel, reported on the economic policy of the government. He took issue with the "plan Mayer," which provided for a liberalization of economic policy and relied on taxation to close what, in this country, we would call "the inflationary gap." His report was followed by a declaration of one of the few economists on the Council, Professor Maurice Byé, who drew attention to the fact that the Council, barging out from its assigned task of suggestions concerning the concrete proposals submitted to it, had launched into a general condemnation of government policy, in which emotion was evident and precision lacking.[14] Byé was voted down by a heavy majority, and the debate became agitated. *Le Monde* of March 11, 1948, reported:

> Yesterday's meeting . . . was particularly stormy and little worthy of an assembly which one believed uniquely preoccupied with technical problems. . . . At one time confusion became so great, that repeated sounding of the bell by the Vice-President, Brousse, did not succeed in reestablishing calm.

The second criticism directed at the Council is related to the first. Its members consider themselves the delegates of the professional groups by which they have been designated rather than as men and women with practical experience in a given field that they would strive to utilize for the general welfare. To be sure, they cannot be

[14] For the report on the meeting, see *Bulletin du Conseil Economique,* deuxième année, No. 10 (March 10, 1948).

recalled, but they know to whom they owe their appointment and on whom they depend for designation for a second term. They are, therefore, inclined to act as automatons, whom the officers of their professional groups can maneuver at will; their speeches in the Council meetings are less calculated to influence the opinion of that body by technical arguments than to provide their organizations with publicity for their views. The Communists who sit in the Council as representatives of the *Confédération Générale du Travail,* the "General Labor Federation," miss no opportunity to make political speeches, introducing topics of foreign policy whenever this can be done.

Third, there is a tendency toward logrolling. Committees as well as the full Council tend to follow the views of the most interested groups, every other group expecting the same courtesy in return. This system works until the point is reached where the demands of one group involve definite sacrifices by another substantial group. Naturally, all groups have acquired the tact not to make such demands and, as a result, a permanent Santa Claus atmosphere prevails. Disagreeable decisions are left to the National Assembly.

Fourth, the Council's plenary assembly resorts too often to decisions by majority vote. This is the natural procedure for a political parliament; however, inasmuch as the moral authority of the "advice" given by the Council to the government, or to the National Assembly, or of the "resolutions" adopted by the Council on its own initiative, depends entirely on the strength of the arguments advanced, the quantitative relation between majority and minority is, artificial as it is anyway, all but irrelevant.

A number of different proposals have been made, by various leaders, to overcome these defects. One of them is the establishment of a permanent central committee, with a small membership, designed to take the place, in all but a few cases, of the plenary assembly. Such a committee, eschewing public deliberations, would be better suited to avoid the pitfalls of partisan propaganda and to maintain close liaison with the government, as well as with the National Assembly and the Council of the Republic. Objections have been raised that such a committee would establish two kinds of

Functional Autonomy after World War II

Council membership, as those not belonging to it would be less influential than those who would belong; unless the committee were large, the smaller groups within the Council could not be represented. For these reasons, Maurice Byé is among those who oppose a permanent committee; Georges Cahen-Salvador and Léon Jouhaux favor it.

A revision of the Council's committee system might also help. At present it is modeled on a system prevailing in the National Assembly, with membership distributed among the groups in proportion to their members. Such proportionality, while natural in a political parliament, hardly commends itself in a body charged with technical advice. Under the present system, for example, only eight of the twenty-four members of the Committee on Agriculture are connected with farming; the remainder can hardly claim any technical competence on the subject. The bulk of the membership should, therefore, in each case consist of people drawn from the professions in question, plus impartial experts, whose number should, in any case, be sharply increased over the few who at present have found refuge among the members of "the group of French thought." Academic economists, for example, are, if they understand economic reality, better experts on questions of economic and social policy than are typical representatives of economic interest groups; in the German *Reichswirtschaftsrat,* much of the constructive work accomplished was due to the initiative of men like Professor Ludwig Heyde. Furthermore, government experts should be called upon for assistance. Close co-operation with them, such as existed in the old Council, could help to bring the new Council into contact with the making of public policy. This would mean less publicity and more utility. It goes without saying that, where the experts disagree, as they usually do, the views of the minority should be fully reported; the final choice between alternatives has to be made by the National Assembly anyway.

Other reform proposals concern the liaison between the Council on the one hand and the National Assembly, the Council of the Republic, and the government on the other. The possibilities provided in this field by the constitution and by the law of October 27,

1946, have been largely ignored. The National Assembly committees should send their reporters regularly into the corresponding committees of the Economic Council; the provision requiring that the *Avis* of the Economic Council be read before the National Assembly discusses a measure should be taken very seriously; the National Assembly should invite the reporters of the Council to take part in its deliberations; there should be delays making it possible for the reports of the Council to be discussed at least by the committee of the National Assembly; and the government should notify the Council in good time of whatever attention has been paid to suggestions, in particular its "resolutions," to which at times the government does not trouble to answer at all.

There remain minor reform proposals concerning, for example, the need for reliable documentation. There being no adequate official service, the Councilors have a tendency to rely on the material provided for them by the research agencies of their respective professional organizations; this leads to considerable differences in regard to the facts and figures used. The discrepancy is not, however, unrelated to the nature of the institution, as representatives of interest groups tend to produce their own information, colored by their own views and interests. The same applies to proposals to bring about a more satisfactory group representation. Certain groups are not represented at all; thus, rent control had to be discussed without representatives of the landlords. It is needless to say that, if all groups receive representation that demand it, the Council membership will have to be increased considerably over the present number of 164. Besides, there will always be dissatisfaction about the number of seats accorded each group. Such quarrels are reminiscent of what Professor Pirenne has to say about the Flemish town during the period of guild rule:

> We find civic constitutions subject, during the 14th century, to perpetual fluctuation. They were continually revised; "members" were added or suppressed, the classification of crafts was modified, and still there was dissatisfaction.[15]

[15] Henri Pirenne, *op. cit.*, pp. 175–76.

Functional Autonomy after World War II

The final conclusions drawn from the practical working of the Council leave little room for praise, more for blame, and most for disappointment. So far as praise is concerned, reference might be made to the reports published by the Council. Some of them are good, others leave much to be desired. Good reports are, however, as likely to be disregarded as bad ones. The government rarely calls upon the Council for advice; the National Assembly does so not infrequently but, it is suggested, more often than not for purposes of delay, or in order to "pass the buck." None of the reports made by the Council has achieved eminence, either of quality or in political repercussions, approaching that of the better known Royal Commissions in Britain. The latter, incidentally, would seem to be in a better position to fulfill the advisory functions of an economic council than any of these councils has proved to be. In the case of the institution with which we are here concerned, reference must be made, however, to the work of its delegation on wages and prices, which was established at the demand of the first Schuman government. It was the task of the delegation to determine to what extent the rise in wages had kept pace with the rise in prices; in France as in the United States the official index of the cost of living was not adequate. The work of this delegation has often been commended; it is said to have succeeded in driving home the fact that nominal wages are not as significant as wage earners usually assume, and that real wages are decisive. This implies that government action to reduce prices, if successful, is more beneficial to workers than a rise in nominal wages offset by an increase in the price level. To have brought about popular acceptance of this proposition, elementary as it is, would be no mean merit.

One of the technical advantages that an economic council may have, according to Dr. Cahen-Salvador, is an integrating effect upon government departments. The latter are inclined to identify themselves with the interests of the particular group with which they are concerned—the Ministry of Agriculture defending the farmers, the Ministry of Labor the workers, and the like. In the Economic Council all these groups meet face to face; they include representatives of consumers, who are overlooked in the organization of ministries but whose interests are often more in accord with the general welfare than those of a particular group of producers. From such meetings there could result the substitution of a more general for a particular point of view. Few would, however, want to say that much has been accomplished along such lines; in fact, the old National Economic Council, in whose work officials from the various government departments participated, was better equipped for the solution of this task than is its successor. In the latter, the mere fact of public deliberations invites the representatives of particular groups to state and restate their point of view, without any serious effort to find common ground. However, we might mention the atmosphere of courtesy, based on personal contacts between representatives of different groups, especially workers and employers, made possible by common council membership, for which the dignified surroundings provided by meetings in the *Palais Royal* provide a suitable background. All this helps to promote better personal relations between representatives of different economic groups, but few would want to contend that this has exercised an appreciable influence on, for example, labor relations in postwar France.

Thus, the record to date of the *Conseil Economique* has not justified the claim that such an institution could remedy the deficiencies of a political parliament. The Council is, in fact, the creature of a political parliament, which has determined its composition as best it could, creating, inevitably, as much dissatisfaction as satisfaction. (It might be noted in passing that, while the Council's term of office was to have been three years, the intention being to consider the composition of the first Council experimental and to adopt a different arrangement later, the necessary legislative action has not been taken, and the first Council continues beyond its term.) Nor has the Council lightened the burden of the legislature; neither has it produced "economic statesmen," supplementing the deficiencies of the political parliament. The visitor to Paris will encounter little praise for the present Council; he is not unlikely to be told that it is another innovation which turned out to be an encumbrance.

Functional Autonomy after World War II

We must now turn to the provisions concerning the National Council of Economy and Labor in Article 99 of the Italian Constitution. Its provisions can best be explained by stating that it differs from the French Economic Council in two respects: It takes in questions of labor by constitutional authorization, whereas the French Council is constitutionally empowered to deal with economic questions alone, although the law establishing it expressly mentions social questions; second, it has the right to initiate legislation. A bill to give effect to these constitutional provisions was introduced in the Senate on March 15, 1949, by the government.[16] It provides for a total of sixty members. The usual difficulties arose in the apportionment of the membership. The Chamber of Commerce of Rome,[17] for example, complains that Chambers of Commerce are not adequately represented, whereas there are to be sixteen members representing government agencies, including nationalized industries. The Chambers of Commerce suggest that there is little need to represent the state before itself; they propose equal representation of state agencies and Chambers of Commerce.

Among the other provisions of the bill it may be mentioned that the introduction of a law is to require a three-fifths majority of the Council, and that its president is to be nominated by the President of the Republic, at the proposal of the Prime Minister. The deliberations are not to be public. These provisions seem to suggest that there is less enthusiasm on the part of the government for the Council than there was during the deliberations in the Constituent Assembly, an assumption that is strengthened by the lack of haste in introducing the bill or in working for its passage. The French experience has been watched closely in Italy; apparently, it did not inspire enthusiasm.[18]

---

[16] Senato della Repubblica, *Disegno di legge,* presentato dal presidente del Consiglio dei Ministri (De Gasperi) di concerto con tutti i Ministri nella seduta del 15 marzo, 1949; Ordinamenti e attribuzioni del Consiglio Nazionale dell' economia e del lavoro.

[17] Le Camere di Commercio e il Consiglio Nazionale dell' economia; Roma Economica, *Bollettino mensile della Camera di Commercio, Industria e Agricoltura di Roma* (August 1949).

[18] The above discussions had to be brief; the interested reader will find further details in Alberto Bertolino, "L'attivita economica, funzioni e forme organizzative

Ferdinand A. Hermens

Reference might also be made to the Bavarian Senate, whose functions are similar to those of the French Council of the Republic. The details are contained in Articles 34-42 of the Bavarian Constitution. One third of the Senators (twenty-one out of sixty) are designated by professional bodies; the remainder represent religious groups, charitable organizations, universities, municipalities and associations of municipalities. The Senate is to give advice on proposed laws, which the government may submit to it; the latter must submit to the Senate the budget, constitutional amendments, and laws to be subjected to a plebiscite. The Senate can introduce bills in the Diet through the government. Lastly, it can within a month, or in the case of emergency procedure within a week, raise reasoned objections to a law passed by the Diet. The constitution says: "The Diet decides, whether it will yield to the objections." It is not required that the Diet's decision be based upon an absolute majority of its members; this renders the position of the Bavarian Senate definitely weaker than that of the French Council of the Republic.

The Bavarian Senate, then, constitutes a case of a second Chamber principally based on economic groups. At first it received much favorable publicity. The dignity of its proceedings was emphasized, and articles appeared in the German press that praised the Bavarian Senate as an escape from the "party monopoly" characteristic of the political parliaments. It must, of course, be borne in mind that the rights of the Senate are limited; this body could hardly afford to press its views in case of a definite conflict with the government and the majority of the Diet. In the first Diet under the constitution, incidentally, the Christian Social Union (C.S.U.) had an over-all majority; its views coincided with those of the Senate on all important matters. In the Diet elected in November 1950, the C.S.U. lost its majority, and the fragmentation typical of P.R. parliaments

---

del lavoro. Il Consiglio Nazionale dell' economia e del lavoro," in Piero Calamendrei and Alessandro Levi, eds., *Commentario sistematico alla costitutzione italiana* (Rome, 1950), pp. 407 ff., in particular pp. 438-40; Giuseppe Alibrandi, "Sull' istituendo Consiglio Nazionale dell' economia e del lavoro," *Il diritto del lavoro*, Nos. 1-2 (1949).

developed. Still, the rightist parties together retained a majority and, though they found it impossible to co-operate in forming a government, the existence of such a majority excludes the possibility of a serious conflict with the Senate. It must be added that in a country which is predominantly agrarian conflicts over economic policy will be less frequent than in an industrial state, apart from the fact that the Federal Republic of Germany, of which Bavaria is a part, has a more important share in economic policy than do the *Länder*.

These considerations make for a comfortable co-existence of the Diet and the Senate. At the same time it is obvious that it would hardly make a difference if there were no Senate. Observers have, in increasing numbers, come to realize this fact. When the author, for the purposes of this study, consulted German economists and political scientists on the Bavarian Senate, those who expressed an opinion agreed that the Senate was unimportant (they were a minority, because most of those approached had heard so little of this body that they had not formed any views about it); some expressed disappointment that it had failed to make a more significant place for itself.

Experimentation with economic representation will continue; in years to come interesting results may be expected from the new Dutch *"Publiekrechtelijke Bedrijfsorganisatie"* (enterprise organization under public law), which is to culminate in a "Social Economic Council."[19] The result is, however, likely to be comparable to the American experience with the code authorities under the National Industrial Recovery Act, so far as the organization of individual industries is concerned, and to the French Economic Council, so far as the central Social Economic Council is concerned, although the latter's limited membership (minimum thirty, maximum forty-five) should guard it against a thoughtless imitation of parliamentary procedure. Democratic countries will keep their promise to allow professional groups to act in freedom, and, as a result, there will not be the cohesion that is needed to create even the appearance

[19] For details, see A. J. S. Douma, *Hoofdzaken en Strijdpunkten van de Publiekrechtelijke Bedriejfsorganisatie* (The Hague, 1950).

of effective common action on the part of the functional bodies created. In dictatorships the ruling party can act as the integrating factor, and, in this case, "corporative" institutions are little more than smoke screens intended to hide a reality from which the conscience of civilized mankind recoils. So far as Italian Fascism is concerned, it is interesting to note that in more serious publications the basic facts were frankly admitted,[20] whereas propaganda destined for popular consumption continued the old theme of the successful establishment of a "corporative state." The situation is similar so far as Russian Communism is concerned. The name "Soviet" means council; the "Soviet Union" is, in theory, a state based upon the councils of workers and peasants. Reality was, however, made tragically clear when in the famous Kronstadt sailors' revolt of 1921 the slogan of the revolutionaries was: "The Soviets without the Communist party!" The Communist party stands, of course, at the base as well as at the top of the pyramid of political power. This the Kronstadt sailors saw, but they failed to realize that this political structure could be eliminated, not by an economic structure of representatives of social groups, but only by an alternative political structure. To proclaim "Soviet" rule in its doctrinal purity amounted to proclaiming a political vacuum.

These considerations take us back to our starting point. The popularity of the demands for functional representation is one of the symptoms of a disease that the proposed solution tries to overcome by medicine derived from the same source. The failure to distinguish between state and society, and to assume that a mere "representation" of social groups would solve a political problem, is widespread. Proportional representation is its institutional embodiment. That system of voting risks taking us back to the divisive forces of society, which true political representation—whose task is, according to Madison, to "refine and enlarge the public view"—is meant to overcome. In practice, P.R. has been one of the conditions of the political disintegration witnessed in so many countries, France in particular, after the end of World War II.

[20] The best example is the article by Francesco Ercole, "La funzione del partito nell' ordinamento corporativo," *Archivio di studi corporativi,* II (1931-1932), 41-71.

Functional Autonomy after World War II

One of the results of such disintegration is that political parties cease to be serviceable bridges between the differences that divide a country; they affirm old divisions, create new ones, and by giving a bad name to the institution of political parties they endanger the essence of democracy. When, for example, in Germany the *Staendestaat* (the corporative state) is again praised as a desirable alternative to the *Parteienstaat* (the parties' state), a vacuum is once more pitted against a reality, undesirable though that reality may be. Nature abhors a vacuum in politics as well as in physics, and the collapse of authority is too easily followed by tyranny.

8

Federalism — The Bonn Model*

By John Brown Mason
FORMERLY OBERLIN COLLEGE

THE geography of Germany has contributed much to the growth of her federalism, although it has also lent itself to intra-Balkanization. In the central and southern upland area—as large a part of the Reich as its northern plains—nature acts as a barrier to communication, while fostering autonomous development of small areas, furthering their cultural individuality, and increasing the difficulties of political unity. The Alps and their foothills in the far South bring out local characteristics again, rather than nation-wide similarities. Germany is also a country of regional diversity in regard to population characteristics, which have long ceased to coincide with political borders. For instance, both the lighthearted Rhinelander and the stolid Pomeranian are (or were) Prussians, although their political outlook tends to differ as much as their degree of natural cheerfulness. Certain pronounced sectional sentiments have had strong effects on the development of federalism, often accentuated by a pronounced religious schism until the recent flood of German refugees from the East and the Balkans tended to lower the dikes of regional religious diversity.

The historical confluence on German soil of Eastern and Western cultural and political tendencies produced uneven results, causing some distinct differences between the eastern and western parts of the country. These are now being accentuated by the contrasting

* This essay was read at the annual meeting of the American Political Science Association in New York on December 28, 1949, before the writer joined the staff of the United States High Commissioner in Germany. The views expressed herein do not, therefore, in any way represent the views of the Department of State.

character and purposes of the Western and Soviet regimes of occupation unless, perchance, a new bond may be formed by the strong desire for national unity.

However, the geographical and cultural divergences between German regions that seem to provide a natural basis for federalism have also proved to be obstacles. At times the quest for German unity seemed to conflict head on with ideas of federalism—rather than to supplement them—reaching an extreme form in the loose association of some 300 independent and mutually suspicious states, principalities, and free cities of the Holy Roman Empire a century and a half ago. Upon this unhappy state of disunity, modern Germans look back with a combination of sorrow, contempt, and fear of possible recurrence.

German unification was finally brought about in the form of a strong federal union—via the earlier and weak North German Confederation—established under Bismarck's leadership and accompanied by the rise of Prussia. But national unity, dear to the Germans as something most difficult to achieve, was brought about by a policy of "blood and iron," after the attempt of the liberal elements to unite the country on a democratic basis had failed dismally.

If the constitution of the Bismarckian Empire had been characterized by strong federalist and weak democratic features, the Weimar Republic presented the opposite picture: a watered-down version of federalism was presented by a constitution that, at the time, was said to echo the march of the working class toward political, economic, and social democracy. When the Hitler steam roller finally flattened the remnants of federalism and crushed democracy, it was unable to kill the seeds of either. Both rose to new life after the double devastation caused by Nazism and war.

Federalism Today

Eleven *Länder* in Western Germany now form the Federal Republic of Germany *(Bundesrepublik)*. Its constitutional basis is the so-called Basic Law adopted by the Parliamentary Council at Bonn on May 8, 1949—the fourth anniversary of the unconditional surrender of Nazi Germany. This intentional coincidence in dates points to two basic facts: the domestic background and cause of Germany's unprecedented downfall from which, it is hoped, a new civil development may arise toward a more permanent democratic and peaceful Republic; and, secondly, the fact that the new constitution was created by a people not yet free but under the control of occupying powers who set in motion and determined the procedure for constitution-making, decreeing for it certain directions and limitations, including provision for a federal structure.

At the same time, the basic disagreement among the wartime Allies resulted in the practical inability of the Germans in the Soviet zone to express or even publicly concern themselves with this first post-Hitler opportunity to create a democratic German constitution. Cynics might claim that the Bonn Constitution, with its strong democratic features, echoes the march of the Western armies of occupation from the Thames, the Seine, and the Mississippi. While the acceptance of the Bonn Constitution[1] does not by itself indicate what exact form it would have taken had the Germans been absolutely free to shape their basic law, the many wide and free discussions before and during the deliberations and the size of the final vote in the Parliamentary Council indicate that, under the given international and domestic conditions, this document represents the preferential will of the large majority of the people, at least in Western (and probably also in Eastern) Germany.

The Allied Influence[2]

Allied interest in the future form of government in Germany has been expressed frequently but not always consistently. The Potsdam Declaration called for the "decentralization of the political structure and the development of local responsibility."[3] The famous Directive

---

[1] Germans speak of the Bonn "Basic Law," or *Grundgesetz*, and refuse to call it a *Verfassung* on the ground that the term presupposes possession of "sovereignty." In contradiction, however, to this argument they do speak of a *Landverfassung* and even a *Gemeindeverfassung*. The American translation "constitution," therefore, is considered a correct translation and is used throughout this discussion.

[2] This topic is discussed in some detail in Carl J. Friedrich, "Rebuilding the German Constitution," *American Political Science Review*, XLIII (June 1949), 465–71, 479–80.

[3] See *Axis in Defeat: A Collection of Documents on the American Policy toward Germany and Japan*, Department of State Publication no. 2423, 1946, p. 13.

Federalism—The Bonn Model

1067 of the United States Joint Chiefs of Staff of April 1945 strongly favored the

establishment throughout Germany of federal German states *(Länder)* and the formation of a central German government with carefully defined and limited powers and functions. All powers shall be vested in the *Länder* except such as are expressly delegated to the Central Government.

The directive also contained these important observations:

Your government does not wish to impose its own historically developed forms of democracy and social organization on Germany, and believes equally firmly that no other external forms should be imposed. It seeks the establishment in Germany of a political organization which is derived from the people and subject to their control, which operates in accordance with democratic electoral procedures, and which is dedicated to uphold both the basic civil and human rights of the individual. It is opposed to an excessively centralized government which through a concentration of power may threaten both the existence of democracy in Germany and the security of Germany's neighbors and the rest of the world. Your government believes that, within the principles stated above, the ultimate constitutional form of German political life should be left to the decision of the German people made freely in accordance with democratic processes.[4]

The British Foreign Minister Mr. Bevin stated his government's position in Parliament on October 22, 1946:

We countenance a German constitution which would avoid the two extremes of a loose confederation of autonomous states and a unitary centralized state. Certain questions would be exclusively reserved to the center. No regional units would be exclusively competent in all the remaining powers. Allowances would thus be made for local differences in traditions, religion, and economic circumstances.[5]

At the Moscow Conference in March 1947, the Allies disagreed strongly on the character of German decentralization. The Soviet Union, logically enough, demanded a German government that was unitary in fact, and which therefore would be susceptible to the influence of the Communist party, strongly and safely embedded in

[4] Directive Regarding the Military Government of Germany, July 11, 1947, Department of State Publication no. 2913.
[5] *The Times* (London), October 23, 1946.

the Soviet zone. France went to the other extreme, favoring a German confederacy, which she believed would be weak and therefore not a danger to her security. The British favored federalism in principle but, perhaps for historical reasons, showed less understanding of it than America would like. The American delegation took the leadership in embodying the basis for decentralized federalism in Germany's future constitution.

The desire of the United States and Great Britain to avoid a charge of violating the Potsdam Agreement, on the one hand, and French policy, on the other, kept the Bi-zonal Organization from developing into a formal provisional government. Continued and increasing disagreement between the Western Allies and the Soviet Union induced the former to prepare for the establishment of a German government based on a German constitution and effective initially in the three Western zones. The terms of the so-called London Agreements on the future political organization of Germany were forwarded to the German Minister-Presidents on July 1, 1948. The Agreements authorized the Minister-Presidents to call a Constituent Assembly, selected by the *Länder* diets, by September 1 of the same year and set forth a procedure for choosing its members. The Agreements also suggested an electoral quotient of 750,000 and provided for a popular referendum on the constitution after it had been approved by the Military Governors. A majority in two thirds of the *Länder* was required to ratify the proposed constitution. The London Agreements stated specifically:

> The Constitutional Assembly will draft a democratic constitution which will establish for the participating states a governmental structure of a federal type which is best adapted to the eventual re-establishment of German unity at present disrupted, and which will protect the rights of participating states, provide adequate central authority, and contain guarantees of individual rights and freedoms.[6]

The German Minister-Presidents accepted the Allied authorization to convene a representative assembly. They proposed, however, that it be called a "Parliamentary Council," as it would draw up a basic

---
[6] See OMGUS press release 7-C-2, Berlin, Germany, July 2, 1948, Document 1.

Federalism—The Bonn Model

law of a provisional nature rather than a full-fledged constitution. The latter would have to wait the day when the Allies would be ready to return sovereignty to the German people.[7]

Strong Federal Features of the Basic Law

The Bonn Constitution or Basic Law is fundamentally federalistic in a number of important respects:

1. It provides for a division of legislative competence between the *Bund* and the *Länder* (Arts. 70-82). The legislative powers of the *Bund* are enumerated and include both exclusive authority and concurrent authority. The *Länder* enjoy all legislative authority not specifically granted to the *Bund,* including education, relations between church and state, police, and internal administration. The *Länder* also have the right to conclude international treaties in those fields in which they possess legislative authority.

2. The constitution provides for a division of fiscal authority.

3. The *Länder* participate in the adoption of the constitution and of its amendments. To be adopted, the constitution had to be approved by the popularly elected Diets in two thirds of the eleven *Länder* in which it was to be initially valid (Art. 144). All *Länder* except Bavaria approved the constitution and did so by large majorities. The Bavarian legislature authorized the government to ratify, if two thirds of the *Länder* should do so. The Weimar Constitution, on the other hand, had been adopted by a unitary constitutional convention. To be valid, amendments to the constitution require a two-thirds vote in both the Federal Council *(Reichsrat)* and the Federal Diet *(Bundestag)*. Under the Weimar regime it was possible for the Reichstag to adopt an amendment by a two-thirds vote even if the Federal Council, representing the *Länder,* opposed. The Weimar dispensation also authorized constitutional

---

[7] At present the *Occupation Statute* amounts essentially to a statement of Allied reserved powers, linked with a grant of the remaining legislative, executive, and judicial powers to the federal and *Land* governments, subject to review by the Allies. The occupation powers were primarily concerned with maintenance of the constitution, foreign relations, foreign trade, reparations, the level of industry, decartelization, disarmament and demilitarization, and the protection and security of the occupation forces. See Arnold Brecht, "Reestablishing German Government," *Annals of the American Academy of Political and Social Science,* CCLXVII (January 1950), 36.

amendments by means of a popular referendum. Amendments to the Bonn Constitution are "inadmissible" respecting the federal form of government, *i.e.,* the division of the *Bund* into *Länder,* the principle of participation of the *Länder* in legislation, and the basic principles upon which the state is founded, that is, civil rights and its democratic and federal character as laid down in Articles 1 to 20.

4. The constitution provides for the establishment of a Federal Constitutional Court (Arts. 92-95), each chamber of the federal legislature electing one half of the court's judges. This tribunal is to decide, *inter alia*

> . . . . in case of differences of opinion or doubts as to the formal and material compatibility of federal law or *Land* law with this Basic Law or on the compatibility of *Land* law with other federal law, at the request of the Federal Government, of a *Land* Government or of one-third of the *Bundestag* members;
> in case of differences of opinion on the rights and duties of the Federation and the *Länder*, particularly in the execution of federal law by the *Länder*, and in the exercise of federal supervision;
> on other public law disputes between the Federation and the *Länder*, between different *Länder.* . . . (Art. 93).

5. The President of the Republic is elected by a federalistic method, *i.e.,* by a federal convention consisting of the members of the Federal Diet and an equal number of members elected by the *Länder* legislatures on the basis of proportional representation. The federal President may be impeached before the Federal Constitutional Court by the Federal Diet *or* the Federal Council (Art. 61). The motion for impeachment can be made by at least one quarter of the members of the Federal Diet or one quarter of the votes of the Federal Council, while the decision to impeach requires a two-thirds majority of the members of the Federal Diet or of the votes of the Federal Council. After the institution of impeachment proceedings, the Federal Constitutional Court—a strongly federalistic institution—may, by interim order, determine that the federal President is prevented from performing the duties of his office; if the President is found guilty of a willful violation of the Basic Law or of any other federal law, it may declare him to have forfeited his

Federalism—The Bonn Model

office (Art. 61, 2). Under the Weimar Constitution only the *Reichstag,* a unitary institution, had the right of impeachment.

6. The constitution provides that the Federal Council (upper chamber) shall consist of members of the *Länder* cabinets. The vote of a *Land* must be cast as a unit, thus enhancing its influence upon the central government. With the disappearance of Prussia, a number of small *Länder*—with a maximum of five votes per *Land*—take the place of President Lowell's "lion among half a dozen foxes and a score of mice," thus allowing for more variety of expression along federal lines. Unlike the situation under the Weimar regime, the members of the national Cabinet are not entitled to place motions before the Federal Council. While, in principle, the Federal Council enjoys only a suspensive veto, this right may weigh heavily on certain occasions. A veto adopted by a two-thirds majority of the Federal Council can be overridden only by a two-thirds vote in the Federal Diet, or lower chamber; and such affirmative vote must embrace at least an absolute majority of the Diet's membership. In certain cases,[8] listed expressly in the constitution, the consent of the Federal Council to federal laws and orders is *required,* thus changing its suspensive veto to an absolute veto. It would therefore appear that in these cases the Federal Council acts as a "genuine" second chamber.

7. In the top federal positions, civil servants from all the *Länder* are to be employed in equitable ratio and persons employed in other federal offices normally are to be selected from the *Länder* in which

---

[8] These laws relate to certain types of taxation (Arts. 105, 3; 106, 3), the equalization of financial burdens between *Bund* and *Länder* (Arts. 106, 4; 107), the structure of *Land* finance administration authorities (Art. 108, 3), possible changes in *Land* administration concerned with the execution of federal laws (Arts. 84, 1; 85, 1), the right of the federal government to give instructions concerning the execution of federal laws (Art. 84, 5), the possible establishment of independent federal authorities at the top, middle, and lower levels and of certain types of public law corporations and institutions (Art. 87, 3), laws concerning the procedure for changes in the existing territories of the *Länder* (Art. 29, 7), and of a law concerning the legal succession and the settlement of former Reich property (Art. 135, 5).

In addition, the consent of the Federal Council is *required* for provisional federal decrees *(Verordnungen)* having the force of law, and of federal individual instructions, in special cases, to the *Länder,* concerning refugees and expellees (Art. 119), and for a federal decree providing details regarding the placement of permanent officials and employees on the retired or waiting lists, or under certain conditions their transfer to another position with less remuneration (Art. 132, 4).

they are employed (Art. 36). This provision is of a federalist character.

8. In case a *Land* fails to fulfill its constitutional or legal obligations toward the *Bund,* "federal sanction" *(Bundeszwang)* on the part of the federal government may force the *Land* to fulfill its duties, but *only* with the approval of the Federal Council. Prior to such a step, of course, the difference must be submitted to the Federal Constitutional Court. The "federal compulsion" of the Bonn Constitution against a *Land* is, therefore, subject to the approval of two distinctly federalistic institutions—the Federal Constitutional Court and the Federal Council. Under the Weimar Constitution, the power of "federal sanction" was taken away from the former *Bundesrat* and given to the Reich President, a unitary institution. A *Land* was able to appeal against the decision of the President in the Court of State or other pertinent court, but the appeal came *after* the intervention by the Reich President. On October 25, 1932, for instance, the Court of State declared unconstitutional the outright dismissal of the Prussian Government on July 20 of the same year by Chancellor von Papen, and its replacement by himself and his deputies.

9. The *Länder* execute their own laws, through their own authorities. The *Länder* also execute the federal laws as their own concern, except as otherwise determined or permitted in the constitution, and in a few cases listed in the constitution the *Bund* authorizes the *Länder* to execute federal laws. In both cases, *Land* execution is supervised by federal authorities: in the first case the federal government exercises supervision to ensure the legal validity of the execution, while, in the second case, the federal government supervises the legality and suitability of the manner of execution.

The Military Governors expressed concern about this very far-reaching administrative prerogative of the *Bund* and stated their intention to watch carefully over its use.[9] But federal supervision is limited to fields actually regulated by federal laws (Arts. 84, 3; 85, 4), in contrast to the more unitary Reich supervision of the constitution of 1871 (Arts. 15 and 4) which was applicable in all

[9] Friedrich, *op. cit.,* XLIII (August 1949), 716.

Federalism—The Bonn Model

fields that could be regulated by federal law, whether they actually were or not. Also, the Bonn Constitution contains much more far-reaching provisions for the settlement of *Bund-Länder* disputes or differences in opinion through the constitutional courts than the Weimar Constitution.

The Federal Diet

The fathers of the Bonn Constitution faced no major problem or disagreement among themselves in working out the constitutional provisions concerning the Federal Diet *(Bundestag)*, the most important organ of the *Bund*. As the center of the federal system of government, it is mentioned first among the federal organs—as in earlier constitutional documents. Elected by the *entire* people in universal, free, equal, and direct elections, its members are the representatives of the *whole* people, not bound by orders and instructions and subject only to their conscience. The *Bundestag* makes the laws for the country as a whole, elects the federal Chancellor, and controls the federal government. As part of and equal partner in the Federal Convention, it also participates in the election of the federal President, its membership making up one half of the Federal Convention, the presidential electoral college.

This participation in the election of the President puts the *Bundestag* in a stronger position than the Weimar *Reichstag*, which had no presidential electoral function. In addition, the federal President is greatly limited in his power to dissolve the *Bundestag*. However, while this fact greatly adds to the importance of the *Bundestag*, an essentially unitary organ, the corresponding loss of power of the old Reich President hits an equally unitary institution. The shift in powers, therefore, does not appear to represent either a decrease or increase in the strength of federalist institutions.

Article 20, dealing with the federation and the *Länder*, provides: "All state authority emanates from the people" and "shall be exercised by the people in elections and plebiscites and by means of separate legislative, executive, and judicial organs." Art. 38, introducing the constitutional section on the Federal Diet *(Bundestag)*, provides that its members shall be "elected by the people in universal, direct, free, equal, and secret elections" and that "they are representatives of the whole people, not bound by orders and instructions, and subject only to their conscience." The Federal Diet is, therefore, the unitary element in the federal government and it is the direct, democratic representative of the people. It is the primary branch of the federal government, limited only by the constitution in the field of legislation, whereas the executive and the judiciary are limited by legislation.

The absolute parliamentary system of the Weimar Republic has been limited in the interest of greater governmental stability and continuity by providing for the so-called "constructive vote of lack of confidence." This is a procedure by which the Federal Diet expresses its lack of confidence in a federal Chancellor, but can do so only by electing a successor by majority vote. A combination of unrelated and heterogeneous elements—such as National Socialists and Communists of the Weimar Republic with nothing in common except opposition to the Cabinet—will be unable to overthrow the Cabinet and leave the country without a helmsman. While this provision detracts from the power of Parliament, the latter is strengthened by an added limitation upon the power of the federal President to dissolve Parliament (Arts. 63, 68), by the apparent denial of the right of self-dissolution of Parliament, and by the new right of Parliament to take part in the election of the federal President.

The Federal Council

The character and status of the Federal Council *(Bundesrat)* were the subject of extended deliberations both at the Herrenchiemsee meeting of a special commission of experts appointed by the Minister Presidents to prepare a constitutional draft and at the Parliamentary Council in Bonn, where opinion was strongly divided in regard to the Federal Council's composition and its tasks. Originally, agreement existed only on the proposition that a second institution should exist alongside the Federal Diet. In these deliberations victory ultimately went to the adherents of the conciliar type of federal representation in the federal government through which

Federalism—The Bonn Model

the *Länder* governments might participate in both the legislation and administration of the federation.

The conciliar type of organ was put through by the more federalistic elements in all parties and adopted by a large majority in the Parliamentary Council, or constitution-making body. It had the support of German tradition from the medieval *Reichstag* to Bismarck's Empire and the Weimar Republic. It was also in line with the fact that the governments of the *Länder* had shared considerably in the establishment of the new government of Western Germany, often because of considerations originating with the occupation powers.

The proponents of a *more* (but not absolutely) centralist organization of government favored a senate of popularly elected representatives of the *Länder*. They admitted the historical tradition in favor of the conciliar type of federal representation, but pointed out that the dynastic units which were united in 1871 in a kind of federation of princes were no longer in existence. They also argued forcefully that a Federal Council consisting of instructed Cabinet members of the *Länder* would never be accepted popularly as a genuine second chamber. In answer to these arguments it was claimed that a second chamber (or second institution) elected by the *Land* diets, or directly by the people, would be only a miniature replica of the elected *Land* parliaments serving as a unit.

A notable minority had favored a second chamber consisting of two elements, one elected directly by the people and one appointed by the *Land* governments. This proposed mixed system, similar to one set up in the constitution of 1849, was said to be unworkable—popularly elected senators, it was argued, would be organized along party lines, while the *Land* government representatives, though party members, would be restrained from joining party groups because of their role as representatives of *Land* governments, which consisted of party coalitions. This argument that popular election would strengthen party discipline is persuasive especially in view of the German custom of strict party discipline, re-enforced by the German list system of proportional representation, which would not allow genuinely "uninstructed" senators to vote regardless of party preferences. "Sons of the wild jackass" are not a German institution and if transplanted would die of loneliness in a disciplined country. *Land* cabinet members, on the other hand, are not likely to be instructed by party caucuses but rather by coalition governments, representing the majority of the *Land* voters—a more federalistic procedure. Whether a mixed system would be desirable from a different point of view is still another question.

Originally, the Social Democratic party favored the senate form of federal representation, while large numbers of the Christian Democratic and the Christian Social Union parties favored the reestablishment of the conciliar system. The mixed system was strongly favored by the Free Democratic party, the largest of the smaller parties, whose chairman, Professor Theodor Heuss, was later elected first President of the new Federal Republic.

Article 51 of the Basic Law provides that the Federal Council shall consist of members of the *Land* cabinets, which shall appoint and recall such members. Contrary to the Federal Council of empire days, the new institution will, therefore, not be a meeting of expert government officials but, as under Weimar, it will be a public platform for the leading *Länder* statesmen which they can use to propagandize the attitudes and proposals of their respective *Land* governments.

Federal President

The status of the President of the Federal Republic differs greatly from that of his predecessor in the Weimar Republic. The Parliamentary Council in Bonn paid special attention to Germany's experience with the dualism of a popularly elected President and a Chancellor and Cabinet responsible to parliament. The federal President is now elected for a period of only five years by a distinctly federalistic method, viz., by a Federal Convention consisting of the members of the Federal Diet and an equal number of members elected upon the basis of proportional representation by the *Land* diets (Art. 54). The President no longer possesses the emergency powers with which he was able, under the Weimar Constitution,

Federalism—The Bonn Model

to suspend civil rights and enforce government decrees—even control local real-estate taxes and municipal and state expenditures; nor does he take part in federal action against the *Länder (Bundesexekution)* or appoint or dismiss the Chancellor at will.

The President of the Weimar Republic had been elected by the people for a period of seven years. The direct method of election and the length of his term reinforced the strong position resulting from certain constitutional powers. These were the power to dissolve the *Reichstag* on his own initiative (Art. 25 of the Weimar Constitution); to compel a state, with the aid of armed forces, to fulfill its duties according to the national constitution or national laws (Art. 48, 1); his dictatorial emergency powers (Art. 48, 2); and his right to appoint and dismiss the Chancellor and Cabinet (Art. 53).

The federalistic character of the new President's position is emphasized not only by the participation of the *Länder* parliaments in his election but also by the constitutional provision that, in case of his inability to perform the duties of his office, his functions are to be exercised by the President of the Federal Council (Art. 57). Under the Weimar Constitution, if the Reich President was prevented from performing his duties, he was represented at first by the national Chancellor. In the case of longer periods of inability, the representation was to be regulated by national law. The same arrangement held in case of a premature vacancy of the presidency (Art. 51).

Internationally, the President is the head of the Federal Republic —the head of state. He concludes treaties in its name with foreign states and accredits and receives diplomatic envoys. He also appoints federal judges and officials, exercises the right of pardon, and promulgates federal laws. In all these functions, however, he needs the countersignature of the Chancellor or the appropriate minister. As in France, the President now occupies a decidedly weak position in contrast to the Chancellor, who is put in a position of definite and dominant leadership, comparable to that of the Prime Minister in Great Britain.

John Brown Mason

Federal and Land *Legislative Powers*

As briefly indicated above, the constitutional provisions for legislation bear a strong federal imprint. As under the Imperial and Weimar Constitutions, today's federal government possesses only the powers specifically granted to it. All others belong to the *Länder* (Art. 70). The *Länder* also have the right to conclude international treaties in those fields in which they possess legislative authority if the federal government concurs (Art. 32, 3).

The *Bund* possesses both exclusive and concurrent legislative authority. The list of its exclusive powers is short. It includes foreign affairs, federal citizenship, passports, immigration and emigration, extradition, currency, weights and measures, customs and foreign trade including international payments, railroad and air traffic, post and telecommunications, federal officials and employees, trade-marks and copyrights, co-operation with the *Länder* in criminal police matters, protection of the constitution, the fight against international crime, and federal statistics (Art. 73). All these affairs are matters that, by their nature, need uniform treatment or regulation. The *Länder* enjoy power to legislate in these fields only if expressly empowered by federal law (Art. 71).

While the power of the *Bund* to exercise concurrent legislation includes a much larger number of fields, ranging from civil and criminal law and laws on economic subjects (including industry, agriculture, and labor) to the fight against infectious diseases (Art. 74), it can legislate in these fields only (1) if the matter cannot be regulated effectively by *Land* legislation, or (2) if regulation by one *Land* would prejudice the interests of other *Länder,* or (3) if federal action is required for the preservation of the legal or economic unity of the country.[10] On the other hand, the *Länder* can legislate in these fields only as long as the *Bund* does not exercise its legislative authority (Art. 72). In effect, therefore, federal legislation is possible in all these important fields. The *Länder* are free

---

[10] See *German Constitutional Proposals,* prepared by the Civil Administration Division, OMGUS (undated; published in 1948). Includes a comparative analysis of draft constitutions by Professor Arnold Brecht.

to regulate these matters until federal legislation is passed. The *Bund* determines the conditions that permit it to enter these fields, but its interpretation is subject to the jurisdiction of the Federal Constitutional Court in case of disputes or differences of opinion.

The legislative initiative lies with the Federal Cabinet, members of the Federal Diet, or the Federal Council. Under the parliamentary system, and as in the past, the overwhelming majority of bills is likely to be introduced by the Federal Cabinet, which must first submit them to the Federal Council. The latter has the right to give its opinions on these bills within three weeks. Bills prepared by the Federal Council are submitted to the Federal Diet by the Federal Cabinet, with a statement of its own views.

The Federal Council may veto bills passed by the Federal Diet, subject to certain rules of procedure, but the veto may be overridden by the Federal Diet. However, as already indicated, a veto passed by a two-thirds majority in the (federalistic) Federal Council can be overridden only by a two-thirds majority of the (unitary) Federal Diet members present at the voting, and these must constitute at least a majority of the entire membership.

Nonfederal or Antifederal Features

1. Section II of the Bonn Constitution on "The *Bund* and the *Länder*" provides not only that the Federal Republic of Germany "is a democratic and social federal state," but also determines that "the constitutional order in the *Länder* must conform to the principles of the republican, democratic and social state based on the rule of law [*Rechtsstaat*] within the meaning of this basic law." The *Bund* must guarantee that the constitutional order of the *Länder* corresponds to the basic rights and provisions just referred to and those listed elsewhere. The federal constitution, therefore, determines the basic features of the constitutions of the *Länder*.

2. The federal constitution invades the normal jurisdiction of the *Länder* when it determines the basic rights of local self-government. It provides that counties *(Kreise)* and communities *(Gemeinden)* "must have a representative assembly resulting from universal, direct, free, equal, and secret elections" (Art. 28, 1). Even more interven-

tionist than the Weimar Constitution, it requires that communities "must be safeguarded in their right to regulate, under their own responsibility, all the affairs of the local community within the limits of the laws" (Art. 28, 2).

3. The Bonn Constitution shows an antifederalist approach when it subjects changes in the geographic boundaries of the *Länder* to the final jurisdiction of the *Bund*. The basic division of the *Bund* into *Länder* is, as mentioned, one of the few constitutional provisions that are not subject to amendment. But the organization as such is to be determined by federal law, with the Federal Council enjoying merely a suspensive veto (Art. 29). The *Länder,* as such, do not participate in this process. The population of the areas that are to switch *Land* jurisdiction is to participate in a referendum on the subject, but not the population of the *Länder,* which are to lose or gain territory. If the law is rejected in at least one area, it becomes subject to a nation-wide referendum, if re-enacted in the Federal Diet. In such a case, a peasant in Bavaria may have to vote on whether Mainz should be a part of Hesse, and the resident of Bremen on whether the Palatinate, formerly a part of Bavaria, should be joined to a neighboring state.

Article 29, which regulates this potential reparceling of *Land* areas, is intended primarily for the *one* reorganization of Germany expected to be necessary to clean up some of the rather arbitrary present boundary lines—a reorganization to be carried through within three years. The requirement for the consent of the Federal Council was omitted to facilitate this reorganization. However, Article 29 provides that in case of other changes, *i.e.*, later territorial changes, only the federal law regulating the procedure shall require the approval of the Federal Council, and not the law about the territorial change itself.

4. From the point of view of the *Länder,* potentially the most important provision of the constitution is Article 30 in Section II on "The *Bund* and the *Länder*." It provides: "The exercise of the powers of the state and the performance of state functions shall be the concern of the *Länder,* insofar as the Basic Law does not otherwise prescribe or permit." This provision would appear to set up

the principle of *Länder* jurisdiction in case of doubt, except where otherwise provided in the constitution. Such exceptions are numerous. Important in this connection is the German equivalent of the "supremacy clause" of the United States Constitution. Article 31 of the German document reads: "Federal law shall supersede *Land* law." This article, giving the *Bund* precedence over the *Länder*, is, of course, conditioned by the requirement that the federal law must be constitutional, *i.e.*, that the federal government has jurisdiction.

The Prerequisites for a Sound Basis for Federalism in Germany

To be sound, effective, and lasting, German federalism must grow out of, and fit in with, the characteristics of the various regions and peoples that make up Germany, due regard being paid to surviving historical patterns which have proved their worth in preserving regional values within national unity. In deciding upon state boundaries, organic units should be preserved or created. It is one thing to merge tiny territorial units resulting from dynastic accidents, to abolish enclaves and exclaves, or to break up Prussia, and quite another thing to carve out new state boundaries primarily to suit the convenience or mood of military occupation authorities. Nor can any goal of the fragmentation of Germany be called federalism.

Federalist provisions in the constitutions of the *Bund* and the *Länder* must be the expression of the popular will or, if the result of compromise, they must gain popular assent. They cannot be the result of orders received from the outside if they are expected to last. Fundamentally, a federal system imposed by foreign dictate would be as much a contradiction in terms, a logical absurdity, and a practical impossibility as a "democracy" set up in response to orders and commands, and threats of "or else. . . ." Fortunately, the federalist character of the Bonn Constitution seems to comply with current German sentiment as much as with Allied directions.

Written constitutional provisions for a division of labor and authority between federal and state governments are of course necessary, but they may be or may become insufficient. They can be reduced to a mere formality if a political group opposed to effective federalism gains control of both the Federal Parliament and all, or most, of the diets; if a coalition of parties opposed to federalism gets into office (as in the early stages of a people's democracy); if a party professing belief in federalism becomes so large, powerful, and uniform in outlook that it is tempted to mold all governments in its own image; and if, regardless of political majorities, too much power and influence is exercised by a civil service trained to such disciplined and tradition-bound views that, in effect, its thinking and actions would be *gleichgeschaltet,* in a rigid uniformity. In such a case, constitutional provisions and divergent state needs or desires may easily become obliterated.

Federalism, like democracy, is assured of effectiveness and longevity only if it is part and parcel of the living constitution of the country, observed in the spirit rather than just in the letter of the law. Each must be meaningful to the people, offer worth-while opportunity, and provide for self-expression in matters close to the home and the hearth, the heart, and the pocketbook, especially in matters such as education, religion, police affairs, socialization, taxation, and the like. There is need for a spirit of enterprise and experiment swelling up from below, a readiness and eagerness to have one's *Land* serve as a social, cultural, and economic laboratory, and to have it lead—or even just grope—where other *Länder* fear to tread because of the weight of tradition, lethargy, or honest disagreement.

German federalism calls for more ideas on the part of the Germans—not only of Bavarians and Württembergers, but also of Rhinelanders and Westphalians. It requires initiative among Hessians, let us say, without orders and directives from Bonn or Berlin, and it demands that the residents of one *Land* respect the constitutional right to actions and attitudes of another *Land* along lines they may oppose or dislike.

If diversity of ideas, initiative close to the grass-roots level, and respect for regional divergences are prerequisites for effective federalism, they are also part of the basis for a more lasting and sound democracy at home and internationally. If Germans living under

Federalism—The Bonn Model

the Bonn Constitution will respect and welcome diversity of political thought and action among the *Länder,* within the unifying framework of a federal constitution, it would seem that they are also more likely to fit into a family of nations consisting of units standing on their own feet and not managed by an almighty *pater familias.* In the past, Germany has tried to make Europe German. The world will be better off, and so, we believe, will Germany herself, if that country becomes European without losing her identity and individual value. If Germans can get along with one another without imposing uniformity of action and thinking on themselves, success of federalism in Germany may prove to be the prototype of that country's role in the international scene.

9

The British Commonwealth as an Example of a Multinational State System

By Adam B. Ulam
HARVARD UNIVERSITY

THE two World Wars have sounded the death knell of old-fashioned imperialism. World War I marked an effective limit to the expansion of the West and, though it was not so realized at the time, the beginning of a rather rapid process of dissolution of the multinational systems, which prior to 1914 had seemed almost permanent pictures of the political map of the world. If the hard test of practical politics rather than that of legal formulas and theories is to be applied to the situation as of today, can we still say that there exists in any meaningful terms a political entity called the Commonwealth of Nations or its French variant, the French Union? Can the new realities, the new social forces, be crowded into a constitutional formula, or is the very process of constitutional reformulation of the old imperial relationships an imposing façade concealing a crumbling structure? The answer can only be given after appraising some of the forces and facts impinging upon the old imperial structures, and determining whether or not they can be reduced to a constitutional mold in a world where there are very many constitutions but very few instances of what might be called true constitutionalism.

The two World Wars have acted as great catalysts of social and political change throughout the world. The aftermath of World War I brought nationalism into the focus of political phenomena, not only as a characteristic of Western culture and of some isolated cultures outside the Western world, but as the central tendency

British Commonwealth as Multinational State System

of the twentieth century. Between the two wars nationalism, and very often militant and integral nationalism, was superimposed upon every social and political issue that was a part of international and domestic policies. Great movements of social reconstruction, which had arisen in the nineteenth century and which had been based upon concepts of loyalties and interests transcending state and national boundaries, now became transformed and distorted by the injection of nationalist orientation. The philosophy of national self-determination that was enunciated at Versailles and that brought the disintegration of the Austro-Hungarian Empire, before 1914 the outstanding example of a multinational constitutional system in Europe, was not an invention of President Wilson but a simple recognition of the ultimate expression of the great historical movement, which ever since the Renaissance has dominated the Western world and which was spreading over Eastern Europe and Asia.

Now nationalism in its modern guise is a stranger to the Lockian world of constitutionalism. As a political movement it is impatient of gradualism and of constitutional formulas and symbols. Nationalism, if agitating various portions of a multinational system, is not only opposed to the reality of domination by one nation within the system but is even impatient of a symbol or fiction of such domination. It is not surprising, therefore, that we find, within a few years after the end of World War I, insistent attempts to define more specifically and to ensure the broadest limits of the autonomy of the self-governing units of the British Empire, which until 1914 were, by and large, content to have their independence from the mother country depend upon convention rather than upon formal statutes and declarations. The feeling which grew up very suddenly after 1918 in the Dominions was not one of hostility toward the British connection or its monarchical connotations (though this did constitute a factor in the Irish Free State and in South Africa) but an expression of the desire that in theory as well as in practice no vestige of doubt should be allowed about the status of the Dominions as free and independent nations.

But effects of the transition extended beyond the realm of legal formulas. In the nineteenth century, the heyday of Britain's power,

Adam B. Ulam

it was easy for some Englishmen of liberal persuasion to envisage a peaceful and friendly demise of imperialism as a natural consequence of the political progress of humanity.[1] The prevailing trend in public opinion in England, while by no means as radically inclined as was Bright, looked throughout the nineteenth century with complacency at the prospect of full maturity of the self-governing colonies. But inherent in the assumption was the notion of quite a different world than the twentieth century was to bring. Toward the end of the nineteenth century and in the beginning years of the twentieth the idea of full independence for the future dominions became more and more supplemented by the notion of a closer and perhaps institutionalized federation between Great Britain and her self-governing colonies in matters like defense, foreign policy, and so on. Here World War I, which in fact marked the fullest possible collaboration between the self-governing units of the empire, marked at the same time, and paradoxically enough, a turn of sentiment toward independent and concrete nationhood for the overseas communities. The Chanak episode showed that South Africa and Canada were no longer willing to have their foreign policy made in London. The empire was in the process of dissolution insofar as the self-governing colonies were concerned, and a commonwealth had to be created to take its place. Already at the Imperial Conference of 1921 various decisions on foreign-policy matters had to be reached through a compromise between the views of those present, rather than through a unilateral decision of the government of the United Kingdom advised only by the Dominions, the normal procedure at previous Imperial Conferences.[2] Thus, an important constitutional precedent was established by convention,

---

[1] John Bright, the most typical representative of the earlier and most optimistic phase of English liberalism, could say: "I believe that if Canada now, by a friendly separation from this country, became an independent state, choosing its own form of government—monarchical, if it liked a monarchy, or republican if it preferred a republic—it would be no less friendly to England, and its tariff would be no more adverse to our manufacturers than it is now. . . . I do not object to that separation in the least; I believe it would be better for us and better for her."— quoted in O. F. Christie, *The Transition from Aristocracy, 1832–1867* (New York, 1928), p. 89.

[2] Eric Walker, *The British Empire* (London, 1943), p. 142.

British Commonwealth as Multinational State System

and the Imperial Conference of 1926 and the Statute of Westminster were to formulate legally what was fast becoming a *fait accompli*—the notion of the Commonwealth as a free association of independent states and the final repudiation of the idea of an imperial federation. The spirit of nationalism was still not appeased, and the Irish Free State and the Union of South Africa were not to be satisfied with the substance of independence but were to go to and through the Statute of Westminster grasping for more and more in the way of concrete symbols of their national separateness.

While the twin forces of nationalism and democracy were modifying the structure of Great Britain's relations with her Dominions, the same combination was making an attack upon Britain's colonial and Indian empires. Again World War I marked the passing of an era. Prior to that conflict, it had been assumed even by the most liberal elements in English public life that the extension of representative institutions to India would be a long and gradual process and that the reins of power there would remain for a long time in the hands of Parliament at Westminster. Unlike the French or the Dutch, the British have never denied, at least in theory, the path of constitutional development to their colonies with self-government as the ultimate, if very distant, goal.[3] A more cynical or Machiavellian imperialism would not have sown the seeds of parliamentary government in India, nor propagated Western political ideas and Western education in Africa and Asia. But British imperialism could be cynical only intermittently, and Britain's commitment to a constitutional development in her most important dependency began even before the Morley-Minto reforms. The latter, despite Morley's dictum at the time that democratic institutions were inapplicable east of Suez, constituted the first step on the tortuous road toward full self-government in India. The full implications of the

[3] It is not argued here that the colonial record of the Dutch and the French is not superior to that of the British in many respects; nor that the former have always denied the rudiments of political representation to the nations under their control. It is simply asserted that, in theory, representative government, even of a very limited form, has from the beginning always figured in the discussions about the future of the colonial, and especially the Indian, possessions of Great Britain, while the same cannot be maintained about the whole course of Dutch or French colonial policy.

reforms were again to be dramatized by World War I, which brought claims for new and far-reaching reforms, going beyond the careful and limited amount of representation granted in India and looking toward dominion status for the empire. Nationalism was becoming a phenomenon that could no longer be localized, and a democracy was in no position to enact the part of an autocracy over another nation. The series of constitutional reforms and would-be reforms instituted in India after 1919, beginning with the Montagu-Chelmsford proposals enacted into the Government of India Act of 1919 and ending with the Government of India Act of 1935, attempted to steer the tide of nationalism into the channel of constitutionalism. Nothing is more indicative of the failure of nineteenth-century preconceptions to deal with the problems of the twentieth century than the fate of those measures. Every concession by Britain in India was regarded as inadequate even before its formal promulgation. That self-government is an art which has to be learned gradually, that national independence for a formerly dependent nation should be an achievement rather than an absolute moral right—all those solid and complacent maxims of the nineteenth century had to yield to the impatient spirit of new nationalism.

The aftermath of 1918 had seen, therefore, the onslaught of the very same forces that were to persist through and after World War II. Nationalism was wreaking havoc in the complicated structure of the British Empire. In addition, the force of social and economic change was thrown behind the fissiparous force of militant nationalism. The relative decline in Great Britain's position as a world power, dating from the early twenties, has to some degree depreciated the strength and prestige of the empire as a whole. And the influence of international Communism was thrown after 1920 behind the militant nationalisms of Asia.

The task of fitting all the disharmonious social and political facts into a neat constitutional formula has occupied British and dominion statesmen ever since 1920, and it is optimistic to assume that the task was finished and concluded with the declaration of 1949. The twenties began to bridge the gap between the theory and the practice of the constitution. When the principles of the Statute of Westminster were first announced and when they became legal realities in 1931, it was difficult to conceive of the next step toward fuller independence of the units of the British Commonwealth without envisaging the end of any conceivable association between its members, and indeed the end of the Commonwealth itself. Yet the process of weakening the formal links of the empire went on during the thirties; it continued throughout and after the war. But the Commonwealth remains even today a meaningful and important organization playing a considerable part in international politics, quite apart from the importance of its member states.

The meaning of "dominion status" had never been defined prior to 1926; and indeed any attempt to do so would have been regarded as an attempt to put down in hard and fast legal formulas an essentially developing and dynamic thing or an attempt to constrain convention by law—an idea rather repugnant to the main trend of British constitutional traditions. Yet indications were not lacking, even before 1926, that some sort of a definition of the status of the Dominions was clearly in order if serious strain was not to be placed upon Great Britain's relations with her self-governing colonies. Considerable conflicts had developed on occasion between representatives of the Crown in the Dominions and their ministries, the two parties being handicapped by differing conceptions of the status and powers of the Governor-General. The Colonial Laws Validity Act of 1865 operated as an uncertain and cumbersome check, at least in theory, upon legislative autonomy of the Dominions. The formal paraphernalia of restraint upon self-government in the new nations were formidable indeed. They included, to mention just the most important elements in the picture, the power of disallowance of colonial legislation held both by the Governor-General and by the Sovereign advised by his British ministers, the Colonial Laws Validity Act, and the Judicial Committee of the Privy Council. Though the power of disallowance had by 1926 practically fallen into desuetude, and the Colonial Laws Validity Act had become a legal nuisance rather than a concrete barrier to full legislative independence, there still remained real grievances and the irritating suggestion of incompleteness in the independent status of the Dominions. General Smuts, who was defeated in the 1924 elections in South Africa because of his supposed subservience to the empire, had said in 1917 that "although in practice there is great freedom, yet in actual theory the status of the Dominions is of a subject character. Whatever we may say, and whatever we may think, we are subject Provinces of Great Britain. That is the actual theory of the Constitution, and in many ways, which I need not specify to-day, that theory still permeates practice to some extent."[4] It is well to recognize the nationalist sensitivity of General Smuts's words, for hardly more than thirty years later another Commonwealth statesman, Mr. Nehru, was to feel almost the same way about the improved and defined status of the Dominions under the Statute of Westminster, and was to demand a considerable advance upon the previous definition.

Dominion status was under discussion between 1926 and 1931, and its definition under the Statute of Westminster is still the legal basis of the status enjoyed by Canada, Australia, South Africa, and New Zealand; more recently, and with some variations, by Ceylon; and, at least for the time being, by Pakistan. It is the cornerstone and the basis of the British Commonwealth of Nations—"The Third British Empire"—and in many ways it suggested to the French and the Dutch, after World War II, the way to deal with their own colonial problems.

The Statute of Westminster once and for all removed even the very theoretical possibility of the Parliament at Westminster legislating for any of the Dominions except by the request and consent of the government of the given Dominion. The legislative autonomy of the Dominions was made complete by annulling for the future the provisions of the Colonial Laws Validity Act of 1865 insofar as the legislative bodies of the Dominions were concerned. It was the intent of the Statute to transform the self-governing part of the British Empire in law, as it was already in fact, into an association of free states "united by a common allegiance to the Crown." The

[4] Quoted in K. C. Wheare, *The Statute of Westminster and Dominion Status* (Oxford, 1938), p. 23.

British Commonwealth as Multinational State System

Crown itself was thus defined not only as the symbol but also as the most concrete legal link of the British Commonwealth of Nations. Under the Statute of Westminster, legal changes touching the succession to the throne or any alteration in the royal titles were to be ratified not only by the British Parliament but also by the Parliaments of all the Dominions, as actually happened in December 1936 upon the abdication of King Edward VIII.

Thus, the series of documents and declarations, beginning with the Balfour Declaration of 1926 and ending with the Statute, established the status of the Dominions as fully self-governing communities with all the essential characteristics of independent states. Constitutionally their legislative bodies became fully autonomous. The Governor-General was no longer an agent of the British Government but solely a representative of the Crown, with his constitutional function similar to that of the King in the United Kingdom; *i.e.*, that of the ceremonial head of the state. Within the space of five years the formal structure of the British Empire was reviewed and rearranged. That the job, which taxed the energies and legal skill of many experts as well as Lord Balfour's metaphysical skill, was largely an acknowledgment of a *fait accompli,* and, as such, a concession to nationalist emotions rather than to concrete and pressing needs, is amply demonstrated by the behavior of Australia and New Zealand. The two most "British" Dominions went along with their fellow members of the Commonwealth, though they never felt that dominion status should be very strictly defined. They were not to ratify the Statute of Westminster till many years after its inception, Australia in 1942 and New Zealand in 1947.

On the other hand, the Statute of Westminster did not go far enough for the Union of South Africa or for the Irish Free State. The Union of South Africa, not satisfied with Section 4 of the Statute of Westminster (which required request and permission by the Dominions for any legislation affecting them), provided in the Status of the Union Act of 1934 that "no Act of the Parliament of the United Kingdom and Northern Ireland, passed after the eleventh day of December 1931 shall extend or be deemed to extend to the Union as part of the law of the Union, unless extended thereto by an Act of the Parliament of the Union."[5] Essentially this provision of the Status of the Union Act added little or nothing to the real legislative powers of the Parliament of the Union. Other provisions of the Act attempted likewise to spell out, in harsh detail, what had already been conceded to the Dominions either by law or by convention. The sole intent of the Act was to remove any implication or hint that might have been construed to suggest a still superior status for the Parliament at Westminster or a status for the Governor-General as anything more than that of the ceremonial head of the state advised solely by his South African ministers. The Status of the Union Act presaged that for South Africa, or at least for a large portion of her citizens, dominion status was not a satisfactory definition of independence.

The case of the Irish Free State, or Eire as it became known in 1937, indicates much more clearly the "looseness" of the Commonwealth even as it existed before 1945. Prior to Mr. De Valera's assumption of power in 1932, the Irish Free State had already pushed dominion status to its extreme limits. Ireland had come into the Commonwealth reluctantly and sullenly. The achievement of self-government could be for her not a consummation of a long and peaceful development, as it was for other Dominions, but only an interlude in the struggle to abolish not only the substance but also the symbolism of her dependent position vis-à-vis Great Britain. Professor Mansergh speculates that even the period of Ireland's willing collaboration in the Commonwealth, the period which ended in 1932, strengthened the fissiparous tendencies within the Commonwealth and hastened latent tendencies in the same direction in Canada and South Africa.[6]

When Mr. De Valera assumed office in 1932 the fragility of the purely constitutional bonds of the Commonwealth became only too obvious. The appurtenances of membership in the Commonwealth and of the connection with the Crown had to go one by one: the oath of allegiance to the King, the office of Governor-General, and the appeal to the Privy Council. In 1937, Ireland became a *de facto*

---

[5] Quoted in Wheare, *op. cit.*, p. 317.
[6] Nicholas Mansergh, *The Commonwealth and the Nations* (London, 1948), p. 199.

republic, its constitution departing in phraseology and form from the established British pattern. But Mr. De Valera refused to sever the connection completely, and the tenuous thread of the External Relations Act remained as the only constitutional link between Ireland and the Crown and hence the Commonwealth.[7] Within the community of free nations of the empire, Mr. De Valera's Ireland became a foreign body forcibly demonstrating that constitutional formulas are not always capable of reconciling national animosities and opposing political and social views.

On the eve of World War II the Commonwealth represented a variety of constitutional forms and stages of development. As a form of political organization, in the accepted sense of the word, the Commonwealth of 1939 could hardly be described as a unit. It was certainly not a federation, which implies an *effective* central organ of legislation. Nor was it, despite the preamble to the Statute of Westminster, a group of freely associated states "united by a common allegiance to the Crown," since one of its members acknowledged neither the Crown (though recognizing one function of its holder) nor the allegiance. The only really relevant description of the Commonwealth in 1939 could be a political one. Such a description would have recognized that, for all practical purposes, Eire was not a member of the Commonwealth; as for the remaining members, they all adhered to the Westminster formula but with varying sets of reservations. Thus, while New Zealand felt that dominion status need not be formally defined and that the relationship between the mother country and the self-governing units of the empire could be safely left to convention, the Union of South Africa had insisted on the most unambiguous legalistic statement of her independence with the unstated premise that even complete secession from the empire was within the rights of the Dominions.

By 1939 the Dominions were independent states. If legislative autonomy is the prime attribute of sovereignty, then the Union of South Africa and Canada were by 1939 independent by law, and

[7] See Executive Authority (External Relations) Act of 1936 reproduced in *The Constitutions of All Countries*, I (London, 1938), 189.

Adam B. Ulam

Australia and New Zealand, though they had not yet adopted the Statute of Westminster, were independent by virtue of the constitutional convention affirmed at the Imperial Conferences of 1926 and 1930. Ireland was in a class by herself, neither in nor out of the Commonwealth, and Newfoundland had had to give up dominion status. As for the four "real" Dominions, the only limitations upon their integral sovereignty persisted in 1939 because of their own preference. The Judicial Committee of the Privy Council sitting in London remained as the supreme court of appeal for the Dominions (excepting some categories of litigation excluded by dominion legislation), but the Judicial Committee is not, from the point of view of the law, a part of the judicial machinery of the United Kingdom since it is a legal appurtenance of the Crown. Insofar as the two federal Dominions and New Zealand were concerned, the Statute of Westminster specifically stated that the procedure for the amending of their constitutions which had been in force prior to the Statute was not to be changed by its passage.[8] Since the procedure required concurrence of the British Parliament on some basic constitutional changes, it might appear that the status of Canada, New Zealand, and Australia was still unequal in regard to that of Great Britain. But it was a constitutional convention, in force even before 1931, that the consent of the Parliament at Westminster would be automatic if requested by the competent constitutional authority in the given Dominion. The reservation in the Statute of Westminster was inserted largely because of the fear of the provinces in Canada and the states in Australia that their constitutional status might otherwise be infringed, and because of New Zealand's oft-repeated wish not to have her *status quo* changed. It is the absence of a similar reservation in regard to South Africa that gives the Union Parliament unfettered powers to change the constitution of the Dominion, and that recently enabled Dr. Malan's government to change the "entrenched" clauses of South Africa's Constitution by less than a two-thirds majority.

Such was the structure of the British Commonwealth that went to war in 1939. It is curious to observe that the response of the

[8] Sections 7 and 8 of the Statute.

British Commonwealth as Multinational State System

Dominions to Great Britain's declaration of war paralleled the extent of their previous assertions of independent status. Eire stayed neutral. In South Africa there was a considerable division of public opinion on whether or not the Union should enter the war. The vote against neutrality, a condition desired by the then Prime Minister, General Hertzog, was close, but it enabled General Smuts to take over and to lead his country through the war. The other Dominions declared war upon Germany without hesitation, but it was done in the manner which suggested that the decision was their own—the decision of independent nations—rather than compliance with the policy of the mother country.[9]

But India was not consulted about entrance into the war. The Congress party immediately ordered its provincial ministries to resign in protest, and provincial self-government in many places had to be suspended for the duration. Thus, India's war effort had to be carried through against the opposition of the most powerful political party in the country.

World War II demonstrated once again the basic weaknesses and strengths of the Commonwealth. When Great Britain herself was in supreme danger, there was no doubt about the response of the Dominions. The war was felt to be the struggle for the preservation of free democratic institutions everywhere, and hence the question of dominion nationalism versus the imperial connection could not really arise. But the war also demonstrated the decline in the strength of Great Britain, perhaps most dramatically to the Pacific Dominions, whose national and political responsibilities were consequently enhanced. The situation was brought home to Australia early in 1942 after the fall of the Dutch East Indies to Japan, when it seemed as if the Dominion, which had hitherto felt secure behind the British fleet, would be exposed to Japanese invasion. There was a brief flurry of bad feeling and strained relations between the

---

[9] In the debate on the issue of war versus neutrality, South Africa rejected the assumption that, since the King in Great Britain was at war, South Africa was constrained to follow. Instead, the Union supported the assumption that "there was no limit to our freedom under the Statute of Westminster as confirmed in our country under the Status Act," but that it was *in the interest of South Africa* to enter the war.—Mansergh, *op. cit.*, pp. 14–15.

Adam B. Ulam

Cabinets in Canberra and in London that centered around Mr. Churchill's rather imperatorial appointment of Mr. Casey, then the Australian Minister in Washington, to a British ministerial post without, it seems, prior consultation with the Australian Prime Minister, Mr. Curtin. The tension soon and happily passed, but the incident, trivial in itself, was a portent of the new era in which the last vestiges of colonialism, both formal and informal, were to disappear from the Commonwealth, and Britain herself was to become in spirit as well as in law merely a senior partner in the enterprise.

The changes that the war brought about in Britain's dependent empire were of more monumental character. The Government of India Act of 1935 was thought at the time of its enactment to settle the status of the subcontinent at least for a decade or two. The Act, though marking a considerable advance in self-government for India, fell considerably short of bestowing dominion status. It became pretty clear right after the beginning of the war, and even more obvious following Japan's entrance into it, that Great Britain, following the conclusion of the conflict, was not going to be able to hold India in a dependent status. It became increasingly clear that the last vestiges of imperial attitude were being dispelled in England by the war, and that the postwar social democracy which England was bound to become, whether under a Conservative or Labour government, would have neither the resources nor the will to keep any of its possessions in a static state of subjection. The only problem was the tempo and the shape of the coming colonial emancipation. Was India to take a place in the Commonwealth or was she going to abandon the British connection? If either of these alternatives was to materialize following the war, how about Ceylon and Burma, which were by 1939 at a stage of colonial self-government that was at least as advanced as that of India? And if they were going to be granted independence, how could the same goal be withheld from other, less advanced, colonies? Could dominion status accommodate the growing nationalism of Asiatic communities? When Sir Stafford Cripps went to India in 1942 on behalf of the War Cabinet to offer dominion status to the Indian leaders if

British Commonwealth as Multinational State System

they would reconcile their own differences and would support the war effort of the Commonwealth, he found hostility to the idea of dominion status as a substitute for full and unequivocal independence. Only a few years before, dominion status had been the fondest expectation of many Indian political leaders. Yet by 1942 it had acquired the connotation of something considerably less than independence. Sir Stafford's attempts to illustrate the completeness of independence under dominion status and the lack of restraint under it on the members of the Commonwealth are significant for two reasons. In the first place, only a few years earlier, they would have shocked a strict legalist; in the second place, they failed to dispel Indian suspicions (though the Cripps mission ultimately failed on other counts).[10]

Mr. Churchill's wartime words that he did not become Prime Minister to preside over the liquidation of the empire now have a very ironic ring. The British Empire has been "dissolved" in the sense that it has been transformed into the Commonwealth—a loose confederation of independent states; and even its dependent units—Britain's colonies—are now officially assured of an eventual advancement into the Commonwealth. By the same token, the Commonwealth still remains a vast laboratory of practical politics, and the experiments that are going on there remain among the most important and fascinating features of contemporary politics.

There are three major spheres of constitutional development within the Commonwealth. There is, in the first place, fuller development and implementation of dominion status insofar as the "old Dominions" are concerned. Canada, Australia, New Zealand, and South Africa now have not only the rights but also the apparatus appropriate to independent nations. This is verified by their own diplomatic representatives to foreign countries and the increasing tendency to have their constitutional decisions and interpretations made at home instead of having them carried, even as a matter of form, to the British Parliament or to the Judicial Committee of the Privy Council. Though the Dominions were already independent nations before 1939, the war gave them the psychology

[10] See a discussion of the point in Mansergh, *op. cit.*, pp. 17–18.

of independent statehood. It may be argued that in some cases, notably in South Africa, this development has been accompanied by a rather aggressive and intolerant nationalism; but, in general, the new status of the Dominions is both natural and in keeping with the spirit of the new Commonwealth.

The second sphere of political development of the former empire is in many ways the most crucial, and its success or failure is likely to be a major factor in world history. It is the attempt to fit the new states of the East, which arose out of the Indian Empire and the colony of Ceylon, into the Commonwealth as willing and equal partners. Here, unlike the case of the old Dominions, it is no longer the problem of finding a few constitutional formulas and convenient symbolism, but the much more engrossing and difficult task of assuaging violent nationalism, which had bred for so long on the hatred of the British master, and of developing a community of interests and ideals that would appeal to those Asiatic nations whose cultural and political traditions and problems are so utterly different from those of the West.

Finally, there is the sphere of constitutional and political development, commonly ignored outside Great Britain, which involves the growing emancipation and gradual extension of self-government in various British colonies. The notion of colonial status as a static condition is no longer applicable, if it ever was, to Britain's colonial possessions. How far the assumptions underlying those reforms—the nineteenth-century notion that self-government can be granted piece by piece with its recipients growing in political wisdom and moderation in the process—are applicable to Nigeria or to Jamaica remains to be seen. But, again, the effort has an importance transcending the fate of the Commonwealth.

The significance of the Commonwealth clearly transcends the future of Great Britain itself, or the fate of its individual members. In the world of today the Commonwealth is the only confederation of several nations that rejects the notion of centralism and that attempts in its own way to be a sort of league of nations, where different races and nationalities are held together only by their willingness to associate and to consult and to respect certain symbols of

British Commonwealth as Multinational State System

this association. It is only right to point out that the present state of the Commonwealth is neither stable nor clearly defined. An organization that has two members engaging in a violent, and at times armed, dispute over a territory, as are India and Pakistan in connection with Kashmir, cannot be said to possess effective unity. On broader issues of foreign policy and defense, the Commonwealth often speaks with many voices. The Crown is no longer an effective symbol of its unity, for one of the members is a republic and another, South Africa, is rather close to becoming one. Clearly a new spirit must be built within the Commonwealth to replace the prevailingly British tone of the era that ended in 1945. Whether time and circumstances will allow it or whether the already elastic formula has been stretched to a point where it is completely meaningless, and the new Commonwealth is a transitory phenomenon in the evolution of independent and separate state systems, remains to be seen.

Constitutionally the new form of the association is even more of a monstrosity than it was under the Statute of Westminster. There have been several attempts at elucidating the status of the inhabitants of what had once been the British Empire, what was more recently the British Commonwealth, and what is now, in deference to the sensitivities of its Asiatic members, simply the Commonwealth. Thus, the British Nationality Act of 1948 [11] establishes dual citizenship throughout the Commonwealth. Previously the expression "British subject" was the common denominator of a Nigerian, Londoner, and New Zealander. Some Dominions, notably Canada, anticipated the action by the British Parliament and introduced the additional category of citizenship for the given Dominion. The Nationality Act sanctioned a more universal application of dual citizenship. An inhabitant of the United Kingdom and of the other eight independent members of the Commonwealth (South Rhodesia being so considered for the purposes of the Act in addition to India and the Dominions) may now be known either as "British subject" or "Commonwealth citizen." For Great Britain proper and her colonies a new category of "citizen of the United Kingdom and

[11] 11 and 12 Geo. VI, c. 56.

Adam B. Ulam

Colonies" is established to parallel dominion citizenships. Thus, the word "citizen," a relative stranger to British constitutional vocabulary, is introduced to dispel any remaining notion that membership in the Commonwealth implies a recognition of its monarchical character or "Britishness."

Even of more profound constitutional importance was the decision reached in April 1949 at a special conference of the Prime Ministers of the Commonwealth in regard to India's position. The startling character of the decision led *The Economist* to entitle a discussion of the impact of the decision *"New Statute"*—an obvious reference to the "Old Statute," which eighteen years before formally sanctioned the now passing stage of the Commonwealth.[12] India announced her decision—and had it accepted by her sister Dominions and Great Britain—to become a "sovereign independent republic" and yet to remain in the Commonwealth recognizing the King as "the symbol of the association of its independent member nations and, as such, the Head of the Commonwealth." India's decision meant, of course, a fundamental change in the constitutional structure of the Commonwealth. The Crown, which by virtue of South Africa's Status Act had become in effect a "divisible Crown" rather than a factor of unity, was now further weakened, and the road was open for the introduction of the republican principle into the Commonwealth, the principle that ultimately may be adopted by Pakistan, Ceylon, and even South Africa.

Second thoughts on India's decision to stay in the Commonwealth and the Commonwealth's acquiescence in the new formula produced some doubts, especially among Australian and New Zealand statesmen, on whether the new formula did not represent a net loss, since in addition to the vagueness and looseness already associated with the Commonwealth it seemed to add complete formlessness to the organization. The argument has run, and it is still not silenced, that in groping for new, and perhaps fictitious, ties one should not weaken the older and more solid ones. An interpretation of the Commonwealth given by Mr. Nehru in answer to an Indian critic may be quoted to support the view expressed above: "The Com-

[12] *The Economist* (London), April 30, 1949.

monwealth itself, as such is not a body, if I may say so; it has no organization through which to function and the King also can have no functions." [13] All that can be said about the declaration now is that it weakens the only sense in which the Commonwealth has had a formal unity and that the advantages it does confer are as yet theoretical and untested by history.

In two cases the Commonwealth has been unable to accommodate its members despite the great latitude of its current constitutional position. Both Eire and Burma have severed completely their connection with Britain. The decision in both cases seems to have been forced by considerations of internal politics rather than by real or fictitious shortcomings of dominion status, which in the case of Ireland had been stretched out to such length that by the time Ireland became officially a republic it came as a letdown.

There have been no postwar constitutional changes in dominion status itself. To be sure, the process of implementing the Statute of Westminster has gone forward in the case of the "old Dominions." In 1939 the Statute was a mold of independent statehood, still unfilled in many cases. Since then Australia and New Zealand have both officially adopted it. More important, the process of curtailing the functions of various institutions located in Great Britain in regard to the Dominions has been going on at a rather rapid pace. The British North America Act of 1949 relieved the British Parliament of the burden of giving its formal assent to changes in the Canadian Constitution. It is not unlikely that the future will see the extension of the same principle to Australia. The Judicial Committee of the Privy Council finds its jurisdiction on dominion cases increasingly restrained. Progress in removing these anachronistic limitations upon the Dominions' formal sovereignty has been caused not so much by pro- or anti-Commonwealth feeling but simply by a desire to resolve constitutional dilemmas, which have especially plagued the two Dominions with federal constitutions. Even so, at least in the case of Canada, the changes have also been prompted by a strong national feeling.

[13] Jawaharlal Nehru, *Independence and After* (a collection of speeches) (New York, 1950), p. 269.

Adam B. Ulam

Along with the formal loosening of institutional ties with Great Britain there has developed an increased assurance and determination on the part of the Dominions to speak as independent nations. In three of the four old Dominions the office of Governor-General is filled by citizens of the given Dominion. Though this is in no sense an innovation since 1939, it is a good indication of the trend. When Mr. Chifley's government recommended Mr. McKell, an active Labour politician, as the Governor-General of Australia and had its recommendation accepted, it demonstrated that there is no restriction on the discretion of a dominion government in choosing the constitutional head of the state.[14]

The Dominions are now independent nations and, more important, they have grown to regard themselves as independent units in international politics. Is then the Commonwealth an optical illusion, a mirage, now deprived even of the legal fiction of unity under the Crown? To answer the question one must take into account considerations transcending purely constitutional points of analysis. Representative institutions are today in danger everywhere in the world. Along with the growing independence of the Dominions and their exercise of the perquisites of sovereignty in international politics, there has developed an increased awareness of the interdependence of their interests in maintaining and preserving their free democratic institutions. The picture has not been without occasional blemishes. In the Union of South Africa these institutions are in danger from conflicts generated by the racial and national structure of the Union. Yet, in general, even in the Asiatic Dominions, it is felt that membership in the Commonwealth is in some deep and yet vague sense a commitment to perpetuate the representative institutions and democratic ideals upon which the Commonwealth is ultimately based.

The spread of those ideals has affected the still dependent "colonial" part of the imperial network. Even during World War

[14] There are, of course, ample precedents for this in the case of the Irish Free State before it dispensed with the Governor-Generalship. Also in South Africa, in 1936, Sir Patrick Duncan, then a minister in the Hertzog-Smuts Cabinet, was appointed to the office.

British Commonwealth as Multinational State System

II far-reaching constitutional reforms were planned and in some cases put into effect. These dealt with various British colonies in Africa and in the Caribbean. The end of the war saw an extension of the reforms to almost every British colony. When Ceylon, the first colony to become a Dominion after the war, assumed that status, the words of the agreement between Ceylon and the United Kingdom clearly implied that dominion status is the logical culmination of colonial development.[15] Representative institutions and, in some cases, semiresponsible government are now being granted to countries that, thirty or forty years ago, were at a most primitive stage of political development. This experimentation on the part of the British Government has not been inhibited by the knowledge that no nationalism is ever satisfied by half measures and that the path of constitutional reform in the colonies is not likely to be easy, nor free of violence, nor rewarding to Britain in terms of gratitude or firm attachment of the colonies once they become nations.

About twenty years ago an American writer asked: "If the Dominions have really become nations how can they form anything properly called either *British* or *Commonwealth?*"[16] History still has not given its answer to this question. To the cynic, or perhaps the realist, the Commonwealth is an empty formula concealing the dissolution of an empire succumbing to the forces of nationalism and social change. To an idealist it is a vast and promising experiment in international collaboration between various races and nationalities. Between the two views there is common ground for considering the Commonwealth as an orderly retreat from imperialism and an attempt to rally those forces and ideas that today are everywhere threatened by a more insidious and incomparably more oppressive imperialism. Within this more modest sphere the

[15] "Whereas Ceylon has reached the stage in constitutional development at which she is ready to assume the status of a fully responsible member of the British Commonwealth of Nations, in no way subordinate in any aspect of domestic or external affairs freely associated and united by common allegiance to the Crown. . . ."—cited in Sir Ivor Jennings, *The Constitution of Ceylon* (New York, 1949), p. 226.

[16] W. Y. Elliott, *The New British Empire* (New York, 1932), p. 16.

Adam B. Ulam

Commonwealth with its machinery of consultation and its periodic conferences is a league of nations rather than a confederation or an alliance; and its future as a multinational organization must depend on the inherent strength of the idea of representative and responsible government that has guided its growth.

10

Constitutional Documents of East-Central Europe[*]

Robert G. Neumann

THE UNIVERSITY OF CALIFORNIA AT LOS ANGELES

THE new constitutions of the countries that now compose the so-called Soviet satellites, and of the ex-satellite, Yugoslavia, are set in a historical background which helps to explain their nature and their draftsmanship. Constitutional government, as it is known in Western Europe and in the United States, is unknown in Eastern Europe, with the exception of Czechoslovakia and of Finland. The latter country, however, is not included in our consideration. Stabs at Western-type constitutionalism have been made occasionally. At a surprisingly early date, in 1879, the so-called Tirnovo Constitution of Bulgaria included many liberal stipulations. Similarly, the Polish Constitution of 1921, which was written primarily in order to curb Josef Pilsudski, was a democratic document. But neither of them prevailed in theory or in practice; and the people of Communist Europe may therefore be expected to take constitutional documents in their stride even if their governments rule as they please and the civil "rights" enumerated thereunder remain a constant mockery of reality.

There is a basic difference between constitutions in a democracy and a dictatorship. In a democracy a constitution, whether written or unwritten, whether supported by judicial review or under a system of legislative supremacy, is designed to limit, to restrain.[1] Constitu-

[*] This essay, although written for this book, was published earlier in the *Journal of Politics*.

[1] Carl J. Friedrich, *Constitutional Government and Democracy* (Boston, 1941), pp. 121 ff.

175

tional government in the Western sense is therefore limited, restrained government. But limitation and dictatorship are mutually exclusive terms, and while satellite Europe has a number of interesting constitutions it does not have constitutionalism.

It follows that constitutions of democratic countries present different questions to the analyst than is the case with those of dictatorships. When studying democratic constitutions, we are concerned with the organization of state and government, with the relations between government and citizens, and with the basic rights of the citizen. This approach will reap few benefits when applied to dictatorships. True, the Soviet and satellite constitutions also circumscribe the institutions of state and government, but this description is often lacking in reality. All Communist constitutions describe their legislatures as the "supreme organ of state power,"[2] but no discussions ever take place there, and no independent decisions are reached. The constitutions of the so-called "People's Democracies" present their respective governments as "the highest organ of state administration,"[3] yet these governments rarely meet, and all decisions are made in the respective Politburos of the Communist parties, or quite often in the Moscow Politburo for which the Cominform serves as a transmitter. It is, of course, quite true that modern democratic government is based on political parties, and they are usually either unmentioned in the constitutions, as in the United States, or mentioned only incidentally and in unimportant places, as in France. But when political parties come to power in a democracy, they express themselves largely through constitutional channels. The Communist parties, which direct affairs in all the countries under consideration, are secret, and the Politburos that make all policy decisions remain obscure. No indication is given in any of these documents of the real seat of power. Only the Hungarian Constitution of 1949 hints at the true state of affairs by proclaiming that "the

[2] Bulgarian Constitution (1947), Art. 15; Albanian Constitution (1946), Art. 37; Hungarian Constitution (1949), Art. 10; Rumanian Constitution (1948), Art. 37; Yugoslav Constitution, Arts. 49, 50. No such provisions are found in the constitutions of Czechoslovakia and Poland. On their nature see *infra*.

[3] Albania, Art. 53; Bulgaria, Art. 38; Hungary, Art. 22; Rumania, Art. 66; Yugoslavia, Art. 77; *infra*.

leading force . . . is the working class *led by its advance guard* and supported by the democratic unity of the whole people" (Art. 56). The nature of this advance guard is coyly kept in the dark, but a study of the equivalent paragraph of the Soviet Constitution [4] reveals it—to nobody's surprise—as being the Communist party.

What is then the purpose of constitutions in "People's Democracies"? For one purpose, at least, we are favored with an explanation by Communist leaders, made with admirable unanimity. In his speech on the draft of the 1936 Soviet Constitution, made before the Extraordinary Eighth Congress of Soviets, Stalin clearly identified the U.S.S.R. Constitution as the expression of that which has already become reality.[5] These words were echoed, almost verbatim, by the Yugoslav Vice-Premier, Edvard Kardelji, on December 2, 1945, when introducing the new Yugoslav Constitution.[6] And on August 17, 1949, Deputy Prime Minister, Matya Rakosi, introducing the Hungarian Constitution, declared:

Thus the new draft constitution is merely a placing on record and a consolidation, in legal form, of what Hungary has in reality already achieved and won.[7]

A second purpose of these constitutions is their propaganda value. The civil-rights provisions in particular serve this purpose, and they are proclaimed by all Soviet apologists as the gospel truth, although they have no validity whatsoever and are condemned by the Communist party in other, more reliable, pronouncements. Thus, when the Polish Socialist, Julian Hochfeld, the *rapporteur* of the Parliament (Sejm) for the *Declaration of Rights and Liberties*,[8] suggested that its purpose was "to prove that the spirit in which the *Sejm* will legislate and write a new Constitution will be that of wisely inter-

---

[4] Art. 126. ". . . the Communist Party of the Soviet Union (Bolsheviks), which is the vanguard of the toilers. . . ."

[5] Joseph Stalin, "On the Draft Constitution of the U.S.S.R.," *Selected Writings* (New York, 1942), pp. 381 ff.

[6] *Politika* (Belgrade), December 3, 1945, as quoted in Michael Boro Petrovich, "The Central Government of Yugoslavia," *Political Science Quarterly*, LXII (December 1947), 519 ff.

[7] *Hungarian Bulletin* (Budapest), August 30, 1949.

[8] Adopted by the Constituent Assembly on February 22, 1947, and still in force.

preted rights and freedoms," he was severely criticized for his un-Marxist approach.[9] More realistic, undoubtedly, is an authoritative Polish commentator, who explained that the Polish declaration created no direct rights which could be claimed by individuals against the state but is merely a promise that the legislature will be guided by certain principles.[10] The picture is further rounded out by the famous speech of Georgi Dimitrov during the election campaign of 1946, in which he accused the opposition of an "improper" campaign and pointedly reminded them of the fate of Draha Mihkailovitch in Yugoslavia,[11] a fate that was later meted out to the opposition leader, Nikola Petkov.

The constitutions of Albania, Hungary, Rumania, and Yugoslavia follow very closely the Soviet model and contain no reminiscences of former constitutional documents that once existed in those countries. This similarity extends not only to individual provisions but also to organization, construction, and sequence. Even the Soviet coat of arms, no masterpiece of heraldic art, has been very nearly copied. However, the Polish and Czechoslovak Constitutions differ in one respect. The Polish Constitution of 1947, known as the "little constitution,"[12] is officially known as "provisional." It is a mixture of old and new, having adopted large sections of the old constitution of 1921.[13] The Czechoslovak Constitution of 1948 is officially permanent, although it too contains many concepts retained from the old democratic constitution of 1920. This is especially expressed in the nominal equality of president, government, and Parliament, which runs counter to established Communist constitutional doc-

[9] Samuel L. Sharp, *New Constitutions in the Soviet Sphere* (Washington, D.C., 1950), p. 32.

[10] K. Grzybowski, *Ustroi Polski Wspolczensnej* (Cracow, 1948), p. 120, as quoted in Sharp, *op. cit.*, p. 33.

[11] Vernon Van Dyke, "Communism in Eastern and Southeastern Europe," *The Journal of Politics,* IX (November 1947), 368 ff. During the same period, "elections" were held in Yugoslavia under the encouraging slogan, "ballots for Tito, bullets for Grol." (Milan Grol was one of the leaders of the opposition.)

[12] The constitution of 1947 is the second "little (provisional) constitution." The first one lasted from 1919 to 1921.

[13] The old provisions are taken over verbatim. Thus, for instance, Article 11 of the new (little) constitution is followed by Articles 20–24 of the 1921 document, and that process is repeated several times. The authoritarian 1935 constitution is ignored.

trine.[14] It may therefore be surmised that the 1948 constitution of Czechoslovakia will have to make way for extensive amendments or will be exchanged for another document, more closely tailored to the Soviet model.

A republican form of government can now be found in every country of Eastern and Central Europe. A change occurred in Albania, Bulgaria, Rumania, and Yugoslavia, but one should bear in mind that Tito, Hoxa, and the late Georgi Dimitrov receive or received a superroyal kind of veneration that satisfies the need for a personification and near deification of the state symbol. However, the peculiar form of republic found in those countries is referred to as a "people's republic." This somewhat trite term, which is applied to all satellite states and Yugoslavia, with the exception of Poland, signifies, as far as one can penetrate the dense fog of the Communist vernacular, a state that has a republican form of government and subscribes to the "people's democratic order." The latter concept was defined by the late Georgi Dimitrov as follows:[15]

1. It "represents the power of the toiling people . . . under the leadership of the working class" (proletariat). This means the class state in which the workers play the dominant role and "the state serves as a tool in the fight of the toilers against the exploiting elements, against all efforts and tendencies, aimed at re-establishing the capitalist order and the bourgeois rule."

2. "The people's democracy is a state in the transitional period, destined to ensure the development of the state on the path to socialism." This means that, although capitalism has been overthrown, the economic roots of capitalism are not yet extirpated. Therefore a relentless class struggle is indicated.

3. "The people's democracy is built in collaboration and friendship with the Soviet Union. . . . Any tendency towards weakening this collaboration with the USSR is directed against the very existence of the people's democracy in our country." This is further elaborated by the statement that the task of a people's democracy includes the "consolidation of the key positions held by the working class, headed by the Communist Party, in all spheres of political, economic, and cultural life." Moreover, the people's democracy stands for internationalism,

[14] See *infra*.
[15] Georgi Dimitrov, "Political Report" (Sofia, 1948), pp. 52–55. This is Dimitrov's speech to the Fifth Congress of the Bulgarian Communist party, December 19, 1948.

which Dimitrov defines as "international collaboration under Comrade Stalin."

Deprived of its excess verbiage, the concept of the people's democracy boils down to two simple criteria. It is a state in which the classless society has not yet been achieved but in which the Communist party has the upper hand and has begun the task of liquidating its opponents. It is also a state that follows the lead of the Soviet Union. A "people's republic" is then the crystallization in legal form of the people's democracy.

One of the consequences of the people's republican system is the condemnation of the doctrine of the separation of powers. Under Communist theory the will of the people must be supreme, and the agencies of government have the function of interpreting it. Vyshinsky explains that

from top to bottom the Soviet social order is penetrated by the single general spirit of the oneness of the authority of the toilers. The program of the All-Union Communist Party (of Bolsheviks) rejects the bourgeois principle of separation of powers.[16]

And Vassil Kolarov, late Prime Minister of Bulgaria, declared that

the source of power in a people's democratic system is the people on whom are bestowed the supreme rights, while the fullest and surest expression of the people's will is the National Assembly.[17]

To establish the doctrine of separation would mean a check on the people's sovereign power, which would be "undemocratic." Says Kolarov:

Whoever preaches a division of the people's power actually places another power next to that of the people. . . . Since two unequally strong powers cannot coexist without struggling for supremacy, the apologists of Montesquieu are in reality working for the domination of the banks and big business.

[16] Andrei Y. Vyshinsky, *The Law of the Soviet State,* trans. H. W. Babb (New York, 1948), p. 318.
[17] Vassil Kolarov, speech on the draft constitution, June 20, 1947 (Sofia, 1947), p. 33.

This remarkable argumentation assumes, of course, that there is one single will of the people which is correctly interpreted by "its most advanced part," the Communist party.

In the question of the relationship between central and regional governments, different approaches may be noted, which depend largely on the ethnic and historical structure of the countries concerned. Albania, Bulgaria, Poland, and Rumania are unitary states. Yugoslavia has a federal regime modeled closely on the Soviet Union, while Czechoslovakia has a peculiar approach all her own. The Federal People's Republic of Yugoslavia is composed of the People's Republics of Serbia, Croatia, Slovenia, Bosnia and Herzegovina, Macedonia, and Montenegro. The People's Republic of Serbia moreover includes the Autonomous Province of Vojvodina and the Autonomous Kosovo-Metohijan Region (Art. 2). The trend toward a federal structure was already quite pronounced during the formative war years. The Anti-Fascist Council of National Liberation (AVNOJ) resolved during its second session on November 29, 1943: "That Yugoslavia be established on a democratic federal principle as a state of equal peoples." [18]

The federal organization of Yugoslavia is almost a carbon copy of the pertinent paragraphs in the Soviet Constitution. Like the U.S.S.R., Yugoslavia has a bicameral legislature—the only such case in the Soviet orbit outside the Soviet Union.[19] The People's Assembly of the F.P.R.Y. (*Narodna skupština*) is divided into a lower house, the Federal Council (*Savezno veće*), and a Council of Nationalities (*Veće Naroda*). The latter house is composed of members elected by the voters in the several people's republics, autonomous provinces, and regions.[20]

According to the constitution, the federal government of Yugoslavia possesses only expressed and enumerated powers, while all

---

[18] As quoted in Petrovich, *op. cit.*, p. 507. Also reprinted in the official gazette, *Službeni List,* February 1, 1945.

[19] For the purposes of this article, Yugoslavia may be considered in the Soviet orbit, as no other country has modeled its constitution more closely on the Soviet precepts.

[20] Art. 54. Each republic elects thirty, each autonomous province twenty, and each autonomous region fifteen members to the Council of Nationalities.

others are reserved to the people's republics.[21] Actually, however, the powers of the central government are overwhelming. Not only does the constitution grant the central authorities vast powers, including all economic matters of national importance, but they also exercise direct administrative control over the republic governments. Like the Soviet Constitution, the fundamental law of Yugoslavia distinguishes between federal and federal-republican ministries in the central government. The federal ministers [22] administer their functions throughout the entire country by means of their own staffs. The federal-republican ministers,[23] on the other hand, exercise their prerogatives through the corresponding ministries of the republics.[24] Even then, however, they may directly administer affairs in the republics if they are of national importance. It may be presumed that the minister of the central government decides what is or is not of national importance.

This arrangement might indeed strike the observer as being a true form of federalism. However, there are some serious objections to such an appraisal. While the form of the state may be federal, the source of all policy rests in the Communist party and especially in the central Politburo, whose decisions are irrevocable and binding on the central as well as the local level. Moreover, the political theories of federalism and of the "people's republics" are in opposition to one another. Federalism, as the term is commonly understood, is a form of limited government. Federalism is also pluralistic in essence. But, as we have seen, the concept of the "people's democratic order" does not permit limitation, and the doctrine of the single popular will cannot easily be reconciled with the idea of

---

[21] Art. 44. Where central government power exists, it is supreme but not necessarily exclusive (Art. 46).

[22] Foreign Affairs, National Defense, Communications, Transport, Post, Foreign Trade.

[23] Art. 86—Finance, Interior, Justice, Industry, Mines, Commerce, Agriculture and Forestry, Labor, Public Works.

[24] Art. 99. Ministries of a republic are either federal-republican or republican. Federal-republican ministries correspond to central departments to which they are subordinated. They are autonomous with regard to some functions and agents of the central government in others. Republican ministries are autonomous.

Constitutional Documents of East-Central Europe

pluralism. The federalism of Yugoslavia, like that of the Soviet Union, is therefore not a true federalism, except possibly in its cultural aspects, but a form of administrative decentralization, which may of course have merits of its own.

If the constitution of Yugoslavia presents a "federal" picture, at least on paper, the approach of the Czechoslovak Republic is much more cautious. The Czechoslovak postwar governments were faced with a high degree of animosity between Czechs and Slovaks. The history of the "independent" state of Slovakia, whose leader, Monsignor Tiso, brought it under Hitler's tutelage, was not forgotten by the Czechs, whose capacity for remembering past grievances is bested only by the Poles and, possibly, the Hungarians. On the other hand, Slovak memories of Czech rule are also somewhat less than happy. Some concessions had to be made.[25] During the abortive uprising against the Germans in the summer of 1944, a Slovak National Council emerged,[26] and later, when the Red Army marched into Slovakia, it used the Council in the reorganization of local government.[27] The Czech (London) government in exile was therefore forced to reckon with the existence of a separate Slovak administrative and policy-making body. Accordingly, in the Košice agreement of April 5, 1945, the right of the Slovaks to be "masters in their land" as an autonomous nation was recognized by the government.

At first the Communists supported the Slovak claims for autonomy, but after their defeat by the (Slovak) Democratic party in 1946 they changed their tune.[28] The eventual solution of this problem takes the form of a compromise, but the "autonomy" of Slovakia is narrowly circumscribed and controlled in such a way as to be lacking in real substance.

[25] For a good summary and analysis, see Samuel L. Sharp, "The Czechs and the Slovaks: New Aspects of an Old Problem," *American Perspective,* I (1947), 311–22.
[26] In Czechoslovak practice the word "nation" (*národ*) denotes the members of the distinct ethnic groups, Czechs and Slovaks. The word people (*lid*) is used when the entire population is meant.
[27] The Slovak National Council was composed of a coalition between the Communists and the Democratic party.
[28] Sharp, *op. cit.,* p. 319; also, *Central European Observer,* June 27, 1947.

Robert G. Neumann

The Fundamental Articles [29] of the Czechoslovak Constitution describe the republic as "a *unitary* State of two Slav nations possessing equal rights, the Czechs and the Slovaks." However, this provision is implemented in a very peculiar fashion. The above-mentioned Articles speak of *equal* rights of Czechs and Slovaks. Yet, there are special Slovak national organs, but the concomitant existence of Czech national organs is missing. There is a Slovak National Council with general legislative powers. Its functions extend primarily to legislation concerning educational, cultural, and welfare matters. It also extends to technical functions of town and country planning and certain trade regulations, but those are overshadowed and narrowly circumscribed by the Uniform Economic Plan, which is in the hands of the central government (Art. 96). The Slovak National Council may also perform such acts as the central parliament, the National Assembly, may confer upon it. The Slovak National Council is convoked and dissolved by the Prime Minister of the Prague government (Art. 102) and may be adjourned by him for no more than three months and not more often than twice a year.

The Slovak "administration" lies in the hands of a Board of Commissioners who "discharge all governmental and executive power in Slovakia, save for matters of foreign affairs, national defense, and foreign trade." The chairman and the members of the Board of Commissioners are *appointed* and *recalled* by the central government which also determines what commissioner shall head a certain executive department (Art. 114). But this is not all. The commissioners are accountable to the central government and must abide by its directives and instructions (Art. 117). Where the act of a commissioner exceeds his competence, the central government may declare it void, and an individual minister may stay the execution of the commissioner's order pending the decision of the central government as a whole (Art. 122).

It must be clear, therefore, that the so-called Slovak "autonomy" is nonexistent in both fact and constitutional theory. It merely exists

[29] The Czechoslovak Constitution of 1948 is divided into a Declaration, twelve "Fundamental Articles," and the Detailed Provisions.

in the field of propaganda. The Slovak "legislature" has, as we have seen, only limited functions which are strictly controlled, while the executive powers are vested in appointees of the central government who are strictly accountable and removable at a moment's notice. That the central government is dominated by Czechs need hardly be stated. Under the Czechoslovak "People's Republic," the Slovaks, whose desire for autonomy is based on their historical, educational, cultural, and religious differences from the Czechs, have less "autonomy" than is granted quite a number of areas living under a colonial administration.

The Soviet doctrine of the "supremacy of the popular will" [30] is strongly expressed in all constitutions under consideration, including the constitutions of the *Länder* in the Soviet zone of Germany.[31] Consequently, they give pre-eminence to their legislatures, which are unicameral except in Yugoslavia. However, this type of "Assembly Government" [32] must be viewed against the background of a single, popular will that is uncontested except by "enemies of the regime" to whom no place can be allowed within the organization of the state. Consequently, assembly government in the Communist sense means that all powers are possessed by the assembly, but that the use of these powers depends on the single "will" of the people which is not formulated in the assembly but in the Politburo. The powers of the Soviet-type assemblies are therefore as real as, say, the power of the French President over the appointment of officers. They do not exist. Nor could they exist. For if they were exercised differently from the will of the leadership, it would mean that there is a possibility of more than one "will of the people," a situation that, according to Kolarov, is impossible.

A recent author has correctly observed that assembly-type governments lend themselves especially well to the entrenchment of

---

[30] See the formulation in the first constitution of the RSFSR (1918); "Authority must belong entirely and exclusively to the toiling masses and their authorized representatives—the Soviets of Worker, Soldier, and Peasant deputies."—Vyshinsky, *op. cit.*, p. 167.

[31] Robert G. Neumann, "New Constitutions in Germany," *The American Political Science Review*, XLII (June 1948), 448–68.

[32] *Gouvernement conventionnel*, a term originating in the French Revolution.

executive supremacy.[33] A peculiar link between executive and legislative authority is the institution of the *Presidium,* which is an invention of the Soviet Constitution and adopted directly from that parent document by the constitutions of Albania, Bulgaria, Hungary, Rumania, and Yugoslavia. Similar but more narrowly conceived institutions exist also in Czechoslovakia and the German *Länder* of the Soviet zone. Poland's Provisional Constitution calls it a *State Council.* Like their Soviet model, the Presidiums of the Communist countries have many functions. One is that of a *collegium president,* as Stalin termed it.[34] This function, which is primarily formal and representative, is performed either by the Presidium as a whole, as in the case of decorations and awards, or by the President of the Presidium, as in the case of the reception of letters of credence from foreign ambassadors. Czechoslovakia, however, has retained the office of the President of the Republic [35] apart from the Presidium of the National Assembly.[36]

The Presidium is elected by the National Assembly in each state, theoretically responsible to it and subject to recall. This approach differs radically from the method by which heads of state are elected in all non-Communist countries. If one may judge by the Soviet experience, the most important role of the Presidium is legislative. When the National Assembly is not in session, which is quite frequently the case, the Presidium exercises most of its legislative functions, and presidial decrees are quite common, though apparently not yet as frequent as in the Soviet Union. In its capacity as a "little assembly" the Presidium carries on the tradition of the "Principal Standing Committee," which is common in a number of European constitutions where it has a much more restricted scope.

Of special interest are the review and interpretative functions of

---

[33] Karl Loewenstein, "The Presidency Outside the United States: A Study in Comparative Political Institutions," *The Journal of Politics,* XI (August 1949), 479.

[34] Vyshinsky, *op. cit.,* p. 330.

[35] Arts. 67–79. All acts of the President must be countersigned by a member of the government to be valid (Art. 77).

[36] Arts. 63–66. The Czechoslovak President of the Republic, not the Presidium, is the state's external representative. Otherwise the Presidium has on the whole the same functions as those of the other Communist countries. The same is true of Poland, but to a narrower degree.

the Presidium, which are also borrowed from the Soviet Constitution. The Presidium is supposed to check on the constitutionality of laws and on the legality of governmental orders and edicts.[37] It also interprets statutes authoritatively. These actions are undertaken in a systematic manner and not as a result of law suits by individuals.[38] As far as the review of legislation and orders are concerned, it appears to belong largely to the realm of legal fiction. All legislative initiative and all executive orders emanate from the government or, in reality, from the Politburo. It is not likely that a Presidium, some of whose members are also members of the government and of the Politburo, will differ in its interpretation from the originator of the legislation or order under review. The legislative acts and orders of regional and local councils, however, may be placed under effective control by this function of the Presidium. On the other hand, the systematic interpretation of statutes is a living feature of the law. It has its origin in the concept of *authentic interpretation; i.e.,* interpretation of statutes by the legislature, which is a familiar feature of countries under the influence of the Roman law. It is natural, therefore, that in the countries here discussed the legislature as a whole, as well as the Presidium, has the right of interpreting statutes. But the Hungarian Constitution, the most recent, goes farther than any other constitution, including that of the U.S.S.R. It gives the Presidium the right to annul or modify bylaws, ordinances, or edicts issued by any organ of government, central or local, not only when they are unconstitutional, but also when they are "detrimental to the interests of the working people." Any local organ of government which infringes upon the constitution or whose activities are "seriously detrimental to the interests of the working people" may also be dissolved by the Presidium (Art. 20, 2, 3). These far-reaching rights may possibly point the way toward future constitutional developments, especially as the Soviet Union has initially effected considerable changes amongst its regional units of government by decree of the

---

[37] Bulgaria, Art. 35; Czechoslovakia, Art. 65; Hungary, Art. 20; Rumania, Art. 44; Yugoslavia, Art. 74.

[38] See Vyshinsky's comment on the difference between the Soviet and United States systems, *op. cit.,* pp. 339 ff.

Presidium rather than by statute, although the constitutionality of such a matter is in doubt.[39]

Following the model of the Soviet Constitution, the basic laws of the satellite and ex-satellite countries describe their respective cabinets (Council of Ministers) as the "Highest Organ of State Administration."[40] This is true, however, only in a purely formal sense. The ministers are indeed in charge of the various departments of government, but legally the control of the Presidium, where it exists, is far greater than is ordinarily the case in the relationship between governments and parliaments in Western parliamentary democracies. Here again it must be remembered that Presidium and government are not two separate centers of policy making but are merely two aspects of the same thing, the unified machinery of control whose sole source of policy is a body of men unknown to the constitution and to a considerable extent to the public at large, the Politburos of the respective Communist parties. In most Communist states some of the most important members of the Politburo and the government are also members of the Presidium, although the presidency of the Presidium is usually left to an unimportant figurehead. But in the Hungarian Constitution of 1949, the Prime Minister and the other ministers are declared ineligible to be members of the Presidium. This innovation may possibly herald a diminution of the Presidium's importance.

The organization of the executive machinery does not differ materially from the system to which those countries were accustomed. Subordinate administrative and local organs receive their orders from their respective ministers as of yore. But it is not always easy to determine where final power of decision rests on the top, as some of the real bosses may not even occupy government offices or be found in second place. Yet there appears to be a tendency of combining real and formal power as, for instance, in Albania, Bulgaria, and

---

[39] The German Volga, the Kalmyk, the Chechen-Ingush, and the Crimean Autonomous Soviet Socialist Republics and the Karachaev Autonomous Region were abolished between 1941 and 1943. (*The New York Times*, November 30, 1945, June 27, 1946). Cf. Julian Towster, *Political Power in the USSR, 1917–1947* (New York, 1948), p. 85.

[40] Bulgaria, Art. 38; Rumania, Art. 66; Hungary, Art. 22; Yugoslavia, Art. 77. Poland and Czechoslovakia have no such provisions.

Constitutional Documents of East-Central Europe

Yugoslavia. A peculiar situation exists in Poland, where the President of the Republic, Boleslaw Bierut, is also General Secretary of the Polish Worker's (Communist) party.[41]

Also interesting is the attitude toward the judiciary. In most countries under discussion the judges are elected by the legislature, appointed by the Presidium or the head of state, or are popularly elected. In effect, however, those appointments are made as they have always been made, by the Minister of Justice. A partial innovation has been the widespread use of lay judges who, comparable to the *Schoeffen* in German and Austrian criminal law, occupy the bench together with learned judges. Jury trials, which have existed in all those countries at various times in the past, have been uniformly abolished.[42]

Because of the absence of judicial review, which is expressly forbidden in one constitution,[43] the interpretative functions of the Presidium, and the direct and heavy-handed control of the Minister of Justice over bench and prosecution staff, the independence of judges is nonexistent. This is not particularly surprising because authoritarian regimes have always considered the control of the judiciary one of their primary tasks. Moreover, none of the countries under discussion, except Czechoslovakia, ever had a completely independent judiciary. However, the constitutions affirm the independence of judges in traditional phrases. Some give an inkling of the truth through the peculiar formulation that the judges shall be independent "in the discharge of their judicial duties," [44] which means that they do not possess personal independence. The Hungarian Constitution of 1949, the newest and presumably "most advanced" of them, declares judges to be independent, but makes judgeships elective and declares all judicial officers "accountable to their electors in respect of their judicial activities." [45] The most

---

[41] The fact is that the Prime Ministers of the satellite countries are often not the true leaders.
[42] It appears to be the tendency in all dictatorships to abolish the jury.
[43] Poland, Art. 24, 3.
[44] Poland, Art. 24, 2; Rumania, Art. 93; Bulgaria, Art. 57.
[45] Art. 39. Judges of the higher courts are elected for five years, the judges of the inferior courts for three years. The judges of the Supreme Court and the presidents of the higher courts are elected by Parliament. All may be recalled.

"perfect" definition of judicial functions under a people's democracy can also be found in the Hungarian Constitution. Article 41 reads:

> The Courts of the Hungarian People's Republic punish the enemies of the working people, protect and safeguard the state, the social and economic order and the institutions of the people's democracy and the rights of the workers and educate the working people in the observance of the rules governing the life of a socialist commonwealth.

In such a setting, the "bills of rights" found in all constitutions except the Polish one, where a separate "Declaration" to that effect exists,[46] do not offer much more than propagandistic blandishments. "Bills of rights" have value only where they afford protection to the citizen against his government, or where they are at the very least expressions of an accepted political theory. Neither, however, is the case in the Communist-controlled countries. In the realm of political theory there is room only for the mystical, collective "will of the people," not for the very real will of individuals. Liberty *against* the "government of the people" is therefore inadmissible by Communist standards. The practice in those countries with regard to civil liberties is so well known that discussion seems quite futile.

The constitutions of the Communist orbit are the legal expressions of the so-called "people's democratic order," which, as we have seen, is a transitional phase toward complete sovietization and the mystical "classless society." These documents must therefore be considered as essentially temporary.[47] However, this transitional character of the constitutions should not arouse any doubts about the stability of those regimes. On the contrary, the transformation through which they are going is developing at an accelerated pace, despite, and perhaps because of, Tito's defections, and pretty much according to plan. Whether the final stage will be complete incorporation into the Soviet Union cannot yet be known to outsiders, but there are many indications which point in that direction.

[46] Cf. *supra*.
[47] C. E. Black, "Constitutional Trends in Eastern Europe, 1945–48," *Review of Politics*, XI (1949), 35.

11

Reflections on the Value of Constitutions in Our Revolutionary Age

By Karl Loewenstein
AMHERST COLLEGE

The Ontological Approach

The epidemic of constitution-making in the wake of World War II has no parallel in history. Since 1945 some fifty-odd nations have equipped themselves with new constitutions.[1] In some countries

[1] The following enumeration is incomplete: *Germany:* two federal constitutions (1949), one each for the Western *(Deutsche Bundesrepublik)* and the Eastern part *(Deutsche Demokratische Republik);* each of the four *Länder* in the United States zone (1945-1946); three in the French zone (in addition to the Saar); five in the Soviet zone (1946-1947); two in the British zone (North-Rhine-Westphalia and Schleswig-Holstein (1950); those in Lower Saxony and Hamburg are in the process of completion. Berlin adopted two constitutions (1946 and 1948). *France:* two constitutions (1946); the first, of April 27, 1946, was rejected by referendum. Other new constitutions in Western Europe are: *Italy* (1947); *Iceland* (1944). In Eastern Europe new constitutions were adopted by the Soviet satellite states of *Yugoslavia* (1946); *Albania* (1946), which was reportedly supplanted by a new constitution in 1950; *Bulgaria* (1947); *Czechoslovakia* (1948); *Rumania* (1948); *Hungary* (1949); *Poland* confined itself to an adaptation of the older constitution of 1920. Latin America has had nine new constitutions since 1945: *Bolivia* (1945); *Brazil* (1946); *Ecuador* (1946); *El Salvador* (1945); *Guatemala* (1945); *Haiti* (1946); *Nicaragua* (1948); *Panama* (1946); *Venezuela* (1947). Among the new constitutions in Asia are: *China* (1946); *Japan* (1946); *Siam* (Thailand) (1949); *Korea* (1948); whether Northern Korea had a constitution is not known. Others, in the British sphere of influence, are *India* (1949); *Ceylon* (1946); *Burma* (1948). In Pakistan and Indonesia, constitutions are under preparation. *Israel,* after a draft constitution (1948), operates on the basis of an *interim* or "little" constitution (1949). *Transjordan* adopted a constitution in 1946.

Reliable texts are not easily obtainable except in the case of Western Europe and Latin America; a good collection of the latter is edited by Russell H. Fitzgibbon, *The Constitutions of Latin America* (Chicago, 1948). For the Arab world, see Helen Miller Davis, *Constitutions, Electoral Laws, and Treaties of the States in the Near and Middle East* (Durham, N.C., 1947). The ambitious undertaking by Amos J. Peaslee, *Constitutions of Nations* (Concord, N.H., 1950), to assemble in three

the new constitution symbolizes statehood and independence attained. In others, a previously serviceable document did not survive the authoritarian hurricane and had to be completely recast in the light of past experience. In others again, the changes in the location of political power caused by revolution required a redefinition of the political organization.

In practically all cases the procedure of constitution-making followed the classical democratic pattern: by elections, everywhere pretending to be free and unconstrained, the people, exercising the *pouvoir constituant,* called into being constituent assemblies or constitutional conventions which, in turn, drafted and adopted the instrument of government. Popular ratification occurred (*France* and some of the *Länder* in *Western Germany*) but was not the rule. In a few instances only the customary procedure was deviated from by injecting into it appointed, instead of popularly elected, constituent bodies. Outwardly at least the entire process seems to reflect the triumph of the ideology of democratic legality.

Though it is historically permissible to distinguish "families" of constitutions which, as a rule, embody similar or identical "patterns of government,"[2] practically all new constitutions are surprisingly alike in structure in that they operate uniformly with the traditional tripartite division of functions into legislative, executive-administrative, and judicial organs of the state. Almost without exception they have a comprehensive and ambitious bill of rights which, in addition to the classical libertarian freedoms from state interference, professes the ideal of social justice to a degree amounting almost to standardization.

Does the seeming universality of the process indicate that at long last, after the dark night of lawless despotism, the bright young day

---

volumes the constitutions of all states seems, at least to the author of this section, a complete and unmitigated failure. Translations are often far from accurate even if obtained from American embassies abroad. The factual data (in some cases even concerning the very date of the constitution) are shot through with crude errors; the introductions of the editor are often without understanding. Much of the tabulatory material is worthless. The bibliographies are neither up to date nor properly selective. Misspellings abound. It is regrettable that the author's efforts have resulted in so amateurish a compilation.

[2] See Karl Loewenstein, *Political Reconstruction* (New York, 1946), pp. 317 ff.

The Value of Constitutions in Our Revolutionary Age

of democratic constitutionalism is dawning? Does the phenomenon of constitutionalism mean that all nations alike attach a paramount importance to a formalized constitutional order, or do they merely follow the laws of diffusion and imitation? And, further, are the constitutions "real" and "living" in the sense that the competitive struggle for political power is actually conducted within the frame offered by the constitution, or is the latter manipulated by the ruling class or classes without permitting the sharing of political power by all sociopolitical forces of the community?

Such questions are rarely asked, since the interpretation and application of a constitution is usually monopolized by relatively small groups of technicians—politicians, lawyers, judges, civil servants—to whom, in a society managed by plural power groups, the constitution serves as the instrument for the attainment and preservation of special interests. "Constitutionalysis" and "constitutionology," to speak with Thomas Reed Powell, overshadow what may be called the ontology of constitutions, that is, the investigation of what a written constitution really means within a specific national environment; in particular, how real it is for the common people, who after all are everywhere, in this alleged age of the common man, the addressees of political power.

The following discussion is a pioneering—and, therefore, most tentative—attempt to implement the customary legalistic and functional analysis by an approach that focuses primarily on the congruity, or lack of it, between political reality and ideological intent of the constitution, or on the distinction between the nominal validity and the actual value of a constitution. The question is: Are the constitutions suitable to satisfy, and do they satisfy, the needs and the aspirations of the people living under them? The volume of new constitutions is an invitation for such a comparative investigation.[3]

---

[3] No student desirous of divesting himself from the stereotypes of constitutional legalism will ignore the work of Max Weber and Guglielmo Ferrero's trilogy: *Bonaparte in Italy* (London, 1939); *The Reconstruction of Europe* (New York, 1941); *The Principles of Power* (New York, 1943). Relevant materials may be found in: John A. Hawgood, *Modern Constitutions since 1787* (New York, 1939); Karl Loewenstein, "The Balance between Legislative and Executive Power," *Chicago*

Karl Loewenstein

The "Climate" of Constitution-making

Constitutions, as the rationally conceived and formalized rules for the exercise and, thereby, for the restraining control of political power, are a relatively recent experience of the *homo politicus*. As long as power was based on the traditional forces of irrational state mysticism—the divinely ordained authority of the legitimate hereditary dynasties and the classes affiliated with them—there was no need for the formalization of the *"lois fondamentales du royaume"* (France), to observe which the traditional power holder was believed to be divinely obligated. The idea of a written constitution was the result of a long-drawn revolutionary struggle for the secularization of political power (Lecky). It was primarily an English discovery [4] in the Puritan revolution when the lower gentry and the middle classes forced on Stuart absolutism their share in political power. For Cromwell, religiously conscious of the inherent moral limitations of political power, the answer was a self-limiting "Instrument of Government" (1653) rather than a "constitution." For the British a written constitution was no necessity, because power shifted to the new social classes pragmatically and without recourse to natural law. But subsequently the increasing ascendancy of natural law gravitated the eighteenth century toward a written constitution as the moral basis of a well-ordered society. The goal was reached, rather for practical than theoretical reasons, first in the American colonies, thereafter in the European key state of France. Here Rousseau's general will provided the moral and the metaphysical incentives, mobilized by the social contract and translated into

---

Law Review, V (1938), 566 ff.; Georges Burdeau, *Traité des sciences politiques* (3 vols.; Paris, 1949, 1950) (Vol. III contains the general theory of constitutions); Maurice Duverger, *Manuel de droit constitutionnel et de la science politique* (Paris, 1948); Dietrich Schindler, *Verfassungsrecht und soziale Struktur* (Zurich, 1932); J. Allen Smith, *The Growth and Decadence of Constitutional Government* (New York, 1930); Samuel L. Sharp, *New Constitutions in the Soviet Sphere* (Washington, D.C., 1950).

[4] See, for example, Egon Zweig, *Die Lehre vom pouvoir constituant* (Tübingen, 1909); Walther Rothschild, *Der Gedanke der geschriebenen Verfassung in England* (Tübingen and Leipzig, 1903); Richard Schmidt, *Die Vorgeschichte der geschriebenen Verfassung* (Leipzig, 1916).

The Value of Constitutions in Our Revolutionary Age

practice by Sieyès' *pouvoir constituant,* both as "subversive" of the existing order as Marxism proved a century later. The constitution was considered the solemn manifestation of the social contract and the functional implementation of the imaginary oath that the general will had taken for its self-realization.

But it is by no means accidental that the climate for the birth of the written constitution was the eighteenth century, fascinated not only by what were believed to be the imperatives of natural law but also by the application of the laws of nature to social dynamics. The science of mechanics was transferred to the science of government. The well-balanced constitution, with its liberty-guaranteeing checks and balances, was intended to establish, by functionally separated powers, the ideal equilibrium of the social forces.[5] In the environment of the Enlightenment the constitution was primarily a moral necessity and a functional achievement only subsidiarily. The constitution itself and the process of constitution-making were surrounded by a sort of collective magic, which belies the rational logicism accompanying it. In their naïve optimism the political theorists and the politicians themselves believed that all that was needed for a well-ordered society was a well-ordered constitution. Well-ordered meant well-equilibrized. Unaware of the demonism of political power, the written constitution would automatically offer the solutions of all social ills and guarantee the happiness of the people living under it. Being a "good" constitution and operated by "good" people it would be self-executing by harmonious cooperation in the interests of the whole society. The first result was the preposterously unworkable French Constitution of 1791, preceded by the greatest seminar in political theory the world has ever known.[6]

The French Revolution did not hesitate to disown the naïve trust of its initiators in human nature and to prove, by streams of blood,

[5] See, for example, *The Federalist,* No. 51, and the interesting observations by Hans J. Morgenthau, *Politics among Nations* (New York, 1949), pp. 125 ff. See also, on the problem of political equilibrium, Carl Schmitt, *Verfassungslehre* (Munich and Leipzig, 1928), pp. 183 f.

[6] See Robert Redslob, *Die Staatstheorien der französischen Nationalversammlung von 1789* (Leipzig, 1912); Karl Loewenstein, *Volk und Parlament nach der Staatsauffassung der französischen Nationalversammlung von 1789* (Munich, 1922).

that functional utility cannot be neglected with impunity, lest political power might become uncontrolled and destroy political liberty. In the search for the magic formula for taming political power while preserving the freedom of the general will, the constitutional laboratory of the Revolution provided the world with all possible "forms of government," that is, the functional co-ordination of powers: constitutionally limited monarchy; parliamentary government and its perversion of assembly government *(gouvernement conventionnel);* the intricate checks and balances of the Directory pattern; and, last but not least, the legalized authoritarianism of the First Consul. But in the process, not surprising with so rational a people as the French, the pristine spell of the sacrosanctity of the constitution as the manifestation of the social contract was definitely lost, never to be recaptured again. The Americans are the only nation which for socioeconomic reasons, irreproducible elsewhere, has retained the original spirit of the constitution as "basic" and irrefragable.

Constitutions in the Nineteenth Century

During the nineteenth century most states "constitutionalized" themselves, following certain prominent patterns such as the United States Constitution in Latin America, the French *Charte Constitutionnelle* (1814) for the semiauthoritarian technique of monarchical legitimism, and the Belgian *Charte* (1831) for the parliamentary constitutional monarchy.[7] But the transcendental value with which the process had been imbued in the eighteenth century was no longer attached either to the creation or the operation of the constitution. What happened was that the industrial and commercial *bourgeoisie* asserted itself as the ruling class and that, wherever it took—or was grudgingly granted—its share in political power, the constitution merely legalized the shift that had occurred before. In spite of the constitutional semantics, popular sovereignty was nominal only, using the representative ideology for

[7] See John A. Hawgood, *Modern Constitutions since 1787* (New York, 1939), pp. 93 ff., 131 ff., who calls the two patterns the "condescended" and the "negotiated" state, respectively.

The Value of Constitutions in Our Revolutionary Age

what was at best an oligarchy of wealth, actually, however, the political monopoly of the propertied classes. The competition for power was conducted at first between the *bourgeoisie* and the royal prerogative, which was successfully whittled away; subsequently, after the victory of the propertied oligarchy, between the latter and the lower middle classes and labor. Its political core was the suffrage rather than the constitution itself. That the constitutions, on the whole, succeeded in rationalizing the power conflict by subjecting it to the regulatory procedures of positive law was due to the fact that they were applied to a relatively self-contained and homogeneous society, not yet exposed to the challenges of social forces basically opposed to the existing distribution of political power. Constitutions function well so long as the competition for power is confined to different groups of the same social class; but they are strained to the limit, and often break, when their rules become insufficient to accommodate the power ambitions of a class excluded by its very rules. The considerable esteem in which the nineteenth century held the constitutions as a method for the peaceful compromise of political dynamics was responsible also for their improved functional utility, devoid of any emotional or transcendental implications. Compared with, for example, the functional matter-of-factness of the Bismarckian Constitution of 1871, the American Constitution reads like a dissertation on political philosophy.

Constitutions after World War I

The magic spell of the constitution was briefly and deceptively recaptured after World War I. The conceptual heritage of the French Revolution—popular sovereignty—gained emotional strength in some of the older states, which were offered an opportunity for wiping the slate clean of the residues of the monarchical tradition. To the host of new states emerging from the ruins of the Czarist, Austro-Hungarian, and Ottoman empires, the constitutions became the symbols of nationhood and independence, in line with Wilson's political ethics of national self-determination, internationally applied. Democratic parliamentarism (France and Britain) had won the war; monarchical authoritarianism had lost. Constitutional democracy was like an incantation invoked everywhere, regardless of how little the professionals and the masses were socially, morally, and politically prepared for it. Constitutions were inspired and carried by the *bourgeoisie,* which subconsciously expected to tame labor by tying it down to constitutionalism. Labor went along because it hoped to gain power by constitutional majorities. A refreshing wind blew over the world, which once again, for a fleeting moment, believed that democratic fundamentalism would be as permanent as it was deemed absolute. The constitutions of this period, no longer confined to functional mechanics, are boldly constructive,[8] filled with the spirit of experimentation and socially conscious in their bills of rights. The Mexican Constitution (1917) in this hemisphere and the Weimar Constitution (1919) are outstanding illustrations. Simultaneously, the new constitutions were functionally perfected, leaving nothing to chance, trying to bridle all potential power elements by legal arrangement. It was, in short, the maximum effort to "constitutionalize" political power.

The Indian summer of constitutional democracy lasted less than a decade. Almost without exception the new constitutions became the victims of the revolt of the masses. The practice of violence, which, in the meantime, had been raised to the rank of a potent political theory, triumphed over the *juste milieu* of bourgeois rationalism. By and large, the constitutions were anachronistic at the time they were written. The error of the *bourgeoisie* consisted in the assumption that labor and the dispossessed lower classes could be paid off with promises or, at the most, token installments of economic security, and that the dominant position which the ruling capitalistic *bourgeoisie* had obtained in its struggle with landed wealth would be permanent.

The aftermath of the brief interlude of constitutional universalism was the dislodgment of constitutional democracy and, with it, of the constitution it had fashioned. Dictatorship spread like wildfire over Europe, sparing only those nations where ingrained tradition of political compromise resisted mass emotionalism, and also over

[8] See Arnold J. Zurcher, *The Experiment with Democracy in Central Europe* (New York, 1933).

The Value of Constitutions in Our Revolutionary Age

Latin America with similarly shallow constitutional habits. Fascism did not require formalization of political power, which, however sweepingly formulated, would have been a limitation on its exercise. Where authoritarianism resorted to the device of a constitution, as in Poland (1935), it served merely as a frame to make the existing configuration of power "legally" unchallengeable.

Constitutions after World War II

The expectation that the nations liberated from Nazi-Fascist despotism would return to their constitutions with jubilation did not materialize. Return they did. What else could they do? But it was a far cry from the democratic *élan* the preceding generation had exhibited. In some marginal states (the Benelux countries and Norway) the existing constitutions, which had been virtually preserved through governments in exile, were put into application without requiring any changes; here the monarchical continuity proved useful.[9] But in the Continental key states of France, Germany, and Italy, the pre-Fascist instruments having been weighed and found wanting, new ones were created. The business of constitution-making was attended to dutifully and without enthusiasm. Very few people in Western Europe will admit that their constitutions partake of the quality of the "higher law," except in the purely formal sense that they establish certain regulatory norms for the conduct of the governmental business. For the tired, neurotic, cynical, disenchanted society of the West, divided against itself, the importance of the written constitution has visibly faded. And in the people's democracies of the East where the powers that be played up to the limit the symbolism of the new order, who would dare to pretend that they embody what democracy prides itself on, the identity of the governors and the governed?

The reasons for the evanescence of the emotional attachment to a constitution lie deeper than the mere mental fatigue of nations after occupation and war. True, the people relish that no longer, in the small hours of the night, will the bell ring for the uncertain fate

[9] See Karl Loewenstein, *Political Reconstruction* (New York, 1946), pp. 138 ff., 168 ff.

arbitrariness may have in store for them. But this generation has seen too much of the viscera of the political process and the demonism of power to put much store by the protection of paper documents. War and postwar inflation have brought about a revolutionary change in social stratification. The bottom has fallen out from under the economic stability of the propertied middle classes, major proportions of which are precariously close to outright proletarianization. There are few antidotes to economic materialism, and what purports to be the "philosophy" of the period—pessimism disguised as existentialism—is not among them. This generation has become alienated from its governments, realizing that political power is the monopoly of party oligarchies, vested-interest cliques, and pressure groups. After the emotionalization by the dictators, the mass mind has not yet found a new center of moral gravity. Liberty the constitutions could and did promise, but not bread and the modicum of economic security the little man yearns for. To him it is the plain and unadorned truth that the political decisions which are vital for the well-being of all no longer occur within the frame of the constitution. The social forces move—and battle—extraconstitutionally, because the constitutions did not even attempt the required solutions.[10] Constitutions are considered stale compromises and extemporizations of the accidental party configuration. It is not difficult to realize that for the cynic, the disillusioned, and the desperate among the laboring and salaried masses the blandishments of Communist collectivism, which they are told has reversed the class situation in their favor, cannot fail to be attractive.

But even the constitutional lawyer whose vision is not blinded by his profession will find little moral comfort in the study of the new constitutions. He realizes with suspicion that those of the Soviet orbit are technically too simple, functionally too straightforward, to allow for a fair adjustment of the power conflict. On the other

[10] A striking illustration is the issue of industrial codetermination in Western Germany, to all intents and purposes the most significant development in management-labor relations in postwar Europe. The Bonn Constitution was prudently silent on it; the federal parliament unable to solve it. When the pressure of the labor unions in coal and steel forced the issue, the *Bundestag* had to yield. The constitutional machinery was used merely for ex post facto ratification.

The Value of Constitutions in Our Revolutionary Age

hand, the Western constitutions, appraised as a group, are stationary and strangely retrospective, overly legalistic and complex, and yet timid and evasive. Both the French Constitution of 1946 and the Bonn Constitution in many respects are merely responsories to 1875 and 1919, respectively, trying to find foolproof answers to past mistakes. In general, these remedial efforts are understandable and commendable. Illustrations are the prohibition of delegated legislation in France (Art. 13), and the "neutralization" of presidential powers by election through a constitutional convention instead of through the people in Western Germany (Art. 54). By the same token, the attempts at rationalizing parliamentary dynamics (vote of nonconfidence and dissolution) and similar efforts to obtain a stable government are useful. Contrariwise, the constitutions reflect diffidence in the people themselves, with the hardly unintended result of playing the actual exercise of political power into the hands of the party oligarchies. Compared with France and Western Germany, Italy's Constitution is much more optimistic and self-confident. With the elimination of the monarchy, Italian parliamentarism could start from scratch without the inhibitions of adverse past experience.

The So-called "Form of Government" [11]

The term "form of government" usually describes the functional arrangement—co-ordination or subordination—of the various organs in the process of determining the will of the state. Here the postwar constitutions did not add anything new to the traditional repertory. None turned to the monarchical solution: in Italy and Bulgaria monarchy was voted out of existence formally by plebiscite; in other Balkan states it was dismissed informally; and India (1949) not only severed the Commonwealth link with the British Crown (though not with Great Britain) but also made short shrift of indigenous residues of monarchical feudalism. All constitutions, those behind the Iron Curtain no less than the others, profess the

[11] For a detailed discussion of the postwar patterns of government, see Karl Loewenstein, "The Presidency Outside the United States," *The Journal of Politics,* XI (1949), 447 ff.

democratic fundamentals; all adhere, with varying accents, to the functional division of powers (though not to their separation). Outwardly they are very similar, and if one would strike off the U.S.S.R. Constitution (1936), chapters I and X, it would be next to impossible to realize that this is the model of a new social order.

The separation-of-powers pattern of government found no favor outside the sphere of influence of the United States, such as in Latin America where, however, more recently a tendency toward approximation to parliamentarism is discernible, or China (1947) and Southern Korea (1948), serving here a protective coloration for unmitigated authoritarian government. The generally favored pattern is parliamentary government in the sense that the government requires the continuous support of a majority party or a coalition of parties (France, Italy, India, Israel, and others). An interesting variation was produced in Western Germany for which the name "demo-authoritarian" may seem appropriate; the Federal Chancellor can be removed from office by vote of confidence only if the absolute majority of all members of the *Bundestag* simultaneously have elected a successor (Art. 67). This implies that the Chancellor is virtually irremovable during the four-year term of the parliament except when the government coalition breaks and a substantial part of it combines with the opposition. Similar efforts to stabilize the government were undertaken in some of the Western German *Länder,* and the same device, though in a most hypothetical manner, figures also in the constitution of Eastern Germany *(Deutsche Demokratische Republik)* (Art. 95, 2). The cabinet system, under which the Prime Minister, by virtue of strict party discipline and the threat of dissolution, is in undisputed exercise of political power between elections, is so much predicated on the interplay of two parties that none of the new constitutions could effectively institutionalize it.

The real surprise, however, is the revival, in the Soviet orbit, of the historically discredited and half-forgotten pattern of assembly government, which not only prevails in the U.S.S.R. itself but also in practically all [12] satellite states including Eastern Germany

---

[12] Albania, Bulgaria, Hungary, Yugoslavia, Rumania. Poland and Czechoslovakia are exceptions, the former having re-established, with some streamlining, the con-

The Value of Constitutions in Our Revolutionary Age

(German Democratic Republic and *Länder*). Why the Soviets abandoned their previous (1918, 1923) undisguised rule of the new proletarian agencies in favor of the more orthodox assembly government cannot be discussed here. But the archdemocratic pattern of the omnipotence of the popularly elected assembly, free from any checks and balances and, therefore, also from conformance with the separation of functions, lent itself perfectly to the rule of the single party, confirming the historical experience that assembly government is the convenient façade behind which the dictatorship of a person, group, party, or ruling clique can be disguised. Since the rule of the assembly is nominal only—it meets rarely and at great intervals—the Presidium, its permanent steering committee, is a logical innovation.[13] At least in Eastern Germany, where the pretense of the multiple-party state is maintained, assembly government is implemented by the "block technique,"[14] the prearranged (by persuasion, pressure, and other means) unanimity of the parliamentary parties and cabinets. The ingenious device serves for the "voluntary" elimination of the opposition and presents to those who wish to believe it the picture of a monolithic democracy. In the Eastern German Republic the technique is even institutionalized in the constitution (Art. 92): Any party with forty deputies *must* be represented in the government according to its strength in the lower house *(Volkskammer)*. Suppression of the opposition certainly is nothing new; but to make a coalition government mandatory in the constitution is evidently the limit of "constitutional" democracy.

The "Living" Constitution: Shadow and Substance

For an ontological evaluation of constitutions it is essential to recognize that the reality of a specific functional arrangement of powers depends to a large measure on the sociopolitical environment to which the pattern is applied. From its own experience the

---

stitution of 1920 (Constitutional Act of February 19, 1947); the latter rewrote the constitution of 1920 in 1948.

[13] See, for example, Hungary (Arts. 19–22), where it is called "Presidential Council." It does not exist, however, in the German Democratic Republic and is seemingly less well endowed with power in Czechoslovakia and Poland.

[14] The leading discussion is Alfons Steiniger, *Das Blocksystem* (Berlin, 1949).

politically advanced Western world is apt to draw the conclusion that, once a constitutional order has been formally accepted by a nation, it is not only valid in the sense of being legal but also real in the sense of being fully activated and effective. If this is the case, a constitution is *normative*. To use a homely simile: The constitution is a suit made to measure and is actually worn. It is, however, an assumption that requires verification in every single case.

There are other cases where a constitution, though legally valid, is actually not lived up to. Its reality and activation are imperfect. This should not be confused with the universally recognized situation that the constitution as written differs from the constitution as applied. Constitutions change, not only by formal constitutional amendments, but even more so, imperceptibly, by constitutional usages. What is aimed at here is the factual state of affairs that a constitution, though legally valid, has no integrated reality. The American Constitution is the law of the land in all the United States, but the Fourteenth Amendment is not fully activated in, for example, Mississippi and Alabama. To continue the simile: It is a ready-made suit which is not worn; it hangs in the closet. In this case the constitution is merely *nominal*.

Finally, there are cases in which the constitution is fully applied and activated, but it is merely the formalization of the existing location and exercise of political power. The mobility of power dynamics, to adjust which is the essential purpose of any constitution, is "frozen" in the interest of the actual power holder. The suit is no suit at all but a fancy dress or a mere cloak. In this case the constitution is nothing but *"semantic."*

The normative constitution prevails in the West where it serves as the procedural frame for the compromise of the power contest. Of the new constitutions, in addition to those of France, Germany, and Italy, those of Israel, India, and Ceylon come under this category, the first because it is manipulated by an intellectually Westernized people, the latter two because of the education the political élite had received in contacts with the British. Burma (constitution of 1947) can hardly be counted here, her experience with self-government being too scanty.

The Value of Constitutions in Our Revolutionary Age

The nominal constitution, on the other hand, is merely a declaration of constitutional intent, a blueprint expected to become a reality in the future. Its habitat is in nations where Western constitutionalism is implanted into a colonial and/or agrarian-feudal social structure. Literacy, of course, is indispensable for the reality of a constitution. But even where literacy is extensive it may seem that the rationality of Western constitutionalism is alien, at least for the time being, to the Asiatic or African mind. This situation prevails definitely in states accustomed to authoritarianism like China (Chiang Kai-shek's constitution of 1947), Southern Korea (1948) and Siam, and possibly also in the Philippines and most of the Arab states. But it is also not uncommon in Latin America where, however, Brazil, Argentina, Chile, Colombia, Uruguay, and Cuba must explicitly be exempted and ranked with Western normativism. The borderline may often be fluid. In the Latin American *ambiente*, constitutions are frequently abolished and rewritten, or suspended by the state of siege, according to shifts of the power cliques temporarily in control of the army.[15] The existence or nonexistence of a constitution does, as a rule, not much affect the life of the business community or the common people.

The case of Japan (constitution of 1946) defies classification. Even the older (1889) constitution was not normative in the sense that it served as the frame for the orderly adjustment of the power conflict. In spite of its Westernized "neutrality," it was wholly subservient to the ruling groups of industrial and agrarian feudalism and the army. The new constitution is S.C.A.P. inspired, S.C.A.P. dictated, and S.C.A.P. enforced, the democratically elected Diet operating as a mixed chorus. In the political vacuum of foreign occupation, under a foreign general as pseudo-Mikado and with party dynamics strictly controlled by him, there can hardly be a reality of the constitution even for a nation so adaptable as the Japanese.

Finally, where the written constitution is advisedly used for "legalizing," stabilizing, and perpetuating an existing configuration

---

[15] Venezuela's Constitution of 1947 (now suspended) is the twenty-second in one hundred and thirty-six years.

of power, it cannot serve as the procedural frame for the competitive power elements. This is probably the generic characteristic of all or most authoritarian constitutions, with the instruments of the years VIII and X in France or the constitution of Napoleon III (1852) as historical and the Pilsudski Constitution of 1935 as more recent examples. The existence of the written constitution is merely the face-saving gesture demanded by the present-time universal belief in democratic legitimacy. If no constitution existed at all, the prevailing power monopoly of a person, group, class, or party would not be changed to a substantial degree. At the most, such constitutions regulate the assignment of high-level jurisdictions as the formal basis for the orderly conduct of the governmental business no state can do without. In the narrow sense of the term these instruments are positivist in that they "freeze" the existing power situation. Actually their purpose is semantic camouflage.

Under this category come most of the Soviet satellite constitutions,[16] but equally so those of other states of quasi-feudal structure (Egypt, Iran, Iraq). In underdeveloped countries the distinction between the semantic and the nominal constitution cannot always be applied with satisfactory precision.

Comparative Observations on the Functional Structure

1. *The legislative-executive relations.* The legislative-executive relationship—whether operating in co-ordination or in subordination—is the essence of the "form of government." The solutions attempted reveal the differences between the normativism of the West and the semanticism of the East. In the fully developed "people's democracy," exemplified by Hungary (1949), the problem

[16] Samuel L. Sharp, in "Communist Regimes in Eastern Europe," *Foreign Policy Reports,* XXVI, No. 16 (January 1, 1951), 183, states that, "in accordance with Stalinist doctrine, constitutions merely register situations of fact already achieved." This explains convincingly that the still existing differences of the constitutions in the Soviet-controlled area, between themselves as well as with the Soviet prototype, are due to the gradualism of evolution toward the Soviet pattern. Hungary, as the latest formulation (1949), is closest and without Westernized pretenses of objectivity. It may be added that the comparative affinity of the Eastern German constitutions (which Sharp does not discuss) to the Western system is occasioned by the desire not to antagonize the Western Germans directly. Therefore, the multiple-party system is nominally preserved.

offers no difficulty. In the place of co-ordination and co-operation there exists, by a curious inversion characteristic of assembly government, a strictly hierarchical system of subordination. The parliament, allegedly "the highest state organ" (Art. 10), is completely dominated by its presidium (called "Presidential Council of the People's Democracy," Arts. 20 and 21), which, in turn, completely controls the Council of Ministers, spoken of as the "highest organ of state administration" (Art. 22) and controlling the local councils hierarchically. All levels are of course linked together by the Communist party (or, in other satellites, the National Front) concerning which the document is semantically silent. No simpler, less complex, and more direct technique for the exercise of political power ever has been put on paper.

In the Western climate, on the other hand, the executive-legislative relationship continues to remain the core of constitutional engineering. There is no longer the eighteenth-century illusion that government and parliament could be harmoniously equilibrized or mutually balanced. The alternatives are either a strong government superior to the parliament, at the expense of responsiveness to public opinion, or a government continually dependent on the whims of the parliamentary parties. The controlling viewpoint is the avoidance of cabinet crises occasioned by the lack of stability of the party coalition supporting the government.

The framers of the new constitutions were visibly impressed by the one hundred-odd cabinets that had occurred under the Third Republic in France within sixty-five years and the twenty-odd under Weimar within fourteen years. A sizable number thereof, being accidental and without deeper political implications, could have been avoided by rationalized parliamentary procedures. Consequently, technical efforts are now made to limit them by the injection of cooling-off periods between the motion for, and the vote of, nonconfidence, or the requirement of a minimum of signatures for the former (Italy, Art. 94) and of absolute majorities for the latter (France, Art. 45; Germany, Bonn, Arts. 67, 68). But the danger of recurrent cabinet crises seems somewhat overemphasized. The record will disclose that many, if not the majority, of the cabinet changes were occasioned by justified demands of the opposition for a change in legislative policies to which the new government conformed. This, after all, is the inherent function of parliamentary government. The exceptional situation under Weimar, to the effect that heterogeneous and basically antidemocratic opposition parties combine "unconstructively" for the overthrow of the government without being able or willing to form an alternative government, may not easily present itself elsewhere. Moreover, breaks in governmental continuity are often mitigated by the "replastering" technique in constituting the new cabinets. Outside France the record of governmental stability since 1945 leaves little to be desired, perhaps with the exception of Belgium while laboring under the singular pressure of the *question constitutionnelle* (the struggle for the removal of Leopold III). Moreover, it may seem doubtful whether cabinet crises are actually the congenital vice of parliamentarism, or whether it is the inability of any "pattern of government" to reconcile political opposites refusing to agree on the socioeconomic fundamentals of the common existence. The common people, with their unstunted sense of realities, are much more aware of this basic dilemma than the politicians and party manipulators themselves.

At any rate, the search for the magic formula to establish a crisis-proof system continues, but the circle remains as unsquared as before. Where the distrust of the strong executive is nationally ingrained as in France, the recourse to unmitigated parliamentarism seems the lesser evil. The French rely largely on the skill of their parliamentarians. Where, as in Germany, the strong executive is an article of national faith, the legislature—and with it the democratic fundamentals—have to foot the bill. The Germans try to ward off spontaneous eruptions of the power conflict by making the Chancellor quasi-irremovable during the four-year term of the *Bundestag* and strengthening his hands, with the *dolus eventualis* of authoritarian government, by the ominous "legislative emergency powers" (Art. 81), under which even if defeated he can operate without parliamentary support for at least six months. The historically less inhibited Italians trust the natural balance of the political forces and the fear of Communism holding together the artificial majority of the Christian Democrats. Evidently parliamentary crises are the price to pay for multiple parties, which Continental politics seemingly cannot be disabused of.

2. *Dissolution.* In the authentic form of parliamentary government,[17] dissolution is the democratic fulcrum of the entire process of adjusting power conflicts by making the electorate the ultimate policy-determining factor. Compared with the period after 1919 dissolution takes a serious beating in the new constitutions even though the French have at long last cautiously revived it (Arts. 51, 52). The curbs to which it is subjected in France and Bonn, Germany, come under the same heading of the search for the crisis-proof constitution. Only in Italy (Art. 88) does the institution preserve its genuine plebiscitary function. Five years of experience in France have demonstrated that the party oligarchies, shifting power among themselves, are as afraid of the people as before, meaning the Communists to the left and the De Gaullists to the right. In Germany, likewise, where dissolution has been resorted to frequently under the empire and Weimar, it seems destined to wither on the vine. Moreover, as F. A. Hermens has emphasized,[18] dissolution loses much of its plebiscitary effect if conducted under proportional representation, which tends to stabilize the existing party pattern. Dissolution, of course, is incompatible with assembly government except in the remote contingency of self-dissolution (Hungary, Art. 18, 1).[19]

3. *Position of the President.* Within the same context of legislative-executive relations the position of the President has been noticeably weakened in comparison with 1919 and after. Because of its greater democratic prestige, popular election is no longer favored

---

[17] Robert Redslob's *Die parlamentarische Regierung* (Tübingen, 1918) (French edition, *Le Régime parlementaire* [Paris, 1924]), most influential after 1919, is now almost forgotten.

[18] Ferdinand A. Hermens, *Mehrheitswahlrecht oder Verhältniswahlrecht?* (Munich, 1949); *Europe between Democracy and Anarchy* (Notre Dame, 1951). See also Maurice Duverger, *L'Influence des systèmes électoraux sur la vie politique* (Paris, 1950).

[19] See also the equally unlikely case of dissolution in Art. 95, 6, of the Eastern German Constitution.

except where, as in Latin America, the American pattern is followed. The President is generally confined to state integrating and ceremonial functions. He retains, however, the designation of the Prime Minister (France, Italy, Israel, India); in Western Germany this function has shifted to the *Bundestag* by election (Art. 63) and in Eastern Germany the strongest party automatically is charged to name the executive-designate (Art. 92). The discretionary powers of the President in dissolution are completely eliminated in France (Arts. 51, 52) and severely restricted by the mechanization of the entire procedure in Western Germany (Arts. 58, 63, 4). Assembly government as a rule dispenses with the office altogether, its functions being performed by the Presidium; for reasons of expediency, however, the office is retained without an actual share in power, in the U.S.S.R., Eastern Germany, Poland, Czechoslovakia, and Yugoslavia.

4. *Second chambers.* Except in federal states the unicameral organization is now generally preferred. The final emasculation of the British House of Lords by the Labour government is paralleled by the powerless Council of the Republic in France and reflected, to some extent, in the position of the Federal Council *(Bundesrat)* under Bonn, which, while strengthening the position of the territorial subdivisions in matters affecting them, is confined to a suspensive veto in federal affairs and without influence on federal political dynamics. Italy has seen fit to restate full-fledged bicameralism with political equality of the Chamber and the Senate, the latter based on a spurious effort to achieve a different composition by "Regions" and, at least in theory, capable of overthrowing the government.

If an "upper" house were to serve as the brake on, or balance of, accidental party fluctuations within the lower house, it would require a different composition, based on corporate units, specific social strata, more mature age groups, or meritorious individual personalities. But this traditional function of the second chamber has become largely obsolete; an exception is the strictly consultative Senate in Bavaria (constitution of 1946, Arts. 34 ff.). While, thus, the decay of the second-chamber technique is a universal phenomenon, it may seem regrettable that corporativism, whose natural location would be the second chamber, though discredited by totalitarian abuse, has not been given the chance of a democratic trial; the Economic Council in France is weaker than other applications (in Czechoslovakia and Weimar Germany) after 1919. The professional stratification of socioeconomic life in organized power groups is one of the undeniable realities of countries professing a free economy; the powerful combines of labor, co-operatives, management, agriculture, civil servants, professional and other interest groups, deprived of legitimate participation in the formation of public policies, are forced to operate either through political parties or to exert power outside the constitution itself. On this score the postwar constitutions have not been able to face realities.

Under assembly government in nonfederal states the second chamber is at variance with the political doctrine and has been discarded everywhere.

5. *Federalism.* Federalism is on the decline, and this in spite of various institutionalizations in the West and the East. Experience in the oldest and best integrated federal states, the United States and Switzerland, demonstrates that, whatever strength of tradition and emotional values of political theory federalism is still imbued with, the economic imperatives of the technological state require unified if not uniform economic policies throughout the entire territory and do not brook that kind of economic fragmentation which goes with effective member-state sovereignties.[20] To point it up sententiously: A state with a federal income tax is no longer a genuinely federal state. On the other hand, the realization is equally general that, even in relatively small areas, decentralization enhances administrative efficiency. Federalism as an organizational device cannot be divorced from the general political philosophy of the age. Federalism is a product of liberal thinking. It applied the (relative) freedom of the individual to the (relative) freedom of organization of territorial entities. It thrives as long as a free economy thrives.

[20] The case of Switzerland is particularly illustrative. The partial revision of the constitution in 1947 (Arts. 31 ff.) practically not only modified the policy of economic *laissez faire* but subjected the entire economic life of the Swiss confederation to federal control.

Karl Loewenstein

Speaking again sententiously: Economic planning is the DDT of federalism. Constitutions, therefore, that take their federal premises too seriously can hardly escape becoming anachronistic.

However, federalism is essential and indispensable where strong tendencies of multinational or tribal diversity prevail. The Indian Constitution, trying to organize and govern a multinational subcontinent, could not operate without evolving a sort of superfederalism, being applied, in terms of the First Schedule to Article 1, to at least three different categories of states and territorial subdivisions with different legal status in regard to their relations to the Union. This kind of "quantitative" federalism obviously is imperative for the growing together of literally hundreds of socially widely divergent separate communities. Federalism in India, and also in Burma, likewise a "Union," seems a method of social integration rather than of perpetuated diversification.

Of the Iron Curtain constitutions, only that of Yugoslavia follows the Soviet federal pattern. But if the inclusive evidence permits an evaluation, the emphasis, as in the U.S.S.R., is on cultural autonomy rather than political self-government. How far the new collectivist way of life, emanating from planning, has succeeded in overcoming the age-old nationalism of the Croats, Montenegrins, and Macedonians, and their resentment of Serb ascendancy, remains to be seen. Whatever may be the degree of effectiveness of cultural autonomy, the social-planning mechanism extends uniformly to all subdivisions. With the older type of federalism in the West it has evidently nothing in common but the name. Federalism of the five *Länder* in Eastern Germany is wholly semantic, as can be easily seen from the unitarian constitution of the German Democratic Republic.

Nor is federalism in Western Germany any longer the genuine article, belying the endless labor of the military governments and the Germans in fashioning it. On the surface the constitution of Bonn is less unitarian than Weimar. But the facts of economic interdependence of the area militate against genuine federalism, except in certain cultural matters. Actually the elaborate and ambitious *Land* constitutions of the Western zones mean little for the

The Value of Constitutions in Our Revolutionary Age

people. The decisive socioeconomic issues, such as economic policies, social security, codetermination, and tax distribution, devolve on the federal government in Bonn. In Italy the new "Regions"[21] remain to date a dead letter (except, to a limited extent, in Sicily, Sardinia, and Alto Adige), and this for the same reasons as elsewhere; namely, that local autonomy cannot but be subservient to nation-wide economic and social policies. Federalism in Latin America (Argentina, Brazil, Venezuela, Mexico) finally never amounted to much in practice because of the constitutionally legalized and frequently used practice of federal intervention.

6. *Suffrage, electoral system, and political parties.* Democratic equality for the formation of the will of the state is no longer problematic. Universal suffrage with, in some instances, a considerably lowered voting age is the general standard. All censitory vestiges have disappeared. But it is indicative of the existing cleavage between constitutional nominalism and political reality that, while proportional representation is universally favored, the operative technique of this (and any) electoral system, the political party, is almost universally ignored. Political parties are mentioned, it is true, in the Bonn (Art. 21) and the Italian (Art. 49) Constitutions as recognized instruments for the formation of the political will of the people. But the fact is carefully ignored that proportional representation, more than any other electoral system, puts the actual exercise of political power into the hands of the party oligarchies and their bureaucracies, which are entirely beyond popular control. The ubiquitous result is the political vacuum in which the party-manipulated parliaments everywhere operate. The general lack of prestige of the political congeries called political parties cannot fail to be reflected in the waning respect the people have for the parliaments themselves.

It is readily admitted that the integration of the political party into the mechanism of the frame of government—recognition of the party within the bill of rights as a phenomenon of the individual right of political association is, of course, merely declaratory—is one of the most difficult aspects of constitutional renovation. The

[21] See Pietro Virga, *La regione* (Milan, 1949).

issue may, for the time being, be inaccessible to legal formulas. But it is equally obvious that silence of all constitutions on the emergence of new elites—in the West the party bosses and their bureaucracies, the parliamentary oligarchies, and, in the East, the powerful layer of the officials of the state party and the managerial technicians of the state-owned industries—is a much more potent reality than the ubiquitously proclaimed "sovereignty of the people" (France, Art. 3, 1; Italy, Art. 1, 2; Germany, Bonn, Art. 20, 2). Sovereignty actually is located in the political parties.[22] The statement (Germany, Bonn, Art. 38, 1) that the individual deputies in parliament represent the entire nation is a piece of undiluted semantics.

The situation is aggravated by the visibly declining emphasis on participation of the people in the political process. It is confined to elections of the parliament at regular intervals or in the (rare) case of dissolution. Initiative and referendum—the latter only in connection with the amending process (France, Art. 90; Italy, Art. 138) —are conspicuous by their absence in Western Europe, let alone elsewhere, probably because of the inconclusive result of direct democracy in the constitutions after 1919. Monopolization of political power by the party oligarchies makes the new constitutions less democratic than their predecessors.

In the monopolization of the popular will by the single or state party, the people's democracies are more honest, and probably can afford to be. The constitution is not a blueprint to be activated in the future, but it closely reflects, and is synchronized with, the actual power configuration reached in the particular country. The paramount function of the single party is admitted and exalted. No longer an abstraction, it is a stark reality, incorporated in the frame of government proper. In the Soviet Constitution of 1936 the Communist party as "the vanguard of the toilers" is an official

---

[22] Constitutional theory, on the other hand, has become widely aware of the changed situation. See, for example, Pascal Arrighi, *Le Statut des partis* (Paris, 1948); Pedro J. Frias, *El ordenamiento legal de los partidos politicos* (Buenos Aires, 1944); Wilhelm Grewe, *Zum Begriff der politischen Partei*, Festgabe für Erich Kaufmann (Stuttgart, 1950), pp. 65 ff.

state organ (Arts. 126, 141). Since in the earlier elaborations of the Soviet system the transition to the single-party state was not completed, the Communist party (or its equivalent) could not yet be given the privileged position. But in the Hungarian Constitution (1949) the "People's Democracy bases itself on the organization of the class conscious workers" and "the leading force in [such] political and social activities is the working class" (Art. 56, 2). Of the thirty-six times the "workers," "working class," or "class conscious workers" are mentioned in this document, not a few refer to the workers as activators of political power rather than as its addressees. And the constitution of the German Democratic Republic could openly assign (Art. 92) the position of the Minister-President to the strongest party because the power apparatus could by now be trusted to identify this as the Socialist Unity party.

7. *Constitutional amendment.* In this revolutionary age constitutions, however carefully projected into the future, cannot aspire to make permanent their political solutions In this they differ from the optimism of the eighteenth century; the Directory Constitution of 1795 was practically unamendable. Consequently, the process of constitutional amendment everywhere is kept sensibly elastic, neither too rigid to invite, with changing conditions, revolutionary rupture, nor too flexible to allow basic modifications without the consent of qualified majorities. However, the amending procedure is rationalized in the sense that it can no longer be "bypassed." In France the Constitutional Committee (Arts. 91 ff.) determines whether a law passed by the National Assembly requires a revision of the constitution; this is a sort of substitute for judicial review of the constitutionality of statutes. In Western Germany the amendment requires the effective change of the text of the constitution (Art. 79, 2). All the more surprising is the increasing illusion that certain fundamentals can be made "unamendable" (republican form of government, Italy, Art. 139; France, Art. 95; federal structure and basic rights, Germany, Bonn, Art. 79, 3). The Indian provision (Sec. 305), to the effect that certain minorities (Muslims, Scheduled Castes, etc.) shall not be

deprived of their seats in the federal and state legislatures for a period of ten years, is one of functional utility rather than of governmental philosophy.

8. *Judicial power and the judicialization of political power.* Western constitutionalism believes traditionally in the clear-cut separation of the judicial function from the other two branches of government and, correspondingly, in the independence of the judiciary secured by tenure. The Soviet approach deliberately discards the separation of powers in whatever form and under whatever disguise. Assembly government, therefore, does not countenance any *capitis diminutio* either by an independent judiciary or by judicial review of legislation. In spite of some face-saving semantics the judicial function is strictly subordinated to the legislative by election and recall through the parliament, for example in the German Democratic Republic (Arts. 130, 131) or Hungary (Art. 39).

In the West serious efforts were undertaken to protect appointment and promotion of the judiciary from extraneous influence or political pressure. Neutralization of the patronage by the political parties is sought in France through the Supreme Council of the Magistrature (Arts. 83 ff.), and in Italy by the creation of the magistrature as an autonomous organization, charged with the exclusive responsibility for the composition and supervision of the judiciary (Arts. 104 ff.). Western Germany has gone furthest in setting up the judicial branch as co-equal with the other two. While the technical arrangements may seem impeccable, they do not go into the core of the problem. In Germany the judges are public officials and, therefore, not independent of the state. De-Nazification has not succeeded in breaking their class consciousness. Basically the independence of the judiciary resolves itself into the sociological dilemma of a judicial caste, a situation with which the American public in its own environment is thoroughly familiar.

Judicial review of the constitutionality of laws that previously had been recognized only for federal-state relations is now viewed with more favor. In Italy (Art. 134) and Germany, Bonn (Art. 93), it is assigned to a special Constitutional Court. It is generally implied in the judicial function in Japan (Art. 76, 3, 8), while

The Value of Constitutions in Our Revolutionary Age

in France it is attenuated to the determination, by the Constitutional Committee acting only on a joint request by the President and the Council of the Republic, whether a law passed by the National Assembly would actually require a constitutional amendment (Arts. 91 ff.). Unavoidable differences of opinion in the interpretation of the new constitutions may well call for an objective judicial decision; but it may seem doubtful whether the institution will integrate itself into political life as the unique regulatory force it is in the United States.

But perhaps more important may become what may be called the judicialization of political power; namely, the efforts to tame the power conflict by subjecting political dynamics to judicial decisions. In Italy (Arts. 134 ff.) and Germany, Bonn (Art. 93), the constitutional tribunal is charged with deciding "conflicts of jurisdiction between the powers of the state" or, in the German version, "disputes concerning rights and duties of the supreme federal organs." Insofar as such conflicts are determinable by positive constitutional norms—the rare exception—judicialization may lead to beneficial results. If, however, jurisdictional attributions of the constitution are being used by the various state organs—for example, by the President against the government or by the government against the parliament—in the competition for political power, the belief that power aspirations can be "decontaminated" by legal formulas may seem to overtax the function of the judiciary. Seemingly the poor showing of the German Supreme Court in an analogous power conflict between the Prussian and the Reich Governments in 1932 was no deterrent. In older and wiser countries the courts exercise self-restraint by refusing to pass on "political questions" or *actes de gouvernement,* which the Germans call *"justizlose Hohheitsakte."* [23] The basic issues of the power process are not justiciable. Reliance on normative legality may impede rather than promote the need for political compromise.

9. *The function of the bill of rights.* Particularly pertinent for the inquiry into the ontological meaning of the constitutions are

---

[23] See, for example, Werner Weber, *Weimarer Verfassung und Bonner Grundgesetz* (Göttingen, 1949).

the principles contained in the bill of rights. In the earlier development of written constitutions the libertarian and equalitarian postulates of the bills of rights were as important as the functional arrangements of the frame of government. The French Declaration of 1789 has assumed the quality of a superconstitutional validity and reality even if the constitution, as, for example, that of 1875, did not contain a restatement or failed to refer to it *expressis verbis*. The (second) constitution of 1946, therefore, could confine itself to a global incorporation by confirming it in the preamble, with some additional socioeconomic rights which the revolutionary fathers could not foresee. But during the nineteenth century, when liberalism was taken for granted, the accent shifted definitely to the functional organization, which, if properly arranged, could be expected to accommodate any socioeconomic system the majority desired to establish by constitutional means. That the Bismarckian Constitution of 1871 failed to register a bill of rights was not due to the authoritarian neglect of the framer but rather to the belief generally adhered to in the period that a constitution should confine itself to functional arrangements and that the main virtue of the declaration of rights consisted in symbolizing the state under the rule of law.

The constitutions after World War I, in whose elaboration the Socialist parties shared for the first time, appear more alerted toward the need of implementing the classic catalogue of libertarian and equalitarian freedoms from the state by a new socioeconomic pattern of economic security and social justice. But again the concept prevails that, beyond certain programmatic aspirations, the decision should be left to the social and political forces contending for power within the framework of the constitution itself. The sociopolitical content of the bills of rights became more important but still not important enough actually to determine and control the functional arrangements in the form of government.

Nothing is more indicative of the parting of the roads between West and East after World War II than the changed position of the bill of rights. In most of the "people's democracies" the relationship between the functional and the ideological parts of the constitution is reversed. What is variously called socioeconomic structure or organization [24] is not only separated from the classical libertarian rights and freedoms—whose actuality under a police state is obviously nominal—but is moved forward into the body of the functional provisions and, thus, considered as binding as the latter. Nationalization of natural resources, state ownership of the means of production, economic planning, the foreign-trade monopoly of the state, and the restrictions on private ownership and property that go with them are no longer programmatic aspirations; they are now part and parcel of the structure of government necessitating a new type of administrative organization. The functional organization is conditioned on the socioeconomic pattern.

In the West the program of the bills of rights has not materially advanced beyond what was reached after World War I. The bills are still large-scale and pretentious catechisms of socioeconomic, cultural, and educational postulates, nowhere raised to the rank of subjective rights the individual can enforce against the state or, what amounts to the same, implying duties of the state to carry out and implement the program by positive legislation. Moreover, without corresponding judicial protection even most of the libertarian freedoms are of paper value only. On the other hand, Bonn, Germany, is more advanced in converting the basic rights into positive rules of law immediately binding legislation, administration, and adjudication (Art. 1, 3) and opening, by way of a general clause, access to the courts for redress against any violation of the constitutionally guaranteed private sphere by governmental or administrative action (Art. 19, 4).

What may seem more important is the twilight zone in which the political philosophy moves. The bills of rights are as articulate and comprehensive as they are evasive on the decisive social issues of labor-management relations and the property complex as the key to the alternatives of private capitalism or socialization, *laissez*

---

[24] Hungary (social structure, Arts. 4–9); Rumania (social and economic structure, Arts. 5–15); Yugoslavia (socioeconomic organization, Arts. 14–20); Bulgaria (public economic organization, Arts. 6–14). In the German Democratic Republic the break with the tradition is less visible because the economic order (Arts. 19–29) is placed together with other categories of rights under a common heading, "Substance and Limits of Sovereignty."

faire or planning. These temporizations are due, of course, to the structure of the party coalition, which was primarily responsible for them (in the three key states dominated by the Christian Democrats). That the elusiveness of the socioeconomic program deprives the most vital parts of the constitution of attraction for the masses can be easily realized by a comparison with Great Britain, where the unformalized character of the basic order permitted the general election of 1945 to become the plebiscite inaugurating a social revolution of the first magnitude.

On the Craftsmanship of Constitutions

The sociological implications of the craftsmanship in writing a constitution—the drafting skill and the "style" [25]—are still unexplored. The symbolic value of the American Constitution, no less than its functional utility, derives to a considerable degree from the unusually felicitous combination of form and content. Craftsmanship is conditioned, besides national traditions, on the sociological and professional composition of the constituent assembly; the intellectual climate of the period; and foreign influences or even foreign intervention (as in the cases of the recent Japanese and German constitutions). A nation starting its constitutional life from scratch is probably less inhibited than a people whose new constitution is merely another link in the traditional chain of the national manifestations of the political will, as in Germany or in France. The indifferent craftsmanship of the French Constitution of 1875, merely a bundle of unrelated organic laws, reflects the *"attente monarchique."* Instruments drafted by an individual leader for his own use are, as a rule, consistent and responsive to the actual power configuration, as evidenced by Napoleon's Constitution of the year VIII or Bismarck's Constitution of 1871.[26] The craftsmanship of constitutions emanating from party coalitions is bound to reflect the

---

[25] See Heinrich Triepel, *Vom Stil des Rechts* (Heidelberg, 1947). The issue is of practical importance, for example, in dealing with the positive validity of preambles, which are a common feature of most recent constitutions.

[26] Unique in the history of constitution-making is the poetic vision incorporated by Gabriele d'Annunzio in his constitution for Fiume, *"La reggenza italiana del Carnero"*; see *Il Popolo d'Italia*, September 1, 1920.

The Value of Constitutions in Our Revolutionary Age

compromises of conflicting aspirations. It is also fairly obvious that the more a constitution aims at ultimately "neutralizing" and regularizing the power process by injecting into it checks and balances, the more complex it must become, and complexity taxes drafting skill. Since the Iron Curtain instruments merely confirm the existing power situation, they can afford to be simple, straightforward, and direct and can dispense with the complex strategy of distributing functions among various state organs to avoid abuse of power by any one of them. Regarding their stylistic craftsmanship a considered judgment is possible only for one who can read the originals; in translation they all sound alike and are alike drab. The French Constitution of 1946, owing to its being grafted on a previous instrument, does not live up to the national reputation, while both the constitution of Italy and the (draft) constitution of Israel are distinguished by clarity and logical arrangement.

A related problem is that of elaborateness and length. The ideal constitution will contain *only* the essentials of the national political order—organs, functions, jurisdictional delineation—but, at the same time, *all* the essentials. If a constitution wishes to be crisis proof—that is, in practice, to avoid deadlocks between the constituted organs—it can leave nothing to chance and must spell out all contingencies. In trying to be "gapless" it approximates the substance of a code that is necessarily more lengthy and complex. Other constitutions, setting greater store by the wisdom and moderation of their manipulators to compromise the power conflict, need be less specific. Once again the semantic constitutions of the East have the advantage of brevity and conciseness in the functional arrangements because they are not likely to be exposed to the strain of competitive political forces.

On the whole, the recent vintage of constitutions is more verbose and articulate than the previous families of constitutions. But here the national "style" tradition comes into focus. Anglo-Saxon legal training and habits of statutory formulation, which try to cover all foreseeable eventualities, are responsible for the length and the minutiae of the Indian Constitution whose 315 articles and 8 schedules fill a book, with the Burmese Constitution of 234 articles running a close second. Much of this is, of course, due to the conditions of a multinational federalism and religious differences. In the West the Bavarian Constitution of 1946 holds the record in the number of words without claiming the palm of craftsmanship.

There is no evidence that any of the new constitutions will attain either the symbolic value or the rank of a piece of classic literature that distinguishes the American Constitution. They are instruments written by lawyers for lawyers. Excessive legalism in craftsmanship necessarily minimizes the appeal to, and the emotional attachment of, the people. This, in turn, cannot fail to reflect adversely on the potential integration of the new constitutions in the minds of the people as the addressees of political power.

The People and the Constitution

At this point the crucial question may be raised: What do constitutions, in our time, mean to the people? Are they "living" in the sense that they are essential for the life not of the professionals manipulating them but of the common people? Or, somewhat more emotionally pointed up: Is the constitution instrumental for the pursuit of happiness of the people? There is no parallel to the phenomenon of the American Constitution as a living reality for the American people, which, beyond its well-advertised quality as a social myth, is essential because it served, and still serves, for the peaceful (and at times even playful) adjustment of the power conflict. It is, of course, a patriotic distortion to attribute the absence of the class struggle in this country to the constitution; rather, the reverse is true. The continued congruity between constitutional form and socioeconomic substance can be preserved because there is no social class to which the functional organization of the constitution denies its share in political power. With the exception of the War between the States no major social conflict has challenged it. The New Deal was accommodated within the constitutional frame with relative ease.

The new constitutions will find it difficult to integrate themselves in the minds of the people. They mean next to nothing, or very little, to the little man ground between the nether and the upper millstones. To be sure, most people value the return of legal se-

The Value of Constitutions in Our Revolutionary Age

curity and administration conducted without galling arbitrariness. But the constitutions are indifferent toward the realities of the life of the people, incapable of satisfying the minimum of social justice and economic security that the common people believe themselves entitled to, the pretentious bills of rights to the contrary notwithstanding. The vital issues are no longer decided by constitutional processes but by the pressure groups operating outside and often in opposition to them. The constitution cannot, and does not, bridge the gap between poverty and wealth. Everywhere, with the possible exception of Britain and the marginal monarchies of Western and Northern Europe, the people distrust their governments, their officials, their parties and parliaments, and their constitutions. What is true for the sophisticated West may even be truer for the East wherever the education of the masses for the Communist eschatology is still incomplete. If the constitution means little for the citizen in Bordeaux or Frankfurt, how much can it mean for the illiterate coolie in Shanghai? The moral crisis of this age cannot fail to vitiate the moral value of a constitution that fails to provide tangible remedies for tangible grievances.

The actual value of a constitutional order can be tested only in the wear and tear of the political process. Predictions, therefore, are mere speculations. Since the constitutions in the Soviet orbit are formalizations of the specific power entrenchment of single-party control and not destined to serve for free power competition, they will not last a day longer than Communist coercion will last. This may be long, and longer than the people living thereunder would desire. How the new constitutions in the West will stand up under the strain of a serious economic or political crisis remains to be seen. In spite of hectic efforts to make them crisis- and shockproof, the inherent defects of the representative parliamentary system have not been exorcised. Authoritarianism remains the skeleton in the closet, except in a political environment with the traditional wisdom of the parliamentary elite trained to govern and, perhaps, the stabilizing influence of respected monarchies.

But obviously the causes for the ambivalence of Western constitutionalism lie deeper than in the inadequacy of functional arrangements. We have not yet begun to investigate the ontological causality between the form of government a constitution endorses and the socioeconomic structure of the society to which it is applied. The inquiry is hampered by still existing residues of the naïve optimism of the eighteenth century that a functionally well-constructed constitution can adjust peacefully any power conflict. That much can be learned from the crude materialism of the Soviet-orbit constitutions; viz., that a definitely chosen socioeconomic pattern requires a commensurate institutionalization of the power situation. The Communists realized that not every constitution can accommodate any form of society, and that a specific society requires a specific constitutional order. The concept that the constitution, confined to the jurisdictional determination of authority, can be "neutral" and "objective" toward the power process is as much a by-product of liberal relativism as is the concept that the written constitution itself is a child of liberal rationalism. In the light of our—admittedly limited —historical experience, it seems likely that an inner congruity exists between constitutional form and societal substance.

To state the thesis in more concrete terms: Athenian direct democracy was predicated on the nontechnological economy of a small and socially homogeneous community based on slavery. The absolute monarchy of the prerevolutionary period corresponded to the social stratification of landed wealth and the hereditary privilege of an aristocratic society. Parliamentary democracy, or rather oligarchy, was suitable for the dominance of the middle-class *bourgeoisie,* rooted politically and economically in *laissez faire.* Liberal constitutionalism could afford to raise the rule of law to the dignity of an absolute value. When finally the laboring masses, unwilling to abide by the rules of liberal capitalism, claimed their share of economic and political power, this form of government was bound to become inadequate. The transformation of capitalism into all-out socialism by planning and nationalization of the natural resources, the means of production and trade, required the authoritarian form of government for the new ruling class. It is most unlikely that this will be more than a transitional stage in the never-ending political experimentation of mankind. On his appointed day the new Montesquieu will arise.

APPENDIXES

A

Constitution of the French Republic, *October 27, 1946* . *page* 226
>English translation by the French Embassy,
Press and Information Division,
610 Fifth Avenue, New York 20, N.Y.

B

Constitution of the Italian Republic, *December 27, 1947* . . 248
>Reprinted from the United States Department of State
Documents and State Papers, April 1948, pp. 46–63.
English translation by
Howard McGaw Smyth and Kent Roberts Greenfield.

C

Basic Law of the Federal Republic of Germany (West Germany), *adopted by the Parliamentary Council, May 8, 1949* . 283
>English translation by Military Government.

D

Statute of Westminster, 1931, *December 11, 1931* 325
>An Act (22 Geo. V, c. 4) to give effect to
certain resolutions adopted by the Imperial Conferences
held in the years 1926 and 1930.

E

Communique and Declaration of the Commonwealth Prime Ministers' Conference, *April 27, 1949, on the Status of the Republic of India in the Commonwealth* 329
>Text supplied by the British Information Services,
30 Rockefeller Plaza, New York 20, N.Y.

F

Statute of the Council of Europe, *May 5, 1949* 331

A

Constitution of the French Republic
October 27, 1946

English translation by the French Embassy, Press and Information Division, 610 Fifth Avenue, New York 20, N.Y.

THE National Constituent Assembly has adopted,
The French people have approved,
The President of the Provisional Government of the Republic promulgates the following Constitution:

PREAMBLE

On the morrow of the victory of the free peoples over the regimes that attempted to enslave and degrade the human person, the French people proclaim once more that every human being, without distinction as to race, religion or creed, possesses inalienable and sacred rights. They solemnly reaffirm the rights and freedoms of man and of the citizen ordained by the Declaration of Rights of 1789 and the fundamental principles recognized by the laws of the Republic.

They further proclaim as most vital to our time the following political, economic and social principles:

The law shall guarantee to women equal rights with men, in all domains.

Anyone persecuted because of his activities in the cause of freedom shall be entitled to the right of asylum within the territories of the Republic.

Everyone shall have the obligation to work and the right to obtain employment. No one may suffer in his work or his employment because of his origin, his opinions or his beliefs.

Constitution of the French Republic

Everyone may defend his rights and interests by trade-union action and may join the union of his choice.

The right to strike may be exercised within the framework of the laws that govern it.

Every worker, through his delegates, may participate in collective bargaining to determine working conditions, as well as in the management of the enterprise.

All property and all enterprises that now have, or subsequently shall have the character of a national public service or of a monopoly in fact, must become the property of the community.

The Nation shall ensure to the individual and to the family the conditions necessary to their development.

The Nation shall guarantee to all, and particularly to the child, the mother, and the aged worker, protection of health, material security, rest, and leisure. Any individual who, because of his or her age, his or her physical or mental condition, or because of the economic situation, shall find himself or herself unable to work, shall have the right to obtain from the community the means for a decent existence.

The Nation shall proclaim the solidarity and equality of all the French people with respect to burdens resulting from national disasters.

The Nation shall guarantee equal access of children and adults to education, professional training, and culture. The establishment of free, secular, public education on all levels, shall be a duty of the State.

The French Republic, faithful to its traditions, shall abide by the rules of international public law. It shall not undertake wars of conquest and shall never use force against the freedom of any people.

On condition of reciprocal terms, France shall accept the limitations of sovereignty necessary to the organization and defense of peace.

France shall form with the peoples of her Overseas Territories a Union based upon equality of rights and privileges, without distinction as to race or religion.

The French Union shall be composed of nations and peoples who shall place in common or coordinate their resources and their efforts in order to develop their respective civilizations, further their well-being, and ensure their security.

Faithful to her traditional mission, France shall guide the peoples for whom she has assumed responsibility, toward freedom to govern themselves and toward the democratic administration of their own affairs; rejecting any system of colonization based upon arbitrary power, she shall guarantee to all equal access to public office and the individual or collective exercise of the rights and liberties hereinabove proclaimed or confirmed.

Constitutions since World War II

THE INSTITUTIONS OF THE REPUBLIC

TITLE I—SOVEREIGNTY

Article 1

France shall be a Republic, indivisible, secular, democratic, and social.

Article 2

The national emblem shall be the tricolor flag, blue, white, and red, in three vertical bands of equal dimensions.

The national anthem shall be the "Marseillaise."

The motto of the Republic shall be "Liberty, Equality, Fraternity."

Its principle shall be: government of the people, for the people, and by the people.

Article 3

National sovereignty belongs to the French people.

No section of the people, nor any individual may assume its exercise.

The people shall exercise it, in constitutional matters, through the vote of their representatives or through the referendum.

In all other matters, they shall exercise it through their Deputies in the National Assembly, elected by popular, equal, direct and secret ballot.

Article 4

All French subjects and nationals of both sexes, who are majors and enjoy civil and political rights, may vote under the conditions prescribed by law.

TITLE II—PARLIAMENT

Article 5

Parliament shall be composed of the National Assembly and the Council of the Republic.

Article 6

The duration of powers of each Assembly, its mode of election, the conditions of eligibility, and the rules of ineligibilities and incompatibilities of office, shall be determined by law.

However, the two Chambers shall be elected on a territorial basis, the National Assembly by direct popular vote, the Council of the Re-

Constitution of the French Republic

public by the communal and departmental collectivities, by indirect popular vote. The Council of the Republic shall be renewable one half at a time.

Nevertheless, the National Assembly may itself elect, by proportional representation, Councillors whose number shall not exceed one sixth of the total number of members of the Council of the Republic.

The number of members of the Council of the Republic may not be less than 250 nor more than 320.

Article 7

War may not be declared without a vote by the National Assembly and the preliminary opinion of the Council of the Republic.

Article 8

Each of the two Chambers shall pass upon the eligibility of its members and the regularity of their election; each one shall accept the resignation of its own members.

Article 9

The National Assembly shall convene by law every year on the second Tuesday in January.

The total duration of the recesses of the session may not exceed four months. Adjournments of more than ten days shall be considered as a recess.

The Council of the Republic shall sit at the same time as the National Assembly.

Article 10

The meetings of the two Chambers shall be public. Reports of the debates in extenso, as well as parliamentary documents, shall be published in the "Journal Officiel."

Each of the two Chambers may convene in secret committee.

Article 11

Each of the two Chambers shall elect its Secretariat every year, at the beginning of its session, by proportional representation of the political parties.

When the two Chambers shall meet together to elect the President of the Republic, their Secretariat shall be that of the National Assembly.

Article 12

When the National Assembly is not in session, its Secretariat, exercising control over the actions of the Cabinet, may convoke Parliament; it must do so upon the request of one third of the Deputies or of the President of the Council of Ministers.

Article 13

The National Assembly alone shall pass the laws. It may not delegate this power.

Article 14

The President of the Council of Ministers and the members of Parliament shall propose legislation.

Bills introduced by members of the National Assembly shall be filed with its Secretariat.

Bills introduced by members of the Council of the Republic shall be filed with its Secretariat and sent without debate to the Secretariat of the National Assembly. They shall not be admissible if they might result in the reduction of revenues or the creation of new expenditures.

Article 15

The National Assembly shall study the bills submitted to it through committees whose number, composition and scope it shall determine.

Article 16

The proposed Budget shall be submitted to the National Assembly.
It may include only such provisions as are strictly financial.
An organic law shall regulate the mode of presentation of the Budget.

Article 17

The Deputies of the National Assembly shall have the power to initiate expenditures.

However, no proposals which tend to increase appropriations already decided upon, or to create new ones, may be presented during the discussion of the Budget and of prospective or supplementary appropriations.

Article 18

The National Assembly shall regulate the accounts of the Nation.
It shall be assisted in this task by the "Cour des Comptes."*
The National Assembly may entrust to the "Cour des Comptes" all investigations and studies concerning public revenues and expenditures or the management of the funds in the treasury.

---

* Highest Court of Accounts.

Constitution of the French Republic

Article 19

Amnesty may be granted only by a law.

Article 20

The Council of the Republic shall examine, in order to give its opinion thereon, the bills passed on first reading by the National Assembly.

It shall give its opinion not more than two months after receipt of each bill sent it by the National Assembly. When the Budget Law shall be under discussion, this period may be reduced, if need be, to the time taken by the National Assembly for its consideration and vote. When the National Assembly shall have adopted a rule for emergency procedure, the Council of the Republic shall give its opinion within the same period of time as that provided for debate in the National Assembly by the rule of that body. The time limits specified in the present Article shall be suspended during recesses of the session. They may be extended by a decision of the National Assembly.

Should the opinion of the Council of the Republic be in agreement with that of the National Assembly or should it not have been given within the time limits specified in the preceding paragraph, the law shall be promulgated in the text as voted by the National Assembly.

Should the opinion of the Council of the Republic not be in agreement with that of the National Assembly, the latter body shall examine the bill on second reading. It shall dispose definitively and absolutely of the amendments proposed by the Council of the Republic, accepting or rejecting them in whole or in part. Should these amendments be totally or partially rejected, the second reading of the bill shall be voted upon by public ballot* and by an absolute majority of the members of the National Assembly whenever the vote on the whole bill has been taken under the same conditions by the Council of the Republic.

Article 21

No member of Parliament may be prosecuted, sought by the police, arrested, detained, or tried because of opinions expressed or votes cast by him in the exercise of his office.

Article 22

No member of Parliament may be prosecuted or arrested during his term of office for a criminal offense or a misdemeanor except upon

---

* For a description of the various methods of voting used in the French National Assembly, see "Règlement de l'Assemblée Nationale," Ch. XIII, Art. 74 to 85.

authorization from the Chamber of which he is a member, unless it be a case of flagrante delicto. The detention or prosecution of a member of Parliament shall be suspended if the Chamber of which he is a member so demands.

Article 23

Members of Parliament shall receive compensation for their services to be ascertained in relation to the salary of a given category of civil servants.

Article 24

No one may be a member of the National Assembly and of the Council of the Republic at the same time. Members of Parliament may not be members of the Economic Council nor of the Assembly of the French Union.

TITLE III—THE ECONOMIC COUNCIL

Article 25

An Economic Council, whose statute shall be determined by law, shall examine the bills within its purview in order to give its opinion thereon. The National Assembly shall send such bills to this Council before considering them.

The Economic Council may also be consulted by the Council of Ministers. It must be consulted concerning the establishment of any national economic plan for full employment and the rational utilization of material resources.

TITLE IV—DIPLOMATIC TREATIES

Article 26

Diplomatic treaties duly ratified and proclaimed shall be enforced even though they be contrary to French domestic laws, and no legislative acts, other than those necessary to ensure their ratification, shall be required for their enforcement.

Article 27

Treaties relative to international organization, peace treaties, commercial treaties, treaties that involve national finances, treaties relative to the personal status and property rights of French citizens abroad, and those that modify French domestic laws, as well as those that call for the cession, exchange, or addition of territories, shall not become final until duly ratified by a legislative act.

Constitution of the French Republic

No cession, no exchange, and no addition of territory shall be valid without the consent of the populations concerned.

Article 28

Diplomatic treaties duly ratified and proclaimed having authority superior to that of domestic legislation, their provisions shall not be abrogated, modified or suspended without previous formal denunciation through diplomatic channels. Whenever a treaty such as those mentioned in Article 27 is concerned, such denunciation must be approved by the National Assembly, except in the case of commercial treaties.

TITLE V—THE PRESIDENT OF THE REPUBLIC

Article 29

The President of the Republic shall be elected by Parliament.

He shall be elected for seven years. He shall be eligible for re-election only once.

Article 30

The President of the Republic shall appoint in the Council of Ministers, the Councillors of State, the Grand Chancellor of the Legion of Honor, ambassadors and envoys extraordinary, members of the High Council and of the Committee for National Defense, rectors of the universities, prefects, directors of the central administrative services, high ranking officers and Government representatives in the Overseas Territories.

Article 31

The President of the Republic shall be kept informed of international negotiations. He shall sign and ratify all treaties.

The President of the Republic shall accredit ambassadors and envoys extraordinary to foreign powers; foreign ambassadors and envoys extraordinary shall be accredited to him.

Article 32

The President of the Republic shall preside over the Council of Ministers. He shall order the minutes of their meetings to be recorded and shall keep them in his possession.

Article 33

The President of the Republic shall preside, with the same prerogatives, over the High Council and the Committee for National Defense, and shall be the Commander-in-Chief of the armed forces.

Article 34

The President of the Republic shall preside over the High Council of the Judiciary.

Article 35

The President of the Republic shall exercise the right of pardon in the High Council of the Judiciary.

Article 36

The President of the Republic shall promulgate the laws within ten days after their text, as finally adopted, has been sent to the Government. This interval may be reduced to five days if the National Assembly declares a state of emergency.

Within the time limit fixed for promulgation of a law, the President of the Republic, in a message stating his reasons, may ask that it be reconsidered by both Chambers; this reconsideration may not be refused.

Should the President of the Republic not promulgate a law within the time limit fixed by the present Constitution, the President of the National Assembly shall promulgate it.

Article 37

The President of the Republic shall communicate with Parliament by means of messages addressed to the National Assembly.

Article 38

Every act signed by the President of the Republic must be countersigned by the President of the Council of Ministers and by a Minister.

Article 39

Not more than thirty and not less than fifteen days before the expiration of the term of office of the President of the Republic, Parliament shall elect a new President.

Article 40

Should, in application of the preceding Article, the election take place during the period when the National Assembly is dissolved in conformance to Article 51, the powers of the President of the Republic in office shall be extended until a new President is elected. Parliament shall elect this new President within ten days after the election of the new National Assembly.

In this case, the President of the Council of Ministers shall be desig-

Constitution of the French Republic

nated within fifteen days after the election of the new President of the Republic.

Article 41

Should the President of the Republic be unable to exercise his office for reasons duly established by a vote of Parliament, or in the event of a vacancy caused by death, resignation or any other circumstance, the President of the National Assembly shall assume his functions during the interim. He, in turn, shall be replaced in his duties by a Vice President.

The new President of the Republic shall be elected within ten days, except under the conditions specified in the preceding Article.

Article 42

The President of the Republic shall not be responsible except for high treason.

He may be indicted by the National Assembly and arraigned before the High Court of Justice under the conditions set forth in Article 57 below.

Article 43

The office of President of the Republic shall be incompatible with any other public office.

Article 44

Members of the families that once reigned over France shall not be eligible for the Presidency of the Republic.

TITLE VI—THE COUNCIL OF MINISTERS

Article 45

At the beginning of the term of each legislature, the President of the Republic, after the customary consultations, shall designate the President of the Council of Ministers.

The latter shall submit to the National Assembly the program and the policy of the Cabinet he intends to constitute.

The President of the Council and the Ministers may not be appointed until the President of the Council receives a vote of confidence from the National Assembly by public ballot and by an absolute majority of the Deputies, except in the case a force majeure shall prevent the National Assembly from meeting.

The same procedure shall be followed during the term of the legislature in the event of a vacancy caused by death, resignation, or any other circumstance, except in the case set forth in Article 52 below.

Article 51 shall not be applied as the result of any ministerial crisis occurring within the fifteen-day period after the appointment of the Ministers.

Article 46

The President of the Council and the Ministers chosen by him shall be appointed by a decree of the President of the Republic.

Article 47

The President of the Council shall ensure the enforcement of the laws.

He shall appoint all civil and military officials except those specified in Articles 30, 46, and 84.

The President of the Council shall supervise the armed forces and shall coordinate all measures necessary for national defense.

The acts signed by the President of the Council and mentioned in the present Article, shall be countersigned by the Ministers concerned.

Article 48

The Ministers shall be collectively responsible to the National Assembly for the general policy of the Cabinet and individually responsible for their personal actions.

They shall not be responsible to the Council of the Republic.

Article 49

Request for a vote of confidence may not be made except after deliberation by the Council of Ministers; it can be made only by the President of the Council.

A vote of confidence may not be taken until one full day after the request has been made to the Assembly. The vote shall be taken by public ballot.

The Cabinet may not be refused a vote of confidence except by an absolute majority of the Deputies in the Assembly.

Refusal to give such a vote shall automatically result in the collective resignation of the Cabinet.

Article 50

Passage of a motion of censure by the National Assembly shall automatically result in the collective resignation of the Cabinet.

The vote on such a motion may not be taken until one full day after the motion has been made. It must be taken by public ballot.

Constitution of the French Republic

A motion of censure may be adopted only by an absolute majority of the Deputies in the Assembly.

Article 51

Should, in the course of an eighteen-month period, two ministerial crises occur under the conditions set forth in Articles 49 and 50, the Council of Ministers, with the concurrence of the President of the Assembly, may decide to dissolve the National Assembly. Its dissolution shall be proclaimed by a decree of the President of the Republic, in accordance with this decision.

The provisions of the preceding paragraph may not be applied before the expiration of the first eighteen months of the term of the legislature.

Article 52

In the event of dissolution, the Cabinet, with the exception of the President of the Council and the Minister of the Interior, shall remain in office to carry on current business.

The President of the Republic shall appoint the President of the National Assembly as President of the Council. The latter shall appoint the new Minister of the Interior with the approval of the Secretariat of the National Assembly. He shall appoint as Ministers of State members of political parties not represented in the Government.

General elections shall take place not less than twenty and not more than thirty days after dissolution.

The National Assembly shall convene by law on the third Thursday after its election.

Article 53

The Ministers shall have access to the two Chambers and to their Committees. They must be heard upon request.

During discussions in the Chambers, they may be assisted by Committee members designated by decree.

Article 54

The President of the Council of Ministers may delegate his powers to a Minister.

Article 55

In the event of a vacancy caused by death or any other circumstance, the Council of Ministers shall call upon one of its members to exercise temporarily the functions of the President of the Council of Ministers.

TITLE VII—THE LEGAL RESPONSIBILITY OF MINISTERS

Article 56

The Ministers shall be legally responsible for crimes and misdemeanors committed in the exercise of their office.

Article 57

The Ministers may be indicted by the National Assembly and arraigned before the High Court of Justice.

The National Assembly shall decide this question by secret ballot and by an absolute majority of its members, with the exception of those who may be called upon to participate in the prosecution, investigation, or judgment of the case.

Article 58

Members of the High Court of Justice shall be elected by the National Assembly at the beginning of the term of each legislature.

Article 59

The organization of the High Court of Justice and its rules of procedure shall be determined by a special law.

TITLE VIII—THE FRENCH UNION
SECTION I—PRINCIPLES

Article 60

The French Union shall be composed, on the one hand, of the French Republic which comprises Metropolitan France and the Overseas Departments and Territories, and, on the other hand, of the Associated Territories and States.

Article 61

The position of the Associated States within the French Union shall, in the case of each individual State, depend upon the Act that defines its relationship to France.

Article 62

The members of the French Union shall place in common all their resources so as to guarantee the defense of the whole Union. The Government of the Republic shall coordinate these resources and direct such policies as will prepare and ensure this defense.

Constitution of the French Republic

SECTION II—ORGANIZATION

Article 63

The central organs of the French Union shall be: the Presidency, the High Council and the Assembly.

Article 64

The President of the French Republic shall be the President of the French Union; he shall represent its permanent interests.

Article 65

The High Council of the French Union, under the chairmanship of the President of the Union, shall be composed of a delegation of the French Government and of the representatives that each Associated State shall accredit to the President of the Union.

Its function shall be to assist the Government in the general conduct of the affairs of the Union.

Article 66

The Assembly of the French Union shall be composed half of members representing Metropolitan France and half of members representing the Overseas Departments and Territories and the Associated States.

An organic law shall determine the mode of representation of the different sections of the population.

Article 67

The members of the Assembly of the Union shall be elected by the Territorial Assemblies for the Overseas Departments and Territories; for Metropolitan France, two thirds shall be elected by the National Assembly representing Metropolitan France and one third by the Council of the Republic also representing Metropolitan France.

Article 68

The Associated States may appoint delegates to the Assembly of the French Union within the limitations and conditions determined by a law and by an act individual to each State.

Article 69

The President of the French Union shall convoke the Assembly of the French Union and shall close its sessions. He must convene it upon the request of half its members.

The Assembly of the Union may not sit during recesses of Parliament.

Article 70

The rules set forth in Articles 8, 10, 21, 22, and 23 shall be applicable to the Assembly of the French Union under the same conditions as prevail for the Council of the Republic.

Article 71

The Assembly of the French Union shall examine the bills or proposals submitted to it by the National Assembly or the Government of the French Republic or the Governments of the Associated States, in order that it may give its opinion thereon.

The Assembly shall be empowered to express its opinion on resolutions proposed by one of its members and, if these resolutions are accepted for deliberation, to instruct its Secretariat to send them to the National Assembly. It may submit proposals to the French Government and to the High Council of the French Union.

In order to be admissible, the proposed resolutions referred to in the preceding paragraph must concern legislation pertaining to the Overseas Territories.

Article 72

Legislative powers with regard to penal law, civil liberties, and political and administrative organization in the Overseas Territories, shall rest with Parliament.

In all other matters, the French law shall be applicable in the Overseas Territories only by an express provision to that effect, or if it has been extended to the Overseas Territories by decree, after consultation with the Assembly of the Union.

Moreover, in derogation to Article 13, special provisions for each Territory may be enacted by the President of the Republic in the Council of Ministers, after preliminary consultation with the Assembly of the Union.

SECTION III—THE OVERSEAS DEPARTMENTS AND TERRITORIES

Article 73

The legislative regime of the Overseas Departments shall be the same as that of the Departments of Metropolitan France, save for exceptions determined by law.

Constitution of the French Republic

Article 74

The Overseas Territories shall be granted a special statute which takes into account their particular interests with relation to the general interests of the Republic.

This statute and the internal organization of each Overseas Territory or group of Territories shall be determined by law after the Assembly of the French Union has expressed its opinion thereon, and after consultation with the Territorial Assemblies.

Article 75

The status of the respective members of the French Republic and of the French Union shall be subject to change.

Modifications of status and passage from one category to another within the framework established in Article 60 may take place only as the result of a law passed by Parliament, after consultation with the Territorial Assemblies and the Assembly of the Union.

Article 76

The representative of the Government in each Territory or group of Territories shall be vested with the powers of the Republic. He shall be the administrative head of the Territory.

He shall be responsible to the Government for his actions.

Article 77

An elective Assembly shall be instituted in each Territory. The electoral regime, composition and powers of this Assembly shall be determined by law.

Article 78

In the groups of Territories, the management of matters of common interest shall be entrusted to an Assembly composed of members elected by the Territorial Assemblies.

Its composition and its powers shall be determined by law.

Article 79

The Overseas Territories shall elect representatives to the National Assembly and to the Council of the Republic under the conditions determined by law.

Article 80

All subjects of the Overseas Territories shall be citizens with the same status as French nationals of Metropolitan France or of the Overseas

Territories. Special laws shall determine the conditions under which they may exercise their rights as citizens.

Article 81

All French nationals and subjects of the French Union shall have the status of citizens of the French Union, and thereby they shall be ensured the enjoyment of the rights and liberties guaranteed by the Preamble of the present Constitution.

Article 82

Citizens not claiming French civil status, shall retain their personal status so long as they do not renounce it.

This status may in no case constitute a ground for refusing or restricting the rights and liberties pertaining to the status of French citizens.

TITLE IX—THE HIGH COUNCIL OF THE JUDICIARY

Article 83

The High Council of the Judiciary shall be composed of fourteen members:
—The President of the Republic, President;
—The Keeper of the Seals, Minister of Justice, Vice President;
—Six members elected for six years by the National Assembly, by a two-thirds majority and chosen outside its membership, six alternates being elected under the same conditions;
—Six members designated as follows:
  —Four judges elected for six years under conditions provided by law, and representing each judicial branch, four alternates being elected under the same conditions.
  —Two members appointed for six years by the President of the Republic and chosen outside the membership of Parliament and the judiciary, but from among the members of the legal profession, two alternates being designated under the same conditions.

The decisions of the High Council of the Judiciary shall be determined by majority vote. In case of a tie, the President shall cast the deciding vote.

Article 84

Upon nomination by the High Council of the Judiciary, the President of the Republic shall appoint the judges, with the exception of those in the Office of the Public Prosecutor.

In accordance with the law, the High Council of the Judiciary shall

Constitution of the French Republic

ensure the discipline of these judges, their independence, and the administration of the courts.

These magistrates shall hold office for life.

TITLE X—LOCAL ADMINISTRATIVE UNITS

Article 85

The French Republic, one and indivisible, shall recognize the existence of local administrative units.

These units shall comprise the Communes, the Departments, and the Overseas Territories.

Article 86

The framework, the scope, the eventual regrouping, and the organization of the Communes, Departments, and Overseas Territories shall be determined by law.

Article 87

The local administrative units shall be free to govern themselves by councils elected by popular vote.

Decisions made by the councils shall be carried out by their mayor or by their president.

Article 88

The coordination of the activities of Government officials, the representation of the national interests, and the administrative control of these units shall be ensured, within the departmental framework, by delegates of the Government appointed in the Council of Ministers.

Article 89

Organic laws shall further extend the liberties of the Departments and Municipalities; for certain large cities, these laws may establish rules of operation and an administrative structure different from those of small towns, and they may include special provisions for certain Departments; they shall determine the conditions under which Articles 85 to 88 above shall be applied.

Laws shall likewise determine the conditions under which local offices of the central administrative services shall function, in order to bring the administration closer to the people.

TITLE XI—AMENDMENT OF THE CONSTITUTION

Article 90

Amendment of the Constitution shall take place according to the following procedure:

Constitutions since World War II

The amendment must be decided upon by a resolution adopted by an absolute majority of the members of the National Assembly.

This resolution shall stipulate the purpose of the amendment.

Not less than three months later, this resolution shall have a second reading under the same rules of procedure as govern the first reading, unless the Council of the Republic, to which the resolution has been referred by the National Assembly, shall have adopted the same resolution by an absolute majority.

After this second reading, the National Assembly shall draw up a bill to amend the Constitution. This bill shall be submitted to Parliament and adopted by the same majority and according to the same rules established for any ordinary legislative enactment.

It shall be submitted to a referendum unless it has been adopted on second reading by a two-thirds majority of the National Assembly, or by a three-fifths majority of each of the two assemblies.

The bill shall be promulgated as a constitutional law by the President of the Republic within eight days after its adoption.

No constitutional amendment affecting the existence of the Council of the Republic may be adopted without the concurrence of said Council or recourse to a referendum.

Article 91

The President of the Republic shall preside over the Constitutional Committee.

The Constitutional Committee shall include the President of the National Assembly, the President of the Council of the Republic, seven members elected by the National Assembly at the beginning of each annual session, by proportional representation of the political parties and chosen outside its own membership, and three members elected under the same conditions by the Council of the Republic.

The Constitutional Committee shall determine whether the laws passed by the National Assembly imply amendment of the Constitution.

Article 92

Within the period allowed for promulgation of a law, the Committee shall receive a joint request to examine the law from the President of the Republic and the President of the Council of the Republic, the Council having so decided by an absolute majority of its members.

The Committee shall examine the law, shall strive to bring about agreement between the National Assembly and the Council of the Republic, and, if it does not succeed, shall decide the matter within five days after it has received the request. This period may be reduced to two days in case of emergency.

Constitution of the French Republic

The Committee shall be competent to decide only on the possibility of amending the provisions in Titles I through X of the present Constitution.

Article 93

A law which, in the opinion of the Committee, implies amendment of the Constitution shall be sent back to the National Assembly for reconsideration.

Should Parliament adhere to its original vote, the law may not be promulgated until the Constitution has been amended according to the procedure set forth in Article 90.

Should the law be judged as conforming with the provisions in Titles I through X of the present Constitution, it shall be promulgated within the period specified in Article 36, said period being prolonged by the addition of the periods specified in Article 92 above.

Article 94

In the event of occupation of all or part of the metropolitan territory by foreign powers, no procedure of amendment may be undertaken or continued.

Article 95

The republican form of government may not be the object of a proposed amendment.

TITLE XII—TEMPORARY PROVISIONS

Article 96

The Secretariat of the National Constituent Assembly shall be responsible for ensuring the continuity of national representation until the meeting of the Deputies of the new National Assembly.

Article 97

In exceptional circumstances, the Deputies of the National Constituent Assembly in office may, until the date specified in the preceding Article, be called together by the Secretariat of the Assembly, either on its own initiative, or upon the request of the Government.

Article 98

The National Assembly shall convene by law on the third Thursday following the general elections.

The Council of the Republic shall meet on the third Tuesday following its election. The present Constitution shall take effect on that date.

Until the meeting of the Council of the Republic, the organization of the Public Powers shall be governed by the Law of November 2, 1945, the National Assembly assuming the powers conferred on the National Constituent Assembly by that law.

Article 99

The Provisional Government constituted under the terms of Article 96, shall tender its resignation to the President of the Republic, as soon as he has been elected by Parliament under the conditions set forth in Article 29 above.

Article 100

The Secretariat of the National Constituent Assembly shall be responsible for preparing the meeting of the Assemblies created by the present Constitution and, especially, for providing, before the meeting of their respective Secretariats, the premises and administrative facilities necessary to the exercise of their functions.

Article 101

During a period of not more than one year after the meeting of the National Assembly, the Council of the Republic may officially deliberate as soon as two thirds of its members shall have been proclaimed elected.

Article 102

The first Council of the Republic shall be renewed entirely within the year following the renewal of the Municipal Councils, which renewal shall take place within one year after the promulgation of the Constitution.

Article 103

Until the organization of the Economic Council and during a maximum period of three months dating from the meeting of the National Assembly, the application of Article 25 of the present Constitution shall be suspended.

Article 104

Until the meeting of the Assembly of the French Union and during a maximum period of one year dating from the meeting of the National Assembly, the application of Articles 71 and 72 of the present Constitution shall be suspended.

Article 105

Until the promulgation of the laws provided for in Article 89 of the present Constitution, and without prejudice to the provisions fixing the

Constitution of the French Republic

status of the various Overseas Departments and Territories, the Departments and Communes of the French Republic shall be administered in accordance with the laws now in force, except for Paragraphs 2 and 3 of Article 97 of the Law of April 5, 1884, for the enforcement of which the State police shall be placed at the disposal of the mayors.

However, any action taken by the prefect in his capacity as representative of the Department, shall be subject to the permanent supervision of the president of the Departmental Assembly.

The provisions of the preceding paragraphs shall not be applicable to the Department of the Seine.

Article 106

The present Constitution shall be promulgated by the President of the Provisional Government of the Republic within two days after the date of the proclamation of the results of the referendum, and in the following manner:

"The National Constituent Assembly has adopted,

"The French people have approved,

"The President of the Provisional Government of the Republic promulgates the following Constitution:

(Text of the Constitution)

The present Constitution, considered and adopted by the National Constituent Assembly, approved by the French people, shall be enforced as the Law of the State.

Paris, October 27, 1946.

("Journal Officiel," October 28, 1946)

Note: This English translation of the Constitution, prepared by the French Embassy, Press and Information Division, has been revised for the third printing.

B

Constitution of the Italian Republic
December 27, 1947

Reprinted from the United States Department of State
Documents and State Papers, April 1948, pp. 46–63.
English translation by
Howard McGaw Smyth and Kent Roberts Greenfield

THE PROVISIONAL HEAD OF THE STATE

HAVING SEEN the resolution of the Constituent Assembly which, in the session of December 22, 1947, approved the Constitution of the Italian Republic;

HAVING SEEN the XVIII final provision of the Constitution;

Promulgates the Constitution of the Italian Republic in the following text:

FUNDAMENTAL PRINCIPLES

Article 1

Italy is a democratic Republic founded on labor.

Sovereignty belongs to the people, who exercise it within the forms and limits of the Constitution.

Article 2

The Republic recognizes and guarantees the inviolable rights of man, whether as an individual or in social groups through which his personality develops, and requires the fulfilment of inalienable duties of political, economic, and social solidarity.

Article 3

All citizens have equal social dignity and are equal before the law, without distinction of sex, of race, of language, of religion, of political opinion, of personal and social condition.

Constitution of the Italian Republic

It is the task of the Republic to remove the obstacles of an economic and social order which, limiting in fact the liberty and equality of citizens, prevent the full development of the human personality and the effective participation by all workers in the political, economic, and social organization of the country.

Article 4

The Republic recognizes the right of all citizens to work and promotes the conditions which render this right effective.

Every citizen has the duty to develop, according to his own capabilities and his own choice, an activity or function which contributes to the material or spiritual progress of society.

Article 5

The Republic, one and indivisible, recognizes and promotes local autonomy; it gives effect to the most ample administrative decentralization in the services which depend on the state; it adjusts the principles and the methods of its legislation to the requirements of autonomy and decentralization.

Article 6

The Republic protects linguistic minorities with appropriate norms.

Article 7

The state and the Catholic Church are, each in its own order, independent and sovereign.

Their relationships are regulated by the Lateran Pacts. Modifications of the pacts, which have been accepted by the two parties, do not require the procedure of constitutional amendment.

Article 8

All religious confessions are equally free before the law.

Religious confessions other than the Catholic have the right to organize according to their own statutes, in so far as they do not conflict with the Italian juridical order.

Their relationships with the state are regulated by law on the basis of agreements with the appropriate representatives.

Article 9

The Republic promotes the development of culture and scientific and technical research.

It protects the scenic beauty and the historic and artistic patrimony of the nation.

Article 10

The Italian juridical order conforms to the generally recognized norms of international law.

The juridical condition of the foreigner is regulated by law in conformity with international norms and treaties.

The foreigner, who in his own country is prevented from effectively exercising the democratic liberties guaranteed by the Italian Constitution, has the right of asylum under conditions established by law.

Extradition of the foreigner for political offenses is not admitted.

Article 11

Italy repudiates war as an instrument of offensive action against the liberty of other peoples and as a means for the resolution of international controversies; it consents, on conditions of parity with other states, to limitations of sovereignty necessary to an order for assuring peace and justice among the nations; it promotes and favors international organizations directed toward that end.

Article 12

The flag of the Republic is the Italian tricolor: green, white, and red, in three vertical bands of equal dimensions.

PART I: RIGHTS AND DUTIES OF CITIZENS

TITLE I: CIVIL RELATIONS

Article 13

Personal liberty is inviolable.

No form of arrest, inspection, or personal search is admitted nor any other restriction whatsoever of personal liberty, except by warrant of judicial authority and only in cases and modes provided by law.

In exceptional cases of necessity and urgency, indicated positively by law, the police authority may adopt provisional measures which must within forty-eight hours be communicated to the judicial authority and, if this authority does not within the succeeding forty-eight hours validate them, they are understood to be revoked, and they remain without any effect.

Any physical or moral violence to persons who are in any way subject to restrictions of liberty is punished.

The law establishes the maximum limits of preventive imprisonment.

Constitution of the Italian Republic

Article 14

The domicile is inviolable.

Inspections or searches or distraints cannot be executed except in cases and according to methods established by law and in accordance with the guarantees prescribed for the protection of personal liberty.

Verifications and inspections for reasons of public health and safety or for economic and fiscal purposes are regulated by special laws.

Article 15

Liberty and secrecy of correspondence and of every other form of communication are inviolable.

Limitation upon them may take place only by means of a warrant of the judicial authority stating the reasons and within the guarantees established by law.

Article 16

Every citizen may move and travel freely in any part whatsoever of the national territory, except for generally applicable limitations which the law establishes for reasons of health or security. No restriction may be determined by political reasons.

Every citizen is free to leave the territory of the Republic and to return to it, subject only to legal obligations.

Article 17

Citizens have the right to assemble peaceably and without arms.

Notice is not required for meetings even in places open to the public. For meetings in public [private] places, notice shall be given to the authorities who may forbid them only for well-established reasons of public security or safety.

Article 18

Citizens have the right to meet freely, without authorization, for whatever purposes are not forbidden to individuals by the penal laws.

Secret associations are prohibited, and those which pursue even indirectly military aims by means of organizations of military character.

Article 19

All have the right freely to profess their own religious faith in whatever form, individual or collective; to propagate it and to conduct worship in private or in public, provided this does not involve rites contrary to morality.

Article 20

The ecclesiastical character and religious purpose or the purpose of worship of an association or institution may not be the cause of special legislative restrictions or of special fiscal burdens upon its constitution, its legal capacity, or any form of its activity.

Article 21

Everyone has the right freely to manifest his own thought by word, by writing, and by every other means of dissemination.

The press may not be subjected to authorization or censure.

A distraint may be exercised only by warrant of judicial authority with statement of reasons in case of crimes, for which the press law expressly authorizes it, or in case of violation of the norms which the law itself prescribes for those designated as responsible.

In such cases, when there is absolute urgency and opportune intervention of the judicial authority is not possible, a distraint on the periodical press may be executed by police agents of the courts. These must immediately, and in any case within not more than twenty-four hours, present charges before the courts. If the judicial authority does not sustain the charge within the succeeding twenty-four-hour period, the distraint is understood to be revoked and without effect.

The law may provide, with norms of a general character, that the means by which the periodical press is financed be made known.

Printed publications, entertainments, and all other manifestations contrary to good morals are prohibited. The law establishes provisions adequate to prevent and to repress violations.

Article 22

No one may be deprived for political reasons of legal capacity, of citizenship, or of his name.

Article 23

No forced loan may be imposed on person or estate except on the basis of law.

Article 24

Everyone may act at law for the protection of his own rights and legitimate interests.

The right of defense is inviolable at every stage and level of procedure.

The poor are assured, by appropriate institutions, of the means of action and defense before any court.

Constitution of the Italian Republic

The law determines the conditions and the methods of reparation for judicial errors.

Article 25

No one may be removed from his natural judge as established in advance by law.

No one may be punished except by virtue of a law in force before commission of the act.

No one may be subjected to police measures except in cases prescribed by law.

Article 26

The extradition of a citizen may be granted only when it is expressly prescribed by international conventions.

In no case may it be granted for political offenses.

Article 27

Penal responsibility is personal.

The accused is not considered guilty until final conviction.

Penalties may not consist of treatment contrary to humane feeling and must be directed toward the reeducation of the condemned.

Capital punishment is not permitted except in cases prescribed by military law of war.

Article 28

In accordance with the penal, civil, and administrative laws, the officials and agents of the state and of public bodies are directly responsible for acts committed in violation of rights. In such cases the civil responsibility extends to the state and to public bodies.

TITLE II: ETHICAL-SOCIAL RELATIONS

Article 29

The Republic recognizes the rights of the family as a natural society based on marriage.

Marriage is founded on the moral and juridical equality of the parties, within the limitations established by law to guarantee the unity of the family.

Article 30

It is the duty of parents to support, instruct, and educate their children, even if born out of wedlock.

In case of incapacity of parents, the law provides who shall acquit their tasks.

The law assures to children born out of wedlock every juridical and social protection compatible with the rights of the members of the legitimate family.

The law lays down the norms and the limits for the investigation of paternity.

Article 31

The Republic, by economic measures and other provisions, facilitates the development of the family and the fulfilment of the tasks pertinent thereto, with particular regard to large families.

It protects maternity, infancy, and youth, favoring the institutions necessary for this aim.

Article 32

The Republic protects health as a fundamental right of the individual and as an interest of society and guarantees free care to the indigent.

No one may be obliged to undergo a given treatment for illness except by provision of the law. In no case may the law violate the limits imposed by respect for the human personality.

Article 33

The freedom of art and science and freedom of instruction in them is affirmed.

The Republic lays down general standards for instruction and institutes state schools of all orders and grades.

Organized groups and private persons have the right to establish schools and educational institutions without burden to the state.

The law, in fixing the rights and obligations of non-state schools which request parity, must assure full liberty to them and must assure to their students a scholastic treatment equipollent to that of students of the state schools.

A state examination is required for admission to the various orders and grades of school, or for passing any of them, and in order to qualify for practice of a profession.

Institutions of higher learning, universities and academies, have the right to give themselves autonomous regulations within limits established by the laws of the state.

Article 34

The school is open to all.

Elementary instruction, imparted for at least eight years, is obligatory and gratuitous.

Constitution of the Italian Republic

Those of capacity and merit, even if without means, have the right to attain the highest grades of study.

The Republic renders this right effective by means of scholarships, allowances to families, and other aids which must be assigned by competition.

TITLE III: ECONOMIC RELATIONS

Article 35

The Republic protects labor in all its forms and applications.

It looks after the development and the professional advancement of workers.

It promotes and favors international agreements and organizations designed to affirm and regulate the rights of labor.

It recognizes freedom of emigration, except for obligations established by law in the general interest, and it protects Italian labor abroad.

Article 36

The worker has the right to a compensation proportionate to the quantity and quality of his labor and in any case sufficient to assure him and his family a free and dignified existence.

The maximum length of the work day is established by law.

The worker has the right to a weekly rest and to annual paid vacations and may not renounce them.

Article 37

The working woman has the same right and, for equal labor, receives the same compensation as the working man. The conditions of labor must permit the fulfilment of her essential functions in the family and assure to mother and child a special adequate protection.

The law establishes the minimum age for paid labor.

The Republic protects the labor of minors with special norms and guarantees to them, for equal work, the right to equal wages.

Article 38

Every citizen unable to work and deprived of the means necessary to live has the right to support and to social assistance.

Laborers have the right to provisions and assured means adequate to their living requirements in case of accident, sickness, disability and old age, and involuntary unemployment.

Those unable to work and the disabled have the right to education and to a beginning in a profession.

Organs and institutions established or assimilated by the state provide for the fulfilment of the tasks contemplated in this article.

The freedom of private charity is affirmed.

Article 39

The organization of trade unions is free.

No other obligation may be imposed on a trade union except that of registering at local or central public offices, in accordance with the norms established by law.

A condition for registration is that the statutes of the unions sanction an internal organization on a democratic basis.

Registered trade unions have legal personality. They may, being represented as units in proportion to their membership, stipulate collective labor contracts with obligatory efficacy for all those members of the category of labor to which the contract refers.

Article 40

The right to strike is exercised within the sphere of the laws which regulate it.

Article 41

Private economic initiative is free.

This may not develop in conflict with social utility or in such a manner as to cause damage to security, to liberty, to human dignity.

The law determines the appropriate programs and controls in order that public and private economic activity may be directed and coordinated toward social ends.

Article 42

Property is public or private. Economic goods belong to the state, to organized groups, or to individuals.

Private property is recognized and guaranteed by law, which determines the methods of its acquisition and enjoyment and the limitations designed to assure its social functioning and render it accessible to all.

In cases prescribed by law, and on the basis of compensation, private property may be expropriated for reasons of general interest.

The law establishes the norms and limits of legitimate and testamentary succession and the rights of the state in inheritance.

Article 43

For the purpose of general utility the law may originally reserve or may transfer, by means of expropriation and with indemnity, to the state, to public bodies, or to communities of workers or of utilizers, specified enterprises or categories of enterprises which relate to essential public services or to sources of energy or to situations of monopoly and which have a character of preeminent general interest.

Article 44

For the purpose of securing a rational exploitation of the soil and of establishing just social relationships, the law imposes obligations and restrictions on private property in land; it fixes limits to its extension according to the region and agrarian zone; it promotes and requires reclamation, the transformation of latifundia, and the reconstitution of productive units; it aids the small and medium-scale proprietor.

The law frames provisions in favor of the mountainous zones.

Article 45

The Republic recognizes the social function of cooperation conducted on the basis of mutuality and without purposes of speculation for private gain. The law promotes and favors its extension by suitable means and assures its character and permanence, subject to appropriate controls.

The law provides for the protection and development of artisanship.

Article 46

With a view to the economic and social advancement of labor and in harmony with the requirements of production, the Republic recognizes the right of workers to collaborate, in ways and within limits established by law, in the management of business enterprises.

Article 47

The Republic encourages and protects saving in all its forms; it disciplines, coordinates, and controls the administration of credit.

It favors the direction of popular savings to residential property, to property in productive land, directly cultivated, and to direct and indirect investment in the great productive enterprises of the country.

TITLE IV: POLITICAL RELATIONSHIPS

Article 48

All citizens, men and women, who have reached the age of majority, are electors.

The vote is personal and equal, free and secret. Its exercise is a civic duty.

The right to vote may not be limited except for civil incapacity or by reason of irrevocable penal sentence or in cases of moral unworthiness indicated by law.

Article 49

All citizens have the right to associate freely in political parties in order to compete by democratic methods to determine national policy.

Article 50

All citizens may submit petitions to the Chambers in order to request legislative provisions or to explain general needs.

Article 51

All citizens of either sex may hold public offices and elective positions on the basis of equality, according to requirements established by law.

The law may, for admission to public offices and to elective positions, equalize the status of Italians not belonging to the Republic with that of citizens.

Whoever is called to elective public functions has the right to devote to them the time necessary for their performance and to retain his job.

Article 52

Defense of the fatherland is a sacred duty of the citizen.

Military service is obligatory within the limits and procedures established by law. Its fulfilment does not prejudice the job of the citizen or his exercise of political rights.

The organization of the armed forces is informed by the democratic spirit of the Republic.

Article 53

All are bound to contribute to public expenses in proportion to their taxable capacity.

The system of taxation conforms to the criteria of progressivity.

Article 54

All citizens are in duty bound to be faithful to the Republic and to observe its Constitution and laws.

Citizens to whom public offices are entrusted are bound to perform their official duties with discipline and honor, swearing an oath in cases established by law.

Constitution of the Italian Republic

PART II: THE ORGANIZATION OF THE REPUBLIC

TITLE I: THE PARLIAMENT

SECTION I: THE CHAMBERS

Article 55

The Parliament is composed of the Chamber of Deputies and of the Senate of the Republic.

The Parliament assembles in joint session of the members of the two Chambers only in cases established by the Constitution.

Article 56

The Chamber of Deputies is elected by universal and direct suffrage, in the proportion of one deputy for 80,000 inhabitants or for fractions greater than 40,000.

Eligible as deputies are all electors who on the day of election have reached their twenty-fifth birthday.

Article 57

The Senate of the Republic is elected on a regional basis.

To each Region is attributed one senator for 200,000 inhabitants or for a fraction greater than 100,000.

No Region may have a number of senators less than six. The Valle d'Aosta has a single senator.

Article 58

The senators are elected by means of universal and direct suffrage by the electors who have attained their twenty-fifth birthday.

Those electors are eligible as senators who have attained their fortieth birthday.

Article 59

Whoever has been President of the Republic is by right senator for life unless he renounces the right.

The President of the Republic may nominate as senators for life citizens who have brought renown to the fatherland by merits of the highest order in the social, scientific, artistic, or literary fields.

Article 60

The Chamber of Deputies is elected for five years, the Senate of the Republic for six.

Constitutions since World War II

The term of either Chamber may not be extended except by law and only in case of war.

Article 61

The elections of new Chambers take place within seventy days of the end of the term of the preceding ones. The first meeting takes place within not less than twenty days of the elections.

The powers of the preceding Chambers are extended until the new Chambers have met.

Article 62

The Chambers meet by right on the first day of February and of October that is not a holiday.

Each Chamber may be exceptionally convoked on the initiative of its President or that of the President of the Republic or on that of one third of its members.

When one Chamber meets in exceptional session, the other is also by right convoked.

Article 63

Each Chamber elects from among its members its President and Presidential Bureau.

When the Parliament meets in joint session, the President and Presidential Bureau are those of the Chamber of Deputies.

Article 64

Each Chamber adopts its own regulations by absolute majority of its members.

The sessions are public; nevertheless each of the two Chambers and the Parliament of the united Chambers may determine to meet in secret session.

The decisions of each Chamber and of the Parliament are not valid if there is not present an absolute majority of their members, and if not adopted by a majority of those present, except when the Constitution prescribes a special majority.

The members of the Government, even if not members of the Chambers, have the right and, upon request, the obligation to attend the sessions. They must be heard whenever they request it.

Article 65

The law determines cases of ineligibility for, and of incompatibility with, the office of deputy or that of senator.

No one may at the same time belong to both Chambers.

Constitution of the Italian Republic

Article 66

Each Chamber judges the credentials of its members and unanticipated causes of ineligibility or incompatibility.

Article 67

Every member of Parliament represents the nation and exercises his function without restraint of mandate.

Article 68

The members of Parliament may not be prosecuted for opinions expressed or votes cast in the exercise of their functions.

No member of Parliament may, without authorization of the Chamber to which he belongs, be subjected to penal proceedings; nor may he be arrested, or otherwise deprived of personal liberty, or subjected to personal or domiciliary search, unless he be taken in the act of committing a crime for which the warrant or the order to seize is obligatory.

Like authorization is required for the arrest or for holding under arrest a member of Parliament in execution even of an irrevocable sentence.

Article 69

The members of Parliament receive a compensation established by law.

SECTION II: THE ENACTMENT OF LAWS

Article 70

The legislative function is exercised collectively by the two Chambers.

Article 71

The initiative in legislation appertains to the Government, to each member of the Chambers, and to the organs and bodies on which it may be conferred by constitutional enactment.

The people exercise initiative in legislation by proposal of a bill drafted in the form of articles and supported by at least 50,000 electors.

Article 72

Every bill, having been presented to one Chamber, is, in accordance with its rules and regulations, examined by a committee and then by the Chamber itself, which approves it article by article and then by final vote.

Constitutions since World War II

The regulations will establish a shortened procedure for bills of declared urgency.

The regulations may also provide in what cases and what forms the examination and approval of bills are to be referred to committees, including standing committees composed to reflect the proportions of the parliamentary groups. Furthermore in such cases, until the moment of definitive approval, a bill is to be submitted to the Chamber, if the Government, or one tenth of the members of the Chamber, or one fifth of the members of the committee, request that it be discussed and voted upon by the Chamber itself, or else that it be considered for final approval by roll call. The regulations shall determine the forms of publicity to be given to the labors of the committees.

Normal procedure for examination and direct approval by the Chamber is always adopted for bills pertaining to the Constitution and the electorate, and for those delegating legislative power, authorizing the ratification of international treaties, or approving the budget or expenditures.

Article 73

The laws are promulgated by the President of the Republic within one month of their approval.

If the Chambers, each by an absolute majority of its own members, declare the urgency of a law, it is promulgated within the time which that law itself establishes.

The laws are published immediately after promulgation and take effect on the fifteenth day following publication, except when the laws themselves establish a different period.

Article 74

The President of the Republic, before promulgating a law, may by means of a message stating the reasons request a new decision of the Chambers.

If the Chambers again approve a law, it must be promulgated.

Article 75

Popular *referendum* is established to determine the abrogation, total or partial, of a law, or of an act having the force of law, when it is demanded by 500,000 electors or by five regional Councils.

The *referendum* is not permitted for tax laws or laws on the budget, for laws of amnesty and of pardon, or for laws authorizing the ratification of international treaties.

All citizens who are eligible as electors of the Chamber of Deputies have the right to participate in the *referendum*.

Constitution of the Italian Republic

The proposal submitted to *referendum* is approved if the majority of those eligible have participated in the voting, and if it has received a majority of votes validly cast.

The law determines the methods and procedures of carrying the *referendum* into effect.

Article 76

The exercise of the legislative function may not be delegated to the Government except after determination of principles and of governing criteria and only for a limited time and for defined objectives.

Article 77

The Government may not, without delegation of power by the Chambers, issue decrees which have the force of ordinary law.

When, in extraordinary cases of necessity and urgency, the Government on its own responsibility adopts provisional measures having the force of law, it must on the same day present them for conversion into law by the Chambers which, even if dissolved, are convoked for the purpose and assemble within five days.

The decrees lose effect as of the date of issue if not converted into law within sixty days of their publication. The Chambers may nevertheless regulate by law juridical relationships arising from decrees not converted into law.

Article 78

The Chambers decide upon the state of war and confer upon the Government the necessary powers.

Article 79

Amnesty and pardon are conceded by the President of the Republic on the basis of laws enacted by the Chambers delegating such power.

They may not apply to crimes committed subsequently to the proposal of delegation.

Article 80

The Chambers authorize by law the ratification of international treaties which are of a political nature, or which provide for arbitration or judicial regulation, or which involve changes of the territory, or charges on the finances, or modifications of the laws.

Article 81

The Chambers approve each year the budget and the account of expenditures presented by the Government.

Provisional exercise of the budget may not be conceded except by law and for periods which total not more than four months.

After approval of the budget by law, new taxes and new expenditures may not be established.

Every other law which involves new or greater expenditures must indicate the means to meet them.

Article 82

Each Chamber may provide for investigations of matters of public interest.

For this purpose it nominates from among its members a committee formed to reflect the proportions of its various groups. The committee of investigation proceeds in its inquiries and in its examinations with the same powers and subject to the same limitations as apply to the judicial authority.

TITLE II: THE PRESIDENT OF THE REPUBLIC

Article 83

The President of the Republic is elected by Parliament in joint session of its members.

Three delegates for each Region, elected by the Regional Council in such manner as to assure representation of minorities, participate in the election. The Valle d'Aosta has a single delegate.

The election of the President of the Republic takes place by secret ballot and requires a two-thirds majority of the assembly. After the third ballot an absolute majority is sufficient.

Article 84

Any citizen may be elected President of the Republic who has reached his fiftieth birthday and who enjoys civil and political rights.

The office of President of the Republic cannot be held contemporaneously with any other office whatsoever.

The salary and the endowment of the President are determined by law.

Article 85

The President of the Republic is elected for seven years.

Thirty days before the expiration of the President's term of office, the President of the Chamber of Deputies convokes the Parliament in joint session, together with the regional delegates, to elect the new President of the Republic.

Constitution of the Italian Republic

If the Chambers are dissolved, or if their term has less than three months to run, the election takes place within fifteen days from the meeting of the new Chambers. In the meantime the powers of the President in office are extended.

Article 86

The functions of the President of the Republic, in each case in which he cannot perform them, are exercised by the President of the Senate.

In case of permanent disability, death, or resignation of the President of the Republic, the President of the Chamber of Deputies announces the election of a new President of the Republic within fifteen days, except for the longer period provided for when the Chambers are dissolved or when their term has less than three months to run.

Article 87

The President of the Republic is the head of the state and represents the national unity.

He may send messages to the Chambers.

He announces the elections of new Chambers and signifies the date of their first meetings.

He authorizes the presentation to the Chambers of bills initiated by the Government.

He promulgates the laws, and he issues decrees having the force of law, and regulations.

He announces the popular *referendum* in cases provided for by the Constitution.

He nominates, in the cases indicated by law, the officials of the state.

He accredits and receives diplomatic representatives, ratifies international treaties after securing, when it is needed, the authorization of the Chambers.

He has command of the Armed Forces; presides over the Supreme Council of Defense constituted according to law; declares the state of war on decision by the Chambers.

He presides over the Superior Council of the Judiciary.

He may concede pardons and commute penalties.

He confers the decorations of the Republic.

Article 88

The President of the Republic may, having heard their respective Presidents, dissolve both Chambers or only one of them.

He may not exercise such a power within the last six months of his term.

Article 89

No act of the President of the Republic is valid unless countersigned by the Ministers proposing it, who assume responsibility for it.

Acts which have the force of legislation and other acts indicated by law are countersigned also by the President of the Council of Ministers.

Article 90

The President of the Republic is not responsible for acts performed while exercising his functions, except high treason or offenses against the Constitution.

In such cases he is impeached by Parliament in joint session, by absolute majority of its members.

Article 91

The President of the Republic, before taking office, swears, in the presence of Parliament in joint session, an oath of fidelity to the Republic and of observance of the Constitution.

TITLE III: THE GOVERNMENT

SECTION I: THE COUNCIL OF MINISTERS

Article 92

The Government of the Republic is composed of the President of the Council and of the Ministers who collectively constitute the Council of Ministers.

The President of the Republic nominates the President of the Council of Ministers and on his proposal nominates the Ministers.

Article 93

The President of the Council of Ministers and the Ministers, before assuming their functions, swear an oath in the hands of the President of the Republic.

Article 94

The Government must have the confidence of the two Chambers.

Each Chamber accords or revokes confidence by means of a motion stating the reasons and voted by roll call.

Within ten days of its formation the Government presents itself to the Chambers to obtain their confidence.

An opposing vote by one or by both of the Chambers on a motion of the Government does not carry with it the obligation of resigning.

Constitution of the Italian Republic

The motion of lack of confidence must be signed by at least one tenth of the members of the Chamber and may not be placed in discussion until three days after its presentation.

Article 95

The President of the Council of Ministers directs the general policy of the Government and is responsible for it. He maintains unity of political and administrative direction, and promotes and coordinates the activity of the Ministers.

The Ministers are responsible collectively for the acts of the Council of Ministers, and individually for the acts of their respective departments.

The law provides for the organization of the presidency of the Council and it determines the number, attributes, and organization of the ministries.

Article 96

The President of the Council of Ministers and the Ministers are impeached by Parliament in joint session for crimes committed in the exercise of their functions.

SECTION II: PUBLIC ADMINISTRATION

Article 97

The public offices are organized according to legal dispositions in such fashion as to assure effectiveness and impartiality of administration.

The spheres of competence, attributes, and appropriate responsibilities of officials are determined in the organization of the offices.

Admission to positions in the public administration is by means of competition except in cases established by law.

Article 98

Public employees are exclusively at the service of the Nation.

If they are members of Parliament they may not receive promotion except by reason of seniority.

Limitations of the right of affiliation with political parties may be established by law as regards judges, professional military officers in active service, police functionaries and agents, and diplomatic and consular representatives abroad.

SECTION III: AUXILIARY ORGANS

Article 99

The National Council of Economy and Labor is composed, in accordance with methods established by law, of experts and of representatives of the productive categories, in such a way as to take account of their numerical and qualitative importance.

It is a consultative organ of the Chambers and of the Government for the matters and in accordance with the functions attributed to it by law. It can initiate legislation and contribute to the elaboration of economic and social legislation according to principles and within limitations established by law.

Article 100

The Council of State is an organ of juridical-administrative advice and an organ for safeguarding justice in administration.

The Court of Accounts exercises a preventive control to assure the legitimacy of acts of the Government, and also audits the administration of the budget. It participates, in cases and under procedures established by law, in control over the financial administration of bodies to which the state regularly contributes. It reports directly to the Chambers on the results of the audit so executed.

The law provides for the independence of the two institutions and of their members as against the Government.

TITLE IV: THE JUDICIARY

SECTION I: JURISDICTIONAL ORGANIZATION

Article 101

Justice is administered in the name of the people.
The judges are subject only to the law.

Article 102

The judicial function is exercised by regular judges instituted and regulated by the norms governing the judicial order.

Extraordinary judges or special judges may not be instituted. There may only be instituted, for stipulated subjects, specialized sections attached to the regular judicial organs, and in these sections may participate qualified citizens not drawn from the magistracy.

The law regulates the cases and forms governing the direct participation of the people in the administration of justice.

Article 103

The Council of State and the other organs of administrative justice have jurisdiction for the protection of legitimate interests as against the public administration and, in particular subjects indicated by law, for the protection also of subjective rights.

Constitution of the Italian Republic

The Court of Accounts has jurisdiction in matters of public accounting and in other matters specified by law.

Military courts in time of war have jurisdiction established by law. In time of peace they have jurisdiction only for military crimes committed by members of the Armed Forces.

Article 104

The judiciary constitutes an autonomous order independent of every other power.

The Superior Council of the Judiciary is presided over by the President of the Republic.

The first president and the general procurator of the Court of Cassation are of right members.

The other members are elected: two thirds by all the regular judges from those belonging to the various categories; one third by Parliament in joint session from the regular university professors of law and lawyers who have had fifteen years of practice.

The Council elects a vice president from the members chosen by Parliament.

The elective members of the Council remain in office four years and are not immediately reeligible.

So long as they are in office they may not be inscribed in the professional registers nor belong to Parliament or to a Regional Council.

Article 105

In accordance with the norms of the judicial order, the following matters pertain to the Superior Council of the Judiciary: appointments, assignments and transfers, promotions, and disciplinary measures in regard to judges.

Article 106

The nomination of judges takes place by competition.

The law on the judicial organization may permit the nomination even by election of honorary judges for all functions attributed to individual judges.

Upon designation by the Superior Council of the Judiciary there may be called to the office of Counselor of Cassation, on the ground of outstanding merit, regular university professors of law and lawyers who have had fifteen years of practice and who are inscribed in the special registers of those practicing in the superior courts.

Article 107

Judges are irremovable. A judge may not be exempted or suspended from service or assigned to another seat or function except as a result of decision by the Superior Council of the Judiciary, adopted either for just cause and with the guaranty of defense as established by the judicial organization, or with the consent of the judge himself.

The Minister of Justice has authority to institute disciplinary action. Judges differ only in diversity of function.

The Public Prosecutor enjoys for his office the guarantees established according to the norms of the judicial order.

Article 108

The norms governing the judicial order and each magistracy are established by law.

The law assures the independence of judges of special jurisdictions, of the Public Prosecutors attached to such courts, and of outsiders who participate in the administration of justice.

Article 109

The judicial authority has the judicial police directly at its disposal.

Article 110

Except as regards the competence of the Superior Council of the Judiciary, the organization and functioning of the services relating to justice pertain to the Minister of Justice.

SECTION II: NORMS REGARDING JURISDICTION

Article 111

All measures pertaining to jurisdiction must be accompanied by a statement of reasons.

Appeal for violation of law is always admitted from sentences and from measures infringing personal liberty which are pronounced or taken by regular or special courts. This norm may be departed from only in the case of sentences of military courts in time of war.

From decisions of the Council of State and of the Court of Accounts, appeal is admitted only on grounds of jurisdiction.

Article 112

The Public Prosecutor has the obligation of administering penal action.

Article 113

The judicial protection of rights and of legitimate interests against acts of the public administration is always permitted before either ordinary or administrative courts.

Constitution of the Italian Republic

Such judicial protection may not be excluded, or limited to particular means of impugnment, or apply simply to specified categories of acts.

The law determines which courts may annul acts of the public administration in cases and with effects provided for by the law itself.

TITLE V: THE REGIONS, THE PROVINCES, THE COMMUNES

Article 114

The Republic is divided into Regions, Provinces, and Communes.

Article 115

The Regions are constituted as autonomous bodies with their own powers and functions according to the principles fixed by the Constitution.

Article 116

Particular forms and conditions of autonomy, in accordance with special statutes adopted as constitutional laws, are attributed to Sicily, to Sardinia, to Trentino-Alto Adige, to Friuli-Venezia Giulia, and to Valle d'Aosta.

Article 117

Within the limits of the fundamental principles established by the laws of the state, the Region legislates in regard to the following matters, provided that such legislation is not in conflict with the interest of the Nation or of other Regions:

Organization of the offices and of the administrative bodies dependent on the Region;
Communal boundaries;
Urban and rural local police;
Fairs and markets;
Public charities and health and hospital assistance;
Professional instruction, training of artisans, and scholastic assistance;
Museums and libraries of local bodies;
City matters;
Tourist trade and hotel industry;
Street railways and automobile lines of regional interest;
Thoroughfares, aqueducts, and public works of regional interest;
Lake ports and lake navigation;
Mineral and thermal waters;
Quarries and peat bogs;
Hunting;

Fishing in domestic waters;
Agriculture and forests;
Artisanship;
Other subjects indicated by the constitutional laws.

The laws of the Republic may delegate to the Regions the power to issue norms for their execution.

Article 118

The administrative functions pertaining to the subjects listed in the preceding article reside in the Regions, except those of exclusively local interest which by the laws of the Republic may be attributed to the Provinces, the Communes, or other local bodies.

The state may by law delegate to the Region the exercise of other administrative functions.

The Region normally exercises its administrative functions by delegating them to the Provinces, to the Communes or other local bodies or by making use of their officials.

Article 119

The Regions have financial autonomy within forms and limits established by the laws of the Republic which coordinate this regional autonomy with the finances of the state, of the Provinces, and of the Communes.

To the Regions are assigned their own taxes and quotas of the taxes of the treasury in relation to the needs of the Regions for the expenses necessary to fulfil their normal functions.

In order to provide for specified ends, and particularly for the development of the South and of the Islands, the state by law assigns special contributions to individual Regions.

The Region has its own domain and patrimony according to forms established by the laws of the Republic.

Article 120

The Region may not levy import or export duties or duties on the transit trade between Regions.

The Region may not adopt provisions which hinder in any way the free circulation of persons and things among the Regions.

It may not limit the right of citizens to exercise their professions, employments, or labor in any part of the national territory whatsoever.

Article 121

The organs of the Region are the Regional Council, the Executive Committee (*Giunta*) and its President.

Constitution of the Italian Republic

The Regional Council exercises the power of legislation and regulation attributed to the Region and the other functions conferred on it by the Constitution and the laws. It may propose bills to the Chambers.

The Executive Committee (*Giunta*) is the executive organ of the Region.

The President of the Executive Committee (*Giunta*) represents the Region; he promulgates regional laws and regulations; he directs the administrative functions delegated by the state to the Region, conforming to the instructions of the central Government.

Article 122

The system of elections, the number and cases of ineligibility and incompatibility of the regional councilors, are established by laws of the Republic.

No one may belong at the same time to a Regional Council and to either Chamber of Parliament or to another Regional Council.

The Council elects from its membership a President and a presidential bureau for its own labors.

The regional councilors cannot be called to answer for opinions expressed or votes cast in the exercise of their functions.

The President and members of the Executive Committee (*Giunta*) are elected by the Regional Council from its own members.

Article 123

Every Region has a constitution which, in harmony with the Constitution and with the laws of the Republic, establishes the norms relative to the internal organization of the Region. The regional constitution regulates the right of initiative and of *referendum* on laws and administrative provisions of the Region and the publication of regional laws and regulations.

The regional constitution is enacted by the Regional Council by absolute majority of its members, and it is approved by legislative action of the Republic.

Article 124

A Commissioner of the Government, residing in the capital of the Region, supervises the administrative functions exercised by the state and coordinates them with those exercised by the Region.

Article 125

The control of the legitimacy of the administrative acts of the Region is exercised, in decentralized form, by an organ of the state according to modes and within limits established by the laws of the Republic. In specified cases the law may admit control on the basis of general merit, solely with the effect of prompting, by formal demand, a re-examination of the decision on the part of the Regional Council.

Within the Region are established organs of administrative justice of the first grade in accordance with the order established by law of the Republic. Sections may be established with seats in other places than the regional capital.

Article 126

The Regional Council may be dissolved when it performs acts contrary to the Constitution or commits grave violations of the laws, or if it fails to respond to the request of the Government to replace its Executive Committee (*Giunta*) or President when they have committed analogous acts or violations.

It may be dissolved when, by reason of resignations or through the impossibility of forming a majority, it is not in a position to function.

It may also be dissolved for reasons of national security.

A dissolution is executed by a decree of the President of the Republic stating the reasons, after hearing a committee of deputies and senators constituted for regional questions according to procedures established by law of the Republic.

With the decree of dissolution is nominated a Commission composed of three citizens who are eligible for the Regional Council, which Commission announces new elections within three months, and provides for ordinary administration within the competence of the Regional Executive Committee (*Giunta*) and for such acts as cannot be postponed. These acts are subject to ratification by the new Regional Council.

Article 127

Every law passed by the Regional Council is communicated to the Commissioner, who, except in case of opposition on the part of the Government, must approve it within a period of thirty days from its submission.

The law is promulgated within ten days from the date of approval, and becomes effective not earlier than fifteen days from its publication. If a law is declared urgent by the Regional Council, and the Government of the Republic consents, its promulgation and date of effect are not subject to the specified terms.

The Government of the Republic, when it considers that a law passed by a Regional Council exceeds the competence of the Region or conflicts with the interests of the nation or with those of other Regions, returns it to the Regional Council within the period fixed for approval.

Constitution of the Italian Republic

When the Regional Council approves it anew by an absolute majority of its members, the Government of the Republic may, within fifteen days from communication of that fact, submit the question of its legitimacy to the Constitutional Court, or the question of the general merit of the regional law, because of conflicts of interests, to the Chambers. In case of doubt the Court decides the issue of competence.

Article 128

The Provinces and the Communes are autonomous bodies within the scope of principles fixed by the general laws of the Republic which determine their functions.

Article 129

The Provinces and the Communes are also territorial units of state and regional decentralization.

The Provinces may be subdivided into districts (*circondari*) with exclusively administrative functions for the sake of further decentralization.

Article 130

An organ of the Region, constituted in accordance with procedures established by the law of the Republic, exercises, likewise in a decentralized form, the control of legitimacy over acts of the Provinces, Communes, and other local bodies.

In cases specified by law, control on the issue of general merit may be exercised in the form of a request stating reasons, submitted to the deliberative bodies for re-examination of their decisions.

Article 131

The following Regions are constituted:

Piedmont	Marche
Valle d'Aosta	Lazio
Lombardy	Abruzzi e Molise
Trentino-Alto Adige	Campania
Venetia	Puglia
Friuli-Venezia Giulia	Basilicata
Liguria	Calabria
Emilia-Romagna	Sicily
Tuscany	Sardinia
Umbria	

Article 132

By constitutional enactment, the Regional Councils having been heard, arrangements may be made for the fusion of existing Regions or the creation of new Regions with a minimum of one million inhabitants, when request for such arrangements is made by as many Communal Councils as represent at least one third of the interested populations, and when the proposal is approved by *referendum* of the majority of the populations themselves.

By means of a *referendum* and by law of the Republic, the Regional Councils having been heard, consent may be given that Provinces and Communes which so request it be detached from one Region and joined to another.

Article 133

Changes of provincial boundaries and the institution of new Provinces within the area of the Region are established by law of the Republic, on the initiative of the Communes, the Region itself having been heard.

The Region, having heard the interested populations, may by its own enactment establish within its own territory new Communes and change their boundaries and names.

TITLE VI: CONSTITUTIONAL GUARANTIES

SECTION I: THE CONSTITUTIONAL COURT

Article 134

The Constitutional Court decides:

on controversies regarding the constitutionality of laws, and of acts having the force of law, emanating from the state and the Regions;

on conflicts arising over constitutional assignment of powers within the state, between the state and Regions, and between Regions;

on impeachments of the President of the Republic and of the Ministers, according to the norms of the Constitution.

Article 135

The Constitutional Court is composed of fifteen judges: one third named by the President of the Republic; one third named by Parliament in joint session; and one third named by the supreme judicial bodies, ordinary and administrative.

The judges of the Constitutional Court are chosen from the magistrates of the superior courts, ordinary and administrative, including magistrates in retirement; from regular university professors of law; and lawyers who have had twenty years of practice.

The Court elects its president from its members.

The judges are nominated for twelve years; they are renewed by instalments in accordance with the norms established by law; and they are not immediately reeligible.

Constitution of the Italian Republic

The office of judge of the Constitutional Court cannot be held concurrently with that of member of Parliament or of a Regional Council, with the practice of law, or with any position or office indicated by law.

In cases of impeachment of the President of the Republic or of Ministers there shall take part, besides the regular judges of the Court, sixteen members who are to be elected at the beginning of each legislature by Parliament in joint session from citizens having the qualifications of eligibility for the Senate.

Article 136

When the Court declares unconstitutional a rule of law, or of an act having the force of law, the rule ceases to have effect from the day following the publication of the decision.

The decision of the Court is published and is communicated to the Chambers and to the interested Regional Councils in order that, where it is considered necessary, provision may be made according to constitutional forms.

Article 137

A constitutional law establishes the conditions, the forms, the time limits for proposing decisions as to constitutionality, and the guaranties of independence for the judges of the Court.

By ordinary law are established the other rules necessary for the establishment and functioning of the Court.

No impugnment of the decisions of the Constitutional Court is admitted.

SECTION II: AMENDMENT OF THE CONSTITUTION—CONSTITUTIONAL LAWS

Article 138

Amendments of the Constitution and other constitutional laws are passed by each Chamber in two successive deliberations at an interval of not less than three months, and they are approved by absolute majority of the members of each Chamber in the second voting.

The laws themselves are submitted to popular *referendum* when, within three months of their publication, a demand is made by one fifth of the members of either Chamber, or by 500,000 electors, or by five Regional Councils. A law submitted to *referendum* is not promulgated unless it is approved by a majority of the valid ballots.

Referendum does not take place if a law has been approved in its second voting by a majority of two thirds of the members of each Chamber.

Article 139

The republican form is not subject to constitutional amendment.

TRANSITIONAL AND FINAL ARRANGEMENTS

I

When the Constitution becomes effective the Provisional Head of the State exercises the attributes and assumes the title of President of the Republic.

II

If at the time of the election of the President of the Republic the Regional Councils have not all been constituted, only the members of the two Chambers will participate in the election.

III

For the initial composition of the Senate of the Republic are nominated as senators, by means of a decree of the President of the Republic, deputies of the Constitutent Assembly who have by law the qualifications to be senators and who:

have been presidents of the Council of Ministers or of legislative assemblies;

have been members of the dissolved Senate;

have been three times elected, including election to the Constituent Assembly;

were declared dismissed in the session of the Chamber of Deputies of November 9, 1926;

have suffered the penalty of imprisonment of not less than five years in consequence of condemnation by the Fascist Special Tribunal for the Defense of the State.

Likewise nominated as senators, by decree of the President of the Republic, are members of the dissolved Senate who were members of the National Consultative Assembly.

Before signature of the decree of nomination the right to be nominated senator may be renounced. Acceptance of candidacy in the political elections implies renunciation of the right to be nominated senator.

IV

For the first elections to the Senate, Molise is considered as a Region in itself with the number of senators which belong to it in proportion to its population.

Constitution of the Italian Republic

V

The disposition in article 80 of the Constitution, in so far as it concerns international treaties which impose charges on the finances or modifications of the law, takes effect from the date of convocation of the Chambers.

VI

Within five years of the effective date of the Constitution, a revision of the special organs of jurisdiction now existing will be undertaken, excepting the jurisdictions of the Council of State, of the Court of Accounts, and of the military courts.

Within one year of the same date provision shall be made by law for the reorganization of the Supreme Military Tribunal with reference to article 112.

VII

Until the new law on the organization of the judiciary bringing it into conformity with the Constitution shall have been issued, the norms of the existing organization will continue to be observed.

Until the Constitutional Court begins to function, the decision of controversies indicated in article 134 takes place within the forms and limits of the norms pre-existent to the date when the Constitution takes effect.

The judges of the Constitutional Court nominated in the initial composition of that court are not subject to the system of partial renewal and remain in office twelve years.

VIII

The elections of the Regional Councils and of the elective organs of provincial administration will take place within one year from the effective date of the Constitution.

Laws of the Republic regulate for each branch of the public administration the transfer of state functions attributed to the Regions. Until provision shall have been made for the reorganization and the distribution of administrative functions among the local bodies, the Provinces and Communes retain the functions which they now exercise, and others the exercise of which the Regions delegate to them.

Laws of the Republic regulate the transfer to the Regions of functionaries and dependents of the state, including those of the central administrations when rendered necessary by the new organization. In setting up their offices the Regions must, except in cases of necessity, draw their personnel from that of the state and of local bodies.

IX

The Republic, within three years from the effective date of the Constitution, will adjust its laws to the requirements of local autonomy and to the legislative competence attributed to the Regions.

X

In the Region of Friuli-Venezia Giulia, referred to in article 116, the general norms of part II, title V, apply. The protection of linguistic minorities in conformity with article 6 remains binding.

XI

Until five years from the effective date of the Constitution, other Regions may be formed, by constitutional enactment modifying the list in article 131, and without recourse to the procedure required by the first paragraph of article 132, but with the obligation to hear the interested populations nevertheless remaining in effect.

XII

The reorganization under any form whatsoever of the dissolved Fascist party is prohibited.

Notwithstanding article 48, temporary limitations are established by law, for a period of not over five years from the effective date of the Constitution, on the suffrage and eligibility of the responsible heads of the Fascist regime.

XIII

The members and descendants of the House of Savoy are not electors and may not hold any public office or elective position.

To the former kings of the House of Savoy, their wives, and their male descendants are prohibited ingress into and sojourn in the national territory.

The properties within the national territory of the former kings of the House of Savoy, of their wives, and of their male descendants revert to the state. Transfers of and the establishments of royal rights on these same properties, which took place after June 2, 1946, are null and void.

XIV

Titles of nobility are not recognized.

The predicates of those existing before October 28, 1922, serve as parts of the proper name.

Constitution of the Italian Republic

The Order of St. Maurice is conserved as a hospital corporation and functions in the modes established by law.

The law regulates the suppression of the Heraldic Council.

XV

When the Constitution goes into effect the legislative decree of the lieutenancy of June 25, 1944, number 151, on the provisional organization of the state, is held to be converted into law.

XVI

Within one year from the effective date of the Constitution, the revision and coordination with the Constitution of the preceding constitutional laws, not until then explicitly or implicitly abrogated, will be undertaken.

XVII

The Constituent Assembly will be convoked by its President to decide, before January 31, 1948, on the law for the election of the Senate of the Republic, on the special regional statutes, and on the press law.

Until the date of the elections of the new Chambers, the Constituent Assembly may be convoked, if there is need to decide on matters placed within its competence by article 2, first and second paragraphs, and article 3, first and second paragraphs, of the legislative decree of March 16, 1946, number 98.

In this period the standing committees continue to function. The committees on legislation submit to the Government the bills transmitted to them, with contingent observations and proposals of amendment.

The deputies may present questions to the Government with request for written reply.

With reference to the second paragraph of the present article, the Constituent Assembly is convoked by its President on the written request of the Government or of at least two hundred deputies.

XVIII

The present Constitution is promulgated by the Provisional Head of the State within five days of its approval by the Constituent Assembly and takes effect on January 1, 1948.

The text of the Constitution is deposited in the town hall of every Commune of the Republic to remain displayed, during the whole of the year 1948, in order that every citizen may have knowledge of it.

The Constitution, furnished with the seal of the state, shall be inserted in the official collection of laws and decrees of the Republic.

The Constitution must be faithfully observed as the fundamental law of the Republic by all the citizens and by the organs of the state.
Given at Rome, this 27th December 1947.

ENRICO DE NICOLA

Countersigned:
 The President of the Constituent Assembly
  UMBERTO TERRACINI
 The President of the Council of Ministers
  ALCIDE DE GASPERI

C

Basic Law
of the Federal Republic of Germany, *as adopted by the Parliamentary Council,* May 8, 1949, and published in the Federal Gazette on *May 23, 1949*

PREAMBLE

Conscious of its responsibility before God and before man, inspired by the resolve to preserve its national and political unity and to serve world peace as an equal partner in a united Europe, the German people,

in the Laender Baden, Bavaria, Bremen, Hamburg, Hesse, Lower Saxony, North-Rhine-Westphalia, Rhineland-Palatinate, Schleswig-Holstein, Wuerttemberg-Baden und Wuerttemberg-Hohenzollern,

has, by virtue of its constituent power, enacted this Basic Law of the Federal Republic of Germany

to give a new order to political life for a transitional period.

It has also acted on behalf of those Germans to whom participation was denied.

The entire German people is called upon to achieve, by free self-determination, the unity and freedom of Germany.

I. BASIC RIGHTS

Article 1

(1) The dignity of man is inviolable. To respect and protect it is the duty of all state authority.

(2) The German people therefore acknowledges inviolable and inalienable human rights as the basis of every human community, of peace and of justice in the world.

(3) The following basic rights are binding on the legislature, on the executive and on the judiciary as directly valid law.

Article 2

(1) Everyone has the right to the free development of his personality, insofar as he does not infringe upon the rights of others or offend against the constitutional order or the moral code.

(2) Everyone has the right to life and to physical inviolability. The freedom of the individual is inviolable. These rights may be interfered with only on the basis of a law.

Article 3

(1) All persons are equal before the law.

(2) Men and women have equal rights.

(3) No one may be prejudiced or privileged because of his sex, his descent, his race, his language, his homeland and origin, his faith or his religious and political opinions.

Article 4

(1) Freedom of faith and conscience and freedom of creed in religion and in philosophy of life (weltanschaulich) are inviolable.

(2) The practice of religion without interference is guaranteed.

(3) No one may be compelled against his conscience to perform military service as an armed combatant. Details are regulated by a federal law.

Article 5

(1) Everyone has the right freely to express and to disseminate his opinion through speech, writing and pictures and, without hindrance, to instruct himself from generally accessible sources. Freedom of the press and freedom of radio and motion-pictures reporting are guaranteed. There is no censorship.

(2) These rights are limited by the provisions of the general laws, the legal regulations for the protection of juveniles and by the right to personal honor.

(3) Art and science, research and teaching are free. Freedom of teaching does not absolve from loyalty to the Constitution.

Article 6

(1) Marriage and family are under the special protection of the state.

(2) The care and upbringing of children are the natural right of parents and their duty, incumbent upon them primarily. The state watches over their performance (of this duty).

(3) Children may be separated from the family against the will of those entitled to bring them up only on the basis of a law, if those so entitled fail to perform their duty, or if, on other grounds, the children are in danger of falling into neglect.

(4) Every mother has a claim to the protection and assistance of the community.

(5) For their physical and mental development and for their position in society, illegitimate children shall, by legislation, be given the same opportunities as legitimate children.

Article 7

(1) The entire educational system is under the supervision of the state.

(2) Those entitled to bring up a child have the right to decide whether it shall receive religious instruction.

(3) Religious instruction shall form part of the curriculum in state and municipal schools, with the exception of non-denominational schools. Religious instruction shall, without prejudice to the state's right of supervision, be given according to the principles of the religious denominations. No teacher may against his will be placed under an obligation to give religious instruction.

(4) The right to establish private schools is guaranteed. Private schools as a substitute for state or municipal schools require the approval of the state and are subject to Land legislation. The approval must be given if the private schools, in their educational aims and facilities, as well as in the professional training of their teaching personnel, are not inferior to the state or municipal schools and if a segregation of the pupils in accordance with the (financial) means of the parents is not fostered. The approval must be withheld if the economic and legal status of the teaching personnel is not adequately ensured.

(5) A private elementary school is to be permitted only if the educational authority recognizes a specific pedagogic interest or if, at the request of those entitled to bring up children, it is to be established as an inter-denominational school (Gemeinschaftsschule), as a denominational or an ideological school, and if a state or municipal elementary school of this type does not exist in the Gemeinde.

(6) Preparatory schools (Vorschulen) remain abolished.

Article 8

(1) All Germans have the right, without prior notification or permission, to assemble peacefully and unarmed.

(2) In the case of open-air meetings this right may be restricted by legislation or on the basis of a law.

Article 9

(1) All Germans have the right to form associations and societies.

(2) Associations, the objects or activities of which conflict with the

criminal laws or which are directed against the constitutional order or the concept of international understanding, are prohibited.

(3) The right to form associations to safeguard and improve working and economic conditions is guaranteed to everyone and to all trades and professions. Agreements which restrict or seek to hinder this right are null and void; measures directed to this end are illegal.

Article 10

Secrecy of the mail as well as secrecy of the postal services and of telecommunications is inviolable. Restrictions may be ordered only on the basis of a law.

Article 11

(1) All Germans enjoy freedom of movement throughout the federal territory.

(2) This right may be restricted only by legislation and only for the cases in which an adequate basis of existence is absent, and, as a result, particular burdens would arise for the general public or in which it is necessary for the protection of juveniles from neglect, for combatting danger of epidemics or in order to prevent criminal acts.

Article 12

(1) All Germans have the right freely to choose their trade or profession, place of work and place of vocational training. The exercise of an occupation or profession may be regulated by legislation.

(2) No one may be compelled to perform a particular kind of work except within the scope of a customary general compulsory public service equally applicable to all.

(3) Forced labor is admissible only in the event of deprivation of freedom ordered by a court.

Article 13

(1) The home is inviolable.

(2) Searches may be ordered only by a judge or, in the event of danger in delay, by other authorities provided by law, and may be carried out only in the form prescribed therein.

(3) In other cases interferences with, and restrictions of, this inviolability may be undertaken only to avert a common danger or mortal danger to individuals and, on the basis of a law, also to prevent imminent danger to public safety and order, especially for the relief of the housing and space shortage (Raumnot), for combatting the danger of epidemics or for the protection of endangered juveniles.

Basic Law of the Federal Republic of Germany

Article 14

(1) Property and the right of inheritance are safeguarded. (Their) scope and limitations are determined by legislation.

(2) Property commits to duties. Its use should at the same time serve the general welfare.

(3) Expropriation is admissible only for the welfare of the community at large. It may be effected only by legislation or on the basis of a law regulating the nature and extent of compensation. The compensation shall be determined after just consideration of the interests of the general public and the parties concerned. In case of dispute regarding the amount of compensation, there is recourse to the ordinary courts.

Article 15

Land, natural resources and means of production may, for the purpose of socialization, be transferred to public ownership or other forms of publicly controlled economy by means of a law regulating the nature and extent of compensation. For the compensation, Article 14, paragraph (3), sentences 3 and 4, applies correspondingly.

Article 16

(1) No one may be deprived of his German citizenship. A person may be deprived of citizenship only on the basis of a law and, against his will, only if he is not thereby rendered stateless.

(2) No German may be extradited to a foreign country. The politically persecuted enjoy the right of asylum.

Article 17

Everyone has the right, individually or jointly with others, to address written requests or complaints to the competent authorities and to the popular representative bodies.

Article 18

Whoever abuses freedom of expression of opinion, in particular freedom of the press (Article 5, paragraph (1)), freedom of teaching (Article 5, paragraph (3)), freedom of assembly (Article 8), freedom of association (Article 9), the secrecy of the mail, of the postal services and of telecommunications (Article 10), the (right of) property (Article 14), or the right of asylum (Article 16, paragraph (2)), in order to attack the libertarian democratic basic order, forfeits these basic rights. The forfeiture and its extent shall be pronounced by the Federal Constitutional Court.

Constitutions since World War II

Article 19

(1) Insofar as, under this Basic Law, a basic right may be restricted by legislation or on the basis of a law, this law must be of general application and not applicable solely to an individual case. Furthermore, the law must specify the basic right and indicate the Article (concerned).

(2) In no case may a basic right be infringed upon in its essential content.

(3) The basic rights also apply to domestic juridical persons insofar as the former, according to their nature, are applicable to the latter.

(4) Should any person's rights be infringed by public authority, he shall have recourse to the courts. Insofar as there is no other jurisdiction, the recourse shall be to the ordinary courts.

II. THE FEDERATION AND THE LAENDER

Article 20

(1) The Federal Republic of Germany is a democratic and social federal state.

(2) All state authority emanates from the people. It is exercised by the people by means of elections and plebiscites and through specific legislative, executive and judicial agencies.

(3) Legislation is subject to the Constitution; the executive power and the administration of justice are subject to the Law.

Article 21

(1) The parties participate in the forming of the political will of the people. They can be freely formed. Their internal organization must conform to democratic principles. They must publicly account for the sources of their funds.

(2) Parties which, according to their aims and the conduct of their members, seek to impair or abolish the libertarian democratic basic order or to jeopardize the existence of the Federal Republic of Germany are unconstitutional. The Federal Constitutional Court decides on the question of unconstitutionality.

(3) Details are regulated by federal legislation.

Article 22

The federal flag is black-red-gold.

Article 23

For the time being, this Basic Law applies in the territory of the Laender Baden, Bavaria, Bremen, Greater Berlin, Hamburg, Hesse,

Basic Law of the Federal Republic of Germany

Lower-Saxony, North-Rhine-Westphalia, Rhineland-Palatinate, Schleswig-Holstein, Wuerttemberg-Baden and Wuerttemberg-Hohenzollern. It is to be put into force in other parts of Germany on their accession.

Article 24

(1) The Federation may, by legislation, transfer sovereign powers to international institutions.

(2) For the maintenance of peace, the Federation may join a system of mutual collective security; in doing so it will consent to those limitations of its sovereign powers which will bring about and secure a peaceful and lasting order in Europe and among the nations of the world.

(3) For the settlement of disputes between nations, the Federation will accede to conventions concerning a general, comprehensive obligatory system of international arbitration.

Article 25

The general rules of international law form part of federal law. They take precedence over the laws and directly create rights and duties for the inhabitants of the federal territory.

Article 26

(1) Activities tending to disturb, and undertaken with the intention of disturbing, the peaceful relations between nations, especially of preparing the conduct of an aggressive war, are unconstitutional. They are to be subject to punishment.

(2) Weapons designed for warfare may be manufactured, transported or marketed only with the permission of the Federal Government. Details are regulated by a federal law.

Article 27

All German commercial vessels constitute a (federally) unified merchant fleet.

Article 28

(1) The constitutional order in the Laender must conform to the principles of the republican, democratic and social state based on the rule of law (Rechtsstaat) within the meaning of this Basic Law. In the Laender, Kreise and Gemeinden, the people must be represented by a body created by universal, direct, free, equal, and secret elections. In Gemeinden, the assembly of the Gemeinde may take the place of an elected body.

(2) The Gemeinden must be safeguarded in their right to regulate, under their own responsibility, all the affairs of the local community within the limits of the laws. The Gemeindeverbaende also shall have the right of self-government within the legally established scope of their functions and in accordance with the laws.

(3) The Federation guarantees that the constitutional order of the Laender conforms to the basic rights and the provisions of paragraphs (1) and (2).

Article 29

(1) The federal territory is to be reorganized by a federal law with due regard to regional ties, historical and cultural connections, economic expediency and social structure. The reorganization should create Laender which, by their size and potentiality, are able to fulfill efficiently the functions incumbent upon them.

(2) In areas which, at the time of the reorganization of the Laender after 8 May 1945, became part, without plebiscite, of another Land, a specific change of the decision reached concerning this jurisdiction can be demanded by popular initiative within one year of the coming into force of this Basic Law. The popular initiative requires the consent of one-tenth of the population qualified to vote in Landtag elections. Should the popular initiative materialize, the Federal Government must, in the draft law regarding the reorganization, include a provision determining to which Land the area concerned shall belong.

(3) After adoption of the law, that part of the law which concerns an area which it is proposed to join to another Land must in each such area be submitted to a referendum. If, pursuant to paragraph (2), a popular initiative has materialized, a referendum must be held in any case in the area concerned.

(4) Insofar as the law is rejected in at least one area, it must then be reintroduced in the Bundestag. Insofar as it is then re-enacted, it shall to that extent require acceptance by referendum in the entire Federal territory.

(5) In a referendum, the majority of the votes cast is decisive.

(6) The procedure is regulated by a federal law. The reorganization should be concluded before the expiration of three years after promulgation of the Basic Law and, should it be necessary in consequence of the accession of another part of Germany, within two years after such accession.

(7) The procedure regarding any other change in the existing territory of the Laender is regulated by a federal law which shall require the approval of the Bundesrat and of the majority of the members of the Bundestag.

Basic Law of the Federal Republic of Germany

Article 30

The exercise of the powers of the state and the discharge of state functions is the concern of the Laender, insofar as this Basic Law does not otherwise prescribe or permit.

Article 31

Federal law overrides Land law.

Article 32

(1) The maintenance of relations with foreign states shall be the concern of the Federation.

(2) Before the conclusion of a treaty affecting the special interests of a Land, this Land must be consulted in good time.

(3) Insofar as legislation falls within the competence of the Laender, these may, with the approval of the Federal Government, conclude treaties with foreign states.

Article 33

(1) Every German has in every Land the same civic (staatsbuergerliche) rights and duties.

(2) Every German has equal access to any public office in accordance with his suitability, ability and professional achievements.

(3) Enjoyment of civil and civic rights (buergerliche und staatsbuergerliche Rechte) and access to public offices, as well as the rights acquired in the public service, are independent of religious denomination. No one may suffer prejudice on account of his adherence or non-adherence to a denomination or philosophy of life (Weltanschauung).

(4) The exercise of state authority (hoheitsrechtliche Befugnisse) as a permanent function shall, as a rule, be entrusted to members of the public service who are pledged to service and loyalty by public law.

(5) Law regarding the public service shall be regulated with due regard to the traditional principles concerning the status of professional civil servants (Berufsbeamtentum).

Article 34

If any person, in exercising a public office entrusted to him, violates his official duty to a third party, responsibility (liability) rests in principle with the state or the public body which employs that person. In a case of willful intent or gross negligence, the (employing body's) right of recourse (against the civil servant or employee) is reserved. With respect to the claim for compensation of damage and to the right of recourse, the jurisdiction of the ordinary courts must not be excluded.

Article 35

All Federal and Land authorities render each other mutual legal and administrative assistance.

Article 36

Civil servants (Beamte) from all Laender shall be employed by the highest Federal authorities in appropriate ratio. Persons employed with the other Federal authorities should, as a rule, be taken from the Land in which they are employed.

Article 37

(1) If a Land fails to fulfill its obligations towards the Federation under the Basic Law or any other federal law, the Federal Government may, with Bundesrat approval, take the necessary measures to force the Land by way of federal compulsion (Bundeszwang) to fulfill its duties.

(2) For the implementation of federal compulsion, the Federal Government or its commissioner has the right to give instructions to all Laender and their administrative agencies.

III. THE BUNDESTAG

Article 38

(1) Representatives to the German Bundestag are elected by the people in universal, direct, free, equal, and secret elections. They are representatives of the whole people, not bound by orders and instructions, and subject only to their conscience.

(2) Any person who has reached the age of twenty-one years is entitled to vote, and any person who has reached the age of twenty-five years may stand for election.

(3) Details are determined by a federal law.

Article 39

(1) The Bundestag is elected for a four-year term. Its legislative term ends four years after its first convening, or with its dissolution. The new election takes place in the last three months of the legislative term or, in case of a dissolution, after sixty days at the latest.

(2) The Bundestag convenes not later than thirty days after the election, but in no case before the end of the legislative term of the previous Bundestag.

(3) The Bundestag determines the closure and resumption of its meetings. The President of the Bundestag may convoke it at an earlier

Basic Law of the Federal Republic of Germany

date. He is bound to do so if one-third of the members, the Federal President or the Federal Chancellor so demand.

Article 40

(1) The Bundestag elects its President, his deputies and the secretaries. It draws up its Rules of Procedure.

(2) The President has charge of, and exercises police power in, the Bundestag building. No search or seizure may take place in the premises of the Bundestag without his permission.

Article 41

(1) The scrutiny of elections is the responsibility of the Bundestag. It also decides whether a representative has lost his seat in the Bundestag.

(2) An appeal to the Federal Constitutional Court against the decision of the Bundestag is admissible.

(3) Details are regulated by a federal law.

Article 42

(1) The deliberations of the Bundestag are public. Upon a motion of one-tenth of its members, or upon a motion of the Federal Government, the public may, by a two-thirds majority, be excluded. The motion is decided in a closed meeting.

(2) Decisions of the Bundestag require the majority of votes cast insofar as this Basic Law does not otherwise provide. For the elections to be held by the Bundestag, exceptions in the Rules of Procedure are admissible.

(3) True records of the public meetings of the Bundestag and of its committees do not entail any responsibility.

Article 43

(1) The Bundestag and its committees may demand the presence of any member of the Federal Government.

(2) The members of the Bundesrat and of the Federal Government as well as persons commissioned by them have access to all meetings of the Bundestag and its committees. They must be heard at any time.

Article 44

(1) The Bundestag has the right and, upon the motion of one-fourth of its members, the obligation to set up an investigating committee which shall take the necessary evidence in public proceedings. The public may be excluded.

(2) The provisions relating to criminal procedure shall essentially apply to the taking of the evidence. Secrecy of the mail, postal services and telecommunications remains unaffected.

(3) The courts and administrative authorities are bound to provide legal and administrative assistance.

(4) The decisions of the investigating committees are not subject to judicial review. The courts are free to appraise and judge the facts on which the investigation is based.

Article 45

(1) The Bundestag appoints a Standing Committee which shall safeguard the rights of the Bundestag in relation to the Federal Government in the interval between two legislative terms. The Standing Committee has also the powers of an investigating committee.

(2) Any wider powers, in particular the right to legislate, to elect the Federal Chancellor, and to impeach the Federal President, are not vested in the Standing Committee.

Article 46

(1) A representative may at no time be proceeded against in the courts or be subjected to disciplinary action or otherwise called to account outside the Bundestag on account of a vote given or an utterance made by him in the Bundestag or one of its committees. This shall not apply in the case of defamatory insults.

(2) A representative may be called to account or arrested for a punishable act only with the permission of the Bundestag, unless he be apprehended while committing the act or in the course of the following day.

(3) Furthermore, the permission of the Bundestag is required in respect of any other restriction of the personal freedom of a representative or for the initiation of proceedings pursuant to Article 18 against a representative.

(4) Any criminal proceedings and any proceedings pursuant to Article 18 against a representative, any detention and any other restriction of his personal freedom, shall be suspended upon the demand of the Bundestag.

Article 47

Representatives are entitled to refuse to give evidence concerning persons who have confided facts to them in their capacity as representatives or to whom they have entrusted facts in this capacity, as well as concerning those facts themselves. Within the scope of this right to refuse to give evidence, the seizure of documents is inadmissible.

Basic Law of the Federal Republic of Germany

Article 48

(1) Any person standing for election to the Bundestag is entitled to the leave necessary for the preparation of his election.

(2) No one may be prevented from accepting and exercising the office of representative. Notice of dismissal or dismissal (from employment) on these grounds are inadmissible.

(3) Representatives are entitled to a remuneration adequate to ensure their independence. They are entitled to free travel in all state-owned transport. Details are regulated by a federal law.

Article 49

Articles 46, 47, and paragraphs (2) and (3) of Article 48 apply to the members of the Presidium and the Standing Committee, as well as to their chief deputies, also in the interval between two legislative terms.

IV. THE BUNDESRAT

Article 50

By means of the Bundesrat, the Laender participate in the federal legislation and administration.

Article 51

(1) The Bundesrat consists of members of the Laender Governments which appoint and recall them. Other members of their Governments may represent them.

(2) Each Land has at least three votes; Laender with more than two million inhabitants have four, Laender with more than six million inhabitants, five votes.

(3) Each Land may delegate as many members as it has votes. The votes of each Land may be given only as a block vote and only by members present or their substitutes.

Article 52

(1) The Bundesrat elects its President for one year.

(2) The President convokes the Bundesrat. He must convoke it if the members for at least two Laender or the Federal Government so demand.

(3) The decisions of the Bundesrat are taken by at least the majority of its votes. It draws up its Rules of Procedure. It deliberates in public. The public may be excluded.

(4) Other members of the Laender Governments or persons commissioned by Laender Governments may belong to the committees of the Bundesrat.

Article 53

The members of the Federal Government have the right and, on demand, the duty to participate in the deliberations of the Bundesrat and its committees. They must be heard at any time. The Bundesrat must be kept currently informed, by the Federal Government, of the conduct of federal affairs.

V. THE FEDERAL PRESIDENT

Article 54

(1) The Federal President is elected, without debate, by the Federal Convention (Bundesversammlung). Every German is eligible who is entitled to vote for the Bundestag and has reached the age of forty years.

(2) The term of office of the Federal President is five years. Re-election for consecutive term is admissible only once.

(3) The Federal Convention consists of the members of the Bundestag and an equal number of members elected by the popular representative bodies of the Laender according to the principle of proportional representation.

(4) The Federal Convention meets not later than thirty days before the expiration of the term of office of the Federal President and, in the case of premature termination, not later than thirty days after this date. It is convoked by the President of the Bundestag.

(5) Upon expiration of the legislative term, the time period provided for in paragraph (4), sentence 1, begins with the first convening of the Bundestag.

(6) The person receiving the votes of the majority of the members of the Federal Convention is elected. If such majority is not obtained by any candidate in two ballots, the candidate receiving most votes in a further ballot is elected.

(7) Details are regulated by a federal law.

Article 55

(1) The Federal President may not be a member of either the Government or a legislative body of the Federation or a Land.

(2) The Federal President may not hold any other salaried office, nor engage in a trade, nor practice a profession, nor belong to the management or the supervisory board (Aufsichtsrat) of a profit-making enterprise.

Basic Law of the Federal Republic of Germany

Article 56

On assuming office, the Federal President takes the following oath in the presence of the assembled members of the Bundestag and the Bundesrat:
"I swear that I shall dedicate my efforts to the well-being of the German people, enhance its prosperity, protect it from harm, uphold and defend the Basic Law and the laws of the Federation, fulfill my duties conscientiously and do justice to all. So help me God."
The oath may also be taken without the religious asseveration.

Article 57

In the event of the Federal President's being prevented from exercising the authority of his office, or in the event of a premature vacancy in the office, this authority shall be exercised by the President of the Bundesrat.

Article 58

Orders and decrees of the Federal President become valid only when countersigned by the Federal Chancellor or the competent Federal Minister. This does not apply in the case of the appointment and dismissal of the Federal Chancellor, of the dissolution of the Bundestag pursuant to Article 63, and of the request pursuant to Article 69, paragraph (3).

Article 59

(1) The Federal President represents the Federation in matters concerning international law. He concludes treaties with foreign states on behalf of the Federation. He accredits and receives envoys.

(2) Treaties which regulate the political relations of the Federation or refer to matters of federal legislation require, in the form of a federal law, the approval or the participation of the respective bodies competent for federal legislation. For administrative agreements the provisions concerning the federal administration apply correspondingly.

Article 60

(1) Unless otherwise provided by law, the Federal President appoints and dismisses the federal judges and the federal civil servants.

(2) In individual cases, he exercises the right of pardon on behalf of the Federation.

(3) He may delegate these powers to other authorities.

(4) Paragraphs (2) to (4) of Article 46 apply to the Federal President correspondingly.

Article 61

(1) The Bundestag or the Bundesrat may impeach the Federal President before the Federal Constitutional Court for willful violation of the Basic Law or any other federal law. The motion for impeachment must be introduced by at least one-fourth of the members of the Bundestag or one-fourth of the votes of the Bundesrat. The decision to impeach requires a majority of two-thirds of the members of the Bundestag or of two-thirds of the votes of the Bundesrat. The prosecution is conducted by a person commissioned by the impeaching body.

(2) If the Federal Constitutional Court finds the Federal President guilty of a willful violation of the Basic Law or of any other federal law, it may declare him to have forfeited his office. Upon institution of impeachment proceedings, the Federal Constitutional Court may, by interim order, rule that the Federal President shall be debarred from exercising the authority of his office.

VI. THE FEDERAL GOVERNMENT

Article 62

The Federal Government consists of the Federal Chancellor and the Federal Ministers.

Article 63

(1) The Federal Chancellor is elected, without debate, by the Bundestag on the proposal of the Federal President.

(2) The person obtaining the majority of votes of the Bundestag members is elected. He is to be appointed by the Federal President.

(3) If the person proposed (for appointment) is not elected, the Bundestag may, within fourteen days of the ballot, elect a Federal Chancellor by more than one half of its members.

(4) If the Federal Chancellor is not elected within this time period, a new ballot shall take place without delay, in which the person receiving the greatest number of votes shall be elected. If the person elected obtains the votes of the majority of the Bundestag members, the Federal President must, within seven days of the election, appoint him. If the person elected does not obtain this majority, the Federal President must, within seven days, either appoint him or dissolve the Bundestag.

Article 64

(1) The Federal Ministers are appointed and dismissed by the Federal President upon the proposal of the Federal Chancellor.

(2) The Federal Chancellor and the Federal Ministers, on assuming office, take before the Bundestag the oath provided in Article 56.

Article 65

The Federal Chancellor determines, and assumes responsibility for, general policy. Within the limits of this general policy, each Federal Minister conducts the business of his department independently and on his own responsibility. The Federal Government decides on differences of opinion between the Federal Ministers. The Federal Chancellor conducts the business of the Federal Government in accordance with Rules of Procedure adopted by it and approved by the Federal President.

Article 66

The Federal Chancellor and the Federal Ministers may not hold any other salaried office, nor engage in a trade nor practise a profession nor belong to the management or, without Bundestag approval, to the supervisory board (Aufsichtsrat) of a profit-making enterprise.

Article 67

(1) The Bundestag may express its lack of confidence in the Federal Chancellor only by electing, by the majority of its members, a successor and by submitting a request to the Federal President for the dismissal of the Federal Chancellor. The Federal President must comply with the request and appoint the person elected.

(2) There must be an interval of forty-eight hours between the motion and the election.

Article 68

(1) If a motion of the Federal Chancellor for a vote of confidence does not obtain the support of the majority of the members of the Bundestag, the Federal President may, upon the proposal of the Federal Chancellor, dissolve the Bundestag within twenty-one days. The right to dissolve lapses as soon as the Bundestag, with the majority of its members, elects another Federal Chancellor.

(2) There must be an interval of forty-eight hours between the introduction of the motion and the vote thereon.

Article 69

(1) The Federal Chancellor appoints a Federal Minister as his deputy.

(2) The Federal Chancellor's or a Federal Minister's tenure of office ends in any case with the convening of a new Bundestag; a Federal Minister's tenure of office ends also with any other termination of the tenure of office of the Federal Chancellor.

(3) At the request of the Federal President, the Federal Chancellor or, at the request of the Federal Chancellor or of the Federal President, a Federal Minister, is bound to continue to transact the business of his office until the appointment of his successor.

VII. THE LEGISLATION OF THE FEDERATION

Article 70

(1) The Laender have the power to legislate insofar as this Basic Law does vest legislative powers in the Federation.

(2) The delimitation of competence between the Federation and the Laender is determined in accordance with the provisions of this Basic Law concerning exclusive and concurrent legislation.

Article 71

In the field of exclusive legislation of the Federation, the Laender have the power to legislate only if, and insofar as, they are expressly so empowered by a federal law.

Article 72

(1) In the field of concurrent legislation, the Laender have the power to legislate as long as, and insofar as, the Federation makes no use of its legislative power.

(2) The Federation has legislative power in this field insofar as a need for regulation by federal law exists because:
   1. a matter cannot be effectively regulated by the legislation of individual Laender, or
   2. the regulation of a matter by a Land law might prejudice the interests of other Laender or of the community at large, or
   3. the preservation of legal or economic unity demands it, in particular the preservation of uniformity of living conditions beyond the territory of an individual Land.

Article 73

The Federation has exclusive legislation on:
1. foreign affairs;
2. citizenship in the Federation;
3. freedom of movement, passports, immigration and emigration and extradition;
4. currency, money and coinage, weights and measures and regulation of time and calendar;
5. the unity of the territory as regards customs and commercial purposes, commercial and navigation agreements, the freedom of

traffic in goods, and the exchanges of goods and payments with foreign countries, including customs and border control;
6. federal railroads, and air traffic;
7. postal services and telecommunications;
8. the legal status of persons in the service of the Federation and of public law corporations directly controlled by the Federal Government;
9. industrial property rights (including patents and trade marks), author's copyrights and publisher's copyrights;
10. co-operation of the Federation and the Laender in the field of criminal police and in matters concerning the protection of the Constitution, the establishment of a Federal Office of Criminal Police, as well as international prevention and repression of crime;
11. statistics for federal purposes.

Article 74

Concurrent legislation extends over the following fields:
1. Civil law, criminal law and execution of sentences, the constitution of courts and their procedure, the Bar, notaries and legal advice (Rechtsberatung);
2. census and registry matters;
3. law pertaining to associations and assemblies;
4. the right of sojourn and of settlement of aliens;
5. the protection of German works of art and of cultural (historic) significance against removal abroad;
6. matters relating to refugees and expellees;
7. public welfare;
8. citizenship in the Laender;
9. war damage and compensation (Wiedergutmachung);
10. assistance to war-disabled persons and to surviving dependents, the care of former prisoners of war and the care of war graves;
11. law relating to the economy (mining, industry, power supply, crafts, trades, commerce, banking and stock exchange, insurance to which civil and not public law applies);
12. labor law, including the relationship between labor and management within an enterprise, the protection of workers and the conducting of employment agencies and exchanges, as well as social insurance, including unemployment insurance;
13. the furtherance of scientific research;
14. law regarding expropriation insofar as it is concerned with the matters enumerated in Articles 73 and 74;

15. transfer of land and real estate, natural resources and means of production to public ownership or to other forms of publicly controlled economy;
16. prevention of the abuse of economic power;
17. furtherance of agricultural and forestry production, safeguarding of food supply, import and export of agricultural and forestry products, deep-sea and coastal fishing and the guarding and preservation of the coasts;
18. transactions in real estate, law concerning land and matters concerning agricultural leases, housing, settlements and homesteads;
19. measures against epidemic and infectious diseases affecting human beings and animals, the admission to medical and other healing professions and healing practices and the traffic in drugs, medicines, narcotics and poisons;
20. protection concerning traffic in food and stimulants as well as in necessities of life, in fodder, in agricultural and forestry seeds and seedlings, and protection of trees and plants against diseases and pests;
21. ocean and coastal shipping and aids to navigation, inland shipping, meteorological services, sea waterways and inland waterways used for general traffic;
22. road traffic, motorized transport and the construction and maintenance of highways used for long-distance traffic;
23. railroads other than federal railroads, except mountain railroads.

Article 75

Within the conditions set forth in Article 72, the Federation has the right to issue general provisions concerning:
1. The legal status of persons employed in the public service of the Laender, Gemeinden and other public law corporations;
2. the general law to govern the press and motion pictures;
3. hunting, the preservation of nature and the care of the countryside;
4. land distribution, regional planning and water conservation;
5. matters relating to registration and identity cards.

Article 76

(1) Bills are introduced in the Bundestag by the Federal Government, by members of the Bundestag or by the Bundesrat.

(2) Bills of the Federal Government are to be submitted first to the Bundesrat. The Bundesrat is entitled to give its opinion on these bills within three weeks.

Basic Law of the Federal Republic of Germany

(3) Bills of the Bundesrat are to be submitted to the Bundestag by the Federal Government, which must add a statement of its own views.

Article 77

(1) Federal laws are passed by the Bundestag. After their adoption, they shall, without delay, be submitted to the Bundesrat by the President of the Bundestag.

(2) The Bundesrat may, within two weeks of the receipt of the adopted bill, demand that a committee composed of members of the Bundestag and Bundesrat be convoked to consider the bill jointly. The composition and the procedure of this committee is regulated by Rules of Procedure which shall be agreed by the Bundestag and shall require the approval of the Bundesrat. The members of the Bundesrat delegated to this committee are not bound by instructions. If the approval of the Bundesrat is required for a law, both the Bundestag and the Federal Government may demand the convocation of the committee. Should the committee propose amendments to the adopted bill, a new vote will be taken by the Bundestag.

(3) Insofar as the approval of the Bundesrat is not required for a law, the Bundesrat may, if proceedings pursuant to paragraph (2) are completed, veto within one week a law passed by the Bundestag. The time period for a veto begins in the case of paragraph (2), last sentence, with the receipt of the bill as readopted by the Bundestag; in all other cases, with the conclusion of the proceedings before the committee provided for in paragraph (2).

(4) Should the veto be adopted by a majority of the Bundesrat votes, it may be rejected by the decision of a majority of the Bundestag members. If the Bundesrat has adopted the veto by at least a two-thirds majority of its votes, the rejection by the Bundestag shall require a majority of two-thirds, and at least the majority of the members of the Bundestag.

Article 78

A law adopted by the Bundestag is deemed to have been passed if the Bundesrat approves it, does not introduce a motion pursuant to Article 77, paragraph (2), does not impose a veto within the time period provided by Article 77, paragraph (3), or withdraws its veto; or, if the veto is overridden by the Bundestag.

Article 79

(1) The Basic Law may be amended only by a law expressly amending or amplifying the text of the Basic Law.

(2) Such a law requires the approval of two-thirds of the Bundestag members and two-thirds of the Bundesrat votes.

(3) An amendment to this Basic Law affecting the organization of the Federation into Laender, the basic participation of the Laender in legislation, or the basic principles laid down in Articles 1 and 20, is inadmissible.

Article 80

(1) The Federal Government, a Federal Minister or the Land Governments may be empowered by a law to issue decrees having the force of law (Rechtsverordnungen). In such cases, the contents, purpose and scope of such powers must be specified in the law. The legal basis must be cited in the decree. If a law provides that such power may be further delegated, such delegation shall require a decree having the force of law (Rechtsverordnung).

(2) Bundesrat approval is required, unless otherwise provided by federal legislation, for decrees having the force of law (Rechtsverordnungen) issued by the Federal Government or a Federal Minister, concerning basic principles and charges for the use of facilities of the federal railroads, of the postal services and of telecommunications, concerning the construction and operation of railroads, as well as for decrees having the force of law (Rechtsverordnungen) issued on the basis of federal laws which require Bundesrat approval or which are executed by the Laender on behalf of the Federation or as matters of their own concern.

Article 81

(1) Should the Bundestag not be dissolved as provided for in Article 68, the Federal President may, at the request of the Federal Government and with Bundesrat approval, declare a state of legislative emergency with respect to a bill, if the Bundestag rejects the bill although the Federal Government has declared it to be urgent. The same applies if a bill has been rejected although the Federal Chancellor had combined with it the motion provided for in Article 68.

(2) If the Bundestag, after a state of legislative emergency has been declared, again rejects the bill or passes it in a version declared to be unacceptable to the Federal Government, the law shall be deemed passed provided that the Bundesrat approves it. The same applies if the bill has not been passed by the Bundestag within four weeks after its reintroduction.

(3) During the term of office of a Federal Chancellor, any other bill rejected by the Bundestag may be passed within a period of six months after the first declaration of a state of legislative emergency in accordance with paragraphs (1) and (2). After expiration of this period, a further declaration of a state of legislative emergency is inadmissible during the term of office of the same Federal Chancellor.

Basic Law of the Federal Republic of Germany

(4) The Basic Law may neither be amended nor wholly or partially repealed or suspended by a law enacted pursuant to paragraph (2).

Article 82

(1) Laws enacted in accordance with the provisions of this Basic Law shall, after countersignature, be engrossed by the Federal President and promulgated in the Federal Gazette. Decrees having the force of law (Rechtsverordnungen) shall be signed by the issuing authority and, unless otherwise provided by law, promulgated in the Federal Gazette.

(2) Every law and every decree having the force of law (Rechtsverordnungen) should specify the date of its becoming effective. In the absence of such a provision, it shall become effective on the fourteenth day after the end of the day on which the Federal Gazette was issued.

VIII. THE EXECUTION OF FEDERAL LAWS AND THE FEDERAL ADMINISTRATION

Article 83

The Laender execute the federal laws as matters of their own concern insofar as this Basic Law does not otherwise provide or permit.

Article 84

(1) If the Laender execute the federal laws as matters of their own concern, they determine the establishment of authorities and administrative procedures insofar as federal laws approved by the Bundesrat do not otherwise provide.

(2) The Federal Government may, with Bundesrat approval, issue general administrative provisions.

(3) The Federal Government exercises supervision to ensure that the Laender execute the federal laws in accordance with the legislation in force. For this purpose the Federal Government may send commissioners to the highest Land authorities and, with their approval or, if this approval is refused, with Bundesrat approval, also to subordinate authorities.

(4) Should shortcomings in the execution of federal laws which the Federal Government has found to exist in the Laender not be corrected, the Bundesrat shall decide, upon request of the Federal Government or of the Land, whether the Land has infringed the law. A decision of the Bundesrat may be challenged in the Federal Constitutional Court.

(5) For the execution of federal laws the Federal Government may, by federal legislation requiring Bundesrat approval, be granted the power to give individual instructions in special cases. They are, except if the

Federal Government considers a case to be urgent, to be addressed to the highest Land authorities.

Article 85

(1) Where the Laender execute the federal laws on behalf of the Federation, the establishment of the administrative agencies remains a concern of the Laender insofar as federal legislation approved by the Bundesrat does not otherwise provide.

(2) The Federal Government may issue, with Bundesrat approval, general administrative provisions. It may regulate the uniform training of civil servants (Beamte) and government employees (Angestellte). The heads of the administrative agencies at intermediate level shall be appointed with its agreement.

(3) The Land authorities are subject to the instructions of the competent highest federal authorities. Except if the Federal Government considers the matter urgent, the instructions are to be addressed to the highest Land authorities. Execution of the instructions is to be ensured by the highest Land authorities.

(4) Federal supervision extends to the legality and suitability of the manner of execution. The Federal Government may, for this purpose, require the submission of reports and documents and send commissioners to all authorities.

Article 86

Where the Federation executes the laws by direct federal administration or through public law corporations or institutions directly under the Federation, the Federal Government issues, insofar as the Law does not make any special provisions, general administrative provisions. It determines, insofar as it is not otherwise provided by the law, the establishment of the administrative agencies.

Article 87

(1) The foreign service, the federal finance administration, the federal railroads, the federal postal services and, in accordance with the provisions of Article 89, the administration of the federal waterways and shipping are conducted as integral parts of the federal administration with their own subordinate administrative offices. Federal border control authorities and central offices for police information and communications, for the compilation of data for the purpose of protecting the Constitution, and for the criminal police may be established by federal legislation.

(2) Social insurance institutions, the sphere of competence of which extends beyond the territory of a Land, are conducted as public law corporations directly under the Federation.

Basic Law of the Federal Republic of Germany

(3) In addition, independent central federal administrative agencies and new public law corporations and institutions directly under the Federation may be established by federal legislation for matters on which the Federation has the power to legislate. Should new functions arise for the Federation in matters in respect to which it has legislative competence, federal administrative agencies at intermediate and lower levels may, in case of urgent need, be established with the approval of the Bundesrat and of the majority of the Bundestag.

Article 88

The Federation establishes a bank of issue as a federal bank.

Article 89

(1) The Federation is the owner of the former Reich waterways.

(2) The Federation administers the Federal waterways through its own agencies. It exercises those state functions relating to inland shipping which extend beyond the territory of a Land and the functions relating to sea-going shipping which are conferred on it by legislation. Upon request, the Federation may delegate the administration of federal waterways, insofar as they lie within the territory of a Land, to this Land, in administration by commission (Auftragsverwaltung). Should a waterway touch the territories of several Laender, the Federation may delegate the administration of it to the Land which is proposed in a request submitted by the Laender concerned.

(3) In the administration, development and construction of waterways, the requirements of soil cultivation and of water conservation shall be safeguarded in agreement with the Laender.

Article 90

(1) The Federation is the owner of the former Reich Autobahnen (auto-highways) and Reich highways.

(2) The Laender, or such self-governing corporations as are competent under Land public law, administer on behalf of the Federation the federal Autobahnen (auto-highways) and other federal highways used for long-distance traffic.

(3) At the request of a Land, the Federation may take under direct federal administration federal Autobahnen (auto-highways) and other federal highways used for long-distance traffic, insofar as they lie within the territory of the Land.

Article 91

(1) In order to avert any imminent danger to the existence or the libertarian democratic basic order of the Federation or of a Land, a

Land may appeal for the services of the police forces of other Laender.

(2) If the Land in which this danger is imminent is not itself prepared or in a position to combat the danger, the Federal Government may place the police in that Land and the police forces of other Laender under its own instructions. This order (Anordnung) has to be rescinded after the elimination of the danger, or else at any time on the demand of the Bundesrat.

IX. THE ADMINISTRATION OF JUSTICE

Article 92

Judicial authority is vested in the judges; it is exercised by the Federal Constitutional Court, by the Supreme Federal Court, by the federal courts provided for in this Basic Law and by the courts of the Laender.

Article 93

(1) The Federal Constitutional Court decides:
1. on the interpretation of this Basic Law in the event of disputes concerning the extent of the rights and duties of any of the highest federal agencies or of other parties granted independent rights by this Basic Law or by Rules of Procedure of the highest federal agencies;
2. in case of differences of opinion or doubts as to the formal and material compatibility of federal law or Land law with this Basic Law or on the compatibility of Land law with other federal law, at the request of the Federal Government, of a Land Government or of one-third of the Bundestag members;
3. in case of differences of opinion on the rights and duties of the Federation and the Laender, particularly in the execution of federal law by the Laender, and in the exercise of federal supervision;
4. on other public law disputes between the Federation and the Laender, between different Laender or within a Land, insofar as recourse to another court is not provided for;
5. in all other cases provided for in this Basic Law.

(2) Furthermore, the Federal Constitutional Court shall act in such cases as are otherwise assigned to it by federal legislation.

Article 94

(1) The Federal Constitutional Court consists of federal judges and other members. Half of the members of the Federal Constitutional Court are elected by the Bundestag and half by the Bundesrat. They may not belong to the Bundestag, the Bundesrat, the Federal Government or corresponding agencies of a Land.

(2) A federal law determines the constitution and procedure of the Federal Constitutional Court and specifies in what cases its decisions shall have the force of law.

Article 95

(1) A Supreme Federal Court is established for the maintenance of the unity of federal law.

(2) The Supreme Federal Court decides cases in which the decision is of fundamental importance for the uniformity of the administration of justice by the high federal courts.

(3) The appointment of the judges of the Supreme Federal Court is decided jointly by the Federal Minister of Justice and a committee for the selection of judges consisting of the Land Ministers of Justice and an equal number of members elected by the Bundestag.

(4) In other respects, the constitution of the Supreme Federal Court and its procedure are regulated by federal legislation.

Article 96

(1) High federal courts shall be established in the spheres of ordinary, administrative, finance, labor and social jurisdiction.

(2) Article 95, paragraph (3), applies to the judges of the high federal courts with the proviso that the Federal Minister of Justice and the Land Ministers of Justice shall be substituted by the Ministers competent in the particular matter. Their service status must be regulated by a special federal law.

(3) The Federation may establish federal disciplinary courts for disciplinary proceedings against federal civil servants and federal judges.

Article 97

(1) Judges are independent and subject only to the law.

(2) Judges definitively appointed on a full-time basis to established court offices may, against their will, be dismissed before the expiration of their term of office, or permanently or temporarily suspended from office or transferred to another position or placed on the retired list, only by the decision of a court and only on grounds and according to the procedures provided for by law. Legislation may set age limits for the retirement of judges who have been appointed for life. In the case of changes in the structure of the courts or their area of jurisdiction, judges may be transferred to another court or suspended from office with the retention, however, of their full salary.

Article 98

(1) The legal status of the federal judges is to be regulated by a special federal law.

(2) If a federal judge, in his official capacity or unofficially, infringes on the principles of the Basic Law or the constitutional order of a Land, the Federal Constitutional Court may, upon request of the Bundestag, rule, with a two-thirds majority, that the judge be transferred to another office or placed on the retired list. In a case of willful infringement, dismissal may also be ordered.

(3) The legal status of the judges in the Laender is to be regulated by special Land legislation. The Federation may issue general provisions.

(4) The Laender may determine that the Land Minister of Justice shall, together with a committee for the selection of judges, decide on the appointment of judges in the Laender.

(5) The Laender may, in conformity with paragraph (2), provide a regulation for Land judges. Land constitutional law in force remains unaffected. The decision concerning a case of impeachment of a judge rests with the Federal Constitutional Court.

Article 99

The decision on constitutional disputes within a Land may be assigned by Land legislation to the Federal Constitutional Court, and the decision of last instance, on such matters as involve the application of Land law, to the high federal courts.

Article 100

(1) If a court considers unconstitutional a law the validity of which is pertinent to its decision, proceedings must be stayed and, if a violation of a Land Constitution is at issue, the decision of the Land court competent for constitutional disputes shall be obtained and, if a violation of this Basic Law is at issue, the decision of the Federal Constitutional Court shall be obtained. This also applies if the violation of this Basic Law by Land law or the incompatibility of a Land law with a federal law is at issue.

(2) If, in litigation, it is doubtful whether a rule of international law forms part of federal law and whether it directly creates rights and duties for the individual (Article 25), the court has to obtain the decision of the Federal Constitutional Court.

(3) If the constitutional court of a Land, in interpreting the Basic Law, intends to deviate from a decision of the Federal Constitutional Court or of the constitutional court of another Land, the (said) constitutional court must obtain the decision of the Federal Constitutional Court. If, in interpreting other federal law, it intends to deviate from the decision of the Supreme Federal Court or a high federal court, it must obtain the decision of the Supreme Federal Court.

Basic Law of the Federal Republic of Germany

Article 101

(1) Extraordinary courts are inadmissible. No one may be removed from the jurisdiction of his lawful judge.

(2) Courts dealing with matters in special fields may be established only by law.

Article 102

The death sentence is abolished.

Article 103

(1) Everyone is entitled to a proper hearing before the courts.

(2) An act may be punished only if the Law defined it as punishable before it was committed.

(3) On the basis of the general criminal laws, no one may be punished for the same act more than once.

Article 104

(1) The freedom of the individual may be restricted only on the basis of a formal law and only with due regard to the forms prescribed therein. Detained persons may be subjected neither to mental nor physical ill-treatment.

(2) Only a judge is (entitled) to decide on the admissibility and extension of a deprivation of liberty. In the case of every such deprivation which is not based on the order of a judge, a judicial decision must be obtained without delay. The police may, on its own authority, hold no one in its own custody beyond the end of the day following the arrest. Further details are to be regulated by law.

(3) Any person temporarily detained on suspicion of having committed a punishable act must, at the latest on the day following the detention, be brought before a judge who shall inform him of the reasons for the detention, interrogate him and give him an opportunity to raise objections. The judge must, without delay, either issue a warrant of arrest, setting out the reasons thereof, or order the release.

(4) A relative of the person detained or a person enjoying his confidence must be notified without delay of any judicial decision ordering or extending a deprivation of liberty.

X. FINANCE

Article 105

(1) The Federation has exclusive legislation on customs and fiscal monopolies.

(2) The Federation has concurrent legislation on:
1. excise taxes and taxes on transactions, with the exception of taxes with localized application, in particular the taxes on real estate acquisition, incremental value and fire protection;
2. the taxes on income, property, inheritance and donations;
3. taxes on real estate and on businesses (Realsteuern), with the exception of the fixing of tax rates;

if it claims the taxes in their entirety or in part to cover federal expenditures, or if the conditions set forth in Article 72, paragraph (2), exist.

(3) Federal legislation on taxes the yield of which accrues in their entirety or in part to the Laender or the Gemeinden (Gemeindeverbaende) require Bundesrat approval.

Article 106

(1) Customs, the yield of monopolies, the excise taxes with the exception of the beer tax, the transportation tax, the turnover tax and levies on property serving non-recurrent purposes accrue to the Federation.

(2) The beer tax, the taxes on transactions with the exception of the transportation tax and turnover tax, the income and corporation taxes, the property tax, the inheritance tax, the taxes on real estate and on businesses (Realsteuern) and the taxes with localized application accrue to the Laender and, in accordance with provisions of Land legislation, to the Gemeinden (Gemeindeverbaende).

(3) The Federation may, by means of a federal law requiring Bundesrat approval, claim a part of the income and corporation taxes to cover its expenditures not covered by other revenues, in particular to cover grants which are to be made to Laender to meet expenditures in the fields of education, public health and welfare.

(4) In order to ensure the working efficiency also of the Laender with low tax revenues and to equalize the differing burdens of expenditure of the Laender, the Federation may make grants and take the funds necessary for this purpose from specific taxes accruing to the Laender. A federal law, requiring Bundesrat approval, shall determine which taxes shall be utilized for this purpose and in what amounts and on what basis the grants shall be distributed among the Laender entitled to equalization; the grants must be transferred directly to the Laender.

Article 107

The final distribution, as between the Federation and the Laender, of the taxes subject to concurrent legislation shall be effected not later than 31 December 1952 and by means of a federal law requiring Bundesrat approval. This does not apply to the taxes on real estate and on businesses (Realsteuern), and the taxes with localized application.

Thereby, each party should be assigned a legal claim to certain taxes or shares in taxes commensurate to their tasks.

Article 108

(1) Customs, fiscal monopolies, the excise taxes subject to concurrent legislation, the transportation tax, the turnover tax and the non-recurrent levies on property are administered by federal finance authorities. The organization of these authorities and the procedure to be applied by them are regulated by federal legislation. The heads of the authorities at intermediate level shall be appointed in agreement with the Land Governments. The Federation may delegate the administration of the non-recurrent levies on property to the Land finance authorities as administration by commission (Auftragsverwaltung).

(2) Where the Federation claims part of the income and corporation taxes it shall thus far administer them; it may, however, delegate the administration to the Land finance authorities as administration by commission (Auftragsverwaltung).

(3) The remaining taxes are administered by Land finance authorities. The Federation may, by federal legislation requiring Bundesrat approval, regulate the organization of these authorities, the procedure to be applied by them and the uniform training of the civil servants. The heads of the authorities at intermediate level must be appointed in agreement with the Federal Government. The administration of the taxes accruing to the Gemeinden (Gemeindeverbaende) may be delegated by the Laender in entirety or in part to the Gemeinden (Gemeindeverbaende).

(4) Insofar as taxes accrue to the Federation, the Land finance authorities shall act on behalf of the Federation. The Laender are liable with their revenues for an orderly administration of these taxes; the Federal Minister of Finance may supervise the orderly administration through authorized federal agents who have the right to give instructions to the authorities at intermediate and lower levels.

(5) The jurisdiction of Finance Courts shall be uniformly regulated by federal legislation.

(6) The general administrative provisions shall be issued by the Federal Government and, insofar as the administration is incumbent upon the Land finance authorities, will require Bundesrat approval.

Article 109

The Federation and the Laender are autonomous and mutually independent with regard to their respective budgets.

Article 110

(1) All revenues and expenditures of the Federation must be estimated for each fiscal year and included in the budget.

(2) The budget shall be established by law before the beginning of the fiscal year. Revenue and expenditure must be balanced. Expenditures shall, as a rule, be approved for one year; in special cases, they may be approved for a longer period. Otherwise, the federal budget law may contain no provisions which extend beyond the fiscal year or which do not concern the revenues and expenditures of the Federation or its administration.

(3) The assets and liabilities shall be set forth in an appendix to the budget.

(4) In the case of federal enterprises commercially operated, only the final result, and not the detailed revenues and expenditures, need be included in the budget.

Article 111

(1) If, by the end of a fiscal year, the budget for the following year has not been established by law, the Federal Government shall, until such a law comes into force, be empowered to effect such payments as are necessary:
- a) to maintain existing institutions established by law and to carry out measures adopted by law;
- b) to meet legal obligations of the Federation;
- c) to continue building projects, procurements and other services, or to grant further subsidies for these purposes, provided that funds have already been approved in the budget of a previous year.

(2) Insofar as revenues, provided by special legislation and derived from taxes, dues and other sources, or working capital reserves do not cover the expenditures mentioned under paragraph (1), the Federal Government may, by way of credits, procure the funds, up to one-fourth of the total amount of the previous budget, which are necessary to conduct current operations.

Article 112

Expenditures exceeding the budget and any extraordinary expenditures require the approval of the Federal Minister of Finance. It may only be given in case of unforeseen and compelling necessity.

Article 113

Decisions of the Bundestag and Bundesrat which increase the budget expenditure proposed by the Federal Government, or include or imply new expenditures for the future, require the approval of the Federal Government.

Article 114

(1) The Federal Minister of Finance must submit to the Bundestag and the Bundesrat an annual account of all revenues and expenditures as well as of assets and liabilities.

Basic Law of the Federal Republic of Germany

(2) This account shall be audited by an Audit Office (Rechnungshof) the members of which shall enjoy judicial independence. The general account and a survey of the assets and liabilities have to be submitted to the Bundestag and the Bundesrat in the course of the following fiscal year, together with the comments of the Audit Office, in order to secure a discharge (Entlastung) for the Federal Government. The auditing of accounts shall be regulated by a federal law.

Article 115

Funds may be obtained by way of credits only in the case of extraordinary requirements and as a rule only for expenditure for productive purposes and only on the basis of a federal law. The granting of credits and providing of securities as a charge on the Federation, the effect of which extends beyond the fiscal year, may be undertaken only on the basis of a federal law. The amount of the credits or the extent of the obligation for which the Federation assumes liability must be determined in the law.

XI. TRANSITIONAL AND CONCLUDING PROVISIONS

Article 116

(1) Unless otherwise provided by law, a German within the meaning of this Basic Law is a person who possesses German citizenship or who has been accepted in the territory of the German Reich, as it existed on 31 December 1937, as a refugee or expellee of German ethnic stock (Volkszugehoerigkeit) or as the spouse or descendant of such person.

(2) Former German citizens, who, between 30 January 1933 and 8 May 1945, were deprived of their citizenship for political, racial or religious reasons, and their descendants, shall be regranted German citizenship on application. They are considered as not having been deprived of their German citizenship if they have taken up residence in Germany after 8 May 1945 and have not expressed a desire to the contrary.

Article 117

(1) Legislation which conflicts with Article 3, paragraph (2), remains in force pending harmonization with this provision of the Basic Law, but not beyond 31 March 1953.

(2) Laws restricting the right of freedom of movement, by reason of the present housing and space shortage (Raumnot), remain in force until repealed by federal legislation.

Article 118

The reorganization of the territory comprising the Laender Baden, Wuerttemberg-Baden and Wuerttemberg-Hohenzollern may be effected, by agreement between the Laender concerned, in a manner deviating from the provisions of Article 29. Failing agreement, the reorganization shall be regulated by federal legislation which must provide for a referendum.

Article 119

In matters relating to refugees and expellees, in particular as regards their distribution among the Laender, the Federal Government may, with Bundesrat approval, issue decrees having the force of law (Verordnungen mit Gesetzeskraft), pending a settlement of the matter by federal legislation. In special cases, the Federal Government may be empowered to issue individual instructions. Except in case of danger in delay the instructions are to be addressed to the highest Land authorities.

Article 120

(1) In accordance with more detailed provisions of a federal law, the Federation bears the expenses for occupation costs and the other internal and external burdens caused by war, and for the subsidies to (alleviate) the burdens of social insurance, including unemployment insurance, and public assistance for the unemployed.

(2) The revenues are transferred to the Federation at the same time as the Federation assumes responsibility for the expenditures.

Article 121

Within the meaning of this Basic Law, a majority of the members of the Bundestag and of the Federal Convention (Bundesversammlung) is the majority of the statutory number of their members.

Article 122

(1) As from the convening of the Bundestag, laws shall be passed exclusively by the legislative authorities recognized in this Basic Law.

(2) Where the competence of legislative bodies and of bodies participating in legislation in an advisory capacity ends in accordance with paragraph (1), such bodies shall be dissolved as of the same date.

Article 123

(1) Law in existence prior to the (first) convening of the Bundestag remains in effect, insofar as it does not conflict with the Basic Law.

(2) The state treaties concluded by the German Reich concerning matters for which, under this Basic Law, Land legislation is competent, remain in force if they are valid and continue to be valid in accordance with general principles of law, subject to all rights and objections of the

interested parties, pending the conclusion of new state treaties by the authorities competent under this Basic Law or until they are otherwise terminated pursuant to the provisions that they contain.

Article 124

Legislation concerning matters within the exclusive legislative competence of the Federation shall become federal law within the area of its application.

Article 125

Legislation concerning matters of concurrent federal legislation shall become federal law within the area of its application
1. insofar as it uniformly applies within one or more zones of occupation,
2. insofar as it concerns legislation by which former Reich law has been amended since 8 May 1945.

Article 126

Differences of opinion concerning the continuing validity of legislation as federal law are settled by the Federal Constitutional Court.

Article 127

Within one year of the promulgation of this Basic Law, the Federal Government may, with the approval of the Governments of the Laender concerned, extend, to the Laender Baden, Greater Berlin, Rhineland-Palatinate and Wuerttemberg-Hohenzollern, legislation of the Bizonal Economic Administration insofar as it continues to be in force as federal legislation under Articles 124 or 125.

Article 128

Insofar as legislation continuing in force provides for powers to give instructions within the meaning of Article 84, paragraph (5), these powers remain in effect until otherwise provided by law.

Article 129

(1) Insofar as legal provisions continuing in force as federal law contain an authorization to issue decrees having the force of law (Rechtsverordnungen) or general administrative provisions, and to perform administrative acts, this authorization passes to the (administrative) agencies henceforth competent in such matters. In cases of doubt, the Federal Government decides in agreement with the Bundesrat; the decision must be published.

(2) Insofar as legal provisions continuing in force as Land law contain such an authorization, it shall be exercised by the (administrative) agencies competent according to Land law.

(3) Insofar as legal provisions within the meaning of paragraphs (1) and (2) authorize their amendment or amplification or the issue of legal provisions in lieu of laws, these authorizations have expired.

(4) The provisions of paragraphs (1) and (2) apply correspondingly whenever legal provisions refer to regulations no longer valid or to institutions no longer in existence.

Article 130

(1) Administrative agencies and other institutions which serve the public administration or the administration of justice and are not based on Land law or state treaties between Laender, as well as the amalgamated management of the South West German railroads and the Administrative Council for the postal services and telecommunications of the French Zone of Occupation, are placed under the Federal Government. The latter, with Bundesrat approval, regulates their transfer, dissolution or liquidation.

(2) The highest disciplinary authority over the personnel of these administrations and establishments is the competent Federal Minister.

(3) Public Law corporations and institutions not directly under a Land, and not based on state treaties between Laender, are under the supervision of the competent highest federal authority.

Article 131

The legal status of persons, including refugees and expellees, who on 8 May 1945, were employed in the public service and who have left service for reasons other than those based on legal provisions concerning civil service or agreed employment regulations (Tarif), and who till now have not been employed or are not employed in a position corresponding to their former position, is to be regulated by federal legislation. The same applies to persons, including refugees and expellees, who, on 8 May 1945, were entitled to a pension or other assistance and who no longer receive any assistance or any adequate assistance for reasons other than those based on legal provisions concerning civil service or agreed employment regulations (Tarif). Pending the coming into force of the federal law, no legal claims may be made, unless otherwise provided by Land legislation.

Article 132

(1) Civil servants (Beamte) and judges who, at the coming into force of this Basic Law, hold appointments for life may, within six months after the first convening of the Bundestag, be placed on the retired list

or waiting list or be transferred to another office with lower remuneration, if they are personally or professionally unsuitable for their office. This provision applies correspondingly also to government employees (Angestellte) whose service cannot be terminated by notice of dismissal. In the case of government employees (Angestellte) whose service conditions provide for termination by notice of dismissal, the period of notice exceeding that required by agreed rules of employment (tarifmaessige Regelung) may be cancelled within the same period (of six months).

(2) These provisions do not apply to members of the public service who are not affected by the provision regarding the "liberation from National Socialism, and militarism" or who are recognized victims of National Socialism, insofar as no serious grounds are to be found in their character.

(3) Persons affected (by the above) have recourse to the courts in accordance with Article 19, paragraph (4).

(4) Details are determined by a decree (Verordnung) of the Federal Government, requiring Bundesrat approval.

Article 133

The Federation succeeds to the rights and obligations of the Bizonal Economic Administration.

Article 134

(1) Reich property becomes in principle federal property.

(2) Insofar as such property was originally intended mainly for administrative functions which, under this Basic Law, are not administrative functions of the Federation, it is, without compensation, to be transferred to the authorities hereafter competent to carry out such functions, and to the Laender insofar as, according to its present, not merely provisional, use, it serves for administrative functions which, under this Basic Law, are hereafter to be fulfilled by the Laender. The Federation may also transfer other property to the Laender.

(3) Property which was placed at the disposal of the Reich by the Laender and Gemeinden (Gemeindeverbaende) without compensation shall again become the property of the Laender and Gemeinden (Gemeindeverbaende), insofar as it is not required by the Federation for its own administrative functions.

(4) Details are regulated by a federal law requiring Bundesrat approval.

Article 135

(1) If, between 8 May 1945 and the coming into force of this Basic Law, a territory has passed from one Land to another, the property in this territory of the Land to which this territory had belonged devolves on the Land to which this territory now belongs.

(2) Property of no longer existing Laender or other public law corporations and institutions, insofar as it was originally intended mainly for administrative functions, or in accordance with its present not merely provisional use serves mainly for administrative functions, devolves on the Land or public law corporation or institution henceforth performing these functions.

(3) Insofar as it is not already included among property within the meaning of paragraph (1), real estate of no longer existing Laender, including appurtenances, devolves on the Land in the territory of which it is located.

(4) Where an overriding interest of the Federation or the particular interest of a territory so requires, an arrangement deviating from paragraphs (1) to (3) may be adopted by federal legislation.

(5) Moreover, the legal succession and the settlement (of property), insofar as it has not been effected by 1 January 1952 by agreement between the Laender or public law corporations or institutions concerned, shall be regulated by federal legislation requiring Bundesrat approval.

(6) Participation of the former Land Prussia in civil law enterprises devolves on the Federation. Details shall be regulated by a federal law which may make deviating provisions.

(7) Insofar as, at the time of the coming into force of the Basic Law, property devolving on a Land or a public law corporation or institution under paragraphs (1) and (3) has been disposed of by the party thereby authorized through a Land law, on the basis of a Land law or in another way, the transfer of property is deemed to have taken place before the act of disposal.

Article 136

(1) The Bundesrat convenes for the first time on the day of the first convening of the Bundestag.

(2) Pending the election of the first Federal President, his functions shall be exercised by the Bundesrat President. He does not have the right to dissolve the Bundestag.

Article 137

(1) The right of civil servants (Beamte), of employees (Angestellte) of the public services and of judges of the Federation, of the Laender and of the Gemeinden to stand for election may be restricted by legislation.

(2). The Electoral Law to be adopted by the Parliamentary Council applies for the election of the first Bundestag, of the first Federal Convention and of the first Federal President of the Federal Republic.

(3) Pending its establishment, the function of the Federal Constitutional Court, pursuant to Article 41, paragraph (2), shall be exercised

Basic Law of the Federal Republic of Germany

by the German High Court for the Combined Area, which shall decide in accordance with its Rules of Procedure.

Article 138

Changes in the regulations of notaries, as they now exist in the Laender Baden, Bavaria, Wuerttemberg-Baden and Wuerttemberg-Hohenzollern, require the approval of the Governments of these Laender.

Article 139

The legal provisions enacted for the "liberation of the German people from National Socialism, and militarism" shall not be affected by the provisions of this Basic Law.

Article 140

The provisions of Articles 136, 137, 138, 139, and 141 of the German Constitution of 11 August 1919 are an integral part of this Basic Law.*

Article 141

Article 7, paragraph (3), first sentence, finds no application in a land where another regulation by land law existed on 1 January 1949.

Article 142

Notwithstanding the provision of Article 31, provisions of Land Constitutions remain in force also insofar as they guarantee basic rights in conformity with Articles 1 to 18 of this Basic Law.

Article 143

(1) Whoever, by force or by threat of force, changes the constitutional order of the Federation or of a Land, deprives the Federal President of the powers accorded to him by this Basic Law, or, by force or by dangerous threats, compels him to exercise his powers or prevents him from exercising them altogether or in a specific manner, or separates from the Federation or from a Land a territory belonging to them, shall be sentenced to penal servitude for life or for not less than ten years.

(2) Whoever publicly incites to an action, within the meaning of paragraph (1), or plots it in connivance with another person, or otherwise prepares it, shall be sentenced to penal servitude up to ten years.

(3) In less serious cases, a sentence of not less than two years' penal servitude in the cases specified in paragraph (1), and of not less than one year's imprisonment in the cases specified in paragraph (2), may be imposed.

* See below, pp. 322–24, "Appendix to Basic Law."

(4) Whoever of his own free will abandons an activity (of this sort) or, in case of participation of several persons, prevents the execution of a plot (of this sort), may not be punished in accordance with the provisions of paragraphs (1) to (3).

(5) Where such an action is directed exclusively against the constitutional order of a Land, the highest Land court competent for criminal cases shall, in the absence of any other provision in Land law, be competent to decide. In other cases, the regional superior court (Oberlandesgericht), in the district of which the first Federal Government has its seat, is competent.

(6) The aforementioned provisions apply pending other regulations by federal law.

Article 144

(1) This Basic Law requires adoption by the popular representative bodies in two-thirds of the German Laender in which it shall for the time being apply.

(2) Insofar as restrictions are imposed on the application of the Basic Law in any of the Laender enumerated in Article 23, paragraph (1), or in a part of any of these Laender, that Land or that part of a Land has the right, in accordance with Article 38, to send delegates to the Bundestag and, in accordance with Article 50, to the Bundesrat.

Article 145

(1) The Parliamentary Council, with the participation of the representatives of Greater Berlin, confirms in a public meeting the adoption of this Basic Law, engrosses and promulgates it.

(2) This Basic Law becomes effective at the end of the day of its promulgation.

(3) It is to be published in the Federal Gazette.

Article 146

This Basic Law becomes invalid on the day on which a Constitution adopted by the German people by means of a free decision becomes effective.

APPENDIX TO BASIC LAW

Articles 136–137–138–139 and 141

of the Section "RELIGION AND RELIGIOUS ASSOCIATIONS" of the Weimar Constitution incorporated into the Basic Law for the Federal Republic of Germany pursuant to Article 140 thereof.

Basic Law of the Federal Republic of Germany

Article 136

Civil and civic rights and duties are neither qualified nor limited by the exercise of religious belief.

The enjoyment of civil and civic rights, and eligibility to public offices, are independent of religious belief.

No one is obliged to reveal his religious convictions. The authorities have the right to inquire into membership in a religious association only so far as rights and duties depend thereon, or a legally ordered statistical investigation makes it necessary.

No one may be compelled to perform any religious act or ceremony, or to participate in religious exercises, or to use a religious form of oath.

Article 137

There is no state church.

Freedom of membership in religious associations is guaranteed. The combination of religious associations within the territory of the Reich is subject to no limitations.

Every religious association regulates and administers its affairs independently within the limits of the law valid for all. It chooses its officers without the intervention of the state or the civil commune.

Religious associations effect incorporation according to the general provisions of the civil law.

Religious associations remain public law corporations insofar as they were such heretofore. Other religious associations are to be granted like rights upon their application, if through their organization and the number of their members they offer a guarantee of permanency. If several such public-law religious associations join in a union, this union is also a corporation of public law.

The religious associations which are public law corporations are entitled to levy taxes on the basis of the civil tax list, according to the standards of the provisions of the state law.

Associations whose function is the common cultivation of a philosophy of life have the same status as religious associations.

Insofar as the execution of these provisions requires further regulation, this is a function of state legislation.

Article 138

Public contributions to religious associations, which rest upon law, contract, or special legal title, are abrogated by state legislation. The fundamental provisions for this are established by the Reich.

Property and other rights of the religious associations and religious unions, in respect to their institutions, foundations, and other property devoted to purposes of worship, education, and benevolence are guaranteed.

Article 139

Sunday and the recognized public holidays remain under legal protection as days of freedom from labor and of spiritual edification.

Article 141

Insofar as there exists a need for religious service and spiritual care in the army, in hospitals, penal institutions, or other public institutions, the religious associations are to be given an opportunity for religious exercises, in connection with which there is to be no compulsion.

D

Statute of Westminster, 1931,
December 11, 1931

An Act (22 Geo. V, c. 4) to give effect to
certain resolutions adopted by the Imperial Conferences
held in the years 1926 and 1930

WHEREAS the delegates of His Majesty's Governments in the United Kingdom, the Dominion of Canada, the Commonwealth of Australia, the Dominion of New Zealand, the Union of South Africa, the Irish Free State and Newfoundland, at Imperial Conferences holden at Westminster in the years of our Lord nineteen hundred and twenty-six and nineteen hundred and thirty did concur in making the declarations and resolutions set forth in the Reports of the said Conferences:

And whereas it is meet and proper to set out by way of preamble to this Act that, inasmuch as the Crown is the symbol of the free association of the members of the British Commonwealth of Nations, and as they are united by a common allegiance to the Crown, it would be in accord with the established constitutional position of all the members of the Commonwealth in relation to one another that any alteration in the law touching the Succession to the Throne or the Royal Style and Titles shall hereafter require the assent as well of the Parliaments of all the Dominions as of the Parliament of the United Kingdom:

And whereas it is in accord with the established constitutional position that no law hereafter made by the Parliament of the United Kingdom shall extend to any of the said Dominions as part of the law of that Dominion otherwise than at the request and with the consent of that Dominion:

And whereas it is necessary for the ratifying, confirming and establishing of certain of the said declarations and resolutions of the said Conferences that a law be made and enacted in due form by authority of the Parliament of the United Kingdom:

And whereas the Dominion of Canada, the Commonwealth of Australia, the Dominion of New Zealand, the Union of South Africa, the

Irish Free State and Newfoundland have severally requested and consented to the submission of a measure to the Parliament of the United Kingdom for making such provision with regard to the matters aforesaid as is hereafter in this Act contained:

Now, therefore, be it enacted by the King's most Excellent Majesty by and with the advice and consent of the Lords Spiritual and Temporal, and Commons, in this present Parliament assembled, and by the authority of the same, as follows:—

1. In this Act the expression "Dominion" means any of the following Dominions, that is to say, the Dominion of Canada, the Commonwealth of Australia, the Dominion of New Zealand, the Union of South Africa, the Irish Free State and Newfoundland.

2. (1) The Colonial Laws Validity Act, 1865, shall not apply to any law made after the commencement of this Act by the Parliament of a Dominion.

(2) No law and no provision of any law made after the commencement of this Act by the Parliament of a Dominion shall be void or inoperative on the ground that it is repugnant to the law of England, or to the provisions of any existing or future Act of Parliament of the United Kingdom, or to any order, rule or regulation made under any such Act, and the powers of the Parliament of a Dominion shall include the power to repeal or amend any such Act, order, rule or regulation in so far as the same is part of the law of the Dominion.

3. It is hereby declared and enacted that the Parliament of a Dominion has full power to make laws having extra-territorial operation.

4. No Act of Parliament of the United Kingdom passed after the commencement of this Act shall extend, or be deemed to extend, to a Dominion as part of the law of that Dominion, unless it is expressly declared in that Act that that Dominion has requested, and consented to, the enactment thereof.

5. Without prejudice to the generality of the foregoing provisions of this Act, sections seven hundred and thirty-five and seven hundred and thirty-six of the Merchant Shipping Act, 1894, shall be construed as though reference therein to the Legislature of a British possession did not include reference to the Parliament of a Dominion.

6. Without prejudice to the generality of the foregoing provisions of this Act, section four of the Colonial Courts of Admiralty Act, 1890 (which requires certain laws to be reserved for the signification of His Majesty's pleasure or to contain a suspending clause), and so much of

Statute of Westminster, 1931

section seven of that Act as requires the approval of His Majesty in Council to any rules of Court for regulating the practice and procedure of a Colonial Court of Admiralty, shall cease to have effect in any Dominion as from the commencement of this Act.

7. (1) Nothing in this Act shall be deemed to apply to the repeal, amendment or alteration of the British North America Acts, 1867 to 1930, or any order, rule or regulation made thereunder.

(2) The provisions of section two of this Act shall extend to laws made by any of the Provinces of Canada and to the powers of the legislatures of such Provinces.

(3) The powers conferred by this Act upon the Parliament of Canada or upon the legislatures of the Provinces shall be restricted to the enactment of laws in relation to matters within the competence of the Parliament of Canada or of any of the legislatures of the Provinces respectively.

8. Nothing in this Act shall be deemed to confer any power to repeal or alter the Constitution or the Constitution Act of the Commonwealth of Australia or the Constitution Act of the Dominion of New Zealand otherwise than in accordance with the law existing before the commencement of this Act.

9. (1) Nothing in this Act shall be deemed to authorise the Parliament of the Commonwealth of Australia to make laws on any matter within the authority of the States of Australia, not being a matter within the authority of the Parliament or Government of the Commonwealth of Australia.

(2) Nothing in this Act shall be deemed to require the concurrence of the Parliament or Government of the Commonwealth of Australia in any law made by the Parliament of the United Kingdom with respect to any matter within the authority of the States of Australia, not being a matter within the authority of the Parliament or Government of the Commonwealth of Australia, in any case where it would have been in accordance with the constitutional practice existing before the commencement of this Act that the Parliament of the United Kingdom should make that law without such concurrence.

(3) In the application of this Act to the Commonwealth of Australia the request and consent referred to in section four shall mean the request and consent of the Parliament and Government of the Commonwealth.

10. (1) None of the following sections of this Act, that is to say, sections two, three, four, five and six, shall extend to a Dominion to

which this section applies as part of the law of that Dominion unless that section is adopted by the Parliament of the Dominion, and any Act of that Parliament adopting any section of this Act may provide that the adoption shall have effect either from the commencement of this Act or from such later date as is specified in the adopting Act.

(2) The Parliament of any such Dominion as aforesaid may at any time revoke the adoption of any section referred to in subsection (1) of this section.

(3) The Dominions to which this section applies are the Commonwealth of Australia, the Dominion of New Zealand and Newfoundland.

11. Notwithstanding anything in the Interpretation Act, 1889, the expression "Colony" shall not, in any Act of the Parliament of the United Kingdom passed after the commencement of this Act, include a Dominion or any Province or State forming part of a Dominion.

12. This Act may be cited as the Statute of Westminster, 1931.

E

Communique and Declaration of the Commonwealth Prime Ministers' Conference,
April 27, 1949, on the Status of the Republic of India in the Commonwealth

Text supplied by the British Information Services,
30 Rockefeller Plaza, New York 20, N.Y.

During the past week the Prime Ministers of the United Kingdom, Australia, New Zealand, South Africa, India, Pakistan and Ceylon, and the Canadian Secretary of State for External Affairs have met in London to exchange views upon the important constitutional issues arising from India's decision to adopt a republican form of constitution and her desire to continue her membership of the Commonwealth.

"The discussions have been concerned with the effects of such a development upon the existing structure of the Commonwealth and the constitutional relations between its members. They have been conducted in an atmosphere of goodwill and mutual understanding, and have had as their historical background the traditional capacity of the Commonwealth to strengthen its unity of purpose, while adapting its organization and procedures to changing circumstances.

"After full discussion the representatives of the Governments of all the Commonwealth countries have agreed that the conclusions reached should be placed on record in the following declaration:—

'The Governments of the United Kingdom, Canada, Australia, New Zealand, South Africa, India, Pakistan and Ceylon, whose countries are united as Members of the British Commonwealth of Nations and owe a common allegiance to the Crown, which is also the symbol of their free association, have considered the impending constitutional changes in India.

The Government of India have informed the other Governments of the Commonwealth of the intention of the Indian people that under the new constitution which is about to be adopted India shall become a sovereign independent republic. The Government of India have, however, declared and affirmed India's desire to continue her full membership of the Commonwealth of Nations and her acceptance of The King as the symbol of the free association of its independent member nations, and as such the Head of the Commonwealth.

The Governments of the other countries of the Commonwealth, the basis of whose membership of the Commonwealth is not hereby changed, accept and recognize India's continuing membership in accordance with the terms of this declaration.

Accordingly the United Kingdom, Canada, Australia, New Zealand, South Africa, India, Pakistan and Ceylon hereby declare that they remain united as free and equal members of the Commonwealth of Nations, freely cooperating in the pursuit of peace, liberty and progress.'

"These constitutional questions have been the sole subject of discussion at the full meetings of Prime Ministers."

Statute
of the Council of Europe,
May 5, 1949

THE Governments of the Kingdom of Belgium, the Kingdom of Denmark, the French Republic, the Irish Republic, the Italian Republic, the Grand Duchy of Luxembourg, the Kingdom of the Netherlands, the Kingdom of Norway, the Kingdom of Sweden and the United Kingdom of Great Britain and Northern Ireland;

Convinced that the pursuit of peace based upon justice and international co-operation is vital for the preservation of human society and civilisation;

Reaffirming their devotion to the spiritual and moral values which are the common heritage of their peoples and the true source of individual freedom, political liberty and the rule of law, principles which form the basis of all genuine democracy;

Believing that, for the maintenance and further realisation of these ideals and in the interests of economic and social progress, there is need of a closer unity between all like-minded countries of Europe;

Considering that, to respond to this need and to the expressed aspirations of their peoples in this regard, it is necessary forthwith to create an organisation which will bring European States into closer association;

Have in consequence decided to set up a Council of Europe consisting of a Committee of representatives of Governments and of a Consultative Assembly, and have for this purpose adopted the following Statute;

CHAPTER I—AIM OF THE COUNCIL OF EUROPE

Article 1

(a) The aim of the Council of Europe is to achieve a greater unity between its Members for the purpose of safeguarding and realising the ideals and principles which are their common heritage and facilitating their economic and social progress.

(b) This aim shall be pursued through the organs of the Council by discussion of questions of common concern and by agreements and common action in economic, social, cultural, scientific, legal and administrative matters and in the maintenance and further realisation of human rights and fundamental freedoms.

(c) Participation in the Council of Europe shall not affect the collaboration of its Members in the work of the United Nations and of other international organisations or unions to which they are parties.

(d) Matters relating to National Defence do not fall within the scope of the Council of Europe.

CHAPTER II—MEMBERSHIP

Article 2

The Members of the Council of Europe are the Parties to this Statute.

Article 3

Every Member of the Council of Europe must accept the principles of the rule of law and of the enjoyment by all persons within its jurisdiction of human rights and fundamental freedoms, and collaborate sincerely and effectively in the realisation of the aim of the Council as specified in Chapter I.

Article 4

Any European State, which is deemed to be able and willing to fulfil the provisions of Article 3, may be invited to become a Member of the Council of Europe by the Committee of Ministers. Any State so invited shall become a Member on the deposit on its behalf with the Secretary-General of an instrument of accession to the present Statute.

Article 5

(a) In special circumstances, a European country, which is deemed to be able and willing to fulfil the provisions of Article 3, may be invited by the Committee of Ministers to become an Associate Member of the Council of Europe. Any country so invited shall become an Associate Member on the deposit on its behalf with the Secretary-General of an instrument accepting the present Statute. An Associate Member shall be entitled to be represented in the Consultative Assembly only.

(b) The expression "Member" in this Statute includes an Associate Member except when used in connexion with representation on the Committee of Ministers.

Statute of the Council of Europe

Article 6

Before issuing invitations under Articles 4 or 5, the Committee of Ministers shall determine the number of representatives on the Consultative Assembly to which the proposed Member shall be entitled and its proportionate financial contribution.

Article 7

Any Member of the Council of Europe may withdraw by formally notifying the Secretary-General of its intention to do so. Such withdrawal shall take effect at the end of the financial year in which it is notified, if the notification is given during the first nine months of that financial year. If the notification is given in the last three months of the financial year, it shall take effect at the end of the next financial year.

Article 8

Any Member of the Council of Europe, which has seriously violated Article 3, may be suspended from its rights of representation and requested by the Committee of Ministers to withdraw under Article 7. If such Member does not comply with this request, the Committee may decide that it has ceased to be a Member of the Council as from such date as the Committee may determine.

Article 9

The Committee of Ministers may suspend the right of representation on the Committee and on the Consultative Assembly of a Member, which has failed to fulfil its financial obligation, during such period as the obligation remains unfulfilled.

CHAPTER III—GENERAL

Article 10

The organs of the Council of Europe are:
(i) the Committee of Ministers;
(ii) the Consultative Assembly.

Both these organs shall be served by the Secretariat of the Council of Europe.

Article 11

The seat of the Council of Europe is at Strasbourg.

Article 12

The official languages of the Council of Europe are English and French. The rules of procedure of the Committee of Ministers and of the Consultative Assembly shall determine in what circumstances and under what conditions other languages may be used.

CHAPTER IV—COMMITTEE OF MINISTERS

Article 13

The Committee of Ministers is the organ which acts on behalf of the Council of Europe in accordance with Articles 15 and 16.

Article 14

Each Member shall be entitled to one representative on the Committee of Ministers and each representative shall be entitled to one vote. Representatives on the Committee shall be the Ministers for Foreign Affairs. When a Minister for Foreign Affairs is unable to be present or in other circumstances where it may be desirable, an alternate may be nominated to act for him, who shall, whenever possible, be a member of his Government.

Article 15

(a) On the recommendation of the Consultative Assembly or on its own initiative, the Committee of Ministers shall consider the action required to further the aim of the Council of Europe, including the conclusion of conventions or agreements and the adoption by Governments of a common policy with regard to particular matters. Its conclusions shall be communicated to Members by the Secretary-General.

(b) In appropriate cases, the conclusions of the Committee may take the form of recommendations to the Governments of Members, and the Committee may request the Governments of Members to inform it of the action taken by them with regard to such recommendations.

Article 16

The Committee of Ministers shall, subject to the provisions of Articles 24, 28, 30, 32, 33 and 35, relating to the powers of the Consultative Assembly, decide with binding effect all matters relating to the internal organisation and arrangements of the Council of Europe. For this purpose the Committee of Ministers shall adopt such financial and administrative regulations as may be necessary.

Article 17

The Committee of Ministers may set up advisory and technical committees or commissions for such specific purposes as it may deem desirable.

Statute of the Council of Europe

Article 18

The Committee of Ministers shall adopt its rules of procedure which shall determine amongst other things:
  (i) the quorum;
  (ii) the method of appointment and term of office of its President;
  (iii) the procedure for the admission of items to its agenda, including the giving of notice of proposals for resolutions;

and
  (iv) the notifications required for the nomination of alternates under Article 14.

Article 19

At each session of the Consultative Assembly the Committee of Ministers shall furnish the Assembly with statements of its activities, accompanied by appropriate documentation.

Article 20

(a) Resolutions of the Committee of Ministers relating to the following important matters—namely:
  (i) recommendations under Article 15 *(b)* [aims of Council];
  (ii) questions under Article 19 [reports of activities];
  (iii) questions under Article 21 *(a)* (i) and *(b)* [publicity];
  (iv) questions under Article 33 [meeting place of Assembly];
  (v) recommendations for the amendment of Articles 1 *(d)*, 7, 15, 20, and 22 [organization];

and
  (vi) any other question which the Committee may, by a resolution passed under *(d)* below, decide should be subject to a unanimous vote on account of its importance, require the unanimous vote of the representatives casting a vote, and of a majority of the representatives entitled to sit on the Committee.

(b) Questions arising under the rules of procedure or under the financial and administrative regulations may be decided by a simple majority vote of the representatives entitled to sit on the Committee.

(c) Resolutions of the Committee under Articles 4 and 5 require a two-thirds majority of all the representatives entitled to sit on the Committee.

(d) All other resolutions of the Committee, including the adoption of the Budget, of rules of procedure and of financial and administrative regulations, recommendations for the amendment of articles of this Statute, other than those mentioned in paragraph *(a)* (v) above, and

deciding in case of doubt which paragraph of this Article applies, require a two-thirds majority of the representatives casting a vote and of a majority of the representatives entitled to sit on the Committee.

Article 21

(a) Unless the Committee decides otherwise, meetings of the Committee of Ministers shall be held:
(i) in private,
and
(ii) at the seat of the Council.

(b) The Committee shall determine what information shall be published regarding the conclusions and discussions of a meeting held in private.

(c) The Committee shall meet before and during the beginning of every session of the Consultative Assembly and at such other times as it may decide.

CHAPTER V—THE CONSULTATIVE ASSEMBLY

Article 22

The Consultative Assembly is the deliberative organ of the Council of Europe. It shall debate matters within its competence under this Statute and present its conclusions, in the form of recommendations, to the Committee of Ministers.

Article 23

(a) The Consultative Assembly shall discuss, and may make recommendations upon, any matter within the aim and scope of the Council of Europe as defined in Chapter I, which (i) is referred to it by the Committee of Ministers with a request for its opinion, or (ii) has been approved by the Committee for inclusion in the Agenda of the Assembly on the proposal of the latter.

(b) In taking decisions under *(a)*, the Committee shall have regard to the work of other European intergovernmental organisations to which some or all of the Members of the Council are parties.

(c) The President of the Assembly shall decide, in case of doubt, whether any question raised in the course of the Session is within the Agenda of the Assembly approved under *(a)* above.

Article 24

The Consultative Assembly may, with due regard to the provisions of Article 38 *(d)*, establish committees or commissions to consider and

Statute of the Council of Europe

report to it on any matter which falls within its competence under Article 23, to examine and prepare questions on its agenda and to advise on all matters of procedure.

Article 25

(a) The Consultative Assembly shall consist of representatives of each Member appointed in such a manner as the Government of that Member shall decide. Each representative must be a national of the Member whom he represents, but shall not at the same time be a member of the Committee of Ministers.

(b) No representative shall be deprived of his position as such during a session of the Assembly without the agreement of the Assembly.

(c) Each representative may have a substitute who may, in the absence of the representative, sit, speak and vote in his place. The provisions of paragraph *(a)* above apply to the appointment of substitutes.

Article 26

The following States, on becoming Members, shall be entitled to the number of representatives given below:

Belgium	6
Denmark	4
France	18
Irish Republic	4
Italy	18
Luxembourg	3
Netherlands	6
Norway	4
Sweden	6
United Kingdom	18

Article 27

The conditions under which the Committee of Ministers collectively may be represented in the debates of the Consultative Assembly, or individual representatives on the Committee may address the Assembly, shall be determined by such rules of procedure on this subject as may be drawn up by the Committee after consultation with the Assembly.

Article 28

(a) The Consultative Assembly shall adopt its rules of procedure and shall elect from its Members its President, who shall remain in office until the next ordinary session.

(b) The President shall control the proceedings but shall not take part in the debate or vote. The substitute of the representative who is President may sit, speak and vote in his place.

(c) The rules of procedure shall determine *inter alia:*
- (i) the quorum;
- (ii) the manner of the election and terms of office of the President and other officers;
- (iii) the manner in which the agenda shall be drawn up and be communicated to representatives;

and
- (iv) the time and manner in which the names of representatives and their substitutes shall be notified.

Article 29

Subject to the provisions of Article 30, all resolutions of the Consultative Assembly, including resolutions:
- (i) embodying recommendations to the Committee of Ministers;
- (ii) proposing to the Committee matters for discussion in the Assembly;
- (iii) establishing committees or commissions;
- (iv) determining the date of commencement of its sessions;
- (v) determining what majority is required for resolutions in cases not covered by (i) to (iv) above or determining cases of doubt as to what majority is required,

shall require a two-thirds majority of the representatives casting a vote.

Article 30

On matters relating to its internal procedure, which includes the election of officers, the nomination of persons to serve on committees and commissions and the adoption of rules of procedure, resolutions of the Consultative Assembly shall be carried by such majorities as the Assembly may determine in accordance with Article 29 (v).

Article 31

Debates on proposals to be made to the Committee of Ministers that a matter should be placed on the Agenda of the Consultative Assembly shall be confined to an indication of the proposed subject-matter and the reasons for and against its inclusion in the Agenda.

Article 32

The Consultative Assembly shall meet in ordinary session once a year, the date and duration of which shall be determined by the Assembly so as to avoid as far as possible overlapping with parliamentary sessions of Members and with sessions of the General Assembly of the United Nations. In no circumstances shall the duration of an ordinary session exceed one month unless both the Assembly and the Committee of Ministers concur.

Article 33

Ordinary sessions of the Consultative Assembly shall be held at the seat of the Council unless both the Assembly and the Committee of Ministers concur that it should be held elsewhere.

Article 34

The Committee of Ministers may convoke an extraordinary session of the Consultative Assembly at such time and place as the Committee, with the concurrence of the President of the Assembly, shall decide.

Article 35

Unless the Consultative Assembly decides otherwise, its debates shall be conducted in public.

CHAPTER VI—THE SECRETARIAT

Article 36

(a) The Secretariat shall consist of a Secretary-General, a Deputy Secretary-General and such other staff as may be required.

(b) The Secretary-General and Deputy Secretary-General shall be appointed by the Consultative Assembly on the recommendation of the Committee of Ministers.

(c) The remaining staff of the Secretariat shall be appointed by the Secretary-General, in accordance with the administrative regulations.

(d) No member of the Secretariat shall hold any salaried office from any Government or be a member of the Consultative Assembly or of any national legislature or engage in any occupation incompatible with his duties.

(e) Every member of the staff of the Secretariat shall make a solemn declaration affirming that his duty is to the Council of Europe and that he will perform his duties conscientiously, uninfluenced by any national considerations, and that he will not seek or receive instructions in connexion with the performance of his duties from any Government or any authority external to the Council and will refrain from any action which might reflect on his position as an international official responsible only to the Council. In the case of the Secretary-General and the Deputy Secretary-General this declaration shall be made before the Committee,

and in the case of all other members of the staff, before the Secretary-General.

(f) Every Member shall respect the exclusively international character of the responsibilities of the Secretary-General and the staff of the Secretariat and not seek to influence them in the discharge of their responsibilities.

Article 37

(a) The Secretariat shall be located at the seat of the Council.

(b) The Secretary-General is responsible to the Committee of Ministers for the work of the Secretariat. Amongst other things, he shall, subject to Article 38 *(d)*, provide such secretariat and other assistance as the Consultative Assembly may require.

CHAPTER VII—FINANCE

Article 38

(a) Each Member shall bear the expenses of its own representation in the Committee of Ministers and in the Consultative Assembly.

(b) The expenses of the Secretariat and all other common expenses shall be shared between all Members in such proportions as shall be determined by the Committee on the basis of the population of Members.

The contributions of an Associate Member shall be determined by the Committee.

(c) In accordance with the financial regulations, the Budget of the Council shall be submitted annually by the Secretary-General for adoption by the Committee.

(d) The Secretary-General shall refer to the Committee requests from the Assembly which involve expenditure exceeding the amount already allocated in the Budget for the Assembly and its activities.

Article 39

The Secretary-General shall each year notify the Government of each Member of the amount of its contribution and each Member shall pay to the Secretary-General the amount of its contribution, which shall be deemed to be due on the date of its notification, not later than six months after that date.

CHAPTER VIII—PRIVILEGES AND IMMUNITIES

Article 40

(a) The Council of Europe, representatives of Members and the Secretariat shall enjoy in the territories of its Members such privileges

Statute of the Council of Europe

and immunities as are reasonably necessary for the fulfilment of their functions. These immunities shall include immunity for all representatives in the Consultative Assembly from arrest and all legal proceedings in the territories of all Members, in respect of words spoken and votes cast in the debates of the Assembly or its committees or commissions.

(b) The Members undertake as soon as possible to enter into an agreement for the purpose of fulfilling the provisions of paragraph *(a)* above. For this purpose the Committee of Ministers shall recommend to the Governments of Members the acceptance of an Agreement defining the privileges and immunities to be granted in the territories of all Members. In addition a special Agreement shall be concluded with the Government of the French Republic defining the privileges and immunities which the Council shall enjoy as its seat.

CHAPTER IX—AMENDMENTS

Article 41

(a) Proposals for the amendment of this Statute may be made in the Committee of Ministers or, in the conditions provided for in Article 23, in the Consultative Assembly.

(b) The Committee shall recommend and cause to be embodied in a Protocol those amendments which it considers to be desirable.

(c) An amending Protocol shall come into force when it has been signed and ratified on behalf of two-thirds of the Members.

(d) Notwithstanding the provisions of the preceding paragraphs of this Article, amendments to Articles 23–35, 38 and 39 which have been approved by the Committee and by the Assembly, shall come into force on the date of the certificate of the Secretary-General, transmitted to the Governments of Members, certifying that they have been so approved. This paragraph shall not operate until the conclusion of the second ordinary session of the Assembly.

CHAPTER X—FINAL PROVISIONS

Article 42

(a) This Statute shall be ratified. Ratifications shall be deposited with the Government of the United Kingdom of Great Britain and Northern Ireland.

(b) The present Statute shall come into force as soon as seven instruments of ratification have been deposited. The Government of the United Kingdom shall transmit to all signatory Governments a certificate declaring that the Statute has entered into force, and giving the names of the Members of the Council of Europe on that date.

(c) Thereafter each other signatory shall become a party to this Statute as from the date of the deposit of its instrument of ratification.

In witness whereof the undersigned, being duly authorised thereto, have signed the present Statute:

Done at London, this 5th day of May, 1949, in English and French, both texts being equally authentic, in a single copy which shall remain deposited in the archives of the Government of the United Kingdom which shall transmit certified copies to the other signatory Governments.

For the Government of the Kingdom of Belgium:
    OBERT DE THIEUSIES.

For the Government of the Kingdom of Denmark:
    GUSTAV RASMUSSEN.
    REVENTLOW.

For the Government of the French Republic:
    ROBERT SCHUMAN.
    R. MASSIGLI.

For the Government of the Irish Republic:
    SEAN MACBRIDE.
    JOHN W. DULANTY.

For the Government of the Italian Republic:
    SFORZA.
    GALLARATI SCOTTI.

For the Government of the Grand Duchy of Luxembourg:
    JOS. BECH.
    A. J. CLASEN.

For the Government of the Kingdom of the Netherlands:
    D. U. STIKKER.
    E. MICHIELS VAN VERDUYNEN.

For the Government of the Kingdom of Norway:
    HALVARD M. LANGE.
    P. PREBENSEN.

For the Government of the Kingdom of Sweden:
    OSTEN UNDEN.
    GUNNAR HAGGLOF.

For the Government of the United Kingdom of Great Britain and Northern Ireland:
    ERNEST BEVIN.
    CHRISTOPHER MAYHEW.

INDEX

Adair, Douglass, 13
Adams, John, 118
American constitutionalism, influence of, 20
Aristotle, 119
Article 48, of Weimar Constitution, comment on, 28
Asiatic Land Tenure and Indian Representation Act, 1946 (South Africa), 49
Assembly government, as interpreted in Communist constitutions, 185, 186; in people's democracies, 210; *see also Régime conventionnel; Gouvernement conventionnel*
Assembly of the French Union, 77
Auriol, Vincent, 100
Australia, increase in size of Senate of, 40; Liberal party in, 41–42; Labour party in, 41 ff.; referendum on constitutional questions in, 64; attitude of, toward Statute of Westminster, 1931, 161; constitutional status of, as Dominion after 1939, 164, 167

Balfour Declaration, 1926, 161
Bardoux, Jacques, 102, 103
Basic Law (Western Germany), electoral provisions of, 61; federal provisions of, 139 ff.; nonfederal or antifederal features of, 149 ff.; other provisions of, 201, 283–324
Beard, Charles A., 13
Beirut, Boleslaw, 189
Belgian *Charte* (1831), 196
Bicameralism, in Italian legislature, 90; in Germany, 144–46; in new constitutions, 210 ff.
Bills of rights, in new constitutions, 5, 22 ff.; changed character of, 67, 218 ff.; in German Basic Law, 78 ff.; in people's democracies, 190, 218, 219; content of, 218, 219; in Western Europe, 219

Bonn Charter, *see* Basic Law (Western Germany)
Bright, John, 156
British Commonwealth, *see* Commonwealth (British)
British constitutionalism, influence of, 20
British Empire, structure of, revised after 1926, 161
British Nationality Act, 1948, some provisions of, 169
British North America Act of 1867 (Canada), amendment of, 45; of 1949 (Canada), effect of, on Parliament of the United Kingdom, 171
British subject, concept of, 169
Bundesrat, see Federal Council
Bundestag, see Federal Diet
Burke, Edmund, 1
Burma, becomes independent state, 171
Byé, Maurice, 123, 125

Cabinet, position of, in contemporary European parliamentary governments, 81 ff.; relation of, to legislature, 81 ff.; collective responsibility of, 82; instability of, in prewar European governments, 82; in people's democracies, 188
(France), relation of legislature to, 74; position under Third Republic, 76; stronger position of, under Fourth Republic, 86; relation of, to National Assembly, 88
(Italy), position of, 90, 110
(Western Germany), composition and powers of, 79, 149; responsibility of, to legislature, 80
Cabinet government, *see* Parliamentary government
Cahen-Salvador, Georges, 123, 125, 128
Canada, electoral reform in, 45 ff.; changes in membership of House of Commons of, 45–46; becomes in-

343

Index

dependent Dominion after 1939, 164, 167; changes in its constitution no longer need formal assent of United Kingdom Parliament, 171
Censure, vote of, in French National Assembly, 88
Ceylon, proportional representation in, 42; representative system of, 43; status of legislature in, 72; comment on, 168
Chamber of Deputies (Italy), composition of, 58; electoral law for, 1948, 58; powers of, 77 ff.
Chanak episode, 156
Chancellor (Western Germany), election of, 80; relationship of, to legislature and President, 91; power of, to dissolve legislature, 91–92
Charte Constitutionnelle (1814), 196
Chiappe, Jean, 102
Chifley, Joseph B., 172
Christian Democratic party (Italy), 59–61, 97, 110, 111, 114
Churchill, Winston, 40, 168
Collective security, acceptance of, in new constitutions, 10
Colonial Laws Validity Act, 1865, 159
Colonies, British, extension of self-government to, 168
Committees, of legislature, powers of, in France, 74; contrasted with position enjoyed in United Kingdom, 74; powers of, in Italy, 110
Common man, American belief in, 33
Commonwealth (British), postwar status of representative legislatures in states of, 71–73; developments in, since World War II, 154 ff.; definition of, 157; position of, on eve of World War II, 163; changing constitutional status of Dominions of, 167 ff.; extension to Asian Dominions, 168; current significance of, 168 ff.; its title changed to "Commonwealth," 169
Commonwealth citizen, concept of, 169
Commonwealth Prime Ministers' Conference, 1949, decisions of, affecting India, 170; communique and declaration of, 329–30

Communes (France), postwar legislation affecting, 102 ff.; (Western Germany), jurisdiction of, 149–50
Communist party (France), 96–97, 102, 103, 104, 155; (Italy), 111; in people's democracies, 176 ff.
Condorcet, Marquis de, 1
Confidence, motions of, in Italian legislature, 77, 89; in United Kingdom Parliament, 87; in French National Assembly, 88; in Western German legislature, 91, 144
Consorzi (Italy), of communes, 110
Constitution, Bismarckian (1871), 197
 (France), local-government provisions of, 97; other provisions of, 201, 226–47
 (Italy), local-government provisions of, 107 ff.; character of, 201; provisions of, 248–82
 (United States), comment on, 197; symbolic value and vitality of, 222
Constitutional Committee (France), comment on, 21; composition and powers of, 75; jurisdiction of, 215
Constitutional Court (Italian), 21; composition and powers of, 77 ff.; (Western Germany), 21; composition and powers of, 78–79, 140
Constitutionalism, revival of, in Western Europe, 94
Constitutions, reasons for decline of, 1 ff.; after World War II, 2 ff., 4, 191, 192, 199 ff.; in authoritarian states, 2; their failure to provide solutions for current problems, 5; common ground in, 17–19; in people's democracies, 175 ff.; contemporary value of, 191 ff.; "families" of, 192; current significance of, 192, 193; ontology of, 193; after World War I, 197 ff.; lack of enthusiasm for, 199; popular apathy toward, 200 ff.; amendment of, 215, 216; craftsmanship in drafting of, 220 ff.; amendment of, 215, 216; weaknesses of, 222–23
 (Democratic), political theory of, 13 ff.
 (Nominal), definition of, 204; areas where prevalent, 205

344

Index

(Normative), definition of, 204
(Semantic), definition of, 204; areas where prevalent, 206
(Written), history of, 194; purpose of, 194, 195; limitations of, 195; reasons for loss of transcendental significance of, 196, 197
Consultative Assembly, of Council of Europe, 11, 29
Convention, its role in determining status of states within the British Commonwealth, 155
Corporativism, in new constitutions, 211
Council of Europe, 11, 30; provisions of Statute of, 331–42
Council of Ministers, *see* Cabinet
Council of States (India), position of, 71
Council of the Republic (France), selection of members of, 56–57; powers of, in relation to National Assembly, 75 ff.; constitutional position of, 87
Cripps, Sir Stafford, 166–67
Crisis government, 2, 8, 92, 208, 209
Cromwell, Oliver, 194
Crown (British), no longer effective as symbol of unity, 169; growing divisibility of, 170
Curtin, John, 166
Czechoslovakia, some provisions of constitution of, 178, 184; recent constitutional history of, 183; problem of Slovak minority in, 183–84

Debré, Michel, 99, 106
Decentralization, constitutional policy toward, in France, 99; desire for, in postwar Italy, 107 ff.
Declaration of Commonwealth Prime Ministers' Conference, 1949, on nature of the Commonwealth, 159; contents of, 329–30
Declaration of the Rights of Man and Citizen, 218
Deconcentration, legislative proposals for, in France, 100 ff.
De Gasperi, Alcide, 110, 111, 112
De Gaulle, Charles, 9, 73, 83
De Gaulle, Pierre, 102

De Gaullists *(Rassemblement du Peuple Française)*, 55
Delegated legislation, in Italy, 90
Democratic constitutionalism, supporters of, in Germany, 25
Democrats, ideology of, in Europe, 19–20
Department (France), creation of, as area of local government, 96; part of system of local government and administration, 97 ff.; postwar legislation affecting, 100
De Valera, Eamon, 162
Dictatorship, in French constitutional history, 87; its spread after World War I, 198 ff.
Dimitrov, Georgi, 179
Dissolution, of legislature, in French Third Republic, 76; in Italy, 77, 84, 89; in German Basic Law, 80, 91–92, 144; in United Kingdom, 87; in French Fourth Republic, 87–88; declining significance of, in new constitutions, 209
Dominions, of British Commonwealth, independent after 1939, 163, 172; changing constitutional position of, 167 ff.
Dominion status, definition of, 159
Dreyfus-Schmidt, Pierre, 101, 105

Economic Council (France), after World War II, 76, 121–24, 211; of 1925 (National Economic Council), defects of, 120–21; (Italy) after World War II, 129 ff.
Economic councils, 4
Economic representation, 117 ff.
Edward VIII, of United Kingdom, 161
Einaudi, Luigi, 112, 114
Eire, attitude of, toward Statute of Westminster, 1931, 162; steps taken by, to weaken Commonwealth tie, 162–63; severs all constitutional connection with United Kingdom, 171
Elections, in France, 56; of Parliament in United Kingdom, 87
Electoral Amendment Act of 1945 (New Zealand), 47
Electoral legislation, after World War II, 36 ff.; in United Kingdom, 37–40;

Index

for Italian communes and provinces, 114
Electoral systems, in new constitutions, 213 ff.
Eliot, T. S., 17
Elite, need for, in a democracy, 118; comment on, 214
Emergency government, 2; *see also* Crisis government
Emergency powers, in postwar constitutions, 28, 208
"Entrenched" clauses, of South Africa Act (Constitution), 48 ff.
European union, 11, 30–33
Executive, strengthening of, 4; relationship to legislature, in Western states, 81 ff., 207, 208; in people's democracies, 206, 207

Federal Convention, serves as presidential electoral college in Germany, 85
Federal Council (Western Germany), selection of members of, 62; powers and composition of, 79–80, 92, 140–41, 144–45, 210; relation to *Länder* governments, 145–46
Federal Diet (Western Germany), election of members of, 61, 62, 143; powers of, 79–80; relation of, to Chancellor, 91; relation of, to Federal Council, 141; representative position of, 143
Federalism, in constitutions after World War II, 6; in Western Germany, 27, 79, 134 ff., 151 ff., 212, 213; in Yugoslav Constitution, 181 ff.; decline of, in postwar constitutions, 211 ff.; in Indian Constitution, 212; in people's democracies, 212
Federalist, The, 19
Federal Republic of Germany, *see* Germany, Western
Federal sanction, in Western Germany, how used, 142
France, voting strength of parties in, 52; electoral and representative changes in, 53 ff.; proportional representation in, 53 ff., 104; role of parties in electoral system of, 54; attitude of parties toward electoral reform in, 55 ff.; electoral law of March 1951, 56; results of elections of June 1951, 56; referendum provisions in constitution of, 64, 65; use of referendum in constitution-making, 65; constituent assemblies (1946), 73; composition of legislature, 73–77; National Assembly, 74–75; Council of the Republic, 74–75, 87; Constitutional Committee, 75; dissolution of legislature in, 75 ff.; position of Cabinet or Council of Ministers, 75–76, 86; economic councils in, 76, 120–21, 122 ff., 124 ff., 128; Assembly of the French Union, 77; President of, under Third Republic, 83; under Fourth Republic, 84; parliamentary government in, 87–88; local government in, 95 ff.; prefects of, 98 ff.; plans for decentralization in, 99 ff.; proposals for deconcentration in, 100 ff.; reform legislation affecting communes of, 102 ff.; majority electoral system in local elections in, 104–5, 113; policy of, toward a central German government, 138
French Revolution (1789), effects of, on local government, 95–96; varieties of forms of government produced by, 195, 196
French Union, 27, 77
Friuli-Venezia Giulia, special regional status of, 108
Functional autonomy, in postwar constitutions, 116 ff.
Functional representation, 122–28; in France, 129–30; in Italy, 130–31; in Bavaria, 131; in the Netherlands, 131; weaknesses of, 131 ff.; in Italian Fascism and Russian Communism, 132

Germany, Eastern, status of federalism in, 212
Germany, Western, electoral legislation of, 61 ff.; elections in, 62; composition of *Bundestag* (Federal Diet), 61, 62, 141, 143–44, 146, 149; composition of *Bundesrat* (Federal Council), 62, 140–41, 144–46; referen-

Index

dum provisions of Basic Law of, 65, 140; legislature of, 78–80, 91–93, 140 ff., 143 ff.; division of powers between *Bund* and *Länder*, 79, 140, 148 ff., President of, under Weimar Republic, 85–86; under Basic Law of Federal Republic, 86, 140; position of Chancellor of, 91–92; Constitutional Court in, 140; Cabinet of, 149; powers of communes of, 149–50; antifederal features of Basic Law of, 150 ff.; status of federalism in, 212

Giunta, Executive Committee of Italian regional government, 108 ff.

Gouvernement conventionnel, 196; *see also* Assembly government

Government of India Act, 1919, 1935, 72, 158

Governor-General, position of, in British Dominions after 1926, 161; office of, filled by Dominion citizens, 172

Great Britain, *see* United Kingdom

Hamilton, Walton, 13
Harrington, James, 19
Havenga, Nicolaas C., 50
Herriot, Edouard, 96
Heyde, Ludwig, 125
Hochfeld, Julian, 177
House of Commons (United Kingdom), Redistribution of Seats Act, 1944, 39; procedural changes in, since World War II, 69–71
House of Lords (United Kingdom), changes in, since World War II, 68–69
House of the People (India), position of, 71
Hungary, constitution of 1949, comment on, 177; Presidium in government of, 187; position of judges under constitution of, 189, 190

Imperial Conference (British), procedure of, 156; decisions of (1921) on foreign policy, 156; significance of (1926), 157

India, representation in, 43–44; suffrage in, 44; referendum in, 64; status of legislation in, 71; attitude of, toward Dominion status, 167; dispute over Kashmir, 169; remains in Commonwealth though a republic, 170; federalism in, 212

"Instrument of Government," 194

Interest representation, 117 ff.; weaknesses of, 118; *see also* Functional representation

Interior, Minister of the, prerogatives of, in France, 96

International law, acceptance of, in new constitutions, 10

Italy, proportional representation in, 57 ff., 111; electoral and representative system of, 57–61, 114 ff.; referendum in, 66; Constitutional Court, 77 ff.; composition and powers of legislature, 77–78, 89–90; powers of President of, 84–86; dissolution of legislature in, 84, 89, 209; power of Cabinet in, 89; parliamentary government in, 89–90, 110; delegated legislation in, 90; bicameralism in, 90, 210; local government in, 107 ff.; status of Regions in, 107 ff., 213; powers of legislative committees in, 110; National Council of Economy and Labor, 129 ff.; character of constitution of, 201

Jefferson, Thomas, 118
Jouhaux, Léon, 122, 125
Judicial Committee of the Privy Council (United Kingdom), 159, 164, 167
Judicial independence, absence of, in people's democracies, 189 ff.
Judicial power, in new constitutions, 216 ff.
Judicial review, of legislation, 4, 21–22, 216, 217; in Italy, 77 ff.; extension of, to "political" decisions, 217
Judiciary, Council of, in France and Italy, 27
Judiciary, position of, in constitutions of people's democracies, 189 ff.; efforts to protect from political influence in West, 216; identification with polit-

Index

ical departments in people's democracies, 216

Kardelji, Edvard, 177
Kashmir, dispute over, 169
King (British), becomes "head" of Commonwealth, 170
Kolarov, Vassil, 180
Košiče Agreement (1945), 183

Labour party (United Kingdom), attitude toward parliamentary reform, 69
Länder, in Western Germany, powers of, under Basic Law, 139–40, 148 ff.; their significance in composition of Federal Council, 141; their legal obligation to central government, 142; administrative powers of, 142–43
Laski, Harold J., 119, 120
Latin America, federalism in, 213
Lecky, William E. H., 194
Legislative supremacy, decline of, in postwar constitutions, 9
Legislature, status and powers of, in postwar constitutions, 67–80; in United Kingdom, 67–71; in Commonwealth (British), 71–73; in India, 71; in Ceylon, 72; in Pakistan, 72; in France, 73–77; in Italy, 77–78; in Western Germany, 78–80, 140 ff.; problem of relationship to executive, 81 ff., 110, 206 ff.; continuing predominance of, in French Fourth Republic, 87; re-emphasis upon supremacy of, in government, 93; danger to stability of, 94; position of, in constitutions of people's republics, 176, 185, 206, 207; in East German Länder, 185; in Western governments, 207, 208
Leopold III, of Belgium, 208
Liberal party (Italy), 112, 114
Local autonomy, in constitutions of people's democracies, 181
Local government, in France, 95–107; in Italy, 107 ff.
Locke, John, 19, 118
London Agreements (1948), 138

Lothian, Marquess of, electoral committee headed by (1932), 44

McKell, William J., 172
Madison, James, 132
Majority electoral system, in Commonwealth countries, 42 ff.; in Ceylon, 43; in India, 43–44; in Canada, 45–46; in New Zealand, 46–47; in French local elections, 104–5; effect of, on French local elections (1949), 113
Malan, Daniel F., 48 ff.
Mansergh, Nicholas, 162
Mazzini, Giuseppe, 19
Menzies, Robert G., 42
Mill, John Stuart, 19, 34
Minister-Presidents, of German Länder governments, call assembly at Bonn to frame Basic Law, 138
Moch, Jules, 105, 106
Monarchy, abolished by plebiscite in Italy and Bulgaria, 201
Montagu-Chelmsford proposals, 158
Moral unity, lack of, in postwar constitutions, 7
Morley-Minto reforms, 157
Morrison, Herbert, 40
Moscow Conference (1947), attitude of, toward a central German government, 137–38
Mouvement Républicain Populaire (France), 55, 97, 121
Multinational organization, in postwar constitutions, 10, 11, 28, 29

National Assembly (France), representation in, 55, 56; powers of, 73 ff.; relation to Cabinet, 74; constitutional position of, 86, 87–88
National Council of Economy and Labor (Italy), comment on, 129 ff.
National Economic Council (France), see Economic Council (France)
Nationalism, 154, 155, 158, 168
Nationalist party (South Africa), 50
National self-determination, effects of, 155

Index

Natives Representative Council (South Africa), 49
Negative revolution, concept of, 16; comment on, 34
Nehru, Jawaharlal, 160, 171
Newfoundland, referendum in (1948), 63, 64; relinquishes "Dominion status," 164
New Zealand, changes in electoral system of, 47; referendum in, 64; attitude of, toward Statute of Westminster, 1931, 161; constitutional position as Dominion after 1939, 164, 167
Nominal constitution, *see* Constitution (Nominal)
Normative constitution, *see* Constitution (Normative)

Occupation Statute, Western Germany, 28

Paine, Thomas, 1
Pakistan, constitution of, 44; government of, 44–45; status of legislature in, 72; dispute over Kashmir, 169
Parliament (United Kingdom), legislative power of, respecting Dominions after 1939, 164; *see also* Legislature
Parliament Act, 1911, 1949 (United Kingdom), 68 ff.
Parliamentary Council of Bonn, adopts Western German Basic Law, 135 ff.
Parliamentary government, mechanical efforts to strengthen, 8–9; stabilization of, 81–94; origin of, 81 ff.; difficulty of transplanting to European Continent, 82; aspects of, in United Kingdom, 87; in Italy, 90, 110
Parties, weaknesses of, 7; attitude toward postwar constitutions, 6–7; their role in the state, 117 ff.; in new constitutions, 213 ff.; lack of prestige of, 213; effect of oligarchies in, 214; in the people's democracies, 214, 215
Party leaders, comment on, 33, 34
People's Assembly (Yugoslavia), composition of, 181
People's democracy, concept of, 179, 180

People's democracies, nature of constitutions of, 190; position of parties in, 214, 215
People's republic, definition of, 179
People's republics, constituent units of Yugoslav federation, 182
Pirenne, Henri, 126
Planning, in constitutions, 24
Pleven, René, 56
Poincaré, Raymond, 83
Poland, constitution of 1921, character of, 175
Popular Front (Italy), 60, 61
Prefect (France), creation by Napoleon I, 96; interference by, with municipal government, 98; professional status of, 99; role of, in local administration, 100 ff.
Premier, *see* Prime Minister
President, position of, in new constitutions, 209, 210
  (France), constitutional position of, under Third Republic, 83; under Fourth Republic, 84
  (Italy), constitutional position of, 84; powers of, 84–85; relationship to Cabinet, 84; power to dissolve legislature, 84; election of, 85; compared with Italian kingship, 86
  (Western Germany), position under Weimar Constitution, 85; under Basic Law of Federal Republic, 85–86; election of, 85, 146; power to dissolve legislature, 91; lacks emergency powers, 146; federal character of office of, 147; powers of, 147–48
President of the Council of Ministers, *see* Prime Minister
Presidium, an executive-legislative link in constitutions of people's democracies, 186; election of, 186; functions of, 187; in Hungarian Constitution, 187
Prime Minister, position of, in new constitutions, 210
  (France), executive powers of, 83; relationship to other ministers, 86; prerogatives of, under Fourth Republic, 86–87; position of, when legislature is dissolved, 88

349

Index

Proportional representation, in United Kingdom, 39–40; in Commonwealth, 40 ff.; in Australian Senate, 40–42; in France, 53 ff.; in Italy, 59 ff.; in French local elections, 104; in Italian local elections, 111; weaknesses of, 132–33

Radical party (France), constitutional views of, 96
Rakosi, Matya, 177
Ramadier, Paul, 99, 105
Referendum, after World War II, 63; in United Kingdom, 63; in Newfoundland, 63, 64; in British Commonwealth countries, 64; in France, 64; in German Basic Law, 65, 140; in Italy, 66, 90–91; in Western Europe, 214
Régime conventionnel, in French Fourth Republic, 88
Regional prefects, under Vichy regime, 101
Regions (Italy), comment on, 6; political organs of, 108 ff.; special status of some, 107, 109
Reichswirtschaftsrat, behavior of, under Weimar Constitution, 119, 125
Representation of interests, *see* Interest representation
Representation of Natives Act, 1936 (South Africa), 48, 49
Representation of the People Act, 1948 (United Kingdom), 38; 1947 (Canada), 45
Republican form of government, in people's democracies, 179
Republican party (Italy), 112, 114
Responsible government, *see* Parliamentary government
Revolution of 1917, 15
Rights, protection of, against subversion, 23–24
Rights, Bill of, *see* Bills of rights
Right-wing Socialists (Italy), 111, 114
Rome, elections in (1946), 112

Sardinia, special regional status of, 108, 109

Schuman, Robert, 101
Schuschnigg, Kurt, 119
Second Chambers, *see* Bicameralism
Select Committee on Statutory Instruments (United Kingdom), powers of, 70–71
Semantic constitution, *see* Constitution (Semantic)
Senate (Bavaria), composition and powers of, 130; attitude toward, 130–31; (Italy) selection of membership in, 59, 60; powers of, 77
Separation of powers, comment on, 94; absence of, in people's democracies, 180
Shop council, in *Land* Hesse, 24
Sicily, regional government and separatist movement in, 107–9
Sieyès, Emmanuel-Joseph, 1, 21, 195
Single-member district plan of representation, *see* Majority electoral system
Slovakia, demand for autonomy for, 183, 184–85; National Council for, in Czech Constitution, 184
Smuts, Jan Christiaan, 160, 165
Social consensus, absence of, in postwar constitutions, 6
Socialist party (France), 103
Socialization policies, in constitutions, 24
Social-market economy, concept of, 25
Sovereignty, limitation of, in constitutions, 28, 29
South Africa Act (Constitution), "entrenched" clauses of, 48 ff.
South Africa, Union of, electoral changes in, 48 ff.; *apartheid* policy of, 48–49; changes in legislative representation, 49; attitude of, toward Statute of Westminster, 1931, 162, 167; changed status of, in Commonwealth, 169
Stalin, J. V., 177
Status of the Union Act (South Africa), 1934, provision of, 162
Statute of Council of Europe, provisions of, 331–42
Statute of Westminster, 1931, comment on, 157; legal effect of, on Dominions of Commonwealth, 161; provisions of, 325–28
Strasbourg Assembly, 11

Index

Suffrage, in new constitutions, 213 ff.
Superprefects (France), 101

Thomas, Ivor, 111
Tirnovo Constitution (1879), character of, 175
Tiso, Monsignor, 183
Tito, of Yugoslavia, 179, 190
Totalitarian rule, causes of, 82
Trentino-Alto Adige, special regional status of, 108, 110

Union of South Africa, *see* South Africa, Union of
United Kingdom, attitude of, toward European unity, 31; comment on constitution of, 31; elections in (1950), 37; proposed use of referendum in, 63; postwar status of Parliament in, 68–71; position of House of Lords since World War II, 68–69; policy of, toward a central German government, 137; position of, in Commonwealth, 159, 165 ff.
United party (South Africa), 50
United States Joint Chiefs of Staff, attitude toward formation of Federal German Republic, 135–36
U.S.S.R., policy of, toward central German government, 137; its constitution serves as model for people's democracies, 178

Val d'Aosta, special regional status of, 108, 109
Von Papen, Fritz, 91
Von Schleicher, Kurt, 92

Weimar Constitution, 66
Western Germany, *see* Germany, Western
Wright, Gordon, 97

Yugoslavia, federal organization of, 181; preponderance of central government in federal system of, 181–82

FEB 1 8 1959